The God Susanoo and Korea in Japan's Cultural Memory

Bloomsbury Shinto Studies

Series editor: Fabio Rambelli

The Shinto tradition is an essential component of Japanese religious culture. In addition to indigenous elements, it contains aspects mediated from Buddhism, Daoism, Confucianism, and, in more recent times, Western religious culture as well—plus, various forms of hybridization among all of these different traditions. Despite its cultural and historical importance, Shinto studies have failed to attract wide attention also because of the lingering effects of uses of aspects of Shinto for the ultranationalistic propaganda of Japan during the Second World War. The Series makes available to a broad audience a number of important texts that help to dispel the widespread misconception that Shinto is intrinsically related to Japanese nationalism, and at the same time promote further research and understanding of what is still an underdeveloped field.

Mountain Mandalas: Shugendo in Kyushu
Allan G. Grapard
The Origin of Modern Shinto in Japan: The Vanquished Gods of Izumo
Yijiang Zhong
Religion, Power and the Rise of Shinto in Early Modern Japan
Edited by Stefan Köck, Brigitte Pickl-Kolaczia, and Bernhard Scheid
The Sea and the Sacred in Japan
Edited by Fabio Rambelli
Shinto, Nature and Ideology in Contemporary Japan
Aike P. Rots
A Social History of the Ise Shrines
Mark Teeuwen and John Breen

The God Susanoo and Korea in Japan's Cultural Memory

Ancient Myths and Modern Empire

David Weiss

BLOOMSBURY ACADEMIC
LONDON • NEW YORK • OXFORD • NEW DELHI • SYDNEY

BLOOMSBURY ACADEMIC
Bloomsbury Publishing Plc
50 Bedford Square, London, WC1B 3DP, UK
1385 Broadway, New York, NY 10018, USA
29 Earlsfort Terrace, Dublin 2, Ireland

BLOOMSBURY, BLOOMSBURY ACADEMIC and the Diana logo are trademarks of Bloomsbury Publishing Plc

First published in Great Britain 2022
This paperback edition published 2023

Copyright © David Weiss, 2022, 2023

David Weiss has asserted his right under the Copyright, Designs and Patents Act, 1988, to be identified as Author of this work.

For legal purposes the Acknowledgments on pp. vii–viii constitute an extension of this copyright page.

Series design by Dani Leigh
Cover image: *Susanoo no mikoto*. History print showing Susanoo, the Shinto god of the sea and storms. MeijiShowa / Alamy Stock Photo

All rights reserved. No part of this publication may be reproduced or transmitted in any form or by any means, electronic or mechanical, including photocopying, recording, or any information storage or retrieval system, without prior permission in writing from the publishers.

Bloomsbury Publishing Plc does not have any control over, or responsibility for, any third-party websites referred to or in this book. All internet addresses given in this book were correct at the time of going to press. The author and publisher regret any inconvenience caused if addresses have changed or sites have ceased to exist, but can accept no responsibility for any such changes.

A catalogue record for this book is available from the British Library.

Library of Congress Control Number: 2021947576

ISBN: HB: 978-1-3502-7118-0
PB: 978-1-3502-7121-0
ePDF: 978-1-3502-7119-7
eBook: 978-1-3502-7120-3

Series: Bloomsbury Shinto Studies

Typeset by Newgen KnowledgeWorks Pvt. Ltd., Chennai, India

To find out more about our authors and books visit www.bloomsbury.com and sign up for our newsletters.

Contents

List of Tables	vi
Acknowledgments	vii
Note to the Reader	ix
Introduction	1

Part 1 Blurred Boundaries and Liminal Identities

1	At the Margin of the Divine Country: Korea in Japanese Cultural Imagination	17
2	A Foil to Set Off the Sun Goddess: Susanoo in the Ancient Sources	47
3	Passion for Transgression: Susanoo's Liminal Character	65

Part 2 Political Mythology: A Genealogy of Susanoo's Connection to Korea

4	"I Do Not Want to Stay in This Land": Susanoo's Sojourn to Korea in the Ancient Court Chronicles	87
5	The God with a Thousand Faces: Susanoo and His Alter Egos in Medieval Mythology	113
6	Korea as a Realm of Death: Susanoo and Korea in Modern Discourses	145

Epilogue After the War: Susanoo in Scholarship, Tourism, and Popular Culture	175
Notes	183
Bibliography	201
Index	229

Tables

2.1	Assignment of Realms to Susanoo and His Siblings in *Nihon shoki* and *Kojiki*	55
2.2	Hirata Atsutane's Equation of Susanoo and Tsukuyomi in *Tama no mihashira*	60
2.3	Ideological Implications of Susanoo's Juxtaposition with Amaterasu in Colonial Discourse	64
4.1	Different Names for the Sword Susanoo Used to Slay the Eight-Headed Serpent in the *Nihon shoki*	90
4.2	Center and Periphery in the Imperial Mythology of Ancient Japan	101
6.1	Center and Periphery in Colonial Discourse	168

Acknowledgments

This is a revised version of my doctoral dissertation accepted by the Faculty of Humanities at the University of Tübingen, Germany. At the same time, this book is the outcome of my lengthy engagement with the god Susanoo, whom I first encountered in an introductory course on Japanese religious and intellectual history I took at the University of Tübingen in 2007.

There are many people who have contributed to this book. Intellectually, it owes its greatest debt to Klaus Antoni, who taught the introductory course mentioned above and supervised my doctoral dissertation. As a teacher, supervisor, and later as a colleague and friend, he has been an inexhaustible fount of inspiration and encouragement. It is impossible to name here all the ways in which Klaus contributed to this book, but he surely lived up to the German term "Doktorvater." My second PhD supervisor You Jae Lee gave me precious feedback on issues of Korean history and supported my research stay at Seoul National University in spring 2014. Heartfelt thanks also go to Moon-Ey Song and Unsuk Han, who allowed me to sit in on their Korean courses and thus helped me to acquire the linguistic skills necessary for the completion of this research project. Bernhard Scheid and Juljan Biontino kindly read the whole manuscript and provided invaluable feedback. Together with Tobias Scholl, Juljan also offered much-needed advice and support during my stay in Seoul.

I received helpful feedback on my research by members of the TUDOKU network comprising scholars from the University of Tübingen, Doshisha University and Korea University during conferences on modern East Asian history in Seoul (2016) and Kyoto (2017). At Rikkyo University, Maeda Ryōzō invited me to become a member of the research project "'National Cultures' and Religiosity in modernizing Germany and Japan" (2018–22), funded by the Japan Society for the Promotion of Science (JSPS), whose members offered important suggestions and comparative perspectives to my research. I am grateful to Aono Masaaki, Erica Baffelli, Hirafuji Kikuko, Itagaki Ryūta, Hwansoo Kim, Kubota Hiroshi, Mizutani Satoshi, Ian Reader, Monika Schrimpf, Birgit Staemmler, Terakawa Machio, Michael Wachutka, and Robert Wittkamp, all of whom provided helpful comments or gave me the opportunity to present my research at different stages of the project. My thanks also go to Fabio Rambelli (who suggested the book's subtitle) and Lalle Pursglove at Bloomsbury for their help in bringing this book into print, as well as to the two anonymous readers for providing insightful suggestions that helped me to sharpen the book's argument.

This book was made possible, thanks to the financial support of many institutions. The German Academic Exchange Service funded my research stays at Doshisha University (October 2009–March 2011, September–October 2017) and Seoul National University (March–June 2014), as well as fieldwork in Shimane Prefecture (May–August 2013). A PhD scholarship of the federal state Baden Württemberg (LGFG) allowed me to focus all my energy on my research from autumn 2012 to winter 2014. This work was also supported by JSPS KAKENHI Grant Number 18KK0004.

My heartfelt gratitude goes to my wife Chizuru and our son Florian for their company and encouragement on the financially unstable and often mentally exhausting path of scholarship. Lastly, I want to thank my parents for their never-ending support over the years. Without them this book would not have been possible.

Note to the Reader

Japanese terms are romanized according to the Modified Hepburn system. Transcriptions from Korean and Chinese follow the McCune–Reischauer and Pinyin (without diacritic markers) systems, respectively. Curly brackets indicate glosses, which are usually written in smaller script in the primary sources. Many of the sources discussed in the following pages consist of several fascicles (Jap. *maki* 巻, Kor. *kwŏn*; literally: "scrolls"). To prevent confusion with the volume numbers of modern editions, fascicles are indicated by Roman numerals. Unless otherwise noted, all translations are by the author.

Like other modern nation-states, Japan and Korea are fond of tracing their roots back to the ancient past. It should be kept in mind, however, that the Korean peninsula was first unified in 668 and the first central state in Japan emerged during the same period (although it would take much longer to consolidate the whole archipelago). Therefore, I have tried to follow William Farris's (1998: 57) advice to "use the words Korea and Japan sparingly" for earlier periods. If they are used nonetheless, they should be understood in a purely geographical sense.

Introduction

In 1910, the year of Japan's annexation of Korea, Emperor Meiji 明治 (1810–1912; r. 1867–1912) announced that colonizers and colonized would henceforth "live together in brotherhood" (Duus 1995: 432). This family metaphor, implying as it did a harmonious, although not necessarily equal, relationship between the two peoples, is a recurrent motif throughout the period of Japanese colonial rule over Korea (1910–45). Japanese scholars, journalists, and politicians used this trope to justify the implementation of a strict assimilation policy on the peninsula with the goal to rob Koreans of their cultural identity and turn them into loyal subjects of the Japanese empire. The Japanese family state with the emperor as "father of the nation" at its apex had turned into a "family-empire" (Uchida 2011: 362).

Imperialist thinkers found a highly welcome visualization of the relationship between the two countries in the sibling relationship of the sun goddess Amaterasu 天照 and her brother Susanoo as depicted in ancient Japanese mythology. In the court chronicles *Kojiki* 古事記 (Record of Ancient Matters; 712) and *Nihon shoki* 日本書紀 (Chronicles of Japan; 720), the immature and unruly Susanoo is contrasted with his serene and radiant sister. After an initial rebellious phase, the mischief-maker mends his ways and submits to his sister's authority. In the colonial context, the identification of Susanoo with Korea and of his sister with Japan suggested itself. This allegory, which was already employed in newspaper articles predating the annexation (Chang 2009: 376; No 2011: 53–4), was publicly embraced by the colonial government in the 1940s. In 1942, for instance, Governor General Koiso Kuniaki 小磯國昭 (1880–1950) explained to a group of Korean schoolchildren that the Japanese could trace their lineage to Amaterasu, whereas the Koreans descended from Susanoo who had appeared on Mount Soshimori in Korea (Scholl 2018: 82). The ideological implications of this statement are clear; the "sibling nation"

Korea was in need of Japanese guidance just as Amaterasu's unruly younger brother depended on his benevolent elder sister's leadership (cf. Suga 2004: 56-7). As Chizuko Allen (2008: 107) rightly remarks, the "parallel of the elder and younger siblings pointed to hierarchical relations just as in the traditional Japanese family."

But how did Susanoo acquire such a central role in defining Japanese-Korean relations during the colonial period? Why did an ancient myth lend itself so readily to a modern imperialistic interpretation? These questions can only be answered by analyzing the history of this myth's reception through the centuries leading up to this specific moment in the two countries' relationship. The present study, therefore, traces the role myths and legends surrounding Susanoo played in Japanese intellectual history from the ancient to the modern period. This genealogical analysis will demonstrate that Susanoo features prominently in Japanese identity discourses long before the annexation of Korea. As early as the medieval period, Susanoo was regarded as a "foreign" deity who had come to the Japanese archipelago from the Asian mainland. In this way, Susanoo came to play the part of a liminal figure in Japanese identity discourses; while the sun goddess Amaterasu represented the center of Japanese collective identity, Susanoo was situated at its margin. In a way, Susanoo marks the boundary between "inside" and "outside" Japan, although—or perhaps, *because*—his own position is ambiguous. He is neither Self nor Other, or to use Victor Turner's (1967) famous expression, he is "betwixt and between." I will argue in this study that it is exactly this liminal position that predestined Susanoo for the task of defining Japan's equally ambivalent relationship to Korea in different historical periods, culminating in Susanoo's elevated position in modern discourses on colonial Korea's role within the Japanese empire.

Myth and Identity: Theoretical Considerations and Aim of This Study

The Meiji Restoration of 1868 marks a dramatic rupture in Japanese history. After governing the archipelago for more than 250 years, the Tokugawa bakufu (1600–1868)—and with it the rigid social stratification and the policy of national isolation[1]—came to an abrupt end. Western ideas flowed into the country, and long-held traditions were challenged and, in many cases, abolished. In this period of rapid social and political change, the Meiji oligarchs utilized the idea of Japan as a family state to create a national identity and a sense of belonging for the masses. This familistic ideology was created by combining ideas of various early modern schools of thought, most importantly National Learning (*kokugaku* 国学) and the Mito 水戸 School. For Motoori Norinaga 本居宣長 (1730–1801), one of the pioneers of National Learning, the myths contained in the *Kojiki* provided "a concrete model for reorganizing Japan" that was "based on the special role of the emperor as a successor and representative of the sun goddess Amaterasu" (Antoni 2016: 133). Norinaga's self-proclaimed disciple Hirata Atsutane 平田篤胤 (1776–1843) extended the idea of the imperial family's divinity to the Japanese people as a whole and thus laid the foundation for the family state ideology. Finally, the Mito School's concept of the "unity of loyalty and filial piety" (*chūkō itchi* 忠孝一致) emphasized the familial ties between the emperor and his subjects. Based on a reinterpretation of the Five Relationships of Confucianism, Mito scholars argued that in Japan the two central relationships of master/vassal and parent/child were one and the same thing. In this way, the emperor was ideologically turned into a father of the whole nation (ibid.: 151, 168–9).

But the architects of this traditionalist state ideology faced one major problem: the imperial institution, which had been politically irrelevant for centuries, was virtually unknown to the common people. Thus, the government authorities were at pains to propagate the new state doctrine and the emperor's elevated position within it throughout the country. This was achieved, for instance, by drawing up public notices that explained the emperor's exalted status in easily understandable language. An early specimen dating from the spring of 1868 reads thus: "In this land called Japan there is one called the Emperor … who is descended from the Sun Deity … This has not changed a bit from long ago and just like the Sun being up in the heavens He is the Master" (quoted in Fujitani 1996: 10).[2] The prominence of the sun goddess as the source of imperial authority can hardly be expressed in clearer words. In the same vein, an imperial edict of 1870 proudly pronounces that "the Heavenly Deities and the Great Ancestress [Amaterasu Omikami] established the throne and made the succession secure. The line of Emperors in unbroken succession entered into possession thereof and handed it on" (quoted in Holtom 1943: 6, brackets in original). In his recent monograph *Amaterasu to tennō* (Amaterasu and the Emperor), Chiba Kei (2011: 13–14, 42–62) traces the conscious effort of the fledgling Meiji government to link the imperial institution to the sun goddess, who had in the latter half of the Tokugawa period been utilized to legitimize various popular uprisings commonly referred to as *yonaoshi* 世直し (renewal of the world). In this way, it became possible to forge a direct link between the populace and the emperor.

The idea of an unbroken line of succession that connected the present emperor with the sun goddess was based on the ancient myths contained in the *Kojiki* and the *Nihon shoki*. Of special importance in this context is a passage of the *Nihon shoki* in which Amaterasu sends her grandson Ninigi down to earth and instructs him to establish a dynasty, which "like Heaven and Earth, [was to] endure for ever." Up to 1945, every Japanese schoolchild had to memorize the sun goddess's proclamation in ancient Japanese (Brownlee 1999: 5).

The mythical foundations of the Japanese state were reinforced by the construction of a national cult centering on Jinmu Tennō 神武天皇,[3] the legendary first emperor, who, according to the *Nihon shoki*, had founded the Japanese state in 660 BCE. In 1873, the Meiji government officially adopted a new imperial calendar, which counted years from the date of Jinmu's alleged founding of Japan. In 1940, huge celebrations were held all over the country to commemorate the 2,600th anniversary of this event, whose fictivity need not be stressed here.[4]

Chiba (2011: 104-9) points out that the Meiji emperor's image changed drastically in the early 1870s. Instead of court robes he started wearing military uniform, stopped using makeup, cut his hair short, and grew a beard. This new image of the emperor as a military leader rather than a high priest was modeled on modern Western sovereigns and disseminated all over the country in the form of a photograph exhibited at schools and other public sites. The emperor's masculinization called for a new political symbol, which Meiji ideologues found in the figure of Jinmu Tennō. Emperor Jinmu thus replaced Amaterasu as the most important idol of national identity. However, by 1940, both mythical figures played an equally important role in the official state ideology, as can be inferred from Prime Minister Konoe Fumimaro's 近衞文麿 (1891-1945) address during the ceremony of the 2,600th anniversary of the founding of Japan:

> When our Imperial founder [the Sun Goddess Amaterasu, progenitor of the imperial line] established the country, began Her rule and made Her grandchild reign over the Eight Provinces, She gave him a divine rescript and the Three Sacred Treasures [also known as the sacred regalia, the three treasures consist of a sword, a necklace of jewels, and a mirror]. The Imperial reign thus established was handed down to the Emperor Jimmu, who ... came to the Throne and ruled over the entire realm with virtue. Since then, all succeeding emperors have

inherited the divine rule, consolidated its foundation and added to the great
Imperial plan straight down to the present—the 2,600th year. (quoted in Ruoff
2010: 16, brackets in original)

These examples show the centrality of the ancient myths in the construction of a modern Japanese national identity. Japan is far from exceptional in this regard, however. Without recourse to the Japanese case, Anthony Smith (2003: 24–5), for instance, defines national identity as "the maintenance and continual reinterpretation of the pattern of values, symbols, memories, *myths*, and traditions that form the distinctive heritage of the nation, and the identification of individuals with that heritage and its pattern" (emphasis added).

While Germany shows parallels to Japan insofar as it acquired its colonies within decades after the founding of a modern nation-state, the nature of Japan's contiguous empire was decidedly different from the far-flung empires of Germany and other Western colonial powers (Morris-Suzuki 1998: 162). Perhaps it is not surprising, therefore, that Japanese policymakers pursued strategies for constructing a collective identity in their new colony Korea that were similar to the ones that had already proved their efficacy in fostering a sense of national unity within Japan. Ernest Gellner (1983: 57) defines nationalism as

the general imposition of a high culture on society, … [the] generalized diffusion of a school-mediated, academy-supervised idiom, codified for the requirements of reasonably precise bureaucratic and technological communication.

This definition applies to the Japanese colonization of Korea as well (Caprio 2009: 8); utilizing the education system (that also played a central role in the dissemination of the Meiji state ideology within the Japanese mainland) and backed by academic scholarship, the Japanese intelligentsia endeavored to incorporate the new Korean subjects into their ideological construct of a Japanese family state.

In this context, the so-called "theory of common ancestry of Japanese and Koreans" (*Nissen dōsoron* 日鮮同祖論; hereafter abbreviated as "theory of common ancestry") fulfilled a crucial function. According to this theory, Japan and Korea were sibling nations with common (pre-) historical roots. As we have seen, the idea that Japan forms a family state guided by the paternal emperor was based on the myths contained in the ancient Japanese court chronicles. A major problem for theorists of common ancestry was that Koreans (in contrast to the often nonliterate societies colonized by Western nations) possessed their own chronicles and their own myths that were quite incompatible with their Japanese counterparts. Worse still, the *Samguk yusa* 三國遺事, a Korean chronicle from the thirteenth century, dated Tan'gun's 檀君 founding of Ancient Chosŏn, the legendary first state on the Korean peninsula, to the year 2333 BCE,[5] that is, more than a millennium earlier than Jinmu's alleged founding of Japan.

Japanese scholars dealt with this problem in different ways. Shiratori Kurakichi 白鳥倉吉 (1865–1942), founder of the discipline of Oriental History (*tōyōshi* 東洋史), argued that the legend of Tan'gun was fabricated by Buddhist priests sometime after 372. The state of Ancient Chosŏn, he maintained, did not exist before approximately the fifth century. This enabled him to demonstrate "that Korea as a unified country developed relatively late in the history of Asia, *and later than Japan*" (Tanaka 1993: 82–5, emphasis added). Most Japanese historians at the time denied Tan'gun's historicity (Kim 2018: 53–5). When the Government-General in 1922 commissioned Japanese and Korean historians to compile an authoritative history of Korea, the question of whether Tan'gun should be included or not proved to be the most controversial subject. While Korean scholars maintained that due to his ideological importance to the Korean people he should be included even if it was not possible to prove his historical existence,[6] their Japanese counterparts argued that it would be inappropriate to include a mythical figure like Tan'gun in a historical chronicle (Kawamura 1996: 16–30). This contrasts sharply with Japanese historians' attitude toward their own founding myths. Although they knew of the fictivity of Jinmu, this did not prevent most academic historians from joining (and in many cases playing an active part) in the festivities of 1940 (Brownlee 1999: 180–5).

The proponents of the theory of common ancestry pursued another strategy. And it is here that Susanoo enters the scene. Several Japanese scholars argued that Tan'gun was in fact none other than the little brother of the Japanese sun goddess. This theory not only allowed the ideological incorporation of the new colonial subjects into the Japanese family state but it was also used to legitimate the primacy of the Japanese, whose ancestral deity was, after all, the elder sister of the Korean founding god. Moreover, the contrast between Susanoo's lack of self-control and Amaterasu's serenity was used as a model for the relationship of the two "sibling" nations: in colonial discourse, the alleged immaturity of the Korean people and their state was often contrasted with Japan's successful modernization, which in turn legitimated Japanese colonial rule. Incidentally, this dichotomy is strikingly similar to that between marginal Izumo and central Yamato as presented in the ancient court chronicles. In both cases, Susanoo is associated with the margin, Amaterasu with the center of imperial authority.

Social and Political Functions of Myth

Why do ancient myths play such a central role in discourses on Japanese and Korean identities? According to Bruce Lincoln (1999: 147), myths are "*ideology* in narrative form" (emphasis in original). They "convey the political and moral values of a culture and ... provide systems of interpreting ... individual experience within a universal perspective" (Doty 1986: 11). Eric Csapo (2005: 134) emphasizes myth's social dimension by defining it as a "collective narrative." Thus,

> A narrative is not a myth the first time it is told, but only a story or an account. What makes a story a myth is the fact that it is received by a given society and that a given society participates in its transmission. ... Thus both in theory and in practice we can never identify any individual creator of a myth. So long as myth is a collective narrative by definition, the only relevant consideration are the mentality and purposes of the society for which the myth is a myth.

Chiara Bottici (2007: 114–15) therefore calls for an "interrelational and phenomenological approach to myth" that takes into account the active role played by audiences in the "process of telling-receiving and retelling of myth." This approach, which is inspired by Hans Blumenberg's (2006) concept of the "work on myth" (*Arbeit am Mythos*), shifts the focus from questions of origin or content to the process of transmission and transformation of myths. Blumenberg (2006: 133, 192, 240–1, 294–5, 299–300) maintains that even the earliest mythical narratives known to us are already products of the work on myth; before they have first been put into writing, they have already passed through a lengthy process of transmission, adaptation, and reformulation. It is thus not possible to draw a sharp line between the genesis and the reception of a myth since both processes are inextricably linked.

Adopting this approach, the present study treats the oldest extant narratives about Susanoo contained in the ancient court chronicles in the same way as later elaborations and reformulations; although these mythological corpuses assumed canonical status early on, they are the result of deliberate selection and rearrangement rather than the faithful reproduction of primordial tales passed on from times immemorial. The aim of the editors of the ancient court chronicles as well as of later exegetes was to harness the ideological potential of the myths for their own political agendas. Myths have "an ordering, a sense giving, an integrative, a legitimating or delegitimating, and a mobilizing function" (Bizeul 2005: 31) and can therefore be powerful tools in the hands of people in power.

Thus, myths continue to fulfill an important function in the construction and maintenance of collective identity—be it familial, ethnic, cultural, or national. Besides myths of common ancestry, what Smith (2003: 212) calls "myths of golden ages" play an important role by providing "a sense of *continuity* between the present and a (preferably glorious) past" (emphasis in original). In the Japanese case, such "golden ages" were identified in the allegedly pure ancient Japan of the Age of the Gods or of Jinmu Tennō's times—an idealized past that scholars of National Learning imagined as free of the tainting influence of the "Chinese Spirit" that was later to enter Japan in the form of Buddhism and Confucianism. The Meiji Restoration was justified as a restoration of imperial rule (*ōsei fukko* 王政復古) and thus as a return to the glorious times of Jinmu or the emperor-governed *ritsuryō* 律令 state of the seventh century, on which the institutions of the early Meiji state were modeled (Wachutka 2012: 11–18, 23–33). Shortly after toppling the Tokugawa bakufu, the fledgling Meiji government promulgated the so-called "edicts to separate *kami* and buddhas" (*shinbutsu bunri no rei* 神仏分離令), which aimed at the institutional eradication of Shintō-Buddhist combinatory practices that had heretofore constituted the norm of Japanese religiosity. These edicts reinforced the connection of Shintō shrines with the imperial institution by purging any deities or religious elements not mentioned in the ancient court chronicles. In this way, the ancient myth-histories[7] were reinvented as sacred texts of Shintō. Based on *kokugaku* notions of a pre-Buddhist golden age, the new government was thus presented as the correction of a temporary aberration and the return to the direct imperial rule of ancient times (Thal 2002: 388–91).

The annexation of Korea, in turn, was viewed as a return to primordial unity under Japanese rule, as depicted in the *Nihon shoki*.[8] Here, we see another important function of myth, namely as a "retrospective pattern" providing "justification by precedent" (Malinowski 1926: 91). Proponents of the theory of common ancestry used the ancient myths to present Japanese rule over the peninsula as the natural state of affairs and Korean independence as a temporary accident of history. Myths are, moreover, "instruments of initiation and bonding, and thereby of *assimilating persons into the grid and group mentality of a society*" (Ellwood 2009: 26, emphasis added). Unsurprisingly, imperialist ideologues endeavored to utilize this integrative potential for the cultural assimilation of Koreans into the Japanese empire.

Tradition, Memory, and Identity

Eric Hobsbawm's concept of the invention of tradition is highly relevant in this context. Hobsbawm (1983: 1) defines an invented tradition as "a set of practices, normally governed by overtly or tacitly accepted rules and of a ritual or symbolic nature, which seek to inculcate certain values and norms of behaviour by repetition, which automatically implies continuity with the past." Rather than being passively inherited from preceding generations, traditions are selectively "fashioned from both material and discursive antecedents," that is, they are *chosen* from a preexisting cultural corpus and rearranged to meet contemporary needs (Vlastos 1998: 12). Scholars who adopt Hobsbawm's concept tend to focus on the selection and reinterpretation of these old ideas for new purposes in a modern context, most commonly that of nation building. Although the present study will address this question as well, it will apply the same methodology to premodern processes of reception, thereby showing that the discursive antecedents on which modern-day ideologues based their invented traditions were themselves the result of the invention of tradition. A large portion of this study is therefore dedicated to a genealogical analysis of the various reinterpretations and reconfigurations Susanoo was subjected to in the course of Japanese intellectual history. Such an approach, I believe, is helpful in grasping the social functions of myth. If myth indeed serves as a precedent justifying the status quo, it loses its raison d'être as soon as it is no longer linked to the everyday experiences of the transmitting group (Bottici 2007: 112, 129, 178–9). It is exactly for this reason that myths continually need to be reconfigured in order to meet present ideological needs: "every historical change creates its mythology" (Malinowski 1926: 92).

The concept of cultural memory, coined by Jan Assmann (1999: 48–56), provides a convenient theoretical framework to describe these processes of selection and reception.[9] For Assmann, cultural memory forms one aspect of a group's collective memory—the other being communicative memory. The latter contains biographical memories, it is informal in nature, and reaches back no further than three to four generations. Cultural memory, on the other hand, reaches back to the primeval times of myth; it is highly formed, narratively structured, and institutionalized. Cultural memory occupies a central position in the construction and maintenance of a group's collective identity and is therefore reactivated and kept alive through rituals, monuments, chronicles, and other objectivations. In this context, myths emerge as "objects of (memory) politics" that are "purposefully employed and disseminated by the leaders of a movement or a state" (Hein-Kircher 2007: 29).

Cultural memory is in a constant state of flux as each change in a group's situation necessitates an adaptation of its cultural memory. Each present imagines its own past. To account for this dynamic nature, Aleida Assmann (2010: 133–42) distinguishes two modes of cultural memory that are in constant mutual exchange: functional and storage memory. The functional memory contains elements that are directly relevant to a group's self-perception at a certain point in time, whereas the storage memory contains an amorphous mass of elements that are no longer (or not yet) relevant to the group's present situation. The latter can thus be considered the former's background; it is from the storage memory that the discursive antecedents for the construction of a new functional memory are unearthed as soon as changes in a group's experienced reality call for modifications of its collective identity.

To illustrate these dynamic processes of selection and reception, the present study examines three interrelated aspects: (1) the myths surrounding Susanoo as presented in the ancient sources, on which all later interpretations (with varying degrees of faithfulness) were based; (2) the reception of these myths (including reinterpretations and reformulations) up to the modern period; and finally, (3) their ideological utilization in the context of Japanese colonial rule in Korea. Thus, this study not only asks questions formulated by Stephen Vlastos (1998: 5), such as "how, by whom, under what circumstances, and to what social and political effect" Susanoo was associated with the colonial Korean subjects and how this notion was "formulated, institutionalized, and propagated." It also examines what discursive antecedents the Japanese intelligentsia could draw upon. What materials did the storehouse of Japanese tradition (or in Aleida Assmann's terms: the storage memory) offer opinion leaders eager to justify colonial rule in Korea? And what strategies did they pursue in choosing from it?

It might seem unusual to focus a study of this kind on an individual deity, rather than on a specific text (for instance, the *Kojiki*), a particular religious or intellectual tradition (such as Shintō or *kokugaku*), or a religious or political institution (obvious examples include the Ise Shrines and the Japanese emperor), but in recent years the number of studies dedicated to individual deities and their roles in religious and political discourses (especially in medieval, but also in ancient and modern Japan) has increased.[10] This trend is probably due to the insight that deities (as discursive antecedents and historical precedents endowed with a special sanctity) possess something akin to an agency of their own (Faure 2016b: 44–5). They are inscribed in various mythical and ritual contexts and though it is possible to reconfigure them by emphasizing certain aspects at the cost of others, a complete remodeling seems hardly possible. After all, myths can only fulfill their social functions as long as they are endowed with a sense of sacred authority. Unconvincingly fabricated interpretations that blatantly contradict discursive antecedents would jeopardize this sense of authority and therefore weaken the myth's legitimating power. Matsumoto Naoki (2016: 18–21, 30–1) calls this authority the "power of myth" and emphasizes that the creators of a new mythology must always move within the constraints of previous mythical traditions in order to safeguard this power. As the present study will show, through all his manifold reinventions, something of the "original" Susanoo of the ancient chronicles (in all his complexity and contradictoriness) remains visible.

Structure of This Study

The present study attempts to answer two interrelated questions: (1) *Why* did Susanoo become a central topic in discourses on Japanese and Korean identity during the colonial period? (2) *How* did he end up in this elevated position within scholarly and public discourses? The first part focuses on the first question by explicating the ideological need filled by Susanoo during the colonial period, whereas the second part is dedicated to a genealogical analysis of the various (re-)formulations and (re-)interpretations the deity and his narrative had undergone up to that point in history, thus tracing Susanoo's way to colonial fame.

The first chapter examines Korea's image in Japanese historical consciousness and cultural imagination. This investigation reveals a highly ambiguous attitude that combines admiration with fear and feelings of superiority. The chapter places special emphasis on the Meiji Restoration, which represents an important turning point marking Japan's adoption of a Western-inspired concept of civilization that went hand in hand with a radical condemnation of (Confucian-based) Asian civilization. It will be argued that this led to modern Japan's contradictory attitude toward its Asian neighbors; on the one hand, Japanese colonial rule was justified through its allegedly superior level of (Western) civilization, and on the other, Japan contrasted itself as an Asian country with the Western colonial powers, picturing itself as the liberator of Asia from Western imperialism. In Korea, this contradictory attitude found expression in concrete colonial policies that hovered between political exclusion and cultural assimilation of the colonial subjects. It was in this historical context that the theory of common ancestry emerged. The chapter examines the role of both academic scholars and agents of State Shintō in the dissemination of this theory and illuminates Susanoo's function in colonial discourses.

During the period of colonial rule over Korea, only historical claims that were based—however loosely—on the ancient Japanese sources were considered legitimate. This is also true for the myth of Susanoo and its modern interpretations. The second chapter, therefore, provides an overview of Susanoo's appearance in the oldest sources. Most important in this context are the court chronicles *Kojiki* and *Nihon shoki* that were considered canonical texts on Japanese history and mythology. These two chronicles are contrasted with a third source: the *Izumo fudoki* of 733. This work, which was created by the local rulers of the Izumo Province rather than by the imperial court, draws an image of Susanoo that differs quite strikingly from the one presented in the court chronicles. Here, Susanoo is depicted as a peaceful and rather insignificant ancestral deity—an image only rarely referred to by prewar and wartime historians. The chapter thus serves as a reminder that ancient Japanese mythology is much more complex and variegated than colonial-period scholars made it appear. Thus, their prioritizing of the court chronicles over the *Izumo fudoki* can already be regarded as a first step in the construction of a politically useful image of Susanoo. In Aleida Assmann's terminology, the Susanoo appearing in the *Izumo fudoki* was relegated to the storage memory. The chapter puts a special focus on Susanoo's function in the court chronicles as a negative foil to set off the sun goddess Amaterasu, since Susanoo fulfilled a similar function in colonial discourses contrasting Japan with Korea.

The third chapter draws attention to Susanoo's liminal character. While the ancient court chronicles clearly associate his sister Amaterasu with the Plain of High Heaven, the uppermost layer in the mythical cosmoses of *Kojiki* and *Nihon shoki*, Susanoo delights in crossing cosmic boundaries. In the course of the mythical narrative, he visits all major realms (including his sister's heavenly abode, the realm of humans, and the peripheral realms of the dead), without entirely belonging to any of these realms. In a similar manner, it is impossible to identify Susanoo unambiguously as a member of either of the two groups of divinities depicted in the ancient court myths: the Heavenly Deities and the Earthly Deities. Besides his crossing of cosmic, spatial, and familial boundaries, Susanoo's fundamental "inbetweenness" also becomes apparent in his transgression of taboos. It is this liminal character, I will argue, that predestined Susanoo for his role in colonial-period discourses. Korean subjects were held in a similar state of perpetual inbetweenness throughout the colonial period; they were no longer allowed to identify as Koreans and not (yet) regarded as fully Japanese. Their liminal status is thus comparable to Susanoo's precarious position in the ancient myths.

The chapters grouped in Part 1 show Susanoo's usefulness in colonial discourses and detect the ulterior political ends of theorists of common ancestry. This may lead to the assumption that Susanoo's connection to the Korean peninsula was nothing more than a modern invention fabricated by colonial-period thinkers to meet the ideological needs of the day. While it cannot be denied that political considerations shaped these scholars', politicians', and opinion makers' interpretations, the second part of this study shows that Susanoo's association with Korea was by no means a modern invention.

As I will demonstrate in the fourth chapter, *Nihon shoki* and *Sendai kuji hongi* 先代旧事本紀 (Chronicle of Old Matters of Former Ages; probably tenth century), arguably the most authoritative sources of myth-history during the ancient period, already link Susanoo to the peninsula. While this link is missing in *Kojiki* and *Izumo fudoki*, it came up as early as the ninth century as a topic of discussion at an imperial court lecture on the *Nihon shoki*. The chapter also emphasizes Susanoo's connection to peripheral realms of the dead that were to ideologically color later interpretations of Susanoo and his connection to Korea. By analyzing the toponyms "Soshimori" and "Kumanari" that link Susanoo to the peninsula in the ancient sources, the chapter serves as the starting point of a genealogy of Susanoo's association with Korea. The fourth chapter thus unearths the earliest discursive antecedents and the textual sources on which colonial-period scholars, journalists, religious thinkers, and politicians would later base their arguments.

Chapter 5 is dedicated to Susanoo's transformation in the medieval period. Within the Buddhist *honji suijaku* 本地垂迹 framework that associated Japanese *kami* 神 with buddhas, bodhisattvas, and other divinities, Susanoo was equated with a large number of foreign deities, most of them connected to notions of pestilence, pollution, or death. Through these associations, Susanoo's negative traits were emphasized, and he was reimagined as a threatening foreign deity. The chapter traces Susanoo's role in Tendai 天台 thought, putting a special focus on developments at Gion 祇園 Shrine in Kyoto and Gakuenji 鰐淵寺 in Izumo Province, and in the mythicoritual framework of Yoshida Shintō, which inherited the network connecting Susanoo with his alter egos and preserved it through the early modern period.

Chapter 6 describes how, from the seventeenth century on, the combinatory paradigm of medieval mythology was increasingly criticized by neo-Confucian scholars and, later, by proponents of National Learning. Both schools of thought endeavored to retrieve a primordial form of Shintō, unadulterated by Buddhist influences. This process culminated in the early Meiji edicts to separate *kami* and buddhas, which marked the end of the combinatory paradigm that had dominated premodern Japanese religiosity. The chapter analyzes how these events affected the perception of Susanoo and his connection to Korea. Special emphasis is placed on Gion Shrine, where in response to the Meiji edicts Susanoo replaced one of his medieval alter egos as the main deity and in the process became linked to Korea and its mythical founder Tan'gun. In 1890, Hoshino Hisashi 星野恒 (1839–1917), a professor at Tokyo Imperial University, used Susanoo's connection to Korea to support his theory of the politico-cultural unity of Japan and Korea in ancient times. His position can be viewed as an early example of the theory of common ancestry, which was to enter the mainstream of scholarly and public discourse after Japan's annexation of Korea in 1910. In the colonial period, Susanoo's connection to the realms of death reappeared and was utilized as a metaphor to depict Korea as a bleak and sinister country that provided a welcome contrast with the rich and shining Japanese mainland. The chapter demonstrates how Japanese intellectuals gleaned fragments from earlier discursive traditions, such as Buddhist, Confucian, and *kokugaku* interpretations of the ancient myths, and reassembled them into a coherent narrative, thus illustrating the mechanisms of political mythology and the construction of cultural memory.

In the epilogue, I consider the postwar fate of Susanoo and his connection to the Korean peninsula, placing special emphasis on the so-called horserider theory that turned the colonial-period theory of common ancestry on its head. I also take a look at Susanoo's role as mascot and tourist attraction in Shimane Prefecture and as a popular character in videogames, showing how his association with Korea has receded from public consciousness as Korea was no longer considered a part of Japan.

Part One

Blurred Boundaries and Liminal Identities

1

At the Margin of the Divine Country: Korea in Japanese Cultural Imagination

Bruce Batten (2003: 102) convincingly argues that "ethnogenesis is a frontier process that results from the interactions between groups." If this is the case, the Korean peninsula's role in the formation of Japanese cultural and ethnic identity can hardly be overstressed. Despite temporal fluctuations, inhabitants of the Japanese islands were in close contact with the various polities on the Korean peninsula throughout most of recorded history and—as the archaeological record shows—even in times predating the advent of written history in both countries. The once commonly held view that "the Corean national genius seems to have left no impress of its own on the civilization which it received from China and handed on to Japan" (Aston [1896] 1956, vol. 1: ix) has been proved wrong by newer archaeological, historical, and linguistic studies (e.g., Lewin 1976).

This chapter provides a short overview of the entangled histories of Japan and Korea with a special emphasis on Japanese perceptions of Korea. I will attempt to show that these perceptions not only played a crucial role in shaping Japanese cultural identity but are also indispensable for an understanding of imperial Japan's ambiguous stance toward its Korean subjects. A helpful theoretical tool in this endeavor is the concept of cultural imagination introduced in a recent study by Sujung Kim (2014: 167–8) to frame Japanese perceptions of Silla 新羅. This concept is inspired by Assmann's studies on cultural memory but stresses the importance of the fictive or imagined dimension of collective memory that is expressed in such forms as myths or legends. Cultural imagination is thus a "conceptual tool used to reveal the persistent image of a specific culture vis-à-vis another cultural world over a long period of time." It is made up of a "network of images, comprised of two modalities that vacillated between resilient images and the fluid perceptions" (ibid.: 163). While Kim limits herself to Japanese perceptions of Silla up to the medieval period and emphasizes negative images of Korea, the present survey includes other polities on the Korean peninsula that were perceived in a much more positive light due to their amicable relations with the Japanese court. Moreover, I cover the early modern and, especially, the modern periods in order to demonstrate both continuities and ruptures between imperial Japan's attitude toward its colonial subjects on the peninsula and earlier perceptions of the neighboring country. Another difference between my and Kim's analysis lies in the types of text that are covered. Partly due to the timeframe of her survey and the institutional context of the deity at the center of her investigation, Kim focuses on Buddhist texts and visual images. The present study considers texts of different religious and philosophical schools as well as historiographic and journalistic sources. This results in a more variegated and complicated picture of Korea in the Japanese cultural imagination than that presented in Kim's work.

In the second half of the chapter, placing special emphasis on Susanoo's role in colonial discourse, I examine how perceptions of Korea were disseminated in both colonial Korea and mainland Japan and how they were used to justify colonial policies.

Japanese Perceptions of Korea Up to the Modern Period

In this section, I introduce three resilient images of the Korean peninsula that, despite being adapted to historical circumstances, remained rather stable over the centuries. These are the perceptions of Korea as (1) a land of riches and advanced civilization, (2) an external threat to Japanese security, and (3) a disobedient Japanese vassal state. In response to historical circumstances, one image could temporally eclipse the others, but the images themselves tended to remain surprisingly stable and resurface in virtually unaltered form time and again, when they could be utilized to explain the respective status quo.

Korea as a Land of Riches and Advanced Civilization

Archaeological artifacts allow us to trace the beginning of cultural exchange between inhabitants of the Korean peninsula and the Japanese islands back at least to the Yayoi period (800 BCE–250 CE), when the inhabitants of the archipelago imported and copied earthenware objects as well as stone objects such as axes, knives, swords, and arrowheads, and later adopted bronze casting technologies and forging techniques from the peninsula.[1] Since smelting technologies were unknown on the archipelago before the late fifth century CE, the Wa 倭[2] depended on the peninsula for the procurement of iron (Barnes 2007: 35). During the same period, from around the final century BCE, Chinese writing entered the archipelago via the Korean peninsula—although it would take many centuries for the first substantial domestically produced texts to appear (Lurie 2011: 17; Wittkamp 2014, vol. 2: 48–9). As Barbara Seyock (2004: 231) has pointed out, the interactions between the peoples around the Korea Straits were so intense during the Middle and Late Yayoi period that the similarities between the cultures of the Wa and the Han 韓 by far outweigh the differences.

The oldest written record of Han–Wa interactions is contained in the *Weizhi Dongyi zhuan* 魏志東夷伝 (Reports on the Wei, Description of the Eastern Barbarians; third century CE).[3] According to this Chinese chronicle, the Wa traded iron with Pyŏnhan 弁韓, one of the polities described as the "Three Han" (*samhan*) in the south of the Korean peninsula. This area was later called Kaya 伽倻 and remained an important center of metal production. The connection between this region and the Wa was so close that the author of the *Dongyi zhuan* believed the area, which was to develop into Kŭmgwan Kaya 金官伽耶,[4] was within the Wa's sphere of influence (Seyock 2004: 16, 133).

The cultural ties between the peninsula and the archipelago became even stronger in the succeeding Kofun period (250–600). In the fifth century, important innovations such as horse breeding, the custom of riding, new techniques of ironworking, gold and silver metallurgy, and stoneware manufacture entered the Japanese islands from the peninsula and contributed to the growth of the Yamato polity (Shiraishi 2004: 332–3). William Farris (1998: 110) ascribes the "influx of Korean-borne goods and services" during the Kofun period to four factors: (1) trade, (2) immigration, (3) the foreign policies of the peninsular states, and (4) plundering by Wa troops on the peninsula. Hence the technological revolution that occurred on the archipelago during this period was closely linked to the political situation on the Korean peninsula.

Considering this historical background, it is not surprising that the *Nihon shoki* describes Korea, first of all, as a land of riches. In one passage that will be treated in more detail in Chapter 4, Susanoo proclaims: "In the region of the land of Kara [Korea] there is gold and silver." Afterward he instructs his son how to build boats. While the passage is not entirely clear, the text seems to imply that these boats were intended to acquire the treasures from the peninsula. This interpretation is supported by a later passage in the same work. In the eighth year of legendary emperor Chūai's reign, the chronicle reports an oracle given by the emperor's spouse Okinaga-tarashi Hime 気長足姫 while divinely possessed. Through his consort's mouth, a deity advises Chūai to stop his military campaigns against the Kumaso of southern Kyushu, since there was a country that possessed "dazzling gold and silver and [treasures of] beautiful colors in abundance," namely Silla, the easternmost of the Korean Kingdoms. If the emperor worshiped the deity, the oracle goes on, he would surely be able to subdue Silla without bloodshed. The emperor does not believe the deity's words and dies shortly afterward (NSK VIII [Chūai 8/9/5–9/2/5], vol. 1: 410–13). However, his spouse, who is more commonly known as Empress Jingū 神功, crosses the sea to subdue the Korean peninsula. This legend, which was to become a central motif in the Japanese cultural imagination of Korea, will be treated in the following sections.

The most significant passage in the *Nihon shoki* that describes Korea as a country of advanced civilization is surely the report of Buddhism's transmission to Japan via Paekche 百濟, the kingdom situated in the southwest of the peninsula. In 552, the chronicle records, the king of Paekche sent an envoy to Japan to present the emperor with a golden statue of Śākyamuni and several Buddhist sutras, emphasizing the merits of this powerful teaching that had already been adopted in the three Korean kingdoms. Rejoicing, the emperor replied that he had "never before heard of such a wonderful teaching" (NSK XIX [Kinmei 13], vol. 2: 416/417). An interesting indicator of Japanese elites' ambivalent attitude toward the Korean peninsula can be observed in the latter's exclusion from the medieval *sangoku* 三国 worldview, which identified India, China, and Japan as the three sacred countries of Buddhism. Although Japanese Buddhists of the time were well aware of Buddhism's transmission via Paekche, within the *sangoku* framework, Korea was either viewed as a part of China or ignored altogether (Toby 2001: 18–19). Sujung Kim (2014: 170) regards the emergence of the three kingdoms model and the exclusion of Korea from it as "both a result of and a response to the tensions involved in overcoming the psychological complex that resulted from existing at the geographical margins vis-à-vis both India, the original land of Buddhism, and China, the center of civilization in the sinosphere." Arguably, this concept served to put Japan on a par with China and thus implicitly above Korea (Blum 2006: 31–3).

Nonetheless, Japanese perceived Korea as a country of advanced civilization up to the modern period. From the late fourteenth to the early sixteenth century, for instance, domainal lords and shōguns repeatedly requested copies of the famed *Tripitaka Koreana*, a collection of Buddhist scriptures (Kang 1997a: 26–8, 51–2, 72). When Toyotomi Hideyoshi 豊臣秀吉 (1537–1598), after unifying the Japanese archipelago under his rule, commanded the invasion of Korea (see below), he formed special units to systematically loot Korean books, objects of craftwork, ceramicists, weapons, movable metal type, gold and silver treasures, and other rare objects (Ha 2015: 323–4). During the Edo period, Japanese scholars and poets vied for the chance to meet members of the Korean embassies. Chosŏn Korea (1392–1910) was perceived as a center of neo-Confucian and Chinese learning. Many aspiring Japanese scholars thus petitioned members of the embassies for a preface to their poetry. Obtaining such a preface could substantially boost a young scholar's career (Lee 2013: 29; Lewis 1985: 27).

Korea as a Threat to Japanese Security

The intense interactions between early polities on the Korean peninsula and the Japanese islands were not always of a peaceful nature, but at times involved the dispatch of Wa soldiers to Korea. The Three Kingdoms period (300–668) was a tumultuous phase of Korean history, which was characterized by nearly incessant warfare between the kingdoms of Paekche in the southwest, Silla in the southeast, and Koguryŏ 高句麗 in the north of the Korean peninsula. As a rule, Yamato's relationship with Paekche seems to have been an amicable one through most of the period, whereas relations with Silla were more hostile.

A stele that was erected in 414 in present-day Jian 集安 in Jilin 吉林 Province of China, the former site of the Koguryŏ capital, to commemorate the deeds of King Kwanggaet'o 廣開土 of Koguryŏ (r. 391–412) informs us that Wa troops fought against the northern kingdom but were defeated and driven out of the peninsula at the beginning of the fifth century. The interpretation of the stele's inscription is complicated by the fact that many characters are defaced due to weathering. This led to vastly different readings by Japanese and Korean scholars after the stele's discovery in 1880: while Japanese historians argued that the stele proved the existence of a Japanese colony on the Korean peninsula, some Korean scholars accused the Japanese of manipulating the stele's inscription and others suggested that Koguryŏ had crossed the sea to attack Japan rather than the other way around. Today, the stele is commonly seen as a piece of state propaganda aiming to depict Koguryŏ as the hegemon in Northeast Asia that was able to protect its alleged vassal states (Silla and Paekche) from incursions by an outside power (Wa). Nonetheless the stele is taken as evidence of Wa troops' involvement in warfare on the peninsula from the late fourth to the early fifth century.[5]

In the latter half of the fifth century, the Wa again sent troops to the peninsula, this time, to assist Paekche in its competition with Silla for influence in Kaya. However, Paekche was weakened by repeated Koguryŏ attacks from the north and could not prevent Silla from conquering large portions of Kaya in the sixth century. The situation became even more desperate when Silla formed an alliance with Tang 唐 in 650, which succeeded in destroying Yamato's ally Paekche in 663 and Koguryŏ in 668 (Farris 1998: 114–20). The Japanese fleet sent to Paekche in 663 was crushed by a Tang armada soon after crossing the Korea Strait. Fearing an invasion of Japan by the combined Silla/Tang forces, the Japanese court hastened to strengthen its defenses: border guards operating a system of signal fires were stationed on the islands of Tsushima and Iki, and in northern Kyushu. Moreover, fortresses were constructed in northern Kyushu as well as in the provinces of Nagato, Tsushima, Sanuki, and Yamato. Bruce Batten (2006: 28, 24) aptly characterized this process as the construction of "Japan's first international boundary," where "no clear line between 'them' and 'us' had existed" prior to the war.

Thus, the Korean peninsula came to be perceived as a threat to Japanese security. However, this negative image was not limited to the fear of a military invasion. Especially from the early eighth century on, the peninsula was also perceived as a source of epidemics. One of the most fatal diseases in premodern Japan was smallpox. In the sixth century, Paekche envoys were accused of having first brought the epidemic to Japan. The most devastating outbreak occurred from 735 to 737 and killed an estimated 25 to 35 percent of the Japanese population (Farris 1985: 53–9, 65–6).

In the medieval period, perceptions of Korea became even more sinister as Japanese elites viewed the peninsula as a "demonic other" that was blamed not only for the outbreak of epidemics but also for piracy on the Japanese coast and even natural disasters such as earthquakes and volcanic activity (Kim 2014: 175–85). This scapegoating can only be understood in the framework of medieval elites' perception of the world as a series of "concentric circles of 'purity' and 'pollution'" extending outward from the Japanese capital "with the degree of 'pollution' increasing the further one moved away from the centre" (Murai 2001: 73). Only buddhas and deities were thought to be able to protect Japan from the dangers entering from the polluted realms beyond its borders—be they military invasions, epidemics, or natural disasters (Batten 2003: 37).

It was against this background that the ideology of Japan as a divine country (*shinkoku*) emerged. Interestingly, the term appears for the first time in the description of Jingū's conquest of the Korean peninsula in the *Nihon shoki*. When the king of Silla observed the approach of the Japanese troops, the chronicle tells us, he exclaimed that these must be the divine warriors from the divine country of Japan he had heard of. Concluding that resistance was futile, he surrendered and promised to annually send tribute henceforth (NSK IX [Chūai 9/10/3], vol. 1: 426–9). The next recorded usage of the term is again related to Silla but differs markedly from the *Nihon shoki*'s chauvinistic narrative. In 869 and 870, two ships from Silla pillaged areas of Kyushu. At the same time earthquakes and other natural disasters occurred in several provinces. In order to restore peace and order to the realm, Emperor Seiwa 清和 (850–881; r. 858–876) ordered temples and shrines throughout the country to perform rituals for the protection of the country. In these prayers for peace, the term *shinkoku* reappears (NSJ XVI [Jōgan 11/12/14]: 254–5). Here the term acquires the new meaning of Japan as a land protected by the deities. This aspect of the *shinkoku* ideology reemerged on a larger scale when Japan faced the Mongol invasions of the late thirteenth century. The numerous rituals conducted by the ruling elites at the time were imbued with the idea that Japan was a sacred country protected by the gods (Rambelli 1996: 393, 407). The Mongols had succeeded in conquering Korea and now mobilized Korean navy forces against Japan. Thus, the perception of Korea as a threat to Japanese security was reaffirmed in Japanese elites' consciousness.

At the end of the eighteenth century, this image resurfaced in a modified form: now Korea's alleged military weakness was regarded as a threat to Japan's security. Concerned about Russia's eastward expansion, Hayashi Shihei 林子平 (1731–1793), a proponent of Dutch studies (*rangaku* 蘭学), wrote a number of works in which he emphasized Korea's strategic importance for the security of Japan from Russian encroachment. This concern lingered in Japanese policymakers' heads and reemerged with force in the 1860s, shortly before the Meiji Restoration, when other Western powers had made their appearance in Japanese waters. Fearing that Korea could be seized by a Western power and used as a base of military operations against Japan, Kido Takayoshi 木戸孝允 (1833–1877), one of the Meiji oligarchs after 1868, together with the Tsushima official Ōshima Tomonojō 大島友之允 (1826–1882), and Katsu Yasuyoshi 勝安芳 (1823–1899), the superintendent of the bakufu navy, urged the bakufu to ensure Japanese security by invading Korea (Kim 1980: 79–80, 94–7).

Korea as a Disobedient Japanese Vassal State

The legend of Empress Jingū's invasion of Korea played a central role in shaping Japanese perceptions of Korea and therefore merits a closer look. Both the *Nihon shoki* and the *Kojiki* (which contains a shorter version of the narrative) record that after her husband's death Jingū performed the ritual of Great Purification and was divinely possessed for a second time. She learned that several deities had been instructing her, the most important among them none other than Amaterasu herself. Divine support secured Jingū's swift victory over the Korean forces (KJK II [Chūai]: 244–7; NSK IX [Chūai 9/2–3], vol. 1: 416–19). The *Kojiki* recounts that after Silla's submission an office for overseas tribute was established in Paekche, and the *Nihon shoki* goes even further by claiming that, intimidated by Jingū's mighty host, the kings of Paekche and Koguryŏ prostrated themselves before the empress and swore from now on to send tribute without cessation (NSK IX [Chūai 9/10], vol. 1: 430/431). The *Nihon shoki* records a further peculiar event that allegedly took place in the forty-seventh year of Jingū's regency. In this year, tribute missions from Paekche and Silla arrived in Japan at the same time. The tribute presented by the Silla envoy was of far superior quality. When the Paekche envoy was questioned, it was found out that the Silla envoy had forced him to switch their tribute goods. Thereupon, Jingū sent an invasion force to the peninsula, which defeated Silla and "pacified" the Kaya states (NSK IX [Jingū 47/4–49/3], vol. 1: 452–7). This episode clearly demonstrates the differing attitudes of Japanese elites toward Silla and Paekche.

More interesting than the narrative itself and what it tells us about its authors' perceptions of the peninsula is its reception. Yi Sŏngsi (2011: 50, 58) links the legend to Pierre Nora's concept of *lieu de mémoire* (site of memory) and demonstrates how the narrative was reinterpreted in each period of Japanese history to explain the present situation. At the end of the eighth century, diplomatic relations between Japan and Silla broke off, when both countries stopped sending official missions (Verschuer 2006: 13). Heian Japan's (794–1185) ruling elites, who were familiar with the legend of Jingū from countless literary adaptations, regarded this as ungrateful behavior on Silla's part. Although Silla had been treated generously by Jingū, they felt, the Korean kingdom resented Japan and had stopped sending the tribute missions they had once promised Jingū (Yi 2011: 39–40). The legend reemerged during the thirteenth century when Japan faced the Mongol invasions. During this period, Sujung Kim (2014: 180) argues, the narrative functioned as "a rhetoric tool for regaining confidence, superiority, and cultural identity" in the face of a national crisis. Against this historical background, the narrative's chauvinistic attitude toward the Korean peninsula became even more emphasized, as the example of the fourteenth century text *Hachiman gudōkun* 八幡愚童訓 (Teachings of Hachiman for Foolish Children) demonstrates. According to this text, Jingū ordered the sentence "The King of Silla is Japan's dog" inscribed on a rock after defeating Silla.

The legend was also used as a "historical precedent" that justified Japanese invasions of Korea. Hideyoshi, for instance, on his way from Kyoto to Kyushu, from where he launched his invasion of Chosŏn Korea in 1592, visited the shrines of Chūai and Jingū in Nagato. From records left behind by many retainers of the domainal lords who led the invasion, we know that they justified their deeds as retribution for Korea's negligence in sending the tribute missions promised to Jingū. The bloodshed on the peninsula was orchestrated as a sacrifice to the war god Hachiman 八幡, who was equated with Jingū's son Ōjin 応神, with whom, according to the legend, she was pregnant when invading Korea (Ooms 1985: 44; Yi 2011: 40–1). Although Hideyoshi's invasion was ultimately unsuccessful, the Tokugawa bakufu spared no effort to present Korea as a vassal state of Japan. The Korean embassies that Chosŏn kings, in response to bakufu requests, sent to Edo to congratulate a new shōgun upon his accession were paraded before the infamous ear mound (*mimizuka* 耳塚) in Kyoto, which was erected to bury the noses and ears of the Korean soldiers and civilians killed in Hideyoshi's wars (Toby 2008: 64–9). Moreover, the embassies are commonly referred to as "tribute missions" even in semiofficial documents compiled by Hayashi Razan 林羅山 (1583–1657), the Confucian advisor to the bakufu (Toby 1984: 41–2, n. 66). These displays of alleged bakufu power were successful in shaping not only elites' but also common people's perceptions of Korea, as can be inferred from local reenactments and numerous woodblock prints of the Korean embassies (Toby 1986). Against this background, the tale of Jingū reemerged as a popular theme of theater plays and woodblock prints (Yi 2011: 41–8). Such diverse intellectuals as the Confucian Arai Hakuseki 新井白石 (1657–1725), the *kokugaku* scholar Hirata Atsutane, and the Mito scholar Aizawa Seishisai 会沢正志斎 (1782–1863) were convinced of the historicity of Jingū and her conquest of Korea (Antoni 2016: 148–9; Kang 1997a: 200–1; Wakabayashi 1986: 306, n. 34).

The legend of Jingū's conquest was often conflated with the alleged existence of a Japanese colony called Mimana 任那 in southern Korea. Seishisai, for instance, writes: "After Jingū Kōgō conquered and incorporated the Three Kingdoms of Korea, an Imperial Magistrate (*fu*) was established to pacify the new territory. This 'Mimana Magistrate' was much like the 'Nagasaki Magistrate' (*bugyō*) of today" (Wakabayashi 1986: 306, n. 34). Apart from the *Nihon shoki*, only the Kwanggaet'o stele mentions a Japanese presence in Mimana Kara 任那加羅 (Kor. Imna Kara) (Szczesniak 1951: 259). Today the term "Mimana" is commonly taken to refer to the Kaya Federation (or a part thereof). The nature of the Japanese presence in this region is still a controversial topic but, considering Pyŏnhan's and Kaya's close ties with the Wa, it seems plausible that the Japanese court did indeed exert a certain (though limited) influence in the region. The Kaya rulers, who desired a counterweight to Silla and Paekche, probably even encouraged Wa engagement on the peninsula (Batten 1986: 212–13).[6]

In the second half of the nineteenth century, both Jingū's conquest and Mimana were raised as historical precedents for a Japanese colonization of Korea. For instance, Hirano Kuniomi 平野国臣 (1828–1864), a loyalist samurai active in the movement to overthrow the bakufu, wrote in the early 1860s that Japan "must reconquer Korea and restore the prefecture of Mimana," and Kido in 1868 called for the reestablishment of Japan's "ancient prefecture of Mimana" (Kim 1980: 82, 124). Empress Jingū's ideological importance for the fledgling Meiji state can be inferred from the fact that her portrait was printed on the first paper money produced by the Meiji government (Yi 2011: 48).

In this way, the narrative of Jingū functioned as a political myth, a component of Japanese cultural memory that in each period was adjusted to the present state of Korean-Japanese relations. With the notable exception of Hideyoshi's invasion, the narrative was used to delegitimize rather than legitimize the status quo. After all, the tale describes Japanese rule over the Korean peninsula as the natural state of affairs. Although no historical Japanese government before the Meiji Restoration could convincingly claim such hegemony over the peninsula, the idea became an important part of Japanese cultural imagination, which reemerged in the modern period, when many Japanese thinkers justified the annexation of Korea as a reunification rather than an imperialistic expansion (e.g., Abe 1928, fasc. I: 52–4; Kita 1979–82: 414–15).

As Heidi Hein-Kircher (2007: 26) points out, "Political myths often flourish in times of crisis, in phases of social and political change, and if deficiencies in identity and legitimacy occur." In the next section, we will turn to exactly such a phase of tremendous social and political change, namely the Meiji period (1868–1912), and examine the changes of Japanese perceptions of Korea during this tumultuous age.

The Meiji Restoration and Beyond: Western Civilization and Asian Backwardness

It has almost become a truism that identity can only emerge and be maintained in a dialectical process of differentiation of the Self from the Other. In this process, the Other can take many forms, it can be known or unknown, attractive, repelling, or threatening—or it might just leave us indifferent (Boesch

1996: 90). This applies not only to individual but also to collective identities since "something is only the *same* if it distinguishes itself as *other* from others" (Waldenfels 2011: 72, emphasis in original). As the preceding discussion of premodern Japanese perceptions of Korea has demonstrated, the peninsula can be regarded as Japan's closest Other throughout most of its history up to the Meiji Restoration. This started to change in the second half of the nineteenth century, when "the West" emerged as a new Other, which has served as an important foil of Japanese national identity ever since.

In the early Meiji period, Japanese intellectuals adopted a Western-inspired concept of civilization, for which the neologism *bunmei* 文明 was coined in order to differentiate it from the Chinese concept of civilization (*ka* 華), which stressed the importance of propriety and Confucian values. *Bunmei*, in contrast, emphasized the idea of progress, defined, first of all, by the ability to create material wealth (Morris-Suzuki 1996: 58). As Japanese elites adopted this new concept of civilization and struggled "to overcome their Western-defined inferiority" (Iida 2002: 4), they regarded the other peoples of East Asia as their "primitive 'Other,'" who could only be transformed into modern societies through Japanese intervention (Weiner 1997: 11). In this process, the image of Korea as a land of riches and advanced civilization was transformed into its opposite as Confucian civilization itself was viewed in a more negative light.[7] The West, on the other hand, was perceived as the "modern Other," effectively placing Japan in the intermediate position of a civilizational triad (Köhn and Schimmelpfennig 2011: 8; Oguma 1998: 645–8).

Japan's attitude toward Asia thus became highly ambiguous: while Japan's cultural superiority as a civilized—that is, westernized—nation served as a justification for the colonization of large portions of Southeast and East Asia (Weiner 1997: 10–14), the fact that Japan was itself an Asian country made it possible to depict Japan's imperial aggression as a liberation of Asia from Western colonialism and to construct "'Asia' as a site of counterhegemonic resistance" (Iida 2002: 16). Alan Christy (2012: 240) provides a succinct summary of Japan's contradictory attitude toward its colonies:

> The ideologies supporting Japanese colonialism were an amalgamation of Western colonial narrative frameworks of the civilized versus the primitive with a narrative of anti-Western, pan-Asian anti-imperialism. As a result, it was possible to hear apologists for Japanese colonialism talk about both the rights of a civilized Japan toward its more primitive neighbors and the responsibilities of an Asian Japan to liberate its Asian brothers from the yoke of the West.

What is more, after decades of rapid modernization and westernization, "Asia became the space to anchor Japan's unique identity" (Tōgō 2011: 165). The Meiji oligarchs were well aware that a wholesale adoption of western civilization was not feasible. Rather they embraced the slogan of *wakon yōsai* 和魂洋才 (Japanese Spirit and Western Knowledge) to allay popular anxieties about the fundamental changes accompanying the government's modernization policy (Oguma 2002: 31–2). In many cases, this allegedly "Japanese" spirit amounted to nothing else than traditional Asian, especially Confucian, ethics.

The family state ideology is a case in point. In 1888, Itō Hirobumi 伊藤博文 (1841–1909), one of the main authors of the Meiji constitution, explained to the Privy Council that in the European nations Christianity formed an axis that unified the people. For Japan, he continued, only the imperial institution could fulfill a comparable function (Maruyama 1961: 28–31). Itō thus attempted to utilize the emperor, an easily recognizable symbol of Japanese tradition, to fill a crucial position in the western-inspired modern nation-state. In the following decades, the emperor's ideological function as "Father of the Nation" became more and more pronounced as the idea of Japan as a homogeneous family state was elaborated by political thinkers. The final form of this state ideology can be seen in the *Kokutai no hongi* 国体の本義 (Cardinal Principles of the National Polity; 1937), a propagandistic work published by the Ministry of Education as a guidebook for teachers of ethics courses. This work clarifies that

> our country [= Japan] is one great family nation [comprising] a union of sovereign and subject, having the Imperial Household as the head family, and looking up to the Emperor as the focal point from of old to the present. Accordingly, to contribute to the prosperity of the nation is to serve for the prosperity of the Emperor; and to be loyal to the Emperor means nothing short of loving the country and striving for the welfare of the nation. Without loyalty there is no patriotism, and without patriotism there is no loyalty. … Of course, in foreign countries, too, there exists a spirit of patriotism. But this patriotism is not of a kind which, like in our country, is from the very roots one with loyalty and in perfect accord with reverence for the deities and the ancestors. (Gauntlett and Hall 1949: 83)

The concept of the family state, which was intended to serve as the state ideology of a modern, Western-inspired nation-state, was clearly built on Confucian paradigms, namely a reinterpretation of the hierarchical relationships of master/vassal and parent/child. At the same time, stubborn adherence to traditional

Confucian ways was regarded as the root of Korea's alleged backwardness. This shows that Japan's ambiguous attitude toward Asia indeed affected the very core of modern Japanese national identity.

Colonized Korea: Caught between Exclusion and Assimilation

The unresolved question of whether Japan belonged to the West or to Asia is also reflected in the policies pursued in Korea, which became a Japanese protectorate in 1905 and was annexed in 1910. Millie Creighton (1997: 212–14, 230) coined the term "*uchi* Others," that is, "inside Others" for contemporary Koreans resident in Japan, the so-called *zainichi* 在日 (Kor. *chaeil*) Koreans. She argues that they occupy a marginal position within Japanese society "because they straddle the division between *uchi* and *soto* (inside and outside)." During the colonial period, it could be argued, all of Korea was placed in a similar position at the margin of the Japanese empire: Koreans were viewed as Other due to their perceived backwardness, poverty, uncleanliness, and laziness (Caprio 2009: 88–91; Duus 1995: 399–406; Henry 2005: 646–53). These stereotypes are reminiscent of the ones Western powers applied to their colonized subjects. Thus, Korea was constructed as a part of "Japan's Orient." Stefan Tanaka (1993) uses this term to describe the way in which Japan constructed an image of Asia that was in many ways similar to the image of the Orient in Western nations. As Edward Said (1995) has shown in his classical study, in Europe these images were supported by the academic discipline of Orientalism. In Japan, the discipline of *tōyōshi* (Oriental History) and its most important proponent, Shiratori Kurakichi, fulfilled a similar function.

Yet, as Duus (1995: 399) points out, "history, language, and culture set limits on the degree to which the Japanese could distance themselves from the Koreans." While the differences between European colonizers and their subalterns were apparent and could readily be used as an affirmation of the superiority of European civilization by contrasting it with the allegedly uncivilized Oriental or African Other, "the Japanese colonisers fully understood that Korea was not an ahistorical void, or a culturally empty space that needed to be filled, but an integral part of their own history as well" (Pak and Hwang 2011: 378–80). The theory of common ancestry, which will be discussed in more detail shortly, even regarded Koreans as belonging to the same ethnic group as the Japanese.

The perceived backwardness of Japan's peninsular brethren was therefore commonly attributed to the alleged corruption of Korean politics and culture rather than to Koreans' racial inferiority (Caprio 2009: 81–9; Duus 1995: 407–13). Many Japanese scholars and politicians of the period were convinced that Korea was incapable of governing itself (Uchida 2011: 154–5). This, they believed, gave Japan not only the right but the moral duty to govern and civilize their peninsular neighbors. If governed competently—that is, by the Japanese—Korea would be able to develop into an enlightened modern nation, just like Japan. Itō Hirobumi, for instance, who served among other things as the first Resident-General of Korea, was convinced that:

> Koreans are great people, you know. In the history of their country there was a period when it was far more advanced than Japan. There is no reason that people with such a history cannot run their country themselves. They are in no way less competent than we [Japanese] are. They are not to blame for the circumstances they are in today. It's their government's fault. If only their country is governed well, then the people will not lack, qualitatively or quantitatively. (Quoted in Takii 2014: 190)

Here, Itō invokes the positive image of Korea as a country of advanced civilization but limits this characterization to an unspecified period in the past, which he, then, contrasts with the allegedly wretched "circumstances [Koreans] are in today." To return to its former greatness, Itō implies, the Korean people depended on Japan's benevolent guidance. As soon as Korea, following Japan's model, became fully modernized, he suggests, it would be able to regain its autonomy and independence (ibid.: 192).

In spite of the existence of positive stereotypes such as the one expressed by Itō, the persistence of traditional Korean culture was regarded as the cause of Korea's stagnation and as an impediment to its successful modernization. Therefore, the colonial government pursued a radical assimilation policy (dōka seisaku 同化政策) with the aim to turn Korean subalterns into loyal subjects of the Japanese empire. This policy, which was pursued with different degrees of intensity throughout the thirty-five years of Japan's colonial rule, extended over all aspects of colonized Koreans' lives (Caprio 2009; Henry 2014).

The most drastic measures of assimilation were taken after the outbreak of the Second Sino-Japanese War in 1937. This entailed the obligatory recitation of the "Pledge of Imperial Subjects," which had been specifically drafted for this purpose, on many occasions such as when Koreans received food rations or purchased train tickets. Korean school children had to recite a simplified version of this pledge in school every day. In some schools, regular "civic days" were introduced, on which pupils had to sing the Japanese national anthem and bow to the national flag. The educational ordinance of 1938 defined three major themes of wartime education in Korea, namely "clarifying the national polity" (*kokutai meichō* 国体明徴), "Japan and Korea as one body" (*naisen ittai* 内鮮一体), and "growing stronger by overcoming hardship" (*ninku danren* 忍苦鍛錬). All three slogans were taken from the "Pledge of Imperial Subjects." Korean language courses were first downgraded to an optional subject and in 1941 abolished altogether. On February 11, 1940, the alleged 2,600th anniversary of the Japanese empire, a program was set in motion that forced Koreans to adopt Japanese names within six months. Failure to comply resulted in exclusion from school and higher education for children and diminished job opportunities for adults (Caprio 2009: 144–5, 153; Chou 1996: 49, 58–60; Pak and Hwang 2011: 390–2).

The assimilation policy also extended to religious matters. As early as 1931, mandatory shrine visits for Korean school children were introduced. Schools that did not participate in these visits were shut down. From 1935 on, all Koreans were forced to worship at shrines. Teachers who refused to worship Amaterasu at a shrine lost their positions. Churches that did not cooperate were closed, their priests and parishioners imprisoned. Having erected Chōsen Grand Shrine (Chōsen Jingū 朝鮮神宮) as the paramount Shintō sanctuary in the heart of Seoul in 1925, the colonial government started an initiative in 1938 with the goal to build one Shintō shrine in every Korean village. Koreans were, moreover, encouraged to erect a household shrine (*kamidana*) for the daily worship of Amaterasu (Aono 2015: 196–7; Chou 1996: 46–8; Hardacre 2017: 431–4).

The aim of this strict assimilation policy was the eradication of Korean cultural identity. This becomes clear if one considers the terms involved. *Naisen*, the first component of the slogan "Japan and Korea as one body," is a contraction of *naichi* 内地 (the interior)—a term commonly used during the colonial period to denote "Japan proper," that is, the archipelago without its colonies—and Chōsen (Kor. Chosŏn 朝鮮), that is, Korea. Contractions of this sort were fashionable during the colonial period. Other examples include *Nissen* 日鮮 (Japan and Korea) as in *Nissen dōsoron*, the theory of common ancestry of Japanese and Koreans, or *Mansen* 満鮮 (Manchuria and Korea). About the latter, Tanaka (1993: 247) remarks that the term "in itself suggests the combination of these two countries into one domain." This is also true for the former two instances, which express the hoped-for assimilation of Korea into the Japanese empire.

Through this phrasing, Japanese policymakers associated the policy pursued in colonial Korea with the biological understanding of the word assimilation as "the conversion of exogenous substances to cell material" or the "transformation of substances absorbed by living organisms into body substance" (Horstmann 1993: 373). Friedrich Nietzsche applied this biological conception to the field of human cognition by stating that:[8]

> All thinking, judging, perceiving as comparison presupposes an "equating" (*Gleichsetzen*) and, earlier still, "equalization" (*Gleichmachen*). Equalization is the same as the assimilation (*Einverleibung*) of acquired matter in the amoeba.[9]

"The drive of assimilation," he claims, "this basic organic function on which all growth depends, adapts what it absorbs from nearby internally: the will to power is at work in this process of subsuming the new under the forms of the old, already experienced."[10] This aptly describes what Japanese policymakers attempted in Korea. The colony was to be swallowed whole and in a very real sense assimilated into the "national body" (*kokutai* 国体)[11] of the Japanese empire to become "one body."[12]

The theory of common ancestry played an important role in this process of assimilation. By claiming a shared cultural, linguistic, and ethnic origin of Japanese and Koreans, the proponents of this theory imagined an ethnic community comprising Korea and Japan. Anthony Smith (1991: 21) cites "a myth of common ancestry" as one of the defining attributes of ethnic communities. He stresses that

> it is myths of common ancestry, not any fact of ancestry (which is usually difficult to ascertain), that are crucial. It is fictive descent and putative ancestry that matters for the sense of ethnic identification. Indeed, Horowitz [1985: 55–92] has likened ethnic groups to "super-families" of fictive descent because members view their *ethnie* as composed of interrelated families, forming one huge "family" linked by mythical ties of filiation and ancestry. Such a linkage between family and nation reappears in nationalist mythologies and testifies to the continuing centrality of this attribute of ethnicity. (Smith 1991: 22)

This explains the centrality of myths surrounding Susanoo within colonial discourses on common ancestry. As Amaterasu's brother, he provided a perfect link to the Japanese imperial family, which, in turn, represented the core and the apex of the Japanese family state. By identifying Susanoo as the national founder of Korea, it was possible to trace the beginning of a Japanese–Korean ethnic community to the mythical past, thus offering a historical precedent for Japanese rule over Korea.

Scholarship and Ideology: The Theory of Common Ancestry

The remainder of this chapter discusses the theory of common ancestry, focusing on its genesis in academic circles, its dissemination to larger audiences both in Korea and in Japan, and its utilization of the myths surrounding Susanoo. Since the late 1960s, the theory of common ancestry of the Japanese and Koreans and its ideological function during the period of Japanese colonial rule in Korea have been scrutinized by several historians. Hatada Takashi (1974: 173), one of the pioneers in this field, argued that the theory was used by the colonial government "as an ideological prop in support of Japanese domination and the assimilation policy." More recently, *Nissen dōsoron* has been described as an "invention of tradition," which projected "the contemporary political unification of Japan and Korea back onto a common historical root" (Suga 2010: 56). The theory's "logical implication," Peter Duus (1995: 420) argues, "was that the separation of the Japanese and the Koreans was unnatural. After all, the doctrine of race as the basis of nationhood urged that related ethnic groups be united in political units." Thus, the theory of common ancestry represents a "colonial view of history which was disseminated and reproduced in order to legitimate and rationalize the Japanese incursion into Korea and to sap the power of Koreans' resistance" (Chang 2009: 367).

While these observations aptly describe the political utilization of the theory of common ancestry during the colonial period, it should be kept in mind that the theory emerged twenty years before Japan's annexation of Korea in a purely academic context. As early as 1890, Hoshino Hisashi, one of the founding professors of the Department of Japanese History (*Kokushika*) at the Imperial University in Tokyo, published a provocative article, in which he suggests that Amaterasu's son Oshihomimi 忍穂耳, who, according to the ancient court chronicles, was the great-great-grandfather of Emperor Jinmu, was in fact of Korean origin. Moreover, he quotes the theory that Susanoo had crossed over to Japan from Korea, where he was worshiped as Tan'gun. At the outset of his article, Hoshino claims that in ancient times Japan and Korea had constituted a single country. This state of Japanese–Korean unity came to an end during the seventh century, when the combined armies of Silla and Tang chased the Japanese troops from the peninsula. Before that time, Hoshino claims, Japan and Korea had formed one ethnical and linguistic entity (*nikkan no jinshu gengo dōitsu nari*) (Hoshino 1890).

At the time of its publication, the article was harshly criticized by *kokugaku* scholars and Shintō activists (Brownlee 1999: 97–8). Nonetheless, Hoshino's fellow professors at the Department of Japanese History of the Imperial University, Shigeno Yasutsugu 重野安繹 (1827–1910) and Kume Kunitake 久米邦武 (1839–1931), supported his position. In *Kōhon: kokushigan* 稿本国史眼 (Manuscript: Views of National History), a book on Japanese history the three professors jointly published in the same year as Hoshino's article, they equate the Plain of the Sea mentioned in the myths of *Kojiki* and *Nihon shoki* with the Korean peninsula. According to their interpretation, the god Izanaki commissioned his son Susanoo with the government of Korea. A passage in the myths relating how Inai 稲永, a brother of Jinmu, enters the ocean is taken to mean that he became the founder of Silla. Rather unsurprisingly, the book describes Jingū's invasion of Korea and the subsequent establishment of a Japanese government in Mimana as historical facts (Shigeno, Kume, and Hoshino 1890, fasc. I: 2, 4, 15–16). Intended as a college textbook, *Kōhon: kokushigan* was the first overview of Japanese history published by state-sponsored historians (Yoshikawa 2017: 42). It became a model for history textbooks used in elementary and middle schools throughout Japan; therefore, its influence on Japanese historical consciousness should not be underestimated (Hatada 1969: 37–8, 185).

It was only with the annexation of Korea in 1910, however, that the theory of common ancestry entered the mainstream of scholarly and public debate. The annexation was promulgated on August 29, 1910. In the weeks before and after this significant date, all leading Japanese newspapers published articles by anthropologists, historians, linguists, and opinion makers who supported the theory of common ancestry. Many of these articles mentioned the mythical and legendary accounts of Susanoo or Jingū as historical precedents for a Japanese colonization of Korea, while others cited the history of Korean mass immigration to Japan in ancient times as a proof of Japan's ability to assimilate new subjects into the Japanese empire (Oguma 2002: 81–6).

After this period of immense public interest in the new colony, Korea all but vanished from public discourse in the Japanese metropole, only to reemerge after the outbreak of the March First Independence Movement of 1919 and its bloody suppression by the Japanese military. During the movement, signatories to a Declaration of Independence submitted a petition to the Government-General in which they emphasized religious, historical, and linguistic differences between Koreans and Japanese, which, they concluded, made cultural assimilation impossible. Notwithstanding, Japanese scholars and intellectuals renewed their efforts to justify the annexation by referring to the theory of common ancestry in the aftermath of the uprising. The Government-General, which had abstained from publicly embracing the theory up to that point, now supported the publication of a new magazine with the telling title *Dōgen* 同源 (The Same Origin), which was dedicated to the propagation of the theory of common ancestry (Oguma 2002: 125–6).

Representative proponents of the theory include the linguist Kanazawa Shōzaburō 金沢庄三郎 (1872–1967), whose 1929 book *Nissen dōsoron* gave the theory of common ancestry its name and who argued that Korean "is nothing but a branch dialect of the Japanese language" (Oguma 2002: 74), and Kita Sadakichi 喜田貞吉 (1871–1939), who worked in the Ministry of Education and circulated the idea of common ancestry not only through his own articles but also as editor of journals such as *Rekishi chiri* 歴史地理 (Historical Geography) or *Minzoku to rekishi* 民族と歴史 (Ethnos and History). Kita, often viewed as the most influential proponent of the theory, described the Koreans as a branch family that had fallen on hard times (in contrast to the splendidly successful Japanese head family) (Kita 1910: 137–40).[13]

An important organ for the dissemination of the theory in Korea was the Seoul-based Chōsen Kenkyūkai 朝鮮研究会 (Korea Research Association), which was founded in 1908 by a number of journalists, educators, professors, and critics from both the colony and the metropole but came to be dominated by settler intelligentsia after the annexation. This group published a large number of works on Korean literature and history with the aim to demonstrate the cultural unity of Japan and Korea in the past and thus contribute to the spiritual fusion of the two peoples in the present (Uchida 2011: 191–8).

Among the general Korean populace, the theory of common ancestry met mostly with indifference, whereas Korean elites reacted in highly diverse ways. Some supported the theory to claim Korean independence from China or the West, others did so to claim equal rights to the colonizers or to gain personal advantages. The most dramatic protest against the theory and the policy of cultural assimilation that was derived from it occurred during the abovementioned March First Movement in 1919. Shortly after the outbreak of this anticolonial uprising, the Provisional Government of the Republic of Korea was formed in Shanghai. One of its activities was the compilation of a "Collection of Historical Materials on Korean–Japanese Relations" to present to the allied powers at a meeting of the Paris Peace Conference in September 1919. This collection refutes the theory of common ancestry by drawing attention to the hostile nature of historical interactions between the two countries. It emphasizes fundamental differences between the national characters of Japan, which is depicted as a "nation of warriors," and Korea, a "nation of scholars." The Provisional Government also published the *Independence Newspaper* (*Tongnip sinmun*), which contained many articles that exposed contradictions in the theory of common ancestry and questioned the viability of cultural assimilation. In doing so, the articles often appropriated aspects of colonial discourse but reversed the hierarchy of Korean–Japanese relations. As in the theory of common ancestry, Korean immigration to ancient Japan was emphasized. But the conclusions Korean authors drew from this phenomenon differed sharply from their Japanese peers: Korean immigrants had brought advanced cultural technologies to Japan, they argued, therefore Korea should be regarded as Japan's teacher. In a similar vein, they pointed out that it was more logical to regard Korea as the main family and Japan as a branch family (Scholl 2018: chap. 5).

The Korean intellectual who engaged most intensively with the theory of common ancestry was arguably the historian Ch'oe Namsŏn 崔南善 (1890–1957). Originally an active member of the independence movement, he later cooperated with colonial authorities on the compilation of a Korean history. In his *Treatise on the Purham Culture* (Ch'oe 1927), written in Japanese, he (re)constructed an ancient culture circle that comprised Manchuria, Korea, and Japan. Like some proponents of the theory of common ancestry, Ch'oe based this culture circle on linguistic similarities in the regions involved. Religiously, the Purham culture was characterized by the worship of heaven as expressed, for instance, in the figure of Tan'gun. In a recent study on the theory of common ancestry and its reception, Tobias Scholl (2018: chap. 7) has pointed out that this allowed Ch'oe to decenter China within East Asian history and claim a central role for Korea in the development of Eastern civilization. While Ch'oe reaffirmed Japanese scholars' claims of cultural and religious affinities between Koreans and Japanese, he rejected assertions of a genealogical connection between the two peoples. Moreover, he described Korean culture as more ancient and therefore primary as compared to Japan. The case of Ch'oe, who was both criticized as a Korean nationalist (and imprisoned for his participation in the anticolonial resistance) by Japanese and branded as collaborator by many Koreans, demonstrates the difficulties facing Korean intellectuals who engaged with the colonial discourse of common ancestry.

In contrast to its lukewarm reception in Korea, the theory of common ancestry enjoyed broad popular appeal in mainland Japan. This is no coincidence, since it offered a means to overcome "one of the greatest contradictions faced by the nationalism of modern Japan," namely that the conception of Japan as a homogeneous family state that differed fundamentally from the Western colonial powers "now faced the contradiction posed by the existence of Koreans and Taiwanese within Japan" (Oguma 2002: xxiii–xxiv). According to Oguma (ibid.: 64), the theory of common ancestry offered a way out of this conundrum by providing "an enlarged version of the homogeneous nation theory that was applied to the entirety of the Great Japanese Empire." It would be more precise to speak of an application of the homogeneous nation theory to Japan and Korea, since the theory of common ancestry, in contrast to pan-Asianism, only included Korea in the Japanese ethnic community, not the other colonies.[14] This was probably due to two interrelated reasons: (1) as already discussed, Korea was indeed a country that had been in close contact with Japan throughout most of its history and (2) the ancient sources (most importantly, the *Nihon shoki*) simply did not provide appropriate myths on which an imagined community that included the other colonies could be based. The latter point emphasizes the difficulty of "inventing traditions" if one cannot build on discursive antecedents in a nation's cultural memory. These qualifications notwithstanding, the thrust of Oguma's observation is right and important.

In Japan, the family state ideology served, among other things, to conquer the spread of liberal ideas and to depict social hierarchization as something natural and even desirable. As Walter Skya (2002: 245) notes, in the family state "the subject was a kind of political child, personally subordinated to the paternal emperor." What is more, the family served as "the model for describing most political and social relationships, not only between the emperor and his subjects, but also between all superiors and subordinated throughout the whole society." The theory of common ancestry, as well, was utilized not only to incorporate Koreans into the Japanese ethnic community but also to legitimate their discrimination within this family empire as something natural. The Confucian concept of family, on which the ideology of the family state was built, implied not only community but also hierarchy:

> In a Japanese family, or indeed in a Korean family, older brother and younger were not equals, nor were brothers and sisters. Even though the Koreans might be described as members of the same family as the Japanese that did not necessarily imply that they should be treated as having full parity with the Japanese. A sense of hierarchy was implicit in the family metaphor, just as it was implicit in the "family state" metaphor that was becoming current in Japanese politics in the 1890s. An assimilationist policy justified by a family metaphor thus permitted the Japanese to subordinate the Koreans, politically and socially, while explaining this differential treatment as natural—just as it was natural that an older brother commands the respect of a younger brother. (Duus 1995: 433)

The Koreans' subordinate position in the Japanese family state was rationalized in various ways. Ōshima Masanori 大島正徳 (1880–1947), an assistant professor of Philosophy at Tokyo Imperial University, for instance, rejected the theory of common ancestry and preferred to regard Koreans as "adopted children, foster children, or foundlings" who should be "spiritually viewed and treated like family" (Ōshima 1918: 14–15). Kita Sadakichi (1910: 137), on the other hand, described the Koreans as a "branch family sharing the same ancestors with our country." Thus, he was able to depict the annexation as the "return" of a "poor branch family" that had "long endured hardships" to the home of its "powerful head family" (ibid.: 140). Although the arguments differ in their assessment of Japanese–Korean ethnic relations, both attempted to ideologically incorporate the Koreans into the Japanese family state—and both placed them in a subordinate position. Ōshima's argumentation, moreover, could be used to support the legitimacy of assimilation policies:

> People brought up in the Japanese family system believed that it was natural for foster children to try to forget their origins, to change their names, and to assimilate into their new families. On the other hand, Japanese migrants identified themselves as foster children when they attempted to assimilate into their host countries. However, this logic was undoubtedly beyond the comprehension of Koreans, who believed in the principle of not adopting anyone with a different surname. (Oguma 2002: 336)

Amaterasu and Susanoo, the unlikely pair of divine siblings, provided a highly welcome visualization of Korean subjects' position within the Japanese family state. While most scholars in this context draw attention to the age gap between the siblings and the different statuses within the family hierarchy that it entails (cf. Allen 2008: 107; Suga 2004: 56–7), an aspect that is rarely discussed is that of gender. In a traditional Japanese or Korean family, an elder sister was unambiguously in an inferior position compared to her younger brothers. Consequently Susanoo—and by inference, the Koreans—should have occupied the superior position within the family state. For this reason, the question of gender was simply not addressed by Japanese intellectuals who associated Susanoo with Korea. This shows the selective reception of myths within colonial discourse. If Japanese–Korean relations were expressed in terms of gender relations, Korea was invariably placed in the female role. For instance, Utsunomiya Tarō 宇都宮太郎 (1861–1922), the general who had brutally subdued the March First Movement in 1919, in the same year published an anonymous article in which he depicted Korea as Japan's reluctant wife (Biontino 2014: 161).

The overall implication of positioning Susanoo as Korea's founding deity was clear enough: for a successful modernization of their country, the politically immature Koreans, or so it was implied, were in need of Japan's benevolent rule, just like Susanoo had depended on his elder sister's guidance. This matches well with the eminent statesman Ōkuma Shigenobu's 大隈重信 (1838–1922) statement that "since the Japanese have the intelligence, experience and wealth ... the Koreans will have to work under Japanese orders" (Oguma 2002: 78–9). A poem written by the infamous pan-Asianist Uchida Ryōhei 内田良平 (1874–1937) on the occasion of the annexation of Korea in 1910 provides a striking example of how the model of Susanoo and Amaterasu was used to describe Korean–Japanese relations. The poem runs thus:

The weeping, wailing, and boisterous god was expelled with a divine expulsion and crossed over to the River Arinare

Starting from today, he might purify himself in the River Arinare and revere the shadow of the heaven-illuminating sun.

Nakiisachi-araburu kami wa kamiyarahi yarahite watase arinare no kawa

Konnichi yori wa arinare kawa ni misogi shite amaterasu hi no kage aoguramu.
(Quoted in Suga 2004: 68)

The "weeping, wailing, and boisterous god" refers to Susanoo, who is described with these terms in the ancient court myths, while "heaven-illuminating sun" is a reference to Amaterasu. "Arinare" is the name of a river supposedly located on the Korean peninsula, which is mentioned in the *Nihon shoki*'s account of Jingū's conquest of the peninsula (NSK IX Jingū [Chūai 9/10/3], vol. 1: 428/429). Uchida's poem alludes to the myth of Susanoo's banishment from his sister's heavenly realm, which will be treated in detail in Chapter 4. This episode marks a turning point in the narrative of Susanoo as related in both the *Kojiki* and the *Nihon shoki*. After this traumatic experience, Susanoo mends his ways, becomes a hero, and, most importantly, submits to his sister's divine authority by offering her a mighty sword. Uchida skilfully links this mythical episode with the account of Jingū's conquest of Korea to drive the message home: Korea was supposed to bow to Japanese rule and thus restore the "natural state" of Japanese–Korean relations as depicted in the ancient Japanese court chronicles.

State Shintō and the Theory of Common Ancestry

It is highly doubtful whether many of Uchida's contemporaries in either Japan or Korea would have understood the dense metaphoricity of his poem. Yet, as we have seen, the theory of common ancestry was disseminated widely through popular media—most importantly, newspapers and magazines—on the occasions of the annexation and the March First Movement. This section deals with questions relating to the dissemination of the theory in Korea. Special emphasis will be placed on the role of State Shintō in this process.

In Korea, the conception that Japanese and Koreans were—or could become—members of the same family can already be observed in newspaper articles predating the annexation. An early example can be found in a newspaper article published in September 1904, that is prior even to the protectorate treaty of 1905. This article suggested the possibility of a Japanese–Korean relationship, which resembled that of a "father to a son, or an elder brother to a younger brother" if the Japanese could overcome their arrogance toward Koreans (quoted in Caprio 2009: 204–5). Even more interesting in the present context is an article published on July 28, 1909 in the *Taehan maeil sinbo* 大韓每日申報 (Korean Daily News), which runs thus: "Just like Korea's Tan'gun and Japan's Amaterasu are siblings, Korea and Japan are sibling nations. Thus, there is no shame for Korea in accepting Japan's protection" (quoted in No 2011: 54). This article expresses the views of the so-called *Singung Ponggyŏnghoe* 神宮奉敬會 (Grand Shrine Worship Assembly), a group of high-ranking pro-Japanese Korean bureaucrats funded by the Korean government that lobbied for the erection of a shrine dedicated to the worship of Tan'gun (whom they regarded as identical with Susanoo), Amaterasu, and King Taejo 太祖 (r. 1392–1398), the founder of the Yi dynasty (1392–1910) (Chang 2009: 376; No. 2011: 53).

During the first meeting of the Kwansei Association for Shrine Priests (*Kwansei shinshoku rengō kai* 関西神職連合会) in February 1906, the ninety-eight participating Shintō activists from the prefectures of Kyushu and Yamaguchi Prefecture decided to petition the Residency-General to erect an official Shintō shrine dedicated to the worship of the imperial progenitress Amaterasu in Korea, in order to "establish the foundations of Japanese national education (*Nihon kokuminteki kyōka* 国民的教化)" (Suga 2004: 54).

The movement initiated by the priests from Kyushu and Yamaguchi soon won the support of the National Association for Shrine Priests (*Zenkoku shinshokukai* 全国神職会). At this time, Tsunoda Tadayuki 角田忠行 (1834–1918), head priest of the Atsuta Jingū 熱田神宮 in Nagoya, proposed that Susanoo rather than Amaterasu should be enshrined at the Korean shrine. Tsunoda, who was a follower of the Hirata School of National Learning, based this proposal on his reading of a passage in the chronicle of Kinmei 欽明 (trad. 509–571; r. 539–571) in the *Nihon shoki* that mentions a "deity who founded the land": when a Paekche prince came to Kinmei's court to inform the emperor of his king's death, a minister advised him to worship this deity to restore peace to the realm (NSK XIX [Kinmei 16/2], vol. 2: 434–9). According to Tsunoda's interpretation, the "deity who founded the land" was none other than Susanoo, whom he identified, in a further step, with Tan'gun. For this reason, Tsunoda argued that Susanoo should be enshrined as the founding deity of Korea. This view was taken up by Fukumoto Nichinan 福本日南 (1857–1921), manager and editor-in-chief of the *Kyūshū nippō* 九州日報 (Kyushu Daily News) and a founding member of the Chōsen Kenkyūkai, who was one of the initiators of the movement. Fukumoto feared that the enshrinement of Amaterasu might convey the impression that Japan regarded Korea as nothing more than a vassal state. If Tan'gun (whom he also identified with Susanoo) was enshrined together with Amaterasu, Fukumoto argued, it would be easier to win over the Koreans' hearts (Suga 2004: 54–60).

While Resident-General Itō Hirobumi showed great sympathy for the idea of constructing a shrine in Seoul, he made it clear that none other than Amaterasu should be enshrined there. He specifically mentioned that it was out of the question to enshrine "Gozu Tennō 牛頭天王." As will be discussed in the second part of this study, Gozu Tennō is a disease deity who was identified with Susanoo in the medieval period and played a significant role in modern period attempts to link Susanoo with Tan'gun. Hence, there can be no doubt that Itō's statement refers to Tsunoda's and Fukumoto's proposal to enshrine Susanoo (ibid.: 60–1).

Over the next two decades, the dispute about what deity to enshrine at the Korean shrine flared up at irregular intervals and was repeatedly debated in the Imperial Diet—the most heated debates occurring after the annexation of 1910 and the March First Independence Movement in 1919. Arguments brought forth against the enshrinement of Susanoo included his statement that he did "not want to stay" in Korea, mentioned in the *Nihon shoki* (see Chapter 4), as well as doubts about Tan'gun's historicity—note that similar doubts were at no point voiced about Amaterasu. When Chōsen Jingū was inaugurated in the Korean capital on October 15, 1925, neither Susanoo nor Tan'gun was enshrined there. Instead, the imperial ancestress Amaterasu and Meiji Tennō, who had achieved the "reunification" of Japan and Korea after two millennia of separation, were installed as the Grand Shrine's main deities (Chang 2009: 377–80; Suga

2004: 88–102). According to Aono Masaaki (2013: 164), Amaterasu was intended to embody the idea of common ancestry, while Meiji symbolized the "opening up of new territory." However, the primary aim of enshrining the imperial progenitress Amaterasu alongside the modern emperor Meiji was surely to emphasize the unbroken imperial line stretching back to the Age of the Gods (Henry 2014: 82). Susanoo and Tan'gun played much more prominent roles than Amaterasu in scholarly and public discourse on common ancestry. The refusal to enshrine one (or both) of the deities therefore points to the Government-General's ambivalent attitude toward the theory of common ancestry.

Takagi Masutarō 高木益太郎 (1869–1929), a parliamentarian and lawyer, was one of the most outspoken supporters of the enshrinement of Susanoo (whom he regarded as identical with Tan'gun) at Chōsen Jingū as a means to heighten the awareness that Koreans and Japanese were compatriots. He took up Hoshino's hypothesis of Susanoo's Korean origin and argued that the deity had first descended to earth in Ch'unch'ŏn 春川 (Jap. Shunsen) in Kangwŏn 江原 (Jap. Kōgen) Province (Chang 2009: 380; Suga 2004: 89–100). Based on this theory, in the late 1920s a movement for the erection of a shrine dedicated to Susanoo in Kangwŏn Province started. Udu 牛頭 Village in Sinbuk 新北 Township of Ch'unch'ŏn District was singled out as the site for this shrine, since this was believed to be the place of Susanoo's descent to earth. In 1931, the settler Yamanaka Tomotarō 山中友太郎 (life dates unknown) handed in a proposal for the construction of a shrine dedicated to Susanoo in Udu Village to the Kangwŏn Province Council. The proposal was favorably received, but due to fiscal problems the construction was not realized. Three years later, Yamanaka handed in a new proposal that met with the same fate. Undeterred, Yamanaka founded a group in 1934 to advance his goal with private funds. This group published and distributed pamphlets, bought the site on which they wanted to build the shrine, and endeavored to win supporters for their plan, both in the metropole and the colony (Aono 1999: 142–5; Iwashita 1941: 195–206). The construction of a shrine "dedicated to the worship of the august soul of Susanoo no Mikoto, the younger brother of the great goddess who founded the nation," they argued in a pamphlet, would "contribute to the prosperity of the nation by venerating [Susanoo] as the great god of Japanese-Korean assimilation (*naisen dōka* 内鮮同化) and thus striving for the complete fusion (*yūgō* 融合) of the two peoples" (Iwashita 1941: 206). In 1935, Kōno Bansei 河野万世 (life dates unknown), a reporter for the *Chosŏn il'il sinmun* 朝鮮日日新聞 (Korean Daily Newspaper), published a book with the title *Shunsen fudoki* 春川風土記 (Local Gazetteer of Ch'unch'ŏn), in which he tried to prove that Udu was indeed the site of Susanoo's descent. He corroborated this view by citing local customs such as the villagers' veneration of Mount Udu as a sacred site (Ch'oe 2008: 114). The movement was also supported and encouraged by several high officials in Korea and Japan. However, it never won the Government-General's approval (Chang 2009: 383–90; Suga 2004: 352–4).

Nonetheless, the movement was successful to a certain extent. In 1938, the Shrine Bureau (*Jinjakyoku* 神社局) permitted the enshrinement of Susanoo in Kōgen Jinja 江原神社. In 1941, this shrine, formerly known as Shunsen Jinja 春川神社, received the rank of a national shrine, third rank (*kokuhei shōsha* 国幣小社), making it the highest-ranking shrine in the province (Aono 1999: 146). In the next year, Koiso Kuniaki[15] was appointed Governor-General of Korea. In July, he gave a lecture to a group of Korean schoolchildren, which rekindled the movement in Ch'unch'ŏn. In this lecture, already mentioned in the introduction, Koiso wholeheartedly endorsed the theory of common ancestry:

> One can say that the mainlanders (*naichijin* 内地人) are descended from Amaterasu Ōmikami and the peninsular people (*hantōjin* 半島人) from Susanoo no Mikoto, and that Tan'gun is in reality identical with Susanoo no Mikoto. And, as you all know, Susanoo no Mikoto descended at the site of Soshimori in Ch'unch'ŏn. (Quoted in Chang 2009: 385)

It is not surprising that this lecture breathed new life into the movement for the establishment of a shrine dedicated to Susanoo in Ch'unch'ŏn. The activists redoubled their efforts and lobbied for the construction of such a shrine. While they succeeded in winning over parts of the press, most importantly the monthly magazine *Chōsen kōron* 朝鮮公論 (Korea Review), they were unable to overcome the critical attitude of historians, archaeologists, and linguists employed at universities both in Japan and Korea. When Koiso returned to Japan to become prime minister in July 1944, the movement subsided (Chang 2009: 385–90).

What makes this movement interesting for the present study is that it shows the degree to which the theory of common ancestry—and of Susanoo as an embodiment of this idea—had entered public discourse in wartime Korea. The movement also demonstrates an interesting reversal of roles in the theory's reception. As we have seen, the theory of common ancestry was first developed by Japanese historians in the 1890s and became a dominant paradigm in academic disciplines such as history, archaeology, linguistics, and anthropology around the time of the annexation. By the 1930s, however, a new generation of scholars started to question this paradigm. On the other hand, Japanese settlers in Korea had traditionally shown a critical attitude toward the colonial government's assimilation policy, fearing that the outcome of such an assimilation process might turn out to be the Koreanization of settlers rather than the Japanization of the Korean population. After the March First Movement, however, many settlers began to collaborate with the Government-General in implementing a reformed version of assimilation policy (Uchida 2011: 132–6, 144–6). The leading role played by settlers and the resident press in the Ch'unchŏn movement is a vivid example of this changed attitude.

Worthy of note is also the audience of Koiso's lecture, namely Korean schoolchildren. The colonial authorities had soon recognized the importance of schools for turning Koreans into loyal subjects of the empire. Thus, Korean schoolchildren were introduced to Japanese myths and essays on Shintō already in elementary school. The significance of fostering a collective identity was grasped especially after the March First Movement of 1919. During the so-called "Cultural Rule" (*bunka seiji* 文化政治), which was implemented after the uprising, the formerly segregated school systems for Koreans and Japanese were merged into a common school system open to both Korean and Japanese schoolchildren. As already pointed out, instruction was conducted in Japanese; and the history class introduced students to Japanese, rather than Korean, history (Caprio 2009: 98–100, 153; Pak and Hwang 2011: 381–2, 387). After the outbreak of the Second Sino-Japanese War in 1937, the Government-General recognized the necessity to "emphasize history, particularly the diplomatic, cultural, and blood connections that the Japanese and Korean peoples have shared from ancient times" in the school curriculum (Caprio 2009: 147). Thus, by the late 1930s, the theory of common ancestry had entered the curriculum of the imperial school system, where it was used to construct a collective identity through ancient Japanese myths and legends.

In contrast to its educational policy, the Government-General's Shintō policy in Korea was highly ambivalent. As the example of Chōsen Jingū shows, the colonial government was not prepared to enshrine Tan'gun or Susanoo at the paramount Shintō sanctuary on the peninsula despite Shintō activists' pleas. This shows a certain reluctance of the Government-General to officially embrace the theory of common ancestry during this period—or, if one accepts Aono's reading that Amaterasu was regarded as the common ancestor, a reluctance to grant Korean deities a place in the Japanese–Korean ancestral chart. Confronted with Governor-General Saitō Makoto's 斎藤実 (1858–1936) refusal to enshrine Susanoo at the Grand Shrine, Shintō activists suggested the enshrinement of Kunitama no Kami 国魂神, that is, "deity of the land soul" instead.[16] As one of the three gods of colonization (*kaitaku sanshin* 開拓三神), this deity was worshiped in the highest-ranking state shrines in all prior colonies. In the case of Chōsen Jingū, the petitioners argued, the term "Chōsen" could be added to the deity's name, thus allowing for the interpretation that the name referred to Tan'gun (Aono 2015: 56–7, 112; Suga 2010: 53–6). As we have seen, the Government-General did not choose this option.

However, in 1929 it sanctioned the enshrinement of Kunitama Ōkami, that is, "great deity of the land soul" in Keijō Jinja 京城神社, a shrine worshiping Amaterasu, which had been established by settlers in Seoul as early as 1898. Moreover, this shrine was raised to the rank of a national shrine, third rank, in 1936. While parishioners might have interpreted this deity as Tan'gun, the colonial government distanced itself from such an interpretation by explicitly forbidding the shrine to add "Chōsen" to the deity's name. During the next decade, in each Korean province one shrine was raised to the rank of national shrine, third rank. All of them followed the example of Keijō Jinja in enshrining both Amaterasu and Kunitama Ōkami (Aono 2013: 165–70; 2015: 106–15; Suga 2010: 57, 64). Susanoo, too, was co-enshrined in many of the national shrines (Mun 2018: 435–7). In this way, the Government-General attempted to accommodate the Korean populace without unambiguously enshrining a "Korean" deity in a Shintō shrine. When the colonial government deliberated the possibility to incorporate native Korean deities into the Shintō pantheon and worship them in shrines, Shintō priests who were active on the peninsula voiced their firm protest, preventing the Government-General from pursuing such a course (Aono 2015: 262–3, 282).

As Albert Memmi (1965: 149–50) has pointed out, "Assimilation is ... the opposite of colonization. It tends to eliminate the distinctions between the colonizers and the colonized, and thereby eliminates the colonial relationship." Echoing Memmi's observation, Suga Kōji (2004: 190) suggests that the apparent reluctance of the Government-General to position itself clearly toward the theory of common ancestry might have been due to the fact that "the theory of common ancestry was a two-edged sword": followed to its logical conclusion, the argument of "Japan and Korea as one body" would eradicate the distinction between colonizer and colonized and thus delegitimize Japanese colonial rule. This shows the inherent contradictoriness of the Japanese colonial project in Korea, which failed to clearly define Koreans' position within the Japanese empire and thus left them in a perpetual state of limbo.

Nevertheless, even if it seems to have been more successful in the metropole than in the colony, the theory of common ancestry provided a much-needed ideological justification for Japan's colonial rule over Korea. As we have seen, Susanoo played an important role in this discourse. But what were the ideological implications of equating Susanoo with the founding deity of Korea? Why did Shintō activists call for the enshrinement of Susanoo at Chōsen Jingū rather than following precedent and lobbying for the installation of the three gods of colonization (or any other of the myriad Shintō deities)? And why did Susanoo appear in virtually all articles propagating the theory of common ancestry of Japanese and Koreans? Some answers to these questions have already been suggested: as Amaterasu's younger brother, Susanoo provided a welcome visualization of the alleged ethnic relationship between Koreans and Japanese, while his younger age implied Korea's allegedly inferior state of development and Koreans' subordinate position within the Japanese empire. While these are certainly the most obvious ideological benefits of associating Susanoo with Korea, the following chapters will try to show that there were other aspects that predestined Susanoo for his role in colonial discourse.

2

A Foil to Set Off the Sun Goddess: Susanoo in the Ancient Sources

And, like bright metal on a sullen ground,
My reformation, glittering o'er my fault,
Shall show more goodly and attract more eyes
Than that which hath no foil to set it off.
—William Shakespeare: *Henry IV, Part First*

Colonial-period interpretations of Susanoo were based on the myths recorded in the ancient court chronicles *Kojiki* (712) and *Nihon shoki* (720). As little brother of the sun goddess Amaterasu, the progenitress of the imperial family, Susanoo plays an important role in both works. Moreover, he appears in the *Izumo fudoki* (733), the local gazetteer of Izumo Province (the eastern part of present-day Shimane Prefecture). Scholars have long marveled at the fact that Susanoo is depicted as a highly contradictory and ambivalent character in the court chronicles,[1] whereas he appears as a much more straightforward and benevolent (though less colorful) deity in the *Izumo fudoki*. The latter image of Susanoo was of little use to colonial-period intellectuals and was therefore mostly ignored in the discourse on common ancestry. Nonetheless, the present chapter will discuss Susanoo's role in the *Izumo fudoki* as well as in the two court chronicles in order to draw attention to the fact that Susanoo's role in ancient mythology was more complex than suggested in colonial discourse. Scholars' selection of "appropriate" sources already constituted a conscious choice in the construction of a useful image of Susanoo. From the perspective of cultural memory, one can say that during the colonial period the peaceful Susanoo of the *Izumo fudoki* was excluded from the functional memory. As we have seen, Susanoo's sibling relationship to Amaterasu was of crucial importance in colonial discourse. Therefore, after providing an overview of Susanoo's role in the three above-mentioned sources, the present chapter will discuss the two deities' relationship in the ancient myths and later interpretations thereof.

Recent scholarship has drawn attention to the differences between the *Kojiki* and the *Nihon shoki*. Kwŏn Dongwoo (2013: 128) in a recent study claims that "even though they are called by the same name, ... the Susanoo of the *Kojiki* and [the Susanoo of the] *Nihon shoki* appear as completely different deities (*mattaku betsu no kami*)."[2] This statement stands in the tradition of scholars such as Saigō Nobutsuna (1973: 285–6; 2005, vol. 1: 13–34) and, especially, Kōnoshi Takamitsu (1999: 82–139; 2008), who argue that each chronicle has to be regarded as a literary work in its own right that conveys a distinct worldview, and that the individual myths can only be understood in the context of this particular worldview. Advocates of this approach, which is usually called *sakuhinron* 作品論 (literary work theory), distance themselves from the comparative approaches of earlier days that were above all interested in reconstructing the "original" form of the myths recorded in the chronicles, often by combining parts of both sources into a new coherent story line. In the last few decades, the *sakuhinron* approach has come to dominate the field. Although some of their claims (like the one by Kwŏn quoted above) seem exaggerated, *sakuhinron* proponents are surely justified in emphasizing the importance of staying true to the sources and distinguishing individual sources clearly. For this reason, the present chapter dedicates separate sections to the myths surrounding Susanoo in the *Kojiki*, the *Nihon shoki*, and the *Izumo fudoki*, highlighting both differences and similarities between the narratives recorded in the individual sources.

Crying Child, Dragon Slayer, and Ruler of the Otherworld: Susanoo in the *Kojiki*

The oldest extant source of Japanese mythology is the *Kojiki*, which was completed in 712. For information on the work's genesis, we have to rely on its preface. Here, the author, a courtier called Ō no Yasumaro 太安万侶 (?–723), asserts that the work was originally commissioned by Tenmu Tennō 天武天皇 (631?–686; r. 673–686), but only completed when Genmei Tennō 元明天皇 (661–721; r. 707–715) gave Yasumaro the order to write it down in 711.[3]

The main text opens with the sequential emergence of several deities at the time "when Heaven and Earth first became active."[4] The youngest pair of these deities, Izanaki 伊耶那岐 and his sister Izanami 伊耶那美, were commanded by the older deities to "form and solidify" the land. Thus, the two deities proceeded to give birth to the Land of the Great Eight Islands and to a large number of deities. As the narrative progresses, these thoroughly mythical episodes give way to legends and, finally, to quasi-historical accounts of the reigns of "emperors," ending with the reign of Suiko 推古 (r. 593–628). Almost all episodes focus on the imperial family and its mythical origins; therefore, the work has been aptly described as "the mythic-historical genealogy of the ruling house" (Wittkamp 2014, vol. 2: 139).

Susanoo 須佐之男 is one of the central characters in the first of the *Kojiki*'s three fascicles. During the birth of the fire deity, the primordial mother Izanami was severely burned and passed away. In an Orpheus-like episode, her husband Izanaki tried to retrieve her from Yomotsu Kuni 黄泉国, one of the afterworlds of Japanese myth.[5] After his return from this realm of death, Izanaki cleansed his body in the mouth of Tachibana River in Himuka (present-day Miyazaki Prefecture). During his purification, several deities came into being. The last of these were the goddess Amaterasu (Heaven Shining),[6] who came into being when Izanaki washed his left eye, the god Tsukuyomi 月読 (Moon Counting), who came into being when he washed his right eye, and Susanoo,[7] who emerged when he washed his nose.

Izanaki was delighted at the birth of these "three noble children" and entrusted the reign over a realm of the cosmos to each of them: to Amaterasu, the rule over the Plain of High Heaven (*takaama no hara* 高天原), to Tsukuyomi, the rule over the Honorable Country of Night (*yoru no osu kuni* 夜之食国), and to Susanoo, the rule over the Plain of the Sea (*unahara* 海原). While the other two deities governed their respective realms as they were told, Susanoo only wept and wailed all the time. This caused the green mountains to wither and the rivers and oceans to dry out. When his father asked him why he was weeping instead of governing his realm, Susanoo replied that he wanted to go to the land of his dead mother, Ne no Katasukuni 根堅州国.[8] Enraged, Izanaki expelled his son.

Thereafter, Susanoo ascended to the Plain of High Heaven to take his leave from his sister. Amaterasu, however, suspected that he had come to steal her realm; therefore, she met him in a warrior's outfit at the bank of the Calm River of Heaven. In order to prove his good intentions, Susanoo suggested performing an *ukei*, a kind of oracle:[9] each deity took an object belonging to the other, chewed it, and spat out divine children. Amaterasu took Susanoo's sword and broke it in three parts that she washed in the True Well of Heaven. When she chewed the parts and exhaled, three female deities were born from her breath. Susanoo repeated the same procedure with his sister's comma-shaped jewels (*magatama* 曲玉) and produced five male deities. Amaterasu declared that, since they were born from her belongings, the five male deities were her children, to which Susanoo responded that the three female deities born from his belongings proved the purity of his heart.

In the flush of victory, he destroyed the divisions between his sister's rice paddies, filled in the ditches, and scattered excrement in the Palace of the Great Harvest Festival. Nonetheless, Amaterasu did not admonish her brother but excused his behavior. Susanoo, however, proceeded to commit an even greater outrage: when Amaterasu was overseeing the weaving of divine garments in the Pure Weaving Hall, he opened a hole in the ceiling and flung the skin of a backward-flayed horse into the hall. Horrified at the sight, a weaving maiden pierced her genitals with the shuttle and died.

When Amaterasu saw this, she became frightened and retreated to the Heavenly Rock Cave, shrouding the whole world in darkness. The eight million deities held council and came up with a plan to lure Amaterasu out of her hiding place. The goddess Ame no Uzume 天宇受売 stomped on an overturned tub in front of the Heavenly Rock Cave. Divinely possessed, she exposed her breasts and genitals. At this sight, the eight million deities broke out in laughter. Surprised about the merrymaking in her absence, Amaterasu peeked out of the Heavenly Rock Cave and was eventually lured out with the help of a mirror. The world was again filled with sunlight.

As punishment for his offenses, the eight million deities imposed a fine of thousand tables full of offerings on Susanoo, cut off his beard and the nails of his fingers and toes, and expelled him from the Plain of High Heaven. Thereupon, Susanoo asked the food goddess Ōgetsu Hime 大気都比売 for something to eat. Obligingly, she took food from her mouth, her nose, and her anus and offered it to him. Considering this food impure, Susanoo killed the goddess in his rage. From the body of the slain food goddess emerged silkworms, rice, millet, red beans, barley, and soybeans.

After this deed, Susanoo descended to the land of Izumo in a place called Torikami 鳥上 at the headwaters of the Hi 簸 River. When he noticed chopsticks floating down the river, he concluded that people must be living upstream. Following the course of the river, he finally met an old couple and a young girl, all of them crying. The man introduced himself as Ashinazuchi 足名椎 (Foot-Stroking Elder), a son of the Great Mountain God. His wife's and daughter's names he gave as Tenazuchi 手名椎 (Hand-Stroking Elder) and Kushinada Hime 櫛名田比売 (Lady Wondrous Rice Paddies), respectively. Originally, the couple had had eight daughters, he explained, but every year the giant eight-headed serpent (*yamata no orochi* 八俣遠呂知) from Koshi 高志 had appeared and devoured one of them. Soon it would come again for their last daughter. Susanoo asked for Kushinada Hime's hand in marriage. Ashinazuchi gladly offered his daughter to Susanoo, but only after the god had introduced himself as Amaterasu's brother. Thereafter, Susanoo turned his bride-to-be into a comb, which he put into his hair, and instructed her parents to brew "eightfold brewed *sake*." Furthermore, they were to build a fence with eight gates and place a trough filled with the strong beverage at each gate. When the preparations were complete, the serpent appeared, drank the *sake*, and fell asleep. Susanoo drew his ten-span sword and chopped the creature to pieces until the Hi River ran red with its blood. In the serpent's middle tail, he found the sword Kusanagi 草那芸, which he offered to his sister Amaterasu.

After this heroic feat, Susanoo built his palace in a place called Suga in Izumo. Clouds gathered over this site and inspired Susanoo to compose a song:

> Eightfold are the clouds that rise
> in Billowing Clouds [Izumo], where eightfold fences
> to surround and shelter my wife
> are eightfold fences made by me.
> Ah, those eightfold fences! (Heldt 2014: 27)

This is the first song mentioned in the narrative of the *Kojiki*. For this reason, Susanoo came to be viewed as the "father of Japanese poetry" (Bentley 2006: 398).[10] Susanoo appointed Ashinazuchi the head of his palace and at length consummated his marriage. The *Kojiki*'s account ends with a list of Susanoo's descendants. The most famous among these is Ōkuninushi 大国主 (Great Land Master), also called Ōanamuji 大穴牟遅 (Great Iron Mines Noble), who takes center stage in the subsequent episodes.

But Susanoo appears one more time, now in his role as ruler of Ne no Katasukuni. To this land, Ōanamuji had to flee from his brothers who were after his blood. In Ne no Katasukuni, he met Susanoo's daughter Suseri Bime 須勢理毘売 and married her. When Suseri Bime announced his arrival to her father, Susanoo called him in and ordered him to spend the night in a room full of snakes. Suseri Bime gave a piece of cloth to her husband that kept the snakes at bay. The next night, Susanoo led Ōanamuji to a room full of wasps and millipedes; again, his wife provided him with a protective piece of cloth. Then Susanoo shot an arrow into a plain and ordered Ōanamuji to retrieve it. When Ōanamuji entered the plain, Susanoo set it on fire. A mouse showed Ōanamuji a hole in the ground where he was safe from the fire. Then it brought him the arrow. Thus, Ōanamuji was able to survive and deliver the arrow to Susanoo. The senior god, who had thought his son-in-law dead, invited him into his house and ordered him to pick the lice from his head. With the help of Suseri Bime, Ōanamuji again got the better of Susanoo, who at length fell asleep. Ōanamuji took this opportunity, bound Susanoo's hair to the rafters and barred the door with a heavy rock. Then he stole Susanoo's weapons and his Gem-studded Zither of Heaven and fled, carrying Suseri Bime on his back. But the zither hit a tree and emitted a reverberating sound that roused Susanoo from his sleep. The mighty god rose with a start, tearing the whole room down. He untangled his hair from the rafters and pursued Ōanamuji and his daughter until he reached the border of his realm: Yomotsu Hirasaka 黄泉比良坂.[11] From here, he shouted after the fleeing couple, instructing Ōanamuji to use the stolen weapons to hunt down his brothers, and make himself master of the land (Ōkuninushi), to take Suseri Bime as his main wife, and to build a mighty palace so tall that its gables should touch the Plain of High Heaven. The passage seems to suggest that Susanoo tests Ōanamuji and finally inaugurates him as his successor.

A Multitude of Variants: Susanoo in the *Nihon Shoki*

The second major source of ancient Japanese mythology is the *Nihon shoki*, which was presented to the court of Genshō Tennō 元正天皇 (680–748; r. 715–724) in 720—a mere eight years after the completion of the *Kojiki*. The *Nihon shoki* was compiled under the supervision of Prince Toneri 舎人 (676–735), a son of Tenmu, and is commonly viewed as the outcome of the history-editing initiative ordered by the latter in 682 (NSK XXIX [Tenmu 10/3/16], vol. 3: 406/407). Although there are many commonalities between the *Kojiki* and the *Nihon shoki*, the latter more closely follows the model of Chinese dynastic chronicles. This pertains not only to the writing style but also to the structure of the work and its endorsement of Chinese concepts like *yin-yang* philosophy (cf. Lurie 2011: 225–50). Hence Saitō Hideki (2006: 59–63) hypothesizes that the *Nihon shoki* was intended to meet the "global standard" of its time, whereas the *Kojiki*'s aim was to create a "local identity." As David Lurie (2011: 243–6) points out, however, it would be anachronistic to regard the *Kojiki* and the *Nihon shoki* as a pair of court chronicles. Two reasons preclude such a view: first, competing works existed during the eighth century that are no longer extant. Second, the *Nihon shoki* succeeded in obtaining official status, was followed by five sequels in the same style, and was studied at official court lectures during the ninth and tenth centuries. The *Kojiki*, on the other hand, was held in markedly lower esteem and viewed as nothing more than a supplementary text for the interpretation of the *Nihon shoki* until its rediscovery by scholars of National Learning in the eighteenth century.[12]

The Sinitic style of the *Nihon shoki* is apparent in its opening passage, which has long been recognized as a pastiche of Chinese works like the *Huainanzi* 淮南子 (Master Huainan; second century BCE) and the *Sanwu liji* 三五暦紀 (Historical Records of the Three Sovereign Divinities and the Five Gods; third century CE) (cf. Kōnoshi 1999: 116–20). The *yin-yang* overtones are unmistakable:

> In ancient times, heaven and earth were not yet separated; the female and the male principles were not yet divided. They formed a chaotic mass like a hen's egg that was dark and hard to discern and contained germs. The clear and bright [parts] expanded thinly and became the heaven, the heavy and murky [parts] lingered and became the earth. The pure and fine parts easily merged, while the coagulation of the dark and murky parts was completed with [greater] difficulty. Therefore, the heaven came into being first and the earth was formed afterward. Thereafter, divine beings were born between them. (NSK I [1, main text], vol. 1: 18/19)

According to Kōnoshi (1999: 120–6) these allusions to *yin-yang* philosophy are more than isolated quotations. Rather, he argues, *yin-yang* cosmology serves as the structuring principle of the *Nihon shoki*'s mythology. Thus, Izanaki 伊奘諾 and Izanami 伊奘冉[13] created the world not according to a command by the deities of the Plain of High Heaven (as in the *Kojiki*) but as embodiments of the male and the female principle.

While this is an apt analysis of the cosmogony presented in the early portion of the *Nihon shoki*'s main text, it ignores one of the most distinctive features of the *Nihon shoki*'s mythology, namely the numerous variant accounts for individual myths that are included in the work. The first two fascicles, which roughly correspond to the *Kojiki*'s first one and are commonly called the "divine age fascicles" (*jindaikan* 神代巻), contain a total of fifty-eight such variants, all of which are introduced with the words "In one writing it is said." The main text of the divine age fascicles is divided into eleven blocks (*dan* 段), after each of which a number of variants is inserted—then the main text picks up the thread of the story where it was interrupted in the preceding block, sometimes in mid-sentence. In contrast to the main text, the variants do not form a coherent story line. Therefore, Kōnoshi (1999: 110–12) in his influential analysis of the divine age fascicles chooses to ignore the variants—which he views as nothing more than explanatory notes.

Matsumoto Naoki (2010) has demonstrated, however, that the variants constitute an integral part of the *Nihon shoki*'s structure. He compares the main text's relationship to the variants with that of a main clause to subordinate clauses, since variants elaborate on information only hinted at in the main text, provide additional information missing from the main text but presupposed in later myth blocks, or even contradict the account of the main text.[14] This interpretation results in a more complex structuring principle than the one proposed by Kōnoshi. According to Matsumoto's analysis, the dual *yin-yang* philosophy stressed in the early portions of the divine age fascicles gives way to the idea of heavenly rulership (more in line with the *Kojiki*'s logic) in later portions, the transition being softened by the interspersed variants.

This complex structure is also reflected in the myth of Susanoo 素戔嗚.[15] In the main text (I [5]),[16] Susanoo and his siblings (the expression "three noble children" does not appear in the *Nihon shoki*) come into the world through the procreation of Izanaki and Izanami. After the primordial mother had given birth to the Land of the Great Eight Islands, to mountains, rivers, grass, and trees, the couple decided to produce someone to rule over the world (*ame no shita* 天下). Thus, Izanami gave birth to the sun goddess Ōhirume no Muchi 大日孁貴 (a gloss provides a number of alternate names for the goddess, including Amaterasu) to whom her parents entrusted the government of heaven (*ame*). Next, Izanami gave birth to the moon god, whom they also sent to heaven to rule beside the sun. Then Izanami gave birth to Hiruko 蛭児 (leech child). This child was malformed and at the age of three years was still unable to stand on his feet; therefore, his parents exposed him in the Heavenly Rock-Camphor-Boat. Lastly, Izanami gave birth to Susanoo. This deity was bold, strong, and cruel. Moreover, he cried all the time, causing many people to die and the green mountains to wither. Therefore, his parents admonished him, saying that he was not fit to rule the world, and at length banished him to the distant Ne no Kuni 根国.[17]

According to the first variant, it was Izanaki alone who created Susanoo and his siblings. When he took a white copper mirror in his left hand, the sun goddess Ōhirume came into being. When he took a white copper mirror in his right hand, the moon god Tsukuyumi 月弓 (Moon Bow) came into being. When he turned his head and looked back, Susanoo came into being. The next variant (I [5, var. 2]) is similar to the main text, but it mentions that after the birth of Susanoo, Izanami died delivering the fire god. Variant six is closest to the *Kojiki*'s account: it relates that Susanoo and his siblings were born when Izanaki cleansed his body after his return from Yomotsu Kuni (the intervening variants

Table 2.1 Assignment of Realms to Susanoo and His Siblings in *Nihon shoki* and *Kojiki*

	Amaterasu	Tsukuyomi	Susanoo
NSK I [5, main text]	Heaven	Heaven (beside the sun)	Ne no Kuni
NSK I [5, var. 1]	Heaven and Earth	Heaven and Earth (beside the sun)	Ne no Kuni
NSK I [5, var. 6]	Plain of High Heaven	Plain of the Blue Sea	World
NSK I [5, var. 11]	Plain of High Heaven	Heaven (beside the sun)	Plain of the Blue Sea
KJK	Plain of High Heaven	Honorable Country of Night	Plain of the Sea

"Amaterasu" and "Tsukuyomi" refer to the sun goddess and the moon god, respectively, even though they are called by different names in some of the variants.
Note: NSK and KJK refer to *Nihon shoki* and *Kojiki*, respectively.

deal with Izanami's demise following the birth of the fire god). In all variants (as well as in the *Kojiki*), Susanoo seems somewhat misplaced in the tale of his siblings' birth. While Amaterasu and Tsukuyomi as sun goddess and moon god form a fitting pair of siblings, the myths do not explicitly associate Susanoo with any natural phenomenon. Moreover, all variants distinguish Susanoo's manner of birth from that of his siblings or even place the birth of Hiruko between that of Susanoo and the sun and moon deities. As shown in Table 2.1, the variants differ with regard to which deity is assigned to govern which mythical realm.

There is a certain overlap between the realms associated with Susanoo and the moon god: each deity is assigned to rule over the Plain of the [Blue] Sea in at least one variant. The overlap between the two deities becomes even clearer if one pays attention to the last variant of the myth block (I [5, var. 11]): in an episode remarkably similar to Susanoo's killing of Ōgetsu Hime in the *Kojiki*, we are told that Tsukuyomi killed the food goddess Ukemochi 保食, who had presented him with food taken from her mouth. When Amaterasu heard of this, she became angry and told the moon god that she did not want to see him face to face anymore.[18] From this time on, the two deities lived separated "one by day and one by night." Together with his peculiar position in the episode narrating the birth of the sun and moon deities, this overlap has been regarded as evidence that points to Susanoo's relatively late incorporation into the court mythology (Matsumura 1954–8, vol. 3: 4–6).

The next myth block relates the story of Susanoo's ascent to the Plain of High Heaven, where he produced children with Amaterasu in order to prove his good intentions (I [6, main text; var. 1–3]; [7, var. 3]). Variants differ with regard to the questions of who suggested the oath, who interpreted its result, who produced which children, and so on.[19]

As in the *Kojiki*, Susanoo wreaked havoc in Amaterasu's realm: in spring, he filled in the ditches (I [7, var. 2; var. 3]), destroyed the sluices (I [7, var. 3]) and the divisions between Amaterasu's rice fields (I [7, main text; var. 2; var. 3]), and sowed seed on the already planted fields (I [7, var. 3]). In autumn, when the grain was ripe, he stretched ropes around the fields, claiming them as his property (I [7, var. 2]), or he let horses loose in the fields (I [7, main text; var. 3]) and set up pointed stakes (I [7, var. 3]). When Amaterasu was about to taste the new rice, he defecated inside the New Palace that had been especially built for the ritual tasting of the newly harvested rice (I [7, main text]). Amaterasu, however, excused her brother's rude behavior.[20] After this, Susanoo threw the skin of a backward-flayed horse into the Pure Weaving Hall, where Amaterasu was weaving divine garments (I [7, main text]) or keeping company with a weaving maiden (I [7, var. 1]). Startled by Susanoo's act of violence, Amaterasu wounded herself (I [7, main text]) or the weaving maiden was killed (I [7, var. 1])—the outcome is the same in both instances: Amaterasu retreated into the Heavenly Rock Cave. After the eight million gods had succeeded in luring her out again, they banished Susanoo from the Plain of High Heaven (I [7, main text]). One variant (I [7, var. 3]) informs us that it was raining incessantly at the time. Therefore, Susanoo made himself a hat and a raincoat from straw and asked the gods for shelter, but none of them offered him hospitality. Suffering bitterly, he descended from the Plain of High Heaven.

The main text of the next myth block (I [8]) offers an account of Susanoo's deeds in Izumo (his slaying of the serpent, the erection of his palace, and his marriage with Kushiinada Hime 寄稲田姫)[21] that is almost identical to the *Kojiki*'s version. Some of the variants differ considerably, however. In the first variant, the motif of serpent slaying is absent: Susanoo just descended to Izumo and married Inada Hime 稲田媛 (Lady Rice Paddies). In another variant (I [8, var. 2]), Susanoo descended not at the headwaters of the Hi River in Izumo but at the headwaters of the E River in Agi, in present-day Hiroshima Prefecture. His bride-to-be was not even born yet, but her parents promised Susanoo her hand in marriage if he managed to defeat the eight-headed serpent. When her birth drew near, the monster came to devour its new victim. Susanoo greeted the creature at the door and in feigned veneration offered it *sake*. Then he proceeded to slay the serpent in its drunken stupor. The new-born child was taken to the headwaters of the Hi River in Izumo, where she was brought up and eventually became Susanoo's bride.[22] The episode of Ōkuninushi's trial at the hands of

Susanoo is not mentioned in the *Nihon shoki*. We are only told that Susanoo eventually entered Ne no Kuni (I [8, main text; var. 5]).

Another Side of Susanoo: The *Izumo Fudoki*

The *Nihon shoki*'s sequel *Shoku Nihongi* 続日本紀 (Chronicles of Japan Continued; 797) records the following imperial edict that was given on the second day, fifth month of the year Wadō 6 (713):

> Good (Chinese) characters must be adopted for the names of provinces, districts and villages in the Home and Outer provinces; the silver, copper, dyes, plants, birds and quadrupeds, fish and insects produced indexed, the fertility of the grounds, the reasons for the names of mountains and rivers, plains and moors, the old legends, and other particulars, recorded and reported. (Snellen 1937: 257)

This led to the compilation of the so-called *Fudoki* 風土記 (Records of Local Customs and Land),[23] local gazetteers of the various provinces that were presented to the imperial court by the officials of the province governments. Today, major portions of only five *Fudoki* are extant—one of them is the *Izumo no kuni fudoki* 出雲国風土記 (hereafter *Izumo fudoki*; 733).[24]

Compared to the *Kojiki* and the *Nihon shoki*, the *Izumo fudoki* depicts Susanoo in a decidedly less glamorous fashion. His heroic fight against the eight-headed serpent is not mentioned at all.[25] Neither is his sibling relation to Amaterasu, as the sun goddess does not appear in the gazetteer. What is more, Susanoo does not play a part in the myth of land-pulling (*kuni-biki*), arguably the most central narrative in the *Izumo fudoki*, which relates the genesis of Izumo. In the *Izumo fudoki*, Susanoo is mentioned mainly as the father of other deities, such as Tsurugi Hiko 都留支日子 (Sword-Prince), Tsukihoko-tooyoru Hiko 衝杵等呼而留比子 (God of the Penetrating Halberd),[26] or Waka-Suseri Hime 和加須世理比売 (Young Lady Suseri), who might be identical with the *Kojiki*'s Suseri Bime.

Only two episodes feature Susanoo as protagonist. One episode relates that he danced, wearing leaves of the *sase* tree on his head; the leaves fell to the ground—consequently the site came to be called Sase. The other episode explains how the township of Susa 須佐 came by its name: "The god Susanoo no Mikoto spoke: 'This land is small, but it is a good place for living. Therefore, I will not attach my name to the trees and stones.' After saying this, he left his spirit to stay quietly at this place. Then he established the Great Rice Field of Susa and the Small Rice Field of Susa" (IF: 242/243).

The Sun and Its Antithesis: Susanoo's Relation to Amaterasu

Considering Susanoo's central role in the mythical plot of the earliest court chronicles, it is not surprising that the deity became the subject of many scholarly discussions.[27] Although Susanoo's role in the imperial myth-histories was interpreted in various ways throughout the centuries, his relationship to Amaterasu tended to occupy a prominent position in most interpretations. Matsumoto Naoki (2003: 252), for instance, describes Susanoo's role in the court myths in the following terms:

> Susanoo is not the protagonist of the [Japanese] founding myth but enters the stage as a secondary character who provides a nice contrast with Amaterasu. … As a worthy opponent he struggles with Amaterasu for a while but in the end has to quit the field in defeat. Thus, his function is to highlight Amaterasu's noble character.

In other words, Susanoo serves as a foil to set off the sun goddess. As the antithesis of Amaterasu, the shady little brother lets his noble sister shine all the more brightly. Kwŏn (2013: 76–84) offers a similar interpretation of Susanoo's function in the *Nihon shoki*. Amaterasu and Susanoo, he argues, serve as a pair of contrasting figures, who represent the dichotomy of good and evil within the *yin-yang* philosophy underlying the divine age fascicles. Susanoo, of course, plays the part of the "evil deity."

Susanoo's adversarial relationship with his sister was already discussed in medieval sources. The Tendai monk Jihen 慈遍 (fl. fourteenth century), an elder brother of Yoshida Kenkō 吉田兼好 (1283?–1352?), the celebrated author of *Tsurezuregusa* 徒然草 (Essays in Idleness; c. 1330),[28] wrote about this topic in his *Tenchi jingi shinchin yōki* 天地神祇審鎮要記 (Primary Record of the Investigation of the Manifest Deities of the World; 1333). He compared Susanoo to Devadatta, a cousin and rival of Śākyamuni, who repeatedly tried to kill the Buddha (Deeg 2005: 313–14, 417–19). In accordance with the Tendai doctrine of original enlightenment, the monk argued for the nonduality of right and wrong and the fluidity of good and evil. According to this reasoning, Devadatta's attempts on Śākyamuni's life served to bring the latter's compassion to the fore. In the same way, Jihen argued, Susanoo's misdeeds brought forth Amaterasu's divine authority (Saitō 2012: 188–90).

In his *Kojikiden* 古事記伝 (Commentaries on the *Kojiki*; completed in 1798), Motoori Norinaga, too, associates Susanoo with evil. The pioneer of National Learning contrasts the "evil deity" Susanoo with his benign siblings

Amaterasu and Tsukuyomi. According to the *Kojiki*, all three deities were born when Izanaki washed off the pollution from his visit in Yomotsu Kuni. While no pollution remained in his eyes (from which Amaterasu and Tsukuyomi were born), Norinaga argues, the stench of the otherworld remained in Izanaki's nose (from which Susanoo was born). For this reason, Susanoo alone turned into an evil deity (MNZ 9: 286).

In the early modern and modern periods, scholars tended to interpret Susanoo and Amaterasu's adversarial relationship from a nature mythological perspective. If Amaterasu was the sun goddess, this left two possible explanations for her antipode Susanoo: either he had to be a moon god or a storm god. While the former hypothesis can be traced to the works of *kokugaku* scholars in the late Edo period, the latter clearly emerged in response to the introduction of the European school of nature mythology in the late nineteenth century. This school of thought goes back to scholars like Adalbert Kuhn (1812–1881), Wilhelm Schwartz (1821–1899), and Friedrich Max Müller (1823–1900), who claimed "that the persons acting in myths have to be interpreted as personifications of natural forces and their interaction as depictions of natural phenomena" (Kohl 1988–2001: 226). In Europe, this school soon fell from favor as its proponents were criticized for their reductionist approach that limited the meaning of myth to the representation of natural phenomena and disregarded any other possible dimensions. Nonetheless, it was one of the dominant schools in mythological studies in Japan during the first half of the twentieth century.

Sun and Moon

As we have seen, Susanoo overlaps with the moon god Tsukuyomi in both the *Kojiki* and the *Nihon shoki*. The question of the two deities' relationship was already addressed by *kokugaku* scholars during the Edo period (1600–1868). Norinaga pointed out that there must be a deep reason for the numerous overlaps between the two deities and suggested that Susanoo and Tsukuyomi might have originally been one and the same deity (MNZ 9: 388).

His student Hattori Nakatsune 服部中庸 (1757–1824) went much further in his *Sandaikō* 三大考 (Treatise on the Great Triad), which was published as a part of Norinaga's *Kojikiden* in 1792. Here, Nakatsune argued that the two deities were indeed identical. Since the *Kojiki* relates that Tsukuyomi reigned over the Honorable Country of Night, Hattori identified this realm with the moon. In a further step, he equated it with Yomotsu Kuni by claiming that the component *yomi* in the moon god's name was identical to the first component

Table 2.2 Hirata Atsutane's Equation of Susanoo and Tsukuyomi in *Tama no mihashira*

Yoru no osu Kuni = Yomi no Kuni (Yomotsu Kuni) = Tsukuyomi no Kuni
=> Susanoo = Tsukuyomi

of Yomotsu Kuni that can be read as both *yomo* and *yomi*. Thus, he was able to equate Yomotsu Kuni with the moon. This, in turn, provided him with a link to Susanoo, who, according to the *Kojiki*, wanted to follow his mother to Yomotsu Kuni[29] and in some variants of the myth was depicted as the god of the sea (whose tides follow the movements of the moon) (SDK: 263–4; cf. McNally 2005: 108–9).

Hirata Atsutane took up and expanded Nakatsune's theory in his famous work *Tama no mihashira* 霊能真柱 (The True Pillar of Spirit; 1813). Like Nakatsune, he viewed the Honorable Country of Night—which he also calls "the Land of Tsukuyomi" (Tsukuyomi no kuni) after its ruler—as identical to the land of Yomi (Yomi no kuni, i.e., Yomotsu Kuni). Atsutane makes this connection appear more convincing by exclusively using the characters for "night" and "view" to write the word *yomi*.[30] Atsutane's hypothesis, which is summarized in Table 2.2, led him to the conclusion that Susanoo and Tsukuyomi were two names for the same deity (TM: 62–3; cf. McNally 2005: 184–5):

Takagi Toshio 高木敏雄 (1876–1922), who is often regarded as the founder of modern mythological studies in Japan, proposed a new theory that linked Susanoo to Tsukuyomi while taking the genesis of the early court chronicles into account. In an article published in 1914, Takagi (1973a: 247–51) argues that Susanoo originally belonged to the Izumo myths that used to be independent from the mythology of the Yamato ruling house. In the mythical tradition of Yamato, on the other hand, a sun deity and a moon deity played important roles. When Izumo came under the political influence of the Yamato dynasty, Takagi hypothesizes, the Izumo deities were incorporated into the mythology of the ruling house. In this process, Susanoo was turned into a brother of the sun and moon deities and partly took over Tsukuyomi's role. Takagi quotes the myth of the killing of the food goddess as evidence for his theory: in its original form, he claims, this tale explained the origin of food, later it was linked with the alternation of sun and moon, and in the last stage, the moon god's role was taken over by Susanoo.

Western scholars such as Karl Florenz (1865–1939) and William George Aston (1841–1911) discussed Susanoo's connection to the moon deity as well. While the former vehemently denied the possibility that Susanoo might be related or even identical to the moon god (Florenz 1901: 319), Aston (1905: 138) pointed out that "the analogy of other mythologies suggests that a god whose relations with the Sun are at one time marital and at another hostile must be the Moon." Aston is thus the only scholar who explicitly bases his interpretation of Susanoo as a moon god on his peculiar relationship with Amaterasu. It seems plausible, however, that Susanoo's antagonistic relationship with the sun goddess motivated many of the other scholars quoted above to identify him as the dark twin of the sun—that is, the moon.

Susanoo as a Storm God

His relationship with the sun goddess occupies a much more prominent position in studies that regard Susanoo as a storm god rather than a moon god. The first scholar who associated Susanoo with wind seems to be Edward Burnett Tylor (1832–1917). The pioneering Victorian anthropologist remarked about Susanoo that "even if the Japanese commentators did not recognise him as the God of Winds, we should see [him] to be such by his description; he is gentle and mild, always with tears in his eyes, but if opposed becomes furious, tearing down everything, uprooting the trees and setting fire to the forests." The nature mythological assumptions underlying this interpretation become apparent when Tylor explains that after eliminating Buddhist and Chinese elements from the *Kojiki*'s account, one is left with "what appears to be a genuine Japanese stratum, containing nature-myths of a clearly marked character."[31] For Tylor, Amaterasu's "purely nature-descriptive character is evident" (Tylor 1877: 55–6). Hence, he concludes that the myth of Amaterasu's hiding in the Heavenly Rock Dwelling is really

> the nature-myth of the Sun driven into hiding by the storm and peeping out from her cloud-cave, when presently the great cloud is rolled away like a rock from a cave's mouth. Following out the same course of ideas, we read of the Wind-god descending to earth and slaying the eight-headed and eight-tailed serpent, who is about to destroy the "lady of the young rice field." The monster is known to the Japanese as being an eight-mouthed river, so the story seems really that of the wind and the flood. (Ibid.: 57)

Some twenty years later, Edmund Buckley (life dates unknown) proposed a similar interpretation. For him, Susanoo was a "Rain-Storm God":

> The following traits indeed indicate that he represents the rain-storm. His name means "Impetuous Male." He was born as Izanagi washed his august nose, that

nose wherein is the breath. The Chinese version of the myth indeed states that the breath of Pan-ku [Pangu 盤古] was transmuted into the wind. He abandons his appointment "to rule over the sea-plain," i.e., the rain-storm blows up in the southwest monsoon from over the sea. … He mounts with great noise heavenwards to the great terror of his sister, Amaterasu, and devastates the country, whereupon Amaterasu retires into a cave and thus plunges the land into "eternal night." In nature-fact, the rain-storm rises from the horizon with thunder, obscures the sun, and spoils the carefully terraced and irrigated rice-fields of Japan. (Buckley 1896: 730–2)

Buckley's article adds two aspects to Tylor's interpretation that were taken up by subsequent treatises. First, it draws attention to parallels in Chinese and Indian mythology, namely the figures of Pangu and Indra. Second, it connects Susanoo's alleged role as storm god with the deity's name. The interpretation of Susanoo's name as "Impetuous Male" follows Basil Hall Chamberlain's (1850–1935) translation of the *Kojiki* into English (1882). Chamberlain bases this translation on the view of the early *kokugaku* scholar Kamo no Mabuchi 賀茂真淵 (1697–1769), quoted by his disciple Motoori Norinaga in his *Kojikiden*. Based on the word *kachisabi*, which is used in the *Kojiki* to describe Susanoo's unruly behavior after his victory in the contest with his sister (KJK I: 62/63), Mabuchi constructs the word *susabi*, which, he claims, has the meaning "to advance" (*susumu*) or "to advance in a wild manner" (*susumi-araburu*). According to Mabuchi, the component "susa" in Susanoo's name has the same meaning, while the component "no-o" means "male of" (MNZ 9: 342).[32]

The storm god hypothesis reached Japan in 1899 and led to the so-called storm god dispute that is often described as marking the beginning of the modern study of myth in Japan.[33] The dispute unfolded between Takayama Rinjirō 高山林次郎 (1871–1902), Takagi Toshio, and Anesaki Masaharu 姉崎正治 (1876–1922), three former students at the Imperial University of Tokyo. It revolved around the question whether or not Susanoo was a storm god. Anesaki, who was to become the first professor of Religious Studies at his alma mater,[34] contended that the myth of Amaterasu and Susanoo's struggle was not concerned with natural phenomena but rather with social questions such as insubordination toward the ruler and the breaking of religious taboos. According to his point of view, Susanoo had to be understood as a deity who rebelled against the social order rather than as a storm god. Takayama and Takagi, on the other hand, argued that Susanoo was indeed a storm god.

In an article first published in 1899, Takagi agrees that the myths surrounding Susanoo address social questions. But he does not accept Anesaki's conclusion that Susanoo has to be understood as the personification of a moral notion. Takagi points to examples of comparably complex and human-like deities in Indo-European mythologies who are nonetheless believed to be based on natural phenomena (such as Indra). Furthermore, he argues that it was only natural to assume that Susanoo was based on a natural phenomenon since this was obviously true for his two siblings: the sun goddess and the moon god. Takagi supports his argument with two pieces of evidence we are already familiar with from Buckley's study: (1) Susanoo's name and (2) Indian and Chinese myths in which the breath of a deity becomes the wind (Takagi 1973b: 141, 158).

Karl Florenz presents exactly the same argumentation in his translation of the divine age fascicles of the *Nihon shoki*, which was under assessment as a doctoral dissertation at the Imperial University of Tokyo at the time the storm god dispute unfolded. Since Takayama, Takagi, and Anesaki were Florenz's students, it seems probable that the young Japanese scholars were influenced by their German teacher, who had studied Sanskrit and Comparative Linguistics at the University of Leipzig, where none other than Friedrich Max Müller, one of the pioneers of the nature mythological approach, was one of his teachers (Satō 1995: 93–5).[35]

The Shady Little Brother of the Sun Goddess: Susanoo in Colonial Discourse

This chapter has shown the complexity and heterogeneity of the myths surrounding Susanoo in the ancient sources. While Susanoo's role in the court mythology of the early eighth century is still a matter of dispute, many scholars point out the significance of Susanoo's relationship to his sister Amaterasu. Contrary to present-day scholarship, the differences between the depictions of Susanoo in the individual sources were not emphasized in studies predating the end of the war. The typical approach of prewar mythologists was rather to combine traits gathered from the various sources into a composite figure that was then understood as the "original" form of Susanoo. Although scholars differed in their interpretations of Susanoo's function in the myths, they tended to see him as the antithesis of the sun goddess—whether this meant that he was a moon god, a storm god, a challenger of Amaterasu's divine order, or just simply her "evil twin" (Faure 2016a: 339). In previous scholarship, the dichotomy between the sun goddess and her shady little brother was expressed on several levels: elder sister vs. younger brother, sun vs. moon/storm, light vs. darkness,

Table 2.3 Ideological Implications of Susanoo's Juxtaposition with Amaterasu in Colonial Discourse

Amaterasu	Susanoo
Senior	Junior
Mature	Immature
Order	Insubordination
Centrality	Marginality
Head family	Branch family (foster children)
Modernity	Backwardness
Japan	Korea

order vs. insubordination, and finally, good vs. evil. By associating Susanoo with Korea, Japanese thinkers of the colonial period added Japan and Korea to this list of antipodes. The relationship of the serene Amaterasu to her immature little brother Susanoo provided a model for the relations between colonizers and colonized. The ideological implications of this juxtaposition are summarized in Table 2.3.

One important function Susanoo fulfills in both *Kojiki* and *Nihon shoki* (but not in *Izumo fudoki*) is to highlight Amaterasu's (and by implication the sun lineage's) splendid serenity by serving as the strongest possible contrast. In the court mythology, Susanoo complements Amaterasu in important ways. While Amaterasu symbolizes central authority, Susanoo is associated with the periphery. While Amaterasu is described as a guarantor of order, Susanoo challenges this order by breaking every rule in an almost systematical way. But in the end, Susanoo's challenge to Amaterasu's authority fails. Defeated, the shady little brother submits to his shining sister's rule. In this way, Susanoo could serve as a figure of identification that convinced regional rulers in the eighth century that it was in their best interest to submit to imperial authority. Twelve centuries later, the theory of common ancestry used the same myths to persuade colonized Koreans to bow to Japan's enlightened rule.

3

Passion for Transgression: Susanoo's Liminal Character

Susanoo's role as a wanderer, border breaker, and rebel connects him to trickster figures that appear in many mythologies around the world. Victor Turner (1968: 580) characterized mythical trickster figures as "liminal personalities." One of their functions in tales all over the world is to complement the ordered world of rules and norms with a more unpredictable dimension of chaos and chance. This chapter will focus on Susanoo's liminal character. Starting from a discussion of Susanoo's ambiguous position between the "Heavenly" and the "Earthly Deities," two groups of divinities mentioned in *Kojiki* and *Nihon shoki*, I will move on to an examination of Susanoo's role as perpetual wanderer and taboo breaker, suggesting that all of these aspects can be viewed as expressions of his fundamentally liminal nature. In the concluding section, I will connect Susanoo's liminal status in ancient mythology with colonized Koreans' precarious position at the margin of the Japanese empire.

Earthly Deities and Heavenly Deities

In the introduction to his translation of the *Kojiki*, Basil Hall Chamberlain points out that three mythical cycles can be distinguished in the chronicle's first fascicle: one centering on Yamato, the second on Tsukushi (Kyushu), and the third on Izumo. He notes that these three mythical cycles "accord but imperfectly together" (Chamberlain [1882] 1982: lxxxv–lxxxvi). While the myths of the Izumo cycle focus on Ōkuninushi and his offspring, both the Tsukushi and the Yamato myths deal with the imperial family descended from Amaterasu through her grandchild Ninigi. Therefore, Japanese researchers often make a further distinction between the myths of the so-called *tenson minzoku* 天孫民族 (people of heavenly ancestry)—comprising the Tsukushi and Yamato cycles—and the myths of the Izumo people (e.g., Matsumura 1951).

In traditional research, the three mythical cycles noted by Chamberlain were commonly regarded as a reflection of a historical battle between different ethnic groups—such as a *tenson* and an Izumo people—with the better end for the Yamato group. As will be discussed in Chapter 6, such interpretations were extremely popular during the first half of the twentieth century, when Japanese historians projected the multiethnic nature of imperial Japan back onto the distant past. However, the genesis of the Yamato central state was a centuries-long process during which the rulers of the Yamato polity gradually extended their sphere of influence over ever-larger portions of West Japan. For the most part, this political unification seems to have been achieved by peaceful means. For local rulers, the benefits of submitting to the Yamato polity included access to trading routes as well as military assistance against external threats (be they real or imagined). It follows from this that the Yamato ruler was (at least in the beginning) nothing more than the first among equals who depended on the goodwill of the local chieftains. According to Bernhard Scheid (2016: 96–7), this historical situation is mirrored in the mythical portions of *Kojiki* and *Nihon shoki*. The compilation of the two court chronicles, he argues, was driven by an "eclectic inclusivism." The aim of these myth-histories was "not to solely declare the mythology of the heartland Yamato as binding for all portions of the realm that had to be governed but, on the contrary, to weave narrative traditions from different regions—including China and Korea—into a single plot so that all potential subjects could identify with parts of the narrative."

In the myths themselves, "Heavenly Deities" (*amatsu kami* 天神) are distinguished from "Earthly Deities" (*kunitsu kami* 国神). The former group of deities resides in the Plain of High Heaven, whereas the latter populates and governs the Central Land of Reed Plains (*ashihara no nakatsu kuni* 葦原中国) situated below the Plain of High Heaven in the cosmoses depicted in *Kojiki* and *Nihon shoki*.[1] This state of affairs comes to an end, however, when Amaterasu sends her grandson Ninigi down to rule over the Central Land of Reed Plains. After witnessing a show of strength by the Heavenly Deities, Ōkuninushi relinquishes his rule over the land on the condition that the Heavenly Deities build him a magnificent palace and worship him there. The palace is built and Ōkuninushi retreats from the world to preside over "hidden matters" (*kakuretaru koto* 幽事) (KJK I: 98–119; NSK II [9], vol. 1: 110–55).[2]

This episode, commonly referred to as the myth of *kuni-yuzuri* 国譲り (cession of the land), has often been interpreted as reflecting a historical struggle between Izumo and Yamato. According to this reading, the deities of the vanquished Izumo polity were later incorporated into the mythology of the Yamato court as Earthly Deities. As such they were attributed an inferior position compared to the Heavenly Deities, to whom the imperial family traced its line and its mandate to rule over Japan. According to Joan Piggott (1989: 62), this myth "sacralised the relationship between Izumo and Yamato." It "sanctified Yamato's paramountcy, but it also guaranteed the continuance of Ohonamuchi's [Ōkuninushi's] cult and the power of its priest-rulers." The retelling of the Izumo myths in the Yamato chronicles, she continues,

> skillfully legitimated the political status quo in the early eighth century: Izumo deities such as Ohonamuchi and Susano-o were appropriately subordinated to Yamato's cult deities; Izumo was described as "the land of darkness" … in contrast to Amaterasu's sunny "high heavenly plain" …;[3] and Ohonamuchi, lord of the land of Izumo, was portrayed as ceding his divine power over Izumo to Amaterasu's descendants. (Piggott 1989: 67–8)

As early as 1914, Takagi Toshio (1973a: 248–51) had expressed a similar view and addressed Susanoo's function within this process. Susanoo, he argues, was originally a creator deity venerated in Izumo. Later, the editors of the court chronicles invented the episode of Susanoo's descent from the Plain of High Heaven to Izumo in order to link the *tenson* and Izumo mythologies. Susanoo's misdeeds in the Plain of High Heaven, Takagi surmises, were also invented at this point to motivate his descent. Since Izumo still held great powers in the religious sphere, the Izumo myths were incorporated in virtually unaltered form into the mythology of the Yamato court.

The historian Tsuda Sōkichi 津田左右吉 (1873–1961), who was famously found guilty of lèse majesté and lost his professorship at Waseda University in 1940 due to his critical views on the imperial myths (Brownlee 1999: 186–9), proposed an even more radical hypothesis. He claimed that the figure of Susanoo was invented from scratch by the "writers of the history of the Divine Age" in order to link the myths of the Yamato court to those of Izumo (Tsuda 1963: 576–95).

The most elaborate argument that attributed Susanoo's contradictory character to his bridging function between two originally separate mythologies was proposed by the eminent mythologist Matsumura Takeo (1883–1969). In Matsumura's opinion, Susanoo was originally one of the major deities of the Izumo pantheon, who was later incorporated into the mythology of the Yamato court as the little brother of the imperial ancestress Amaterasu. The incorporation of a vanquished group's paramount deity into the pantheon of the new rulers as the younger sibling of (and thus in an inferior position to) the latter's highest deity is a strategy Matsumura discovered in many mythologies. He quotes the sibling relationships between Odin and Loki (Scandinavia), Zeus and Poseidon (Greece), and Osiris and Seth (Egypt) as examples. He notes that in all these examples the younger sibling, that is, the deity of the conquered group, shows aggressive behavior toward its elder sibling and defies the latter's authority. Susanoo, he argues, had originally been a tutelary deity of agriculturists and a provider of rain, but when the mythmakers of the Yamato court incorporated him into their mythology, they ascribed traits to him that were contrary to his original character. In the court chronicles, Susanoo was described as a destructive deity in order to show his inferiority to Amaterasu (Matsumura 1951).

While the interpretations introduced above do not lack plausibility, the presupposition on which they are based, namely that the Heavenly and Earthly Deities mentioned in the myths represent two different political, cultural, or ethnic entities of early Japan, is questionable. Comparative studies show that the trope of a struggle between two groups of deities that are close kin can be observed in many Eurasian mythologies, such as that of Greece (Olympians and Titans) and India (Asuras and Devas) (Witzel 2012: 163–4). Burkhard Gladigow (1988–2001: 325) regards such struggles as a typical structuring principle in polytheistic pantheons:

> The gods who are defeated in the battle for the "kingdom in heaven" not only represent an older generation of deities, that is they are "historically earlier," but usually they also have to leave the center of the world: Seth is allocated to the area of outside, Alalu flees to the dark earth, Kronos is banished to a place beneath the earth or dwells at the margin of the world. In this way a regionalization of the mythical world is achieved.

A similar regionalization of the mythical world can be observed in the *Kojiki* and the *Nihon shoki*, where Izumo, the country ruled by the Earthly Deities before Ninigi's descent, is depicted as a peripheral region bordering on the realms of the dead. Izumo thus serves as an antipode to the Plain of High Heaven (Matsumae 1998: 333–5). It is an interesting question why Izumo was selected to represent the margin of the Japanese state, but the struggle of the Heavenly and Earthly Deities has not necessarily to be viewed as the distant echo of a military or political rivalry between Yamato and Izumo.

The ideological implications of this regionalization of the mythical world are more relevant for the aims of the present study. Jonathan Stockdale (2013: 254) draws attention to "the crucial role played by exile in mapping out a Yamato-based constellation of power." Susanoo's banishment from his sister's heavenly realm served not only as a "narrative bridge joining the Izumo section to the central Yamato narrative" but also made it possible to link the Izumo deities genealogically to Amaterasu through her sibling relation with Susanoo, while at the same time politically subordinating them through their descent from an exiled deity. Izumo is thus depicted as a peripheral region, where unwanted persons are exiled to: "the court texts vividly imagine and dramatically assert an entire constellation of power, juxtaposing Amaterasu and Susano-o, Yamato and Izumo, center and margin, royalty and loyalty." Ōkuninushi's cession of the land to the Heavenly Deities has an important function in this context. After all, the Earthly Deity received a splendid palace and the worship of the sun lineage as a reward for his submission. This episode thus reminds its readers that submission and loyalty to the Yamato court is rewarded with privileges and prestige (Stockdale 2013: 255). *Kojiki* and *Nihon shoki* thus legitimate the political order of the late seventh and early eighth century by projecting it back onto a mythical past. The target audience for this myth-history were regional rulers, who were reminded that loyalty to the imperial court paid off.

Lord of In-Between

Susanoo's position in this divine struggle is ambiguous. As Amaterasu's brother, it seems logical to include him in the ranks of the Heavenly Deities, but Susanoo marries the daughter of an Earthly Deity and becomes the progenitor (in some versions the father) of Ōkuninushi. In this way, he serves as a mediator who links the two groups of deities but cannot unambiguously be assigned to either group. This ambiguous position "betwixt and between" links Susanoo to trickster figures in other mythologies.[4] In Norse mythology, Loki occupies a similar position between the gods and their greatest enemies, the giants. Though living among the gods, Loki is closely linked to the giants as well; not only was his father a giant but he also fathers his own children by a giantess (Hyde 2010: 97).

In a study on trickster figures in various mythologies, Lewis Hyde (2010: 6) eloquently describes tricksters as "the lords of in-between": constantly "on the road," they "can move between heaven and earth, and between the living and the dead." This characterization certainly applies to Susanoo. "As wanderer between the worlds" (Wittkamp 2018: 384), Susanoo travels between the various realms of the mythical cosmos (heaven, earth, and the otherworld) without entirely belonging to any of the spheres (Ellwood 1997: 151). This "enduring inbetweenness" is one of the defining traits of trickster figures around the globe (Pelton 1997: 124–5).

Victor Turner (1967: 94) characterizes tricksters as "liminal personalities." Drawing on Arnold van Gennep's famous study on *rites de passage* (1909), Turner associates tricksters with the ambiguous middle phase in rites of passage. Such rites "accompany every change of place, state, social position and age" and are marked by a succession of three phases: (1) separation from the previous state, (2) liminal phase, and (3) consummation of the passage. A good example for such a ritual passage is the transition from youth to adulthood, a process often accompanied by elaborate rites. In the first phase, the initiand is separated from his family, thus dying "as a child." Previously taken-for-granted norms, rules, and limits are removed to enable the initiand's rebirth "as an adult" (Szakolczai 2015: 17–19).

During the liminal phase, initiands occupy an ambiguous position in-between the two states: while already separated from their old state, they are not yet initiated into their new one. Since persons in this liminal situation do not have a defined role and position within society, social norms do not apply to them. Their behavior is thus highly unpredictable (Turner 1967: 94).

> One class of myths which throws into sharp relief many aspects of liminality is that represented by the widely distributed trickster tales. … Tricksters are clearly liminal personalities (threshold men or edge men). … These liminal entities share an antinomian character. They behave as though there were no social or moral norms to guide them. (Turner 1968: 580)

This brings us to a further character trait that links Susanoo to other trickster figures: as vividly expressed in the episode of Susanoo's outrages in the Plain of High Heaven, he is a "notorious border breaker" (Hynes 1997: 33), who seems intent on transgressing every conceivable moral, agricultural, and religious taboo.

Breaker of Taboos

Peter Pörtner (1986: 227–8) calls Susanoo the "Japanese archetype of a taboobreaker," whose "sole ambition" seems to be "to commit crime (almost systematically) against everything which was considered to be sacrosanct by his heavenly relatives." The transgression of taboos is a prominent feature in many trickster tales.

In this context, anthropologist Laura Makarius draws attention to the strict taboo on contact with blood that she observed in tribal traditions in Africa, North America, and Oceania. She shows that this taboo is systematically violated by ritual clowns, whom she regards as "earthly counterpart of the *trickster*" (italics in original). These clowns often use blood to besmear each other or the spectators of their performance. The Navaho, Makarius points out, use a piece of sheepskin drenched in menstrual blood for healing (Makarius 1970: 68, 46, 49). Blood coming from female sexual organs, especially from a consanguine, is regarded as particularly dangerous. This is one of the reasons for the taboo on incest. Why, then, would anybody dare to violate these taboos? Makarius provides an explanation for this seeming contradiction: the taboo against the contact with blood is breached in various ways in order to acquire "the 'overdeterminated' power of blood." Thus, the breach of taboo is thought to endow its perpetrator with magical power (Makarius 1974: 541–2).

A taboo on contact with blood similar to the one described by Makarius can be observed in the oldest Japanese texts and, to a certain extent, is still upheld in Shintō practice (Ellwood 1997: 155). In the myth of Susanoo, at least two breaches of taboo with a potential connection to blood can be discerned: (1) his implied incest with Amaterasu and (2) his throwing of a horse skin into the Pure Weaving Hall.[5]

Claude Lévi-Strauss (1966: 326–9) explained Susanoo's unruly behavior with his desire to commit incest, comparing the Japanese myth to several South American ones.[6] All of these tales are concerned with a crying child who is abandoned by his mother (the fact that Susanoo is a "posthumous child" of Izanami, Lévi-Strauss argues, only changes the date of being left alone) or who considers himself unduly neglected although he has already reached an age when a normal child is supposed to emancipate itself from its parents. It is not difficult, Lévi-Strauss claims, "to recognize in the figure of the crying child that of the asocial hero (asocial in the sense that he refuses to let himself be socialized), who stubbornly clings to nature and to the feminine world." He compares the Japanese tale to a myth of the Central Brazilian Bororo that recounts how a boy raped his mother, when she was out in the woods together with the other women in order to collect palm branches for the penis sheath that male adolescents receive at the time of initiation (Lévi-Strauss 1964: 43–5). Afraid of this new stage in life, the boy "commits incest in order to return to the maternal womb" (Lévi-Strauss 1966: 328–9).

Lévi-Strauss leaves the question of whether Susanoo actually fulfilled his desire to commit incest unanswered, but Bernhard Scheid (2016: 99) in a recent paper argues that Susanoo and Amaterasu "continue the incestuous mode of marriage of their parents." "One need not be a Freudian," Scheid remarks, "to recognize the image of Susanowo breaking a hole in the weaving hall and inserting a carcass into it as a metaphor for rape" (ibid.: 104). Similar interpretations have been proposed by Géza Róheim (1972: 371–2)—who, incidentally, *is* a Freudian—and Allan Grapard (1991: 13). In Japanese scholarship, Susanoo's alleged incest with Amaterasu is mainly addressed in psychological interpretations. Standing in the tradition of Lévi-Strauss, these interpretations often maintain that Susanoo's incest with his sister shows the former's immaturity as well as his dependence on and longing for his mother, which are then redirected toward his sister (Kawai 1996: 79).

Mori Asao (2002: 19–37) draws attention to another aspect of the episode: he convincingly argues that the point of Susanoo's actions in the Plain of High Heaven is to introduce chaos into his sister's pure realm. Susanoo's outrages are true acts of border breaking: he destroys the divisions between Amaterasu's rice paddies and devastates the paddies, thus in effect restoring them to their uncultivated state and rendering them indistinguishable from the surrounding nature. By strewing his excrements in the New Palace for the ritual costing of the new rice, he destroys the purity of this sanctuary, thus eliminating the border between the sacred precinct and its profane surroundings. In the same vein, Mori argues, Susanoo's incest with Amaterasu has to be viewed as the introduction of a mode of sexuality that defies cultural rules into the highly ordered Plain of High Heaven.[7]

All in all, there are many indications that Susanoo's confrontation with Amaterasu in the Plain of High Heaven constitutes "a well-disguised primordial incest" (Witzel 2005: 38).[8] The "hedged formulations" of this episode, which make its interpretation today so difficult, might be deliberate, since its authors shunned a more explicit description of "the transgression of taboos centering around birth, sexuality, and death" in a narrative that associates these actions with the highest deities (Scheid 2016: 112). By treating these topics in a veiled fashion, the imperial ancestress Amaterasu could be depicted as a "virgin mother … untouched by the activities of sexual congress, conception, and childbirth" (Matsumura 1998: 47).

It would be a mistake, however, to reduce the meaning of the whole episode to this single aspect. In his zeal to prove Susanoo's incest with his sister, Róheim (1972: 372), for instance, regards the horse flayed backward as an image for "the penis in erection" with pulled-back foreskin. Nelly Naumann (1979) offers a much more convincing explanation in correlating the act of backward flaying with two magical practices, mentioned in the *Nihon ryōiki* 日本霊異記 (Record of Miraculous Events in Japan; *c.* 822) and the *Kojiki*, that also rest on "reverse" actions, namely reversely drinking rice-wine while reciting spells and reversely clapping hands.

> Both of these magical practices cause death, a quality they obtain just because they are *reverse* actions. The original actions, however, which have been thus reversed into their very opposite, are actions of blessing which, on their part, effect "life." They are benedictions wishing health and longevity, offered with the highly raised wine-cup, and the clapping of the hands accompanying those benedictions. We do not know how such a reverse action would, in fact, have been carried out. The essential point lies solely in the idea that the total reversal of an action will bring forth the total reversal of its original effect … [T]he inferences relating to the nature of these two magical practices as reverse actions and as death magic apply to the *sakahagi* [逆剥; backward flaying] as well insofar as the *sakahagi* too can be considered a reverse action causing death, if only on the mythic plane. (Naumann 1982: 15)

Makarius (1970: 61–2) reports a similar phenomenon with regard to ritual clowns: they often adopt forms of "reverse behaviour" like, for instance, "backward speech." This means that the clowns say the exact opposite of what they mean, or that they do the exact opposite of what they are told. This constitutes the reverse of normal, accepted behavior and can therefore be regarded as a breach of taboo. Thus, the myths centering on Susanoo show striking parallels to the patterns that Makarius associates with tales of tricksters as "magical violators of taboo." However, if the breach of taboos is one of Susanoo's central functions in the narrative, this leaves us with the question of the point of Susanoo's destructive behavior. What did the shady little brother of the sun goddess try to achieve with his transgressions? And why did the author-compilers of the court chronicles report his misdeeds in such detail?

Defining the Divine Order

Hyde (2010: 178) provides an insightful answer to these questions. Like many other scholars, he believes that the story of Amaterasu's retreat into the Heavenly Rock Cave is at its core a myth about the winter solstice: "the dirt and disorder Susa-nö-o has injected into the harvest rituals have initiated some sort of eclipse, which is followed, in turn, by rituals to repair the loss. The sun disappears; then the sun returns." While at first sight Susanoo's actions might seem destructive, they enable not only the rebirth of the sun, but also bring forth the seeds of the five grains, that is, the cultural plants. He introduces chaos into his sister's highly ordered realm, but it is a fertile sort of chaos:

> You get no seeds at all if the sunlight is too pure ever to mingle with the muck of the rice paddies. You get no seeds if shit never enters the New Palace [of the Great Harvest Festival]. And because there is always a hunger seeking for those seeds, whenever humans or gods move to purify life by excluding death, or to protect order completely from the dirt that is its by-product, trickster will upset their plans. When purity approaches sterility, he will tear a hole in the sacred enclosure and drop a dead pony on the virgin weavers, or strew his feces under the Sun Goddess's throne. (Ibid.: 179)

This interpretation is based on Mary Douglas's conception of "dirt" as "matter out of place." According to Douglas ([1966] 2005: 44), dirt is "the by-product of a systematic ordering and classification of matter, in so far as ordering involves rejecting inappropriate elements." All these rejected elements are then subsumed under the label of "dirt." Barbara Babcock-Abrahams (1975: 152) links this concept to the peripheral position of trickster figures. As we have seen, tricksters do not belong to a larger group. From the perspective of any group, they occupy a peripheral position. For this reason, Babcock-Abrahams likens tricksters to "the 'dirt' of the social system" and argues that they represent a "tolerated margin of mess."[9] Since all semiotic systems are defined by what they are not, such a margin of mess is needed as the defining condition of all ordered systems.

Thus, trickster figures give definition to order by acting at its boundaries (Street 1972: 101). This is also true in the case of Susanoo. It has often been remarked that the various forms of destruction Susanoo brought over Amaterasu's rice paddies, correspond almost perfectly with the Heavenly Sins (*amatsu tsumi* 天津罪) enumerated in the ritual prayer of the Great Purification (*ōharae* 大祓) that is recorded in the *Engi shiki* 延喜式, a ritual compendium that was presented to the court in 928 (EGSK VIII, vol. 1: 476–81; cf. Philippi 1990: 45–9).[10] Inbe no Hironari 斎部広成 (fl. ninth century) made the connection explicit when he wrote in his *Kogo shūi* 古語拾遺 (Gleanings from Ancient Stories; 807) that Susanoo's actions in the Plain of High Heaven were the "Heavenly Sins. They are now [recorded in] the words of purification (*harae-kotoba*) of the Nakatomi 中臣." (KS: 193).[11] This is a reference to the ritual prayer of the Great Purification, which was performed by the Nakatomi, the kinship group that held the greatest religious authority at the time. If the episode of Susanoo's misdeeds in the Plain of High Heaven are thus regarded as "a kind of myth of origin for the *ōharae*" (Scheid 2016: 107), one could argue that Susanoo gave definition to the "Heavenly Sins" in a very real sense by committing them. The rules were not even explicit before Susanoo broke—and thus defined—them (Vollmer 1986: 203).

The tale of Susanoo also shows what happens to those who violate the prohibitions: the "'criminal' culture hero" (Babcock-Abrahams 1975: 148) is fined, purified, and banished from Amaterasu's realm. Makarius explains why this is the inevitable consequence of the transgression of taboos. The effectiveness of the violation of taboo rests on the collective recognition of taboo. If all members of society breached a taboo, it would stop being a taboo. Thus, transgressions of taboo have to be individual and exceptional acts in order to remain meaningful. Owing to its fundamentally antisocial nature as a challenge to the very rules on which social order rests, the breach of taboo—even if it yields positive results for society—results in the banishment of its perpetrator (Makarius 1973: 668–70). The same pattern can be observed in the myth of Susanoo, who has been described as an "embodiment of sin." As such he had to be banished to Ne no Kuni—the same realm to which all sins are carried in the ritual prayer of the Great Purification (Saigō 1967: 65).[12]

According to the classicist Karl Kerényi (1956: 185), the trickster's function "is to add disorder to order and so make a whole, to render possible within the fixed bounds of what is permitted, an experience of what is not permitted." However, it would be a mistake to view all trickster tales simply as "mechanisms of social control in the form of 'ritualized rebellion' [or] 'licensed aggression'" (Babcock-Abrahams 1975: 157), since they have the potential to cast doubt on the validity of the rules whose transgression they depict. Brian Street (1972: 97) draws attention to the creative potential of breaking rules. Progress is only possible by going against cherished traditions. "Creation demands the destruction of what went before." In a similar vein, the historian Dieter Langewiesche (2013: 168) emphasizes society's dependence both on rules and their transgression: the former are needed for a functioning state, whereas the latter enables social progress. The trickster's role is therefore not a purely destructive and negative one but can lead to innovation.

In the case of Susanoo, however, the rules are never seriously called into question. In the end, he cannot challenge Amaterasu's authority. His actions seem capricious and their positive results are well hidden in the narrative: Susanoo drives Amaterasu into the Heavenly Rock Cave, but it is the other deities who lure her out again; Susanoo kills the food goddess, but it is another deity, Kamimusuhi, who collects the seeds that grow from her corpse. But if we keep in mind that Amaterasu is the progenitress of the imperial family and that it was Emperor Tenmu who ordered the compilation of the court chronicles to legitimate his claim to the throne he had won in a bloody war of succession (cf. Ooms 2009: 3), it becomes clear that an assault on monarchic power could only be incorporated into the imperially sanctioned myths in a veiled fashion. For these reasons, Susanoo appears in the Japanese tales as the "exception who probes and proves the rules" (Vescey 1997: 119) rather than as the "negation offering possibility" (Babcock-Abrahams 1975: 186). Scheid (2016: 99) rightly characterizes Susanoo as a "classical trickster deity" whose "deeds are opposed to the order of the deities ... [but] nonetheless effect its revitalization and substantiation." Susanoo's introduction of chaos into his sister's realm and the subsequent re-creation of order can be viewed as "the contradictory phases of a single process" that serves to justify and reinforce the imperial order (Yamaguchi 1977: 159). By questioning it, Susanoo ends up defining the divine order represented by his sister, the sun goddess.

This adds a new dimension to the juxtaposition of Susanoo and Amaterasu in the court chronicles. According to Yamaguchi Masao, kingship "integrates chaos with order." On the symbolic plane, it has to incorporate the opposing principles of central authority and marginal reality. In the Japanese court chronicles, these opposing principles are symbolized by Amaterasu and Susanoo. While the consolidation of central authority is Amaterasu's ultimate concern, Susanoo "is oriented in the other direction, away from the center toward the periphery." In this structural model of kingship, Amaterasu and Susanoo are contrasted as complete opposites. This dichotomy is expressed on various levels such as the capital vs. the frontier, static vs. dynamic, normality vs. abnormality, peace vs. violence, government by rule vs. attack by means of trick, order vs. chaos, the sacred vs. sacrilege, and centrality vs. marginality. In sum, Susanoo functions as a "negative expression" of the sun goddess (Yamaguchi 1977: 162, 165–7, 164).

Merging Mythical Traditions: The Creation of a Court Mythology

The preceding discussion has highlighted Susanoo's role as wanderer, border breaker, and rebel and has attempted to get a handle on his elusive personality through Turner's definition of tricksters as liminal figures. But after his second banishment to Izumo, Susanoo mends his ways. He saves a maiden in distress, kills a vile monster, and settles down with his wife. He also puts an end to the rivalry with his sister, presenting her with the mighty sword he has found in the eight-headed serpent's tail. While he had been a villain in the Plain of High Heaven, in Izumo Susanoo appears as a hero and the progenitor of Ōkuninushi, who ruled the Central Land of Reed Plains before the arrival of the sun lineage. In the second half of Susanoo's narrative as presented in the court chronicles, there is no hint of the liminal quality that characterizes the god in the earlier portions of the narrative. It is this incongruity that led scholars like Takagi or Matsumura to suspect that the author-compilers of the *Kojiki* and the *Nihon shoki* had invented Susanoo's negative traits.

In the previous chapter, it has been suggested that Susanoo might have been incorporated into the imperial myth-history at a relatively late date. Both Susanoo's peculiar position in the episode of the sun and moon deities' birth and his overlap with Tsukuyomi lend plausibility to such a hypothesis. Since the depiction of sun and moon deities as rivals is a widespread mythical motif,[13] it is tempting to conclude that in the imperial mythology Susanoo took over Tsukuyomi's role as Amaterasu's rival. There are good reasons to view Susanoo as a figure "that was created for the purposes of an imperial chronicle and that borrows its features from a number of existing deities" (Scheid 2016: 97).

Yet it should be kept in mind that it is highly doubtful whether systematized mythologies of, say, Izumo or Yamato existed before the creation of the court chronicles in the late seventh and early eighth centuries. Recent scholarship suggests that Amaterasu herself was not part of a monolithic block of "Yamato myths" but rather a local deity of Ise that was adopted as imperial ancestress only shortly before the compilation of the imperial court's myth-histories (Mizoguchi 2009: 77–9).[14] The mythmakers could probably draw on a "diverse archive of mythic variants" (Stockdale 2013: 250), comprising earlier versions of court mythology and the mythical traditions of various kinship groups, rather than on systematized mythologies of Yamato, Tsukushi, or Izumo. As the differences between individual myths in *Kojiki* and *Nihon shoki* (and even between the latter's main text and its variants) demonstrate, the tales were at times rewritten beyond recognition in order to integrate them into the overarching plot. All of these factors make it all but impossible to reconstruct proto-forms of the myths contained in the early court chronicles.

Nonetheless, it is possible to draw meaningful conclusions about the mythmakers' political aims from a careful reading of the court chronicles. This chapter has shown that in the court myths, Susanoo plays the role of a liminal figure that adds disorder to the order symbolized by Amaterasu. Through his wanderings in peripheral realms, he complements and highlights his sister's role as unmovable center of authority. Thus, he fulfills an important function in the cultural memory of early Japan; he serves not only as a foil to set off the imperial ancestress, as we have seen in the preceding chapter, but also incorporates regional elites, symbolized by the Earthly Deities, into an "imagined community" (Anderson 1991) centered on the imperial court and its representative, the sun goddess.

Liminal Subjects of the Japanese Empire

This chapter has shown that in the mythical plot of the ancient court chronicles, Susanoo reaffirms and strengthens Amaterasu's authority by showing that there is no alternative to her rigid order. Without the benevolent rule of the sun goddess, the world is reduced to chaos. Aldous Huxley's expression "tolerated margin of mess" vividly describes this process, whereby the center is made to shine even more brightly by being juxtaposed with a deficient margin.

In geographical terms, Izumo fulfills the role of a "tolerated margin of mess" in the court chronicles of the early eighth century, whereas Korea occupied a similar position in modern colonial discourse. Both regions were viewed as peripheral and possibly subversive sites that had to be brought under the control of the central authority. At the same time, their deficiencies served to highlight the superiority of the imperial heartland. For the author-compilers of the court chronicles, Susanoo proved a powerful personification of the margin of empire. As suggested above, it is politically expedient for ruling elites to incorporate the paramount deity of a peripheral region or a vanquished state into the official mythology in a way that allows its members to identify with the central state, but at the same time leaves no doubt about their subordinate position.

In the first half of the twentieth century, apologists for Japanese colonialism faced a similar task with regard to the inhabitants of colonized Korea. Considering the central role of the ancient myths in the construction of a modern Japanese national identity, it is perhaps not surprising that the theorists of common ancestry followed a strategy similar to that of the author-compilers of the eighth-century myth-histories.[15] They discovered Tan'gun as an important identity symbol of the Korean population and endeavored to incorporate him into the Japanese pantheon, thus placing Korea in the same peripheral position at the margin of the Japanese empire that Izumo occupies in the court chronicles. By then, the ancient court chronicles were considered sacred scriptures of the Japanese nation, so it was no longer an option to rewrite them or choose other, more easily utilizable texts for the construction of a cultural memory that included the new colony. As soon as it is put into writing, the flexibility of myth to adapt to new situations is transferred to its exegesis (van Baaren 1984: 223–4). Thus, it became the task of Japanese historians, mythologists, and linguists to "demonstrate" in a scientifically acceptable way that Tan'gun was nothing but an alternate name for Susanoo. The—often complex—argumentations devised by scholars to "prove" the two divinities' identity will be treated in detail in the second part of this study.

This chapter has argued that Susanoo's liminality shows in the fact that he neither belongs to the Heavenly nor to the Earthly Deities (or arguably to both at the same time). As demonstrated by awkward terms like "peninsular persons" (*hantōjin*), coined in the colonial period to distinguish Koreans from "mainland Japanese" (*naichijin*) without granting them cultural autonomy as "Koreans," the Korean populace occupied a similarly ambivalent position within the Japanese empire. Colonized Koreans can therefore be regarded as "liminal subjects" of imperial Japan.

The term liminality has in recent years become popular in postcolonial studies. With regard to the Japanese empire, it has been used to describe the ambivalent positions of Japanese settlers in Korea (Uchida 2011: 25), an Atayal translator and cultural mediator married to a Japanese (Ziomek 2015: 124–5), or Okinawan migrants in Taiwan (Matsuda 2019). The second example is probably most typical for the postcolonial usage of the term, namely as a description of the hybrid identities of individuals who due to special circumstances such as mixed parentage or intercultural marriage find themselves in an in-between space, being neither colonized nor colonizer or colonized as well as colonizer, depending on the perspective one chooses. As reflected in the other two examples, however, liminality can also affect larger social groups or even whole societies (Thomassen 2014: 89).

Liminality refers to an in-between position, either spatially or temporally (Thomassen 2015: 40). While the temporal aspect has already been explained with regard to the tripartite structure of ritual passages, it is important not to confuse spatial liminality with the related concepts of marginality or peripherality. While the latter two terms apply to regions far removed from cultural or political centers, spatial liminality refers to peripheral zones situated between two or more centers (Szakolczai 2015: 23–4; Thomassen 2014: 7–8, 91–2). Korea arguably was in a state of spatial liminality from the late 1870s to 1905, when the regional powers China, Japan, and Russia vied for influence on the peninsula. However, this state of affairs came to an end with Japan's victory in the Russo-Japanese War and Korea's subsequent transformation into a Japanese protectorate in 1905 and into a colony in 1910 (Zöllner 2007: 183–7, 193, 195–7). Thus, Korea was turned from a liminal zone situated between China, Russia, and Japan into a peripheral region of the Japanese empire.

On the other hand, the assimilation policy pursued by the colonial government in Korea placed the Korean population in a perpetual state of (temporal) liminality that was to last throughout the colonial period. While the liminal period in rites of passage is typically limited to a short period of time, under certain circumstances liminality can become "institutionalized" (Thomassen 2014: 82–3). "The institutions constituting a society," Bjørn Thomassen (2015: 54) explains this phenomenon, "were created to deal with an extraordinary situation only to later become permanent." In this manner, whole societies can become "stuck in liminality." This development is encouraged by two crucial points that differentiate liminality in large-scale settings from liminality in ritual passages: "(1) the future is inherently unknown (as opposed to the initiand whose personal liminality is still framed by the continued existence of his home society, awaiting his re-integration); and (2) there are no real masters of ceremony, since nobody has gone through the liminal period before" (Thomassen 2014: 210). A similar process of "permanentization" of liminality can be observed in colonized Korea, owing to the contradictoriness of Japanese policies on the peninsula that combined the rhetoric of assimilation with the practice of discrimination and failed to clarify Koreans' position within the Japanese empire.

As Oguma (1998: 653–4) points out, this divergence between inclusive rhetoric and discriminatory practice was

> glossed over and the ambiguous position of the subjects who were Japanese but were not Japanese was legitimated by raising catchphrases like "gradual progress" or "common ancestry." These catchphrases were intended to resolve the contradiction between the present status and the propagated equality by moving the latter up or down the timeline. In other words, difference and discrimination might exist at the present time, but in the distant future ("gradual progress") or in the distant past ("common ancestry") equality would be or had been achieved.

If one took the theory of common ancestry seriously, Koreans had to be regarded as ethnically identical to their Japanese compatriots. All it would take for them to become truly Japanese "again" was to shed their cultural identity "as Koreans." This is exactly what the Government-General's assimilation policy tried to achieve. Koreans were expected to stop wearing traditional white clothes, stop conducting ceremonies in their traditional form at weddings or funerals, and even stop speaking Korean (Chou 1996: 52–5; Uchida 2011: 333–6). Civil organizations like the Chōsen Kenkyūkai assisted the colonial government's efforts by "proving" in numerous publications that there was nothing worth remembering about Korean history. The myth of Tan'gun was discarded as a fabrication without historical base, and millennia of Korean history were reduced to "a monotonous tale of foreign subjugation, political corruption, and moral decay" (Uchida 2011: 205–6, 198). The goal of this devaluation of Korean history, as Jun Uchida (2011: 202) rightly points out, "was nothing less than engineering collective amnesia." The significance of foundational myths and cultural memory for the preservation of collective identity has been emphasized repeatedly in the course of this study. The erasure of a people's history, in the long run, amounts to the elimination of its cultural identity. Viewed from van Gennep's tripartite structure, the "engineering of collective amnesia" on the Korean peninsula can be interpreted as a means of separating the colonial subjects from their former cultural identity "as Koreans," plunging the whole Korean populace into cultural liminality.

But were there also steps toward a reaggregation "as Japanese"? Indeed, there were. Despite Japanese settlers' protests, Koreans gained more and more rights, especially after the outbreak of the Second Sino-Japanese War, raising their status closer to that of mainland Japanese—and above that of subjects in Japan's other colonies. As Uchida (2011: 378, 382–9, 392–3) convincingly shows in her study on settler colonialism in Korea, Japanese settlers, constantly concerned about their privileged position within the colony, tended to oppose far-reaching assimilation policies, especially the extension of citizenship rights to Koreans. Governor-General Minami Jirō 南次郎 (1874–1955) to a certain extent accommodated their fears by demanding that Koreans "first thoroughly master the essence of being loyal imperial subjects" before "selfishly demanding rights" (ibid.: 387). Nonetheless, Koreans were step by step incorporated as citizens of Japan. They were allowed (or rather forced) to adopt Japanese names (1940), to serve in the Japanese army (on a voluntary basis from 1938, general conscription on the peninsula started in 1944), and there were even plans to grant limited suffrage to Koreans (to go into effect in 1946) (Chou 1996: 62–3; Uchida 2011: 378, 384). These concessions were made at a time when the Japanese government was in desperate need to win Koreans' loyalty and support as the war took a turn for the worse (Oguma 1998: 435). It was during this period that the various aspects of assimilation that had emerged in the first decade of colonial rule—nationalization (*kokuminka* 国民化), Japanization (*Nihonjinka* 日本人化), and imperialization (*kōminka* 皇民化)—were combined into one integrated program under the catchphrase of "Japan and Korea as one body" (Uchida 2011: 360)—a veritable reaggregation of former Koreans as Japanese citizens.

But for colonized Koreans, considerable obstacles remained on the way to become metropolitan citizens. The most important of these was the family registration (*koseki* 戸籍) system that made it possible to distinguish Koreans from Japanese even if they adopted a Japanese name and migrated to Japan. The Japanese family registration system dates from the early Meiji period. It lists all members of a household, their current address, and the location of the register (*honseki*), that is, the regional authority with jurisdiction over the registered family. It is common to transfer the *honseki* to the person's current address when he or she establishes a new family (as in the case of marriage). If the same system had been enforced in Korea, colonial subjects could have simply become mainland Japanese by moving to Japan and transferring their *honseki*. To prevent this from happening, a separate system of family registration was implemented in Korea (and Taiwan). The two systems were never unified, which meant that Koreans—although they possessed Japanese nationality (*kokuseki* 国籍)—were not allowed to transfer their *honseki* to Japan, except in cases of marriage with a Japanese or adoption into a Japanese family. In other words, even if a Korean adopted a Japanese name, became fluent in Japanese, assimilated completely into Japanese culture, and migrated to Japan, his or her Korean origin was still recognizable for the authorities (Oguma 1998: 159–61). The family system alone, therefore, sufficed to render "reintegration as a Japanese" impossible and thus to keep Korean subjects trapped in perpetual liminality. Tessa Morris-Suzuki (1998: 161) provides a convincing explanation of the reasons that led to the establishment of this contradictory system that combined assimilation with discrimination: "The ruling state's urge to exalt and spread the values of its own civilization contended with its desire to maintain the differences that justified unequal access to power." Or, in the words of Albert Memmi (1965: 127), "assimilation and colonization are contradictory."

In the Korean case, the colonized's situation was even more confusing, since the full political integration of Korea into the metropole (mainland Japan) was not the only possible political outcome that was discussed. The idea of Korean self-rule had prominent supporters both in the colony and in the metropole (Uchida 2011: 281–97). Uchida emphasizes the significance of historical consciousness in the arguments brought forth both by advocates of assimilation and of autonomy:

> Advocates of Korean self-rule generally emphasized Korea's distinct history, language, and customs, often contrasting the success of the British system of self-rule with the failure of the French assimilation policy in their colonies. Conversely, their critics stressed the long centuries of contact between Japan and Korea, often evoking the theory of *dōgen dōshu* (same origin, same race). (Ibid.: 284)

For Koreans, their undecided political future within (or outside) the Japanese empire must have further deepened their anguish. Not only were they "stuck in liminality," but there was no way of knowing whether they would emerge from this in-between state as fully integrated metropolitan citizens or autonomous modernized Koreans—or whether they would remain in a cultural limbo indefinitely. While many postcolonial studies emphasize the empowering aspect of liminality for colonial subjects who manage to utilize ambivalent spaces to their advantage,[16] I would like to stress the confusion and insecurity accompanying this state (or rather nonstate); for Koreans living during the colonial period, it was virtually impossible to maintain a meaningful cultural identity—and thus a sense of belonging and direction—within the Japanese empire. As pointed out by Thomassen (2014: 216), "Human life ceases to be meaningful in perpetual liminality."

This chapter has focused on Susanoo's liminal character in the court mythology. Considering the centrality of historical consciousness and cultural memory in colonial discourse on Korea's appropriate position within the Japanese empire, it is understandable how he could become such a powerful model for Koreans' actual or envisioned relation to the metropole. Most importantly, Susanoo could be used to seemingly reconcile the contradictory attitude Japanese thinkers and politicians directed toward their peninsular compatriots, namely their conviction that Koreans shared the same ancestors and to a large extent the same cultural traditions with mainland Japanese, but at the same time were uncivilized brutes in need of Japanese political and cultural guidance. Susanoo's liminal position in the mythological cosmoses of *Kojiki* and *Nihon shoki* mirrors that of Koreans in the Japanese empire. Like the colonized were held in an ambiguous position in-between "Japanese" and "Korean" without being allowed to identify completely as one or the other, Susanoo is caught between the Heavenly Gods and the Earthly Gods without wholly belonging to either group.

As we have seen, in the court mythology of ancient Japan Susanoo fulfills a complementary function with regard to Amaterasu. While Amaterasu represents the stability and integrative force of the center, Susanoo's character is more dynamic, oriented toward the borders of the realm; hence it is not surprising that he came to play an important role in the legitimation of Japan's modern imperialistic expansionism. Moreover, Susanoo's boisterous and immature character serves to accentuate Amaterasu's flawless rule. In the colonial context, Korea, while being regarded as a sibling country, was often used in a similar manner as a foil to set off the allegedly enlightened, progressive, ordered, and wealthy Japan. Descriptions of Koreans as unhygienic, lazy, poor, and undisciplined contributed to the construction of Korea as a "tolerated margin of mess" of the Japanese empire, which made the metropole shine in an even brighter light.

Owing to his structural equivalence to the ideological function of Korea for the Japanese empire, Susanoo lent himself as a personification of the peninsular compatriots. The efficacy of this personification was probably strengthened by the fact that it accorded rather well with previous interpretations of Susanoo, as we will see in the second part of this study. Thus, his association with the colonized Koreans—most clearly expressed in the equation of Susanoo with Tan'gun and the description of Japan and Korea as sibling nations—did not convey the impression of being politically motivated (which, it goes without saying, it was). Rather it seemed to provide a "historical precedent" for the colonial situation. This answers the first question raised at the outset of this study, namely: "*Why* did Susanoo play such a central role in colonial discourse?" The answer, put briefly, is: he filled a political need to justify the status quo by providing a (mythico-) historical precedent.

If it is almost impossible to "invent traditions" from scratch, as argued in the introduction, this raises a second question, namely: "*How* was Susanoo associated with Korea?" Or, to put it differently, "What discursive antecedents could colonial-period scholars, politicians, and opinion makers draw on to bolster their argument of common ancestry?" The second part of this study will try to answer this question through a genealogical analysis of Susanoo's reception—his manifold transformations and reinterpretations—from the ancient through the colonial periods.

Part Two

Political Mythology: A Genealogy of Susanoo's Connection to Korea

4

"I Do Not Want to Stay in This Land": Susanoo's Sojourn to Korea in the Ancient Court Chronicles

At this time, Susanoo no Mikoto, accompanied by his son Itakeru no Kami, descended to the land of Silla and lived at the place Soshimori. Then he raised his voice and said: "I do not want to stay in this land."
—*Nihon shoki*, fasc. I [8, var. 4]

The first part of this study has shed light on the ideological need Susanoo filled in the construction of a collective identity that incorporated Korea into the Japanese family state. It discussed Susanoo's function in the ancient court chronicles as a foil to set off the imperial ancestress Amaterasu and demonstrated his liminal character as a solitary wanderer and taboo breaker. It was this liminality, the third chapter concluded, that predestined Susanoo to serve as a symbol for Korean subjects' liminal position within the Japanese empire.

The whole argument rested on the premise—raised in the introduction—that myths constitute an important component of a group's cultural memory and thus fulfill a critical function in the construction and maintenance of collective identity. Myths can provide the status quo with a legitimating foundation by arguing that "it has always been like this" or "in the good old days it was like this." In other words, they provide a society's present values, ideas, and behavioral norms with an aura of sacred antiquity by shaping a sense of historical continuity (cf. Hein-Kircher 2007: 30).

This implies two things: first, in order to remain relevant, myths have to be adapted to the present circumstances. If there are authoritative texts—like the *Kojiki* and the *Nihon shoki* in Japan (or, for that matter, the Bible in Christian cultures)—this adaptation takes the form of reinterpretation. Second, myths have to be familiar to, and recognized as authentic by, the receiving society. If no one had ever heard of Amaterasu and there had been no written records that proved her antiquity and her connection to the imperial household, she would hardly have sufficed to legitimate the Meiji loyalists' overthrow of the Tokugawa bakufu. This means not only that it would be an utterly useless undertaking to write new myths from scratch (who would believe them?). It also suggests that while myths have to be reinterpreted to connect them with a group's present situation, the need to achieve a sense of historical continuity places substantial constraints on the freedom of such reinterpretations.

The three chapters that form the second part of this study thus attempt to answer the question "How did Susanoo end up in his elevated position in the colonial discourse on common ancestry?" The chapters employ a genealogical approach to trace the roots and development of Susanoo's association with the Korean peninsula in the ancient, medieval, (early modern), and modern periods, respectively. The second part thus attempts to unearth the "discursive antecedents" on which participants in colonial discourse built their arguments. By placing these discursive antecedents in the historical context of their emergence, this genealogy of Susanoo's association with Korea will yield new insights into the workings of cultural memory and add historical depth to the description of collective identity construction in imperial Japan provided in the first part.

Martin Saar (2007: 9) characterizes the genealogical approach as a specific form of critique that "directs the knowledge of an object's historical genesis (*Gewordenheit*) against it in order to compromise and delegitimate the object by clarifying its origin." In this sense, the following genealogy is intended as an implicit critique of colonial-period scholars' and opinion makers' interpretations of Susanoo's connection to Korea. The succeeding chapters will show that colonial-period thinkers did not fabricate politically inspired interpretations of the ancient myths from scratch, but at the same time it will emphasize that the discursive antecedents on which they based their interpretations (including the genesis of the oldest written sources) were themselves more often than not motivated by political aims and deeply implicated in the power politics of their times. I will call this process of politically motivated creation, reinterpretation, and reconfiguration of myths "political mythology."

The present chapter focuses on the ancient period. It will introduce passages from the ancient chronicles *Kojiki*, *Nihon shoki*, and *Sendai kuji hongi* that more or less explicitly link Susanoo to the Korean peninsula. The chapter pays special attention to the toponyms "Soshimori" and "Kumanari," mentioned in *Nihon shoki* and *Sendai kuji hongi*, that were to play a central role in later attempts to link Susanoo with the Korean peninsula. A further topic that will be discussed at some length is Susanoo's connection to Ne no (Katasu) Kuni, one of the mythical afterworlds. As will become clear in subsequent chapters, Susanoo's link to this polluted realm of death was to color later interpretations of Susanoo and the regions associated with him (including Korea).

Susanoo's Connection to Korea in the Ancient Sources

The oldest textual evidence that links Susanoo to Korea can be found in the *Kojiki*, the *Nihon shoki*, and the *Sendai kuji hongi*. As this section will show, the latter two sources are much more fruitful in this respect. This is not surprising since the *Kojiki* generally pays little attention to events outside Japan, whereas the *Nihon shoki* contains detailed accounts of diplomatic relations with the Korean kingdoms and the *Sendai kuji hongi* places special emphasis on myths and legends connected to the Korean peninsula. Although the *Kojiki* was regarded as the most authentic source on Japan's pre-sinicized past by early modern and modern scholars of National Learning, the latter two chronicles were held in much higher esteem in premodern Japan, and the *Nihon shoki* continued to play a much more important role than the *Kojiki* in linking Susanoo with Korea through the modern period.

Kojiki

The *Kojiki* contains only indirect evidence for a possible connection of Susanoo to the Korean peninsula. We are told that Susanoo fathered the deity Ōtoshi 大年 by Kamu-ōichi Hime 神大市比賣, a daughter of the mountain god Ōyamatsumi 大山津見 (KJK I: 72/73). Ōtoshi, in turn, fathered three children whose names suggest a connection to the Korean peninsula, namely Kara no Kami 韓神, Sohori no Kami 曾富理神, and Shirahi no Kami 白日神 (KJK I: 96/97). The first deity's name literally means "god of Kara" or "Korean deity." This name does not reappear in the ancient myths. Kara no Kami has, however, been linked to the *Nihon shoki*'s Itakeru, who will be introduced below (Chamberlain [1882] 1982: 108). "Sohori" is thought to be a Japanese rendering of *sŏbŏl* 徐伐 or *sŏrabŏl* 徐羅伐, the Silla word for "capital" (Kanazawa 1994: 43; Mishina 1972: 260–1).[1] Like in the case of Kara no Kami, there are no narratives associated with this deity in the ancient sources. Sohori no Kami might be connected to (or even identical with) Sono Kami 園神, a deity who, according to the *Engi shiki*, was worshiped inside the Imperial Household Ministry (*kunaishō* 宮内省) alongside Kara no Kami (EGSK IX, vol. 1: 508/509; cf. Yi 2003: 52–5). The last deity's name, Shirahi no Kami, suggests a connection to Silla. While this kingdom is usually rendered as "Shiragi" in Japanese, Dewa Hiroaki (2004) in a recent study lists a number of shrines with connections to Silla throughout Japan that are called by names such as Shiraki, Shirai, Shiraishi, Shirahige, or Shirakuni Shrine.[2] Considering his or her two siblings' obvious connection to Korea, it seems not too far-fetched to propose a similar connection for Shirahi no Kami as well. Even so, the names of these three grandchildren are the only evidence linking Susanoo to the Korean peninsula in the *Kojiki*. As will become apparent in the succeeding chapters, for this reason the *Kojiki* did not play a prominent role in endeavors to connect Susanoo with Korea.

Nihon shoki

The *Nihon shoki* is a much more fruitful source in this regard. Its numerous variants to particular myths provide important information that is not found in the *Kojiki*. In addition to the main text, the *Nihon shoki* records five variants dealing with Susanoo's fate after his banishment from the Plain of High Heaven (NSK I [8], vol. 1: 90–102). These variants provide four different names for the sword Susanoo employed to slay the eight-headed serpent (see Table 4.1).

The appellation Totsuka no Tsurugi 十握剣, which is used in the *Nihon shoki*'s main text as well as in the *Kojiki*, means "ten-span sword" and was commonly used to refer to long swords. It can also be found in the episode of the *ukei* performed by Susanoo and Amaterasu, where it was chewed and transformed into divine children (see Chapter 2). The name provided in the fourth variant (Ama no Haha-kiri no Tsurugi 天蠅斫之剣) is explained in the *Kogo shūi*: "in the ancient language, great serpents were called *haha* 羽々. The name [Ama no Haha-kiri] refers to the slaying of the serpent" (KS: 195).

More interesting for the purposes of the present study are the remaining two names. There are different interpretations for the name Orochi no Ara-masa

Table 4.1 Different Names for the Sword Susanoo Used to Slay the Eight-Headed Serpent in the *Nihon shoki*

Main text	Var. 2	Var. 3	Var. 4
Totsuka no Tsurugi	Orochi no Ara-masa	Orochi no Kara-sai no Tsurugi	Ama no Haha-kiri no Tsurugi

蛇之麁正, mentioned in variant two: while *orochi* means "serpent" and *masa* "splendid," *ara* might mean either "rough" or "shining" (Florenz 1901: 131). But the sword's name has also been linked to Ara Kaya 阿那加耶,[3] one of the five Kaya states in the south-eastern part of the Korean peninsula (Bentley 2006: 179; Yoshino 1972: 322). Both archaeological evidence and Chinese sources suggest that the Kaya Federation was an important center of metal production with close ties to the Japanese islands as early as the Yayoi period. Hence it would not be surprising if a powerful sword was associated with this region in the Japanese court chronicle.

This hypothesis becomes even more plausible when the fourth name that is attributed to the sword is taken into consideration: Orochi no Kara-sai no Tsurugi 蛇韓鋤之劍 means nothing else than "Serpent blade of Korea" (cf. Aston [1896] 1956, vol. 1: 57, n. 1). The word *sai*, translated here as "blade," appears in Old Japanese texts in the meaning of "hoe" or "plough," or, as in this case, in proper names of swords. The Old Japanese word has been linked to the Middle Korean .*salp* "spade" (Naumann and Miller 1995: 411; Robbeets 2005: 194). Considering a later passage in the *Nihon shoki* (NSK XXII [Suiko 20/1/7], vol. 2: 566/567), which mentions "a supreme blade from Wu 呉"[4] (Kure *no masai*), one is surely justified to translate Kara-sai no Tsurugi as "a blade from Korea" (Naumann and Miller 1995: 411). These names suggest a connection of the serpent-slaying myth and its protagonist, Susanoo, to metalworkers of Korean origin (cf. Weiss 2018b).

The last two variants mentioning Susanoo in the *Nihon shoki* provide more direct evidence of the deity's connection to Korea. These variants were to play a central role in virtually all later attempts to associate Susanoo with the Korean peninsula. For this reason, a full translation is provided below:

> [Var. 4:] In one writing it is said: Susanoo no Mikoto's behavior was unseemly. Therefore, all the gods imposed a fine of a thousand tables [of offerings] on him and in the end banished him. At this time, Susanoo no Mikoto, accompanied by his son Itakeru no Kami 五十猛神, descended to the land of Silla and lived at the place Soshimori 曾尸茂梨. Then he raised his voice and said: "I do not want to stay in this land." Finally, he took clay and built a boat with it, boarded it and crossed over to the east until he reached the mountain peak Torikami, which is located at the headwaters of the Hi River in the land of Izumo. Now there was in this place a great serpent that devoured men. Thereupon, Susanoo no Mikoto took his sword Heavenly Serpent Cutter (Ama no Haha-kiri no Tsurugi) and slew this great serpent. Now, when he cut the serpent's tail, the blade [of his sword] became notched. Thereupon, when he split it open and inspected it,

there was a divine sword inside the tail. Susanoo no Mikoto said: "I must not take this and use it for myself." Thereupon, he sent his descendant in the fifth generation Ama no Fukine no Kami 天之葺根神 to offer it up to Heaven. This is the sword now called Kusanagi.[5]

First, when Itakeru no Kami descended from Heaven, he took down with him many seeds of trees. However, he did not plant them in the land of Kara [Korea], but took them all back with him and finally, beginning from Tsukushi, planted them all in the Land of the Great Eight Islands and there was no place he did not turn into green mountains. For this reason, Itakeru no Mikoto is called the meritorious god. He is the great deity who resides in Kii Province.

[Var. 5:] In one writing it is said: Susanoo no Mikoto said: "In the region [literally: island] of the land of Kara (*Kara-kuni no shima* 韓郷之嶋) there is gold and silver. It would not be good if there were no floating treasures (*ukutakara* 浮宝) [i.e., ships] in the land ruled by my son." Thereupon, he plucked out the hair of his beard and, when he strewed it about, it then turned into cedars. Furthermore, he plucked out the hair of his breast and, when he strewed it about, it turned into cypresses. The hair of his bottom turned into pines. The hair of his eyebrows turned into camphor trees. After this had come to pass, he determined how they should be used. Thereupon he said: "These two trees, namely the cedar and the camphor tree, are to be made into floating treasures; the cypress is to be made into timber for beautiful palaces; the pine is to be turned into tools [coffins?] in which the visible green human grass (*utsushiki ao hito kusa* 顕見蒼生) [i.e., humans][6] shall be laid in remote burial-places (*okitsu sutae* 奥津棄戸).[7] The eighty kinds of trees which are to be eaten, I have all planted and made to grow well."

Now Susanoo no Mikoto's son was called Itakeru no Mikoto; his [Itakeru's] younger sisters [were called] Ōyatsu Hime no Mikoto 大屋津姫命 and, next, Tsumatsu Hime no Mikoto 抓津姫命. These three deities also scattered the seeds of trees well. Thereupon they proceeded to the land of Kii.

Thereafter, Susanoo no Mikoto dwelt on the peak of Kumanari 熊成 and finally entered into Ne no Kuni. (NSK I [8, var. 4, 5], vol. 1: 98–102)

As pointed out in the first chapter, the *Nihon shoki* was regarded as the most authoritative historical chronicle throughout the ancient period. As such, it was studied at the so-called *Nihongi-kō* 日本紀講, "lecture-cum-poetry sessions on the *Nihon shoki*," in whose course the meaning of difficult passages or the reading of uncommon words were clarified. These lectures were conducted at the imperial court roughly every thirty years from the early ninth to the latter half of the tenth century (Teeuwen 2007: 87).[8]

The thirteenth-century *Shaku Nihongi* 釈日本紀 reports that the meaning of the term "Soshimori," mentioned in variant 4 as the site of Susanoo's sojourn in Silla, came up as a topic during the third series of lectures held from 878 to 881. At that time, a certain Koreyoshi no Sukune Takahisa 惟良宿祢高尚 (life dates unknown) suggested that the term might refer to the Silla capital.⁹ The *Shaku Nihongi* informs us that Regent (*sesshō* 摂政) Fujiwara no Mototsune 藤原基経 (836–891), arguably the most influential aristocrat of his time, laughed at this suggestion. The text implies that the assembled courtiers hardly took Takahisa's opinion seriously (SNG: 177). Yet Takahisa belonged to a lineage group of Paekche origin. It thus seems probable that he was more knowledgeable about Korean affairs than the rest of the assembled courtiers (Yamaguchi 2012: 172). More important than the question of the validity of Takahisa's hypothesis is the fact that Susanoo's connection to Korea emerged as a topic of discussion as early as the ninth century.

Sendai kuji hongi

The "discovery" of a further ancient source that associates Susanoo with the Korean peninsula also occurred in the context of the *Nihongi-kō*. In 936, the Confucian scholar Yatabe no Kinmochi 矢田部公望 (life dates unknown), who served as head lecturer of the lecture series that took place from 936 to 943, introduced the *Sendai kuji hongi* to the assembled courtiers. This text, he ascertained, had been written by none other than the fabled Shōtoku Taishi 聖徳太子 (572–621) and thus predated both the *Kojiki* and the *Nihon shoki*. The *Sendai kuji hongi* was subsequently held in high esteem since it provided answers to many of the questions raised during succeeding lectures. Up to the early modern period, the work was regarded as the oldest extant Japanese chronicle. As such, it was included in the "three fundamental scriptures" (*sanbu no honsho* 三部本書) of Yoshida Shintō together with the *Kojiki* and the *Nihon shoki* (Scheid 2001: 212, 306–7).

In the seventeenth century, the *Sendai kuji hongi*'s antiquity and Shōtoku Taishi's authorship of the work were questioned. From that time on, the view has prevailed that the work has been created at a later date "by splicing together sentences lifted from the texts of *Kojiki*, *Nihon shoki*, and *Kogo shūi*" (Bentley 2006: 28). This position was based on the *Sendai kuji hongi*'s close resemblance to the other three works, with regard to wording and contents, and on the fact that it contained references to events that occurred after the compilation of the *Nihon shoki*.[10]

Since the *Sendai kuji hongi* contains an elaborate version of the Mononobe 物部 lineage group's mythical origins, which cannot be found in any other source, it is generally believed to have been written by a member of this lineage group, probably during the ninth century (Teeuwen 2007: 89).[11] This theory is supported by the fact that Kinmochi himself was descended from the Mononobe (Kwŏn 2013: 183–9). Since the early Heian period witnessed a veritable "Shōtoku Taishi boom" among Confucian scholars, it was possibly a strategic choice to attribute the work to this paragon of scholarship to endow it with unassailable authority (Saitō 2006: 74).

What makes the *Sendai kuji hongi* relevant to the present study is that its version of the Susanoo myth contains all the elements that link the god to the Korean peninsula. In this way, the *Sendai kuji hongi*'s narrative, although it does not provide any information that cannot also be found in *Kojiki* and *Nihon shoki*, places special emphasis on Susanoo's connection to Korea. These "peninsular (Silla) overtones" (Bentley 2006: 79), which are not limited to the myth of Susanoo but characterize the work as a whole, are further indicators that point to Mononobe involvement in the compilation of the *Sendai kuji hongi*, since the Mononobe seem to have absorbed "a large number of kinship groups and newly formed service-group lineages with roots in the Korean peninsula" (Como 2010: 91).

Regarding Susanoo, the *Sendai kuji hongi* clearly copied from the *Kojiki* and the *Nihon shoki* (or at least used the same sources). However, it arranges this material in a fundamentally different way. As we have seen, the *Kojiki* creates a consistent plot by choosing one mythical account and excluding all material that might contradict it, whereas the *Nihon shoki* includes several variants of particular tales without trying to force them into a consistent story line but differentiates these variants from the more or less consistent plot provided in the main text. The *Sendai kuji hongi*, on the other hand, tries—more or less successfully—to construct a hybrid version that weaves all the available material into one narrative without discriminating between passages from *Kojiki*, *Kogo shūi*, and *Nihon shoki*. Neither does it make a distinction between the latter work's main text and variants. The goal of this strategy was possibly to create an all-encompassing unified mythology out of the various traditions (Kōnoshi 1999: 185–6; Kwŏn 2013: 143–6, 185–91). The result is an often awkward and inelegant text, fraught with contradictions.

The myth of Susanoo as related in the fourth fascicle of the *Sendai kuji hongi* can be summarized thus:

> Susanoo and Amaterasu perform an *ukei* and three female deities are born. Susanoo's behavior is unseemly. Therefore, he is fined and banished from the

Plain of High Heaven. Accompanied by his son Itakeru, Susanoo descends to the place Soshimori in Silla. He builds a boat out of clay and crosses the ocean until he comes to the headwaters of the Hi River in Izumo *and* to the headwaters of the E River in Agi.

He meets Ashinazuchi, Tenazuchi, and their daughter Kushiinada Hime, who inform him about the great eight-headed serpent from Koshi, which has devoured Kushiinada Hime's sisters. Susanoo tricks the monster into drinking strong *sake* and chops it into eight pieces in its drunken stupor. From these pieces emerge eight thunder deities who ascend to heaven. In the serpent's tail, Susanoo discovers the sword "Gathering Clouds of Heaven," which is later called Kusanagi, and offers it up to heaven. The sword Susanoo employs to slay the serpent is called Totsuka no Tsurugi and is now stored in Kibi 吉備. According to another version, the sword is called Orochi no Ara-masa and is now kept in the Isonokami Jingū 石上神宮 (a shrine closely associated with the Mononobe). Susanoo thereupon builds a palace in Izumo and consummates his marriage with Kushiinada Hime, who gives birth to Ōkuninushi. Susanoo takes another wife and fathers children on her.

Susanoo observes that there is gold and silver in Korea. ... (The text that follows is basically identical to the *Nihon shoki*'s variant 5.) Susanoo dwells on the peak of Kumanari and finally enters Ne no Kuni. Itakeru brings seeds of the eighty trees from Heaven. He does not plant them in Korea but on the Great Eight Islands. Today he is venerated in Kii. One version says that his sisters assisted him in the task and are worshiped together with him in Kii. (SKH IV: 61–4)[12]

While in the *Nihon shoki* the variants that link Susanoo with the Korean peninsula are rather marginal insofar as they are not or only poorly connected to the overall plot, the *Sendai kuji hongi* incorporates Susanoo's sojourn in Silla and his curious remark about gold and silver to be found on the peninsula into the overall plot of Susanoo's deeds after his banishment from his sister's realm. Considering the work's prominence as allegedly oldest extant Japanese chronicle, Susanoo's connection to Korea must thus have been known to most aristocrats during the ancient period (people other than aristocrats probably had neither opportunity nor leisure and skill to read the court chronicles).

Susanoo and the Realms of the Dead

Apart from the toponym Soshimori, the peak of Kumanari, to which Susanoo, according to *Sendai kuji hongi* and variant 5 of the *Nihon shoki*, retreated before entering Ne no Kuni, came to play an important role in later discourses on Susanoo's connection to Korea. The reasons for this development will be discussed in the last portion of this chapter. Before moving to this question, Susanoo's connection to the otherworldly Ne no (Katasu) Kuni in the ancient sources merits our attention. As will become apparent in the following chapters, this association with a polluted realm of death was to color later interpretations of Susanoo and his connection to Korea.

The *Kojiki* places special emphasis on Susanoo's connection to the afterworld: here Susanoo not only utters his desire to go to the land of his deceased mother, Ne no Katasukuni,[13] but later even becomes the ruler of this realm. The strangeness of the former passage has often been remarked upon: in the *Kojiki*, Susanoo is born during Izanaki's ritual cleansing. Therefore, he has no mother. Even if we follow Lévi-Strauss's suggestion and regard Susanoo as a "posthumous child" of Izanami,[14] this does not sufficiently explain Susanoo's desire to go to Ne no Katasukuni. After all, Izanami resides not in Ne no Katasukuni but in Yomotsu Kuni after her demise. Another peculiarity of the *Kojiki*'s account is that it does not mention how Susanoo ended up in Ne no Katasukuni.

In the *Nihon shoki*, Susanoo is sent by his parents to Ne no Kuni shortly after his birth, owing to his destructive character (NSK I [5, main text; var. 1; var. 2], vol. 1: 36–9). In the main text, the account of Susanoo's fight with the eight-headed serpent and his subsequent marriage with Kushiinada Hime concludes with the succinct statement: "Finally, Susanoo no Mikoto at length proceeded to Ne no Kuni" (NSK I [8, main text], vol. 1: 94). The last variant dedicated to Susanoo (the one which relates how he turned his hair into trees) provides somewhat more information on Susanoo's retreat to Ne no Kuni; it informs us: "Thereafter, Susanoo no Mikoto dwelt on the peak of Kumanari and finally entered into Ne no Kuni." The same sentence concludes the account of Susanoo's deeds in the *Sendai kuji hongi*.

That the narrative of a major deity's actions is brought to a close by naming a specific location—often an important center of the respective deity's cult—from where he or she is said to have entered one of the various otherworlds, is a common pattern in the mythical portions of *Kojiki* and *Nihon shoki*. Examples include Izanaki, who "his divine task having been accomplished, ... built himself a hidden palace on the island of Awaji 淡路, where he dwelt eternally in silence and concealment" (NSK I [6, main text], vol. 1: 60–2); his spouse Izanami, who was "buried at the village of Arima 有馬 in Kumano 熊野, in Kii Province" after she had died while giving birth to the fire god (NSK I [5, var. 5], vol. 1: 40–2);[15] and the diminutive god Sukunabikona 少彦名, who together with Ōkuninushi created the realm under heaven, "thereafter ... went to the cape of Kumano, and eventually proceeded to Tokoyo no Kuni 常世郷" (NSK I [8, var. 6], vol. 1: 102/103).

Since these accounts often identify a concrete geographic site as the entrance to an otherworld and considering the *Kojiki* and *Nihon shoki*'s interweaving of myth and history, it is not surprising that many scholars have attempted to pinpoint the entrances to the various otherworlds on the map. As we will see in subsequent chapters, the same is true for the "peak of Kumanari," which was variously identified with sites in Kii, Izumo, and on the Korean peninsula. These identifications were by no means unpolitical in nature, since they could serve as an ideological basis for the marginalization (or, more rarely, for the valorization) of the respective region associated with the realm of the dead.[16] Before turning to these questions, however, it is worthwhile to have a closer look at the various otherworld conceptions mentioned in the ancient Japanese sources.

Otherworld Conceptions in Japanese Myth

At least three different otherworlds can be distinguished in the ancient Japanese sources, namely Tokoyo no Kuni, Yomotsu Kuni, and Ne no Katasukuni (*Kojiki*), or Ne no Kuni (*Nihon shoki*, *Sendai kuji hongi*). The first of these otherworlds differs quite markedly from the latter two (or three). Tokoyo no Kuni is a "country of everlasting life" (Naumann 1996: 124) located beyond the sea. It is mentioned in the myths as a site to which deities retreat after their task is finished or to which an imperial envoy is dispatched to obtain the "fragrant fruit that grows out of season" (Aston [1896] 1956, vol. 1: 186). However, its topography is not described and, in contrast to the other two otherworlds, it never serves as the setting of a particular narrative, thus remaining invisible (Wittkamp 2018: 155).

A connection between Yomotsu Kuni and Ne no (Katasu) Kuni is suggested by Susanoo's wish to visit his dead mother in Ne no (Katasu) Kuni, although Izanami in fact resides in Yomotsu Kuni after her demise. A further link between the two otherworlds is that they share a border to the Central Land of Reed Plains: Yomotsu Hirasaka. This term is usually rendered as "Flat Slope" (Antoni 2012: 29), or "Gentle Decline" (Heldt 2014: 16) of Yomi. According to another interpretation, *hira* means "cliff" and *saka* "border" (Masuda 1984: 127–9). What is certain is that Yomotsu Hirasaka marks the border between this world and the otherworld. Izanami cannot pursue her spouse, who had fled from Yomotsu Kuni, further than to this point (KJK I: 48/49; NSK I [5, var. 6, var. 10], vol. 1: 46/47, 56/57). Ōkuninushi also passes this border during his flight from Ne no Katasukuni, forcing Susanoo to abandon his chase (KJK I: 84/85).

Both the term Yomi/Yomo, which is written with characters that refer to an underworld in Chinese, and the term Ne in Ne no (Katasu) Kuni, which is written with the Chinese Character for "root," suggest a subterranean location for these two otherworlds. Apart from the fact that roots usually sprout beneath the surface of the earth, a formulation in the *Engi shiki*'s ritual prayer of the Great Purification suggests a subterranean position of the latter realm, which is here referred to as "land of roots, land of the bottom" (EGSK VIII, vol. 1: 480/481). Consequently, Yomotsu Kuni and Ne no (Katasu) Kuni were commonly believed to represent the lowest plain of a three-layered cosmos—the other two layers being the Plain of High Heaven and the Central Land of Reed Plains (Saigō 1967: 17–18).

But more recent scholarship casts doubt on the subterranean location of these otherworlds.[17] The *Kojiki*'s wording, for instance, suggests that both Yomotsu Kuni and Ne no Katasukuni were situated at the *upper* end of Yomotsu Hirasaka. Moreover, a number of passages in the *Man'yōshū* 万葉集 (Collection of Ten Thousand Leaves), the earliest Japanese anthology of poetry (c. 759), suggest that the otherworlds were believed to be located up in the mountains. This might well be related to the custom of exposing the dead in the mountains (Naumann 1971: 144). It seems likely that the conception of subterranean otherworlds—though probably already familiar from Chinese scriptures at an earlier date—only took root in Japan after the completion of the *Kojiki*.

In conclusion, it seems hardly possible to discern the positions of the respective realms of the dead in the cosmoses of *Kojiki* and *Nihon shoki* (which do not necessarily have to correspond) with any certainty. However, it is certain that they were regarded as realms situated on the cosmic periphery. In this context, an observation by Robin Hard (2004: 22) on Greek mythology is instructive. He remarks that "Homer and Hesiod can speak of a place as lying beneath the earth and at the edges of the earth as if there were no conflict between the two concepts." Hard quotes an example by Hesiod, in which the poet writes that the primordial deity Ouranos "made [some monsters] live beneath the broad-path earth, where they suffered anguish, being set to dwell underground in the furthermost distance, at the bounds of the great earth."

As in the Japanese case, the peripheral, distant position of the otherworld seems to be the decisive point. Whether this distance was conceived along a vertical or a horizontal axis seems to have been a matter of secondary importance. The otherworlds depicted in the oldest sources were thus possibly conceived as lying on the periphery of the Central Land of Reed Plains—situated beneath the Plain of High Heaven on the lower plain of a two-layered cosmos (Masuda 1984: 189). Equally possible is a three-layered cosmos in which Yomotsu Kuni (and possibly

Ne no [Katasu] Kuni) are situated beneath the Central Land of Reed Plains. In the former case, the component "central" (*naka*) in the Central Land of Reed Plains would refer to a horizontal relation of "center / periphery," in the latter to a vertical relation "above / below." Both conceptions imply a hierarchy, which was also to play a decisive role in pinpointing the realms of the dead on the map.

Kumano in Kii Province

The Kumano region in Kii is known, first of all, for the "Three Mountains of Kumano," as the three great shrines of Hongū 本宮, Hayatama 速玉, and Nachi 那智 are commonly called. These shrines not only constituted an important religious center of mountain ascetics (Toyoshima 1998), but they were also the site of the Kumano pilgrimage, which was extremely popular among court aristocrats, especially during the Insei period (1086–1192) (Shinjō 1998: 385).

However, the region is also associated with the realms of the dead in the myths of the *Kojiki* and the *Nihon shoki*. As already mentioned, the *Nihon shoki*, for instance, locates Izanami's grave "at the village of Arima in Kumano, in Kii Province." Moreover, both the *Kojiki* and the *Nihon shoki* locate the grave of Iware Biko's (Jinmu's) elder brother Itsuse 五瀬 on Mount Kamayama 竈山 in Ki (= Kii) no Kuni (KJK II [Jinmu]: 144/145; NSK III [Jinmu], vol. 1: 200/201). Itsuse's death was the result of a wound that was inflicted on him during a skirmish on Iware Biko's legendary eastward expedition. According to the *Nihon shoki*'s account, Iware Biko continued his campaign in the company of his remaining two brothers after having buried Itsuse. In the village Miwa 神 in Kumano, they set to sea, where they met with a violent storm. Indignantly, Iware Biko's two brothers exclaimed that their mother was a goddess of the sea; thereafter one brother, Inai, "plunged into the sea, where he turned into the deity Saimochi 鋤持," whereas the other, Mike-irino 三毛入野, "treading upon the waves, … went to Tokoyo no Kuni" (NSK III [Jinmu], vol. 1: 200–3).

As we have seen, the *Nihon shoki* variant that reports Susanoo's entry to Ne no Kuni via Kumanari is connected to Kii as well. We are told that before Susanoo's retreat to the peak of Kumanari, his son Itakeru and his two sisters "scattered the seeds of trees well. Thereupon they proceeded to the land of Kii." An episode from the *Kojiki* sheds further light on this passage. Here, we are told that Ōanamuji went to "the august place of the god Ōya Biko 大屋毘古 in Ki no Kuni 木国," from where he entered Ne no Katasukuni in order to escape from his murderous brothers (KJK I: 80/81). Since his name is the male form of Ōyatsu Hime, one of Itakeru's sisters in the *Nihon shoki*, Ōya Biko is commonly viewed as Ōyatsu Hime's brother and thus equated with Itakeru (MNZ 9: 442–3; Florenz 1901: 134; Matsumae 1997: 104)—a view that is corroborated by the *Sendai kuji hongi*, which gives Ōya Biko as an alternate name of Itakeru (SKH IV: 72).

These examples show that Kii is closely connected to the various realms of the dead in the myths of *Kojiki* and *Nihon shoki*. Kumano thus played a role similar to that of Susanoo in the mythical portions of *Kojiki* and *Nihon shoki*: while the latter served as a foil to set off Amaterasu, the former can be viewed as a hidden otherworld (*kakure kuni* 幽国) that provided a contrast to the manifest realm (*utsushi kuni* 顕国) of Ise, the site of Amaterasu's shrine (Gorai 1998: 234).

Izumo: Land of the Setting Sun

Izumo's connection to the realms of the dead is even more strongly emphasized in the ancient myths. The *Kojiki* explicitly states that Yomotsu Hirasaka, that is, the site where Izanaki and Ōkuniushi escaped from Yomotsu Kuni and Ne no Katasukuni, respectively, "is now called Iuyazaka 伊賦夜坂 in Izumo Province" (KJK I: 48/49); and the *Izumo fudoki* contains several toponyms that are obviously connected to the realm of the dead. Examples include Yomi no Shima 夜見嶋 (Island of Yomi), Yomi no Saka 黄泉之坂 (Slope of Yomi), and Yomi no Ana 黄泉之穴 (Cavern of Yomi) (IF: 138/139, 172, 212/213).

Contrary to the *Nihon shoki*, the *Kojiki* locates Izanami's grave "on Hiba 比婆 Mountain at the border between Izumo Province and Hōki Province [the western portion of present-day Tottori Prefecture]" (KJK I: 42/43). A fragment of the *Hōki no kuni fudoki* 伯耆国風土記, quoted in *Shaku Nihongi*, relates that the diminutive deity Sukunabikona climbed a millet-stalk on Awashima 粟嶋 (Millet Island) in Ōmi 相見 District in the region of present-day Yonago city; when he was dislodged, he proceeded to Tokoyo no Kuni (SNG VII: 178).[18] Like Izanami's grave, the island is located at the border between Izumo and Hōki and is therefore also mentioned in the *Izumo fudoki* (IF: 156/157). Owing to Hōki's vicinity to Izumo, the cape of Kumano, from where the *Kojiki* lets Sukunabikona enter Tokoyo no Kuni, is commonly associated with Izumo rather than with Kii (Sakamoto et al. 1965–7, vol. 1: 129, n. 18; Aston [1896] 1956: 60; Florenz 1901: 143).[19] This view is supported by the deity's strong connection to Izumo: in both *Kojiki* and *Nihon shoki*, Sukunabikona is said to have arrived in Izumo from beyond the sea; here he assisted Ōkuninushi, the great culture hero of Izumo, in the task of creating or solidifying the land.[20]

Izumo's special connection to the otherworld in *Kojiki* and *Nihon shoki* has not gone unnoticed in previous scholarship. Saigō Nobutsuna (1967: 31–47), for instance, emphasizes that both works were compiled at the Yamato court. In relation to Yamato, he points out, Izumo is situated to the west—in the direction of the sunset. Ise, on the other hand, lies to the east—in the direction of the sunrise. Therefore, Saigō argues, the compilers of the court chronicles depicted the axis Ise–Yamato–Izumo as a horizontal reflection of the cosmological axis Plain of High Heaven–Central Land of Reed Plains–Yomotsu Kuni. In a more recent study, Kanda Norishiro (1992: 15–25) hypothesizes that Yomotsu Kuni and Ne no Kuni originally expressed two completely different conceptions.[21] In the course of the systematization of the myths at the Yamato court, however, Ne no Kuni, which was originally a positive realm closely associated with the Izumo deities Susanoo and Ōkuninushi, was equated with the dark and polluting Yomotsu Kuni. In this way, Kanda argues, the mythmakers at the Yamato court were able to depict Izumo as a realm of death. This negative image, in turn, served to justify the subordination of Izumo at the hands of the Heavenly Deities, that is, the ancestors of the imperial family.

These interpretations do an admirable job in capturing the ideological implications of Izumo's association with the mythical otherworlds. Strangely, this association seems to have been tolerated, if not encouraged, by the local rulers of Izumo, as they included various passages linking Izumo to the land of Yomi in the *Izumo fudoki* (see above). Matsumoto Naoki (2016: 214–61) has convincingly shown that the editors of the *Fudoki* sublimely reinterpreted the official mythology of the court chronicles in their own favor. Their acceptance of Izumo's association to Yomi can thus only mean that they deemed it advantageous for Izumo. While Izumo's role as a foil to set off Yamato (or Ise) surely implied a sinister aspect, at the same time it elevated Izumo to an importance not accorded to any other province in the ancient myths. The same stance was to reappear in the Meiji period, when the head priest of Izumo Shrine emphasized Ōkuninushi's connection to the otherworld to claim his parity with Amaterasu. Izumo's function as an ideological antipode to Ise and Yamato is summarized in Table 4.2.

Table 4.2 Center and Periphery in the Imperial Mythology of Ancient Japan

Center	Periphery
Yamato/Ise	Izumo
Sunrise	Sunset
Light	Darkness
Life	Death

Kumanari and the Korean Peninsula

A third site associated with an otherworld in the ancient sources, and the most relevant for the present study, is the "peak of Kumanari." According to both *Nihon shoki* (NSK I [8, var. 5]) and *Sendai kuji hongi*, Susanoo passed this mountain on his way to Ne no Kuni. In contrast to Kumano and Izumo, this mountain does not correspond to any known site on the Japanese archipelago. However, the *Nihon shoki* mentions the name Kumanari again in the chronicle of Yūryaku 雄略 (trad. 418–479; r. 456–479). This passage suggests that Kumanari was located on the Korean peninsula. Since the toponym Kumanari was to play a central role in later discussions of Susanoo's connection to Korea, I will analyze this passage and its context in some detail before concluding this chapter.

Yūryaku's Generous Gift

The chronicle of Yūryaku in the *Nihon shoki* contains the following entry:

> Year 21 [= 477], spring, third month: When the Emperor heard that Paekche had been defeated by Koma 高麗 [= Koguryŏ], he gave Kumanari 久麻那利 to King Munju 汶洲 [trad. r. 475–477], thus aiding his country. The people at that time all said: "The country of Paekche, although their race has almost been destroyed and they have assembled lamenting at Hesuoto 倉下,[22] they rebuilt their country with the sincere assistance of the Emperor."[23] (NSK XIV [Yūryaku 21/3], vol. 2: 204–6)

Aston ([1896] 1956, vol. 1: 367, n. 2) has aptly commented that "the above narrative must be taken with a few grains of salt," pointing to the role of national vanity as "a powerful stimulus to the mythopœic faculty." That the compilers of the *Nihon shoki* themselves were not entirely convinced of the account's correctness can be inferred from a comment inserted directly after the passage quoted above:

> King Munju was King Kaero's 蓋鹵 [trad. r. 455–475] younger brother by the mother's side. According to an old Japanese record, Kumanari was given to King Mata 末多.[24] This is probably an error. Kumanari is an exclave in the Lower Takori 哆呼利 District in the land of Mimana. (NSK XIV [Yūryaku 21/3], vol. 2: 206/207)

It must be emphasized that in the chronicle of Yūryaku, "Kumanari" is written with different characters than in the myth of Susanoo. While the latter is written with characters meaning "bear" and "become" (thus allowing for alternate pronunciations), the former employs Chinese characters solely for their sound value. The connection between the two passages is thus not as obvious as the romanization makes it appear. To get a better understanding of the rather cryptic entries of the *Nihon shoki* and their historical context, it is helpful to consider how Korean sources describe the period in question. The *Samguk sagi* 三國史記 (1145), the oldest surviving Korean chronicle, is an important point of reference.

The Crisis of Paekche

If we follow the *Nihon shoki*'s chronology, Paekche was defeated by an invading Koguryŏ army in the winter of 476. Yūryaku's generous gift is dated to the spring of the following year (NSK XIV [Yūryaku 20, 21], vol. 2: 204/205). This chronology corresponds reasonably well with the one provided in the Paekche Annals of *Samguk sagi*.[25] According to this source, a Koguryŏ force laid siege to the Paekche capital of Hansŏng (in the region of present-day Seoul) in the 21st year of King Kaero's reign, that is, in 475. The king tried to escape but was captured and executed by Koguryŏ generals (SGSG XXV [Kaero 21/9], vol. 2: 60–2/67–8). King Kaero's successor Munju, however, managed to escape unharmed and went to Silla to seek aid.

> Having obtained a relief force of ten thousand men, Munju returned, and even though Koguryŏ's troops then withdrew, the royal citadel had fallen and the king was already dead. Munju therefore ascended the throne, and although his character was weak and indecisive, he loved the people and they him.
>
> [475] [1st year,] Winter, 10th month. The king ordered that the capital be moved to Ungjin. ...
>
> [3rd year], 9th month. The king went hunting and spent the night outside of the capital; Hae Ku [the Minister of War] sent a thug to the royal resting place who wounded him and, as a consequence, the king died. (Best 2006: 300–3; cf. SGSG XXVI [Munju], vol. 2: 69–70/82)

Munju was succeeded by Samgŭn 三斤 (trad. r. 477–479) and Tongsŏng 東城 (trad. r. 479–501), that is, the *Nihon shoki*'s King Mata. In the annals of these three kings, there is no mention of any assistance provided by Yamato (SGSG XXVI, vol. 2: 69–75/82–4). According to Jonathan Best (2006: 64–5), the *Samguk sagi*'s silence in regard to early relations with the Japanese archipelago is "not surprising":

> Not only did the editors of the *Samguk sagi* have minimal access to Korean records relating to Paekche, but also, in the more copious materials relating to

early Silla that were still available, Japan was consistently represented as a piratical scourge—a characterization that still held validity when the text was compiled in the twelfth century. As a result, both the nature of the extant historical data and of contemporary experience served as disincentives to treat in detail the generally more amicable relationship that evidently existed between the rulers of Paekche and the archipelago. In addition, although it is clear that the Confucian orientation and sinophile worldview of the *Samguk sagi*'s editors countenanced the careful search of Chinese histories for information to incorporate into the text, there is nothing to suggest that they had a comparable knowledge of—or interest in—early Japanese historical sources.

After a thorough analysis of Chinese, Korean, and Japanese written and archaeological sources, Best concludes "that the Yamato exercised significant influence in southern Korea from late in the fourth century to the end of the fifth." He emphasizes, however, that the "early decades of the fifth century mark the zenith of Yamato influence on the peninsula," which declined rapidly after this period (Best 2006: 68, 87). As we have seen, Munju in 475 sought military help in Silla rather than in Kaya, where Yamato influence is supposed to have been strongest. This suggests that Yamato did no longer have the military means to play a significant role in this peninsular conflict. The *Samguk sagi*'s account also casts doubt on the *Nihon shoki*'s claim "that it was only through a … grant of territory from the Yamato government that Munju was able to re-establish the kingdom" (ibid.: 93).

It would certainly be a mistake to accept the *Nihon shoki*'s account as historical fact. Nonetheless, the Yamato court clearly wanted its version to be accepted as true—at least on the archipelago, if not on the continent as well. Therefore, it stands to reason that they followed (no longer extant) Paekche chronicles not only with regard to dates but also to toponyms in order to endow their narrative with a certain historical plausibility. In this context, Ungjin, the new Paekche capital mentioned in the *Samguk sagi*, is highly relevant.

Locating Kumanari on the Korean Peninsula

According to the linguist Yi Pyŏngsŏn (2003: 2), "Toponyms are proper nouns, but at the time they were first applied, they were regular nouns created from the common vernacular language. Therefore, etymological analyses of the names of deities and places mentioned in myths play an important role in the study of ancient Korean-Japanese history, which is characterized by a scarcity of historical documents." While I would not characterize the account of Yūryaku in the *Nihon shoki* as a myth (but neither as a reliable historical account), the etymological approach proves useful in this instance as well.

Most contemporary linguists agree that *kuma* (or *koma*) was the word for "bear" in the old language of Paekche. Based on the Old Japanese *kuma* and the Middle Korean *kwom*, Bentley (2000: 425) reconstructs the Paekche word **kəma ~ *kuma*, pointing out that the vowel of the first syllable is not clear at this stage. Alexander Vovin (2010: 143) argues that the Old Japanese *kuma* is probably a loanword from Paekche.[26]

Nari, on the other hand, is thought to signify "river." Aston ([1896] 1956, vol. 1: 367–8, n. 2) in his translation of *Nihon shoki* remarked that "Kuma [in Kumanari] is for koma, the Corean word for bear, and nari is a dialectical or ancient form of nǎi (pronounced né), river." This hypothesis is confirmed by recent linguistic studies. Based on transcriptions in the *Samguk sagi*, Bentley (2000: 427) reconstructs the Paekche word **nari*, which he sees as cognate to the Middle Korean *nayh* "stream"—a reconstruction that is supported by Vovin's (2010: 207) assertion that "M[iddle] K[orean] :*nayh* 'river' certainly goes back to P[roto] K[orean] **narih*, as confirmed by O[ld] K[orean] *NAli* … 'river.'"[27]

The modern Korean pronunciation for these two characters, which is also used in translations of ancient sources, is Ungch'ŏn 熊川. This name is indeed mentioned in both the *Samguk sagi* and the *Samguk yusa* as an alternate name for Ungjin 熊津 (Bear Port; present-day Kongju), which served as capital of Paekche from 475 to 538 (SGSG XXXVII [Chiri 4], vol. 2: 265/279; SGYS II, III: 73/269, 96/310, 114/345). It seems highly unlikely that the ruler of Yamato was able to "give" his peninsular ally a territory in the center of the latter's domain. However, this preposterous claim matches the pathos of the *Nihon shoki*, which depicts Yūryaku as the savior of Paekche and suggests that fear from retaliation at the hands of Yamato was the only reason that deterred the Koguryŏ troops from annihilating Paekche once and for all (NSK XIV [Yūryaku 19–21], vol. 2: 204–7). The supposition that the Paekche capital was called by a name similar to Kumanari is further supported by the *Zhi-gong tu-juan* 職貢図卷 (Tribute Office Scroll), compiled around 539 by Xiao Yi 蕭繹 (508–555), the later Emperor Yuan 元 of Liang 梁 (r. 552–555). This text transcribes the name of Paekche's capital as Guma 固麻, "a long recognized equivalent for Ungjin" (Best 2006: 128–9; cf. Akiyama et al. 1968: 122) that possibly constitutes an abbreviated form of Kumanari.

A second possibility is that the *Nihon shoki*'s "Kumanari" refers to a port town in the territory of the former Kaya Federation called Ung'chŏn (located in the Chinhae District of present-day Ch'angwŏn city in Southern Kyŏngsang Province). This site must have been known to the compilers of the *Nihon shoki*, since it is mentioned in the chronicle of Keitai 継体 (trad. 458–531; r. 507–531). The relevant passage reports that Ōmi no Kena no Omi 近江毛野臣, a Yamato nobleman, who, as the text informs us, lived in Mimana, was commissioned to resolve a border conflict between Silla and Mimana. "Hereupon, Kena no Omi lodged at Kumanari (Bear River) {One book says he lodged at Kushimura 久斯 牟羅 in Mimana} whereto he summoned the kings of the two countries Silla and Paekche" (NSK XVII [Keitai 23/4], vol. 2: 318/319).

That this site was easily accessible from the Japanese archipelago is evidenced by the fact that it was one of the three ports the Yi government opened to the Japanese in the early fifteenth century (Lee 1984: 191). It seems possible that Yamato exerted some sort of influence in this region during the fifth century. Of course, this does not mean that the Yamato ruler had the power to "give" this territory to Paekche. Ungchŏn's location on the south-eastern coast of the peninsula, moreover, makes it hard to believe that it could ever have been part of Paekche territory. A possible solution to this conundrum is that the writers of the *Nihon shoki* tried to reinterpret the decline of Yamato influence in this region during the fifth century as a generous gift to their peninsular ally. The interweaving with historical events recorded in (no longer extant) peninsular chronicles would have lent further credibility to such a rewriting of history.

All in all, it is doubtful whether the location of Yūryaku's Kumanari can be unambiguously identified with the sources at our disposal. Nonetheless, it seems relatively certain that it was meant to refer to an actual site on the Korean peninsula. It is an altogether different question, however, whether this also applies to the peak of Kumanari mentioned in the tale of Susanoo's retreat to Ne no Kuni. The next section will show that the name Kumanari, interpreted as "bear river," is replete with conceptions that appear in various founding myths from the Korean peninsula, namely the cluster bear/river/mountain. This suggests the possibility that the toponym (and the mythical conceptions it entails) was brought to Japan and introduced into the court mythology by aristocrats with Korean roots.

Bears, Rivers, and Mountains—A Cluster of Motifs in Korean Myth

The "vertical conception" of a male heavenly deity who descends on a mountain peak, marries a female by the river side, and begets the founder of a dynasty is common to many Korean and Japanese myths.²⁸ A trait that seems to be specific to myths from the Korean peninsula, however, is that bears are mentioned in one form or another in many of these myths. This is not surprising, since dreams of a bear were considered a lucky omen presaging the birth of a son (Eberhard 1968: 194; Grayson 2001: 116).

The most famous example of a peninsular myth of this type is, of course, the myth of Tan'gun. In this tale, Hwanung 桓雄, a son of Hwanin 桓因, the Lord of Heaven, descends to a mountain beside a sandalwood tree and at length marries a she-bear whom he has previously turned into a woman, thus begetting Tan'gun, the founder of Old Chosŏn. This myth combines the elements of heavenly descent on a mountain, bear, marriage, and birth of the founder of a dynasty. Admittedly, none of the various versions of the tale seems to mention a river (Grayson 2001: 30–58). The myth of Kim Suro 金首露, first king of Kaya, also contains most of the elements mentioned above: according to the *Samguk yusa*, Suro descended on a mountain, while his consort is at least indirectly associated with water since she arrived by ship from a country beyond the ocean; moreover, we are explicitly told that she dreamt of a bear before giving birth to Suro's heir (SGYS II: 81–4/284–90).

But it is the myth of Chumong 朱蒙 (or Tongmyŏng 東明), the founder of Koguryŏ, in which the cluster bear / river / mountain emerges in its clearest form.²⁹ This myth is already attested in the first-century *Lunheng* 論衡 (Discourses in the Balance) and the third-century *San guo zhi*. The first non-Chinese version is the one engraved in the famous stele of King Kwanggaet'o (414) mentioned in Chapter 1. However, it is an epic poem written in 1193 by the scholar-bureaucrat Yi Kyubo 李奎報 (1168–1244) that constitutes the most elaborate version of the myth. Entitled "The Lay of King Tongmyŏng" (*Tongmyŏng-wang p'yŏn* 東明王篇), this poem is based on a no longer extant text referred to as *Ku-Samguksa* 舊三國史 (Old History of the Three Kingdoms). Since it is richly annotated with passages that are thought to be direct quotes from the *Ku-Samguksa*, the poem is an invaluable source for the study of Korean myth.

According to Yi Kyubo's poem, Haemosu 解慕漱, a son of the Ruler of Heaven, descended to Mount Ungsim 熊心 (Bear Heart) in Puyŏ 夫餘, a Tungus kingdom situated in southern Manchuria, in 59 CE. At a pool of the Ungsim Torrent, he captures Yuhwa 柳花, a daughter of the river god, and impregnates her, before re-ascending to heaven. Kŭmwa 金蛙, the King of Puyŏ, takes Yuhwa to his capital, where she gives birth to an egg. At length, a boy called Chumong hatches from the egg. Owing to an intrigue by Kŭmwa's sons, he has to flee from the capital and founds his own dynasty in a country situated to the south of Puyŏ (Hwang 2009: 161; Rutt 1973; Gardiner 1982b: 39–40).

Similar, though much shorter, versions of the tale are found in *Samguk sagi* and *Samguk yusa*. In both these versions, the story of Haemosu's seduction of Yuhwa is related by the daughter of the river god herself when she meets Kŭmwa. In the *Samguk sagi*, she explains, "I am the daughter of the river god. My name is Yuhwa. I was playing with several of my siblings when a man who said that he was Haemosu,[30] the son of the Ruler of Heaven, lured me away. In a house by the shores of the Yalu River at the base of Ungsim Mountain he seduced me. He then left and has not returned" (SGSG XIII [Tongmyŏng], vol. 1: 328/341).[31] The *Samguk yusa* follows this version rather closely, giving, however, a different name for the mountain:

> The girl told Kŭmwa that one day, when she was playing with her younger siblings, a man came to her and said that he was Haemosu, son of the Ruler of Heaven. She said that he had taken her to a house on the Yalu River just beneath Ungsin 熊神 (Bear God) Mountain, committed adultery with her, and had not returned. (SGYS I: 32)

As Grayson (2001: 78) points out, "Bear motifs, while not central to the workings of the narrative, still remain in the background, colouring the scene." For this reason, the name Ungsim Mountain has been associated with "the bear cult among north Asian peoples" (Song 1974: 49). The importance of the bear in the folklore and customs of Northeast Asian peoples is well documented. Most peoples of the circumpolar zone, stretching from Lapland over North Asia to Greenland and Labrador, shared a complex of beliefs and practices centered on the bear hunt. Despite regional variations, there are astonishing similarities. Central factors of the bear cult include taboos against uttering certain words during the bear hunt, reconciliatory speeches addressed to the bear, taboos against eating certain parts of the bear, and the burial of the bear's skull or bones (Paproth 1976: 11–13). In the accompanying myths, bears are often depicted as ancestors or spouses of humans (e.g., Grayson 2001: 136–55). The bear cult still plays a central role in the customs of Tungusic-speaking peoples in Siberia and Manchuria (Paproth 1976). Thus, it seems plausible that the bear also figured prominently in the mythology of the Tungusic Puyŏ, with whom the myth of Tongmyŏng was associated before it was taken over as the foundation myth of Koguryŏ around the fourth century CE (Gardiner 1988: 165).

Of special interest in the present context is the *Ku-Samguksa* version of the tale, since it mentions not only a "Bear Heart Mountain" but also a "Bear Heart

Torrent" and a "Bear Heart Pool"; thus, it is closest to the *Nihon shoki*'s "peak of Kumanari" if we accept the view that *kumanari* means "Bear River." As in the *Ku-Samguksa*, "peak of Kumanari" might refer to a mountain beside a "Bear River." On the other hand, the "Bear-Heart Mountain" or "Bear God Mountain" is associated with a river (the Yalu) in the other versions as well. Apparently, the authors of *Samguk sagi* and *Samguk yusa*, despite their abridgement of the myth, did not want to destroy the narratological cluster of mountain (the site of the heavenly deity's descent)/bear (bear cult, totemistic conceptions)/river (the site where marriage with the river god's daughter takes place).

But if this complex of motifs originated in Puyŏ, how did it reach the Japanese archipelago? As we have seen, the capital of Paekche in the period after the sack of Hansŏng was called Ungjin (Bear Port) or Ungch'ŏn (Bear River). A connection with the myth of Chumong becomes plausible if one considers that the royal family of Paekche called itself by the name of Puyŏ and traced its lineage to Chumong. According to the *Samguk sagi*, Onjo 溫祚, the founder of Paekche, was a son of Chumong. He was born as the younger of two sons fathered by Chumong on a daughter of the king of Cholbon Puyŏ 卒本扶餘, where Chumong had settled after his flight from Northern Puyŏ. After the death of the former king, Chumong succeeded the throne. When a son born to Chumong while he was still in Northern Puyŏ appeared at his father's court, he, rather than Onjo or his brother, was designated as crown prince. Thereupon, the two brothers took their leave from Cholbon Puyŏ and traveled south, where Onjo's elder brother found his death and Onjo founded Paekche. Thus, the *Samguk sagi* tells us, "because the royal lineage of Paekche—like that of Koguryŏ—descended from Fu-yü [Kor. Puyŏ] forebears, they took Puyŏ as their family name" (Best 2006: 205–8; cf. SGSG XXIII [Onjo], vol. 2: 9–11/23–24). The Paekche dynasty's connection to Puyŏ is confirmed by the *Wei-shu* 魏書 (Book of Wei), a Chinese chronicle from the middle of the sixth century, which claims that "the ancestors of Paekche come from Fuyü" (quoted in Gardiner 1969: 565).[32]

If the ancestors of the ruling class of Paekche did indeed originate in southern Manchuria, they might well have brought their beliefs centered on bears to their new home in the south. The *Samguk yusa* tells us that after the relocation of the capital from Ungjin to Sabi 泗沘 (also called Puyŏ!) in 538, the country was renamed Southern Puyŏ (SGYS II: 73). It seems plausible that the kings of Paekche in this period (when they had recovered to a certain extent from the national crisis caused by Koguryŏ more than half a century earlier) endeavored to show that their country—rather than Koguryŏ—was the legitimate successor to the kingdom of Puyŏ. Probably the former capital at Ungjin was named for similar reasons, that is, to assure oneself of the noble descent and former glory of the kingdom. Such ideas were possibly propagated to Paekche's insular ally by envoys or by the numerous refugees from Paekche who arrived at Japanese shores during the late fifth and the early sixth centuries. But whether the mythical ideas connected with the name "Kumanari" were still understood by the authors of the *Nihon shoki* is difficult to ascertain. Even in the extant versions of the Chumong myth, the "Bear Heart Mountain" and "Bear God Mountain" appear as nothing more than toponyms, after all, retaining at most a faint echo of earlier mythological (and possibly totemistic) conceptions associated with the bear in Northeast Asia.

Summary

This chapter has shown that Susanoo's connection to the Korean peninsula, far from being a modern invention, can be traced back to the ancient period. While some sources, such as the *Kojiki*, the *Izumo fudoki*, and the *Kogo shūi*, do not explicitly link Susanoo with Korea, the more influential *Nihon shoki* and *Sendai kuji hongi* do. Of special importance are the two toponyms Soshimori and Kumanari mentioned in both sources. While I am not aware of any commentary on Kumanari dating from the ancient period, Soshimori was identified (rightly or wrongly) as the capital of Silla as early as the ninth century. In the case of Kumanari, the *Nihon shoki* itself hints in a similar direction by repeating the toponym (albeit written differently) in the chronicle of Yūryaku. In this instance, the name quite clearly refers to a site on the peninsula (possibly Ungjin). Whether this is also true for the "peak of Kumanari" mentioned in the myth of Susanoo must remain open. As suggested in the last portion of the chapter, both the Korean toponym Ungchŏn and the Japanese Kumanari seem to reflect Northeast Asian mythological conceptions centering on the interconnected motifs bear/river/mountain.

A second point that was emphasized in this chapter is Susanoo's (and Izumo's) close association with the otherworld Ne no (Katasu) Kuni in the ancient sources. Arguably, this connection to a sinister realm of death helped to construct Susanoo as a foil to set off Amaterasu. Izumo, it has been argued, fulfills a similar function with respect to Yamato and Ise. As we will see in the following chapter, during the medieval period, Susanoo's connection to both Korea and the afterworld served as the textual basis for his reinterpretation as a foreign deity of disease.

Incidentally, the findings of this chapter confirm Blumenberg's insight that already the earliest myths known to us have undergone a lengthy process of reception before being put into writing. The association of specific geographical sites such as Kumano or Izumo with the mythical realms of the dead reflects the political intention of the mythmakers at the imperial court during the late seventh and early eighth century to depict the present political order as an image of the order of the divine age, thus providing justification by precedent. Such an undertaking only makes sense after a certain degree of political centralization has been achieved and formerly independent polities like Izumo are ideologically incorporated into the central state. Izumo thus came to play the role of a peripheral region (albeit the most exalted peripheral region) of the Yamato state. As will be demonstrated in the following two chapters, the structural similarity of Izumo's position within the Yamato state (as reflected in the court mythology) and Korea's position within the modern Japanese empire resulted in a perception of Izumo and Korea as subordinate and peripheral realms that nonetheless fulfill an important ideological function as a foil to set off the "heartland."

5

The God with a Thousand Faces: Susanoo and His Alter Egos in Medieval Mythology

This chapter deals with Susanoo's transformation in the medieval period. The Japanese Middle Ages are commonly defined as corresponding roughly to the Kamakura and Muromachi periods (1185–1573), but in this chapter I will also discuss earlier developments that started with the decline of the *ritsuryō* system in the later Heian period, and that are indispensable for an understanding of religious and intellectual developments during the medieval period.

Arguably, the most far-reaching innovation in the religious world of medieval Japan was the emergence of the *honji suijaku* paradigm. This model was originally introduced by Buddhist thinkers to incorporate local divinities into their Buddhist worldview. According to this paradigm, humans could not grasp the "essence" (*honji*) of the buddhas, who therefore manifested themselves as "traces" (*suijaku*) in the form of local deities to lead them toward awakening. Theoretically, this framework put the local deities in a subservient position compared to the buddhas and was thus a powerful tool for Buddhist institutions to claim precedence over other religious traditions. However, as Bernard Faure (2016a: 341) has shown, this attempt to co-opt local cults "backfired" as the distinction between essences and traces became increasingly blurred: while intended as a systematization of the religious world, the *honji suijaku* model gave rise to a wild "mythico-ritual proliferation," in whose course local deities and even humans could become "essences," while buddhas might be regarded as "traces."

Recent scholarship moreover emphasizes that the *honji suijaku* model did not just link buddhas and the *kami* mentioned in the ancient court chronicles, as the modern Japanese term *shinbutsu shūgō* 神仏習合 (syncretism of *kami* and buddhas)[1] suggests (Faure 2016a: 2–4, 335–6). *Honji suijaku* is now rather perceived as a "complex and ongoing process," characterized by the coexistence of centripetal and centrifugal tendencies, that brought forth "complicated networks of associations, establishing links between kami and buddhas, but also between kami and other kami, kami and Yin-Yang deities, buddhas and other buddhas, Wisdom Kings, historical culture heroes both from Japan, China, and India, and even demons and witch animals" (Teeuwen and Rambelli 2003: 30, 47).

Iyanaga Nobumi (2003: 176) has likened the relationship between the individual nodes in these networks to reflections in an unlimited number of fragmented mirrors. This is an apt metaphor that visualizes the infinite proliferation of associations between individual deities within the *honji suijaku* paradigm. Since fragmented mirrors do not show a truthful reflection of the person looking into them but rather a distorted image that emphasizes certain aspects at the expense of others, the metaphor also allows us to account for the individuality and diversity of the deities connected in this mythicoritual network. I would argue, however, that in the combinatory world of medieval Japanese religion, there is often no clear distinction between the person looking into the mirror and its reflections. The reflections are not only distorted and fragmented versions of an original, they also introduce new elements that might change the character of the alleged "original."

As we will see in the course of this chapter, Susanoo was mainly associated with so-called *ijin* 異神, that is, "strange" or "foreign gods." This term was coined by Yamamoto Hiroko (1998b: i–ii) to describe medieval deities who are neither mentioned in the ancient myths nor in Buddhist sutras and can therefore be distinguished from *kami*, buddhas, and bodhisattvas. These deities were believed to have come to Japan from somewhere beyond the ocean. In medieval religious discourse, the realms beyond the Japanese shores were often described as shadowy otherworlds rather than as mere foreign countries. They were regarded as polluted realms inhabited by devils, seedbeds for all sorts of calamities, such as contagious diseases or military invasions, that threatened to disrupt order and prosperity on the Japanese archipelago (Batten 2003: 37; Murai 2001: 73). *Ijin* were thus commonly perceived as epidemic deities who had to be placated to prevent the spread of diseases (Yamamoto 1998b: 11–14). Susanoo's association (and, at times, equation) with such sinister deities, unsurprisingly, resulted in an emphasis on the negative aspects of his character and his connection to the realms of the dead (Gotō 2002: 38–41). This development led to the emergence of a distinctly dark image of Susanoo in medieval religious discourse. In this way, his alleged mirror images fundamentally changed the perception of the *kami* Susanoo during the Middle Ages.

Within the *honji suijaku* paradigm, supernatural entities were correlated in various ways and for various reasons. Often, similar names or iconographic representations served as a basis to link two or more divinities (similarity of signifiers); however, deities were also clustered on the basis of similar functions or meanings (similarity of signifieds). These associations were then expressed in particular interpretations (or inventions) of rituals, doctrines, visual representations, and myths (Teeuwen and Rambelli 2003: 48). This chapter will lay special emphasis on medieval myths.

Yamamoto Hiroko (1998a: 4) has coined the term "medieval myths" (*chūsei shinwa* 中世神話) to refer to "tales or statements relating to the creation of the cosmos or the deeds of deities contained in the innumerable commentaries, Shintō texts, legends on the origins of temples and shrines (*jisha engi* 寺社縁起), and tales revealing a deity's 'original essence' (*honji monogatari* 本地物語) that were produced in the medieval period." The *Nihon shoki* plays a central role in the religious discourses of medieval Japan. Not only are motifs and episodes from the *Nihon shoki* quoted and discussed in many medieval treatises, but even tales that are only loosely or not at all related to the ancient court chronicle are often introduced with phrases like "the *Nihongi* 日本紀 says" or "can be seen in the *Nihongi*." Some scholars refer to such tales as "medieval *Nihongi*," stressing both their indebtedness to the ancient chronicle and their originality (Itō 1972: 29–30). These texts situated Japan and its deities in a Buddhist universe, bringing forth a number of competing images of Japan as either (1) a land situated at the periphery of the Buddhist world, (2) one of three centers of Buddhist civilization (the other two being India and China), or (3) a land of the gods.

In this context, it is impossible to draw a sharp distinction between interpretations of ancient myths and the formulation of new ones. As Saitō Hideki (2012: 136) points out, for medieval thinkers such a distinction did not exist: the interpretation of myths was "a creative process that produced new myths; medieval scholars of myth were at the same time 'mythmakers.'" Recent Japanese scholarship on medieval myths strives to overcome the association of mythology with the ancient period. The traditional focus of mythological studies on the narratives of the divine age as recorded in the ancient court chronicles is questioned and replaced by an emphasis on the changeability of myths and their embeddedness in larger historical, social, or cultural changes (Kwŏn 2013: 43). Studies on medieval myths therefore draw attention to the "repetition, transformation, and retranscription" of myths—processes that can be framed as "the work of cultural memory" (Faure 2016b: 31–2).[2] These processes of reception and transformation were enacted by a wide range of ritual specialists including shrine personnel, Buddhist thinkers, "and those who specialized in the

Onmyōdō divination, purification practices, oracular speech, dream incubation, and star cults" (Andreeva 2017: 266–7). A criticism that has been leveled at studies on medieval myths is its "fetishization" of an allegedly unique medieval world (Kim 2020: 8). By subsuming research on medieval texts under the more general rubric of cultural memory, the present study tries to draw attention to medieval myths' continuities with earlier and later mythological discourses. To emphasize the interconnectedness of ancient myths, their interpretation, and the emergence of new myths, I call this process "medieval mythology," since the word "mythology" can refer to both a mythical corpus and the study of myth (Weiss 2018a: 338–9).

Susanoo in Gion: Epidemic Deity from beyond the Sea

Yasaka 八坂 Shrine, located in the famous Gion district in Kyoto, is one of the most popular shrines dedicated to the worship of Susanoo. Up to the modern period, this site was known as Gion Shrine or Kanjin-in 感神院. Both names point to the site's Buddhist dimension. Since the time of its founding, the sanctuary seems to have had close connections to Buddhism. These Buddhist ties were reinforced in the tenth century, when Gion Shrine became a subtemple (*betsuin* 別院) of Enryakuji, the Tendai head temple. In premodern times, the religious site at Gion therefore constituted a "shrine-temple complex" (McMullin 1987: 165) rather than a Shintō shrine. Partly due to these Buddhist associations, Gion Shrine came to play an important part in Susanoo's medieval reinvention as an epidemic deity. Thus, the Gion complex forms a good point of departure for a discussion of Susanoo's transformation in medieval mythology.

The name "Gion" refers to Jetavana, the site of Śākyamuni's first monastery in India. According to legend, this monastery (which in Japanese is called Gion-shōja 祇園精舎) was built by Sudatta, a wealthy disciple of Śākyamuni. Sudatta bought the site on which the monastery was to be built from its owner at an exorbitant price: he had to cover the whole precinct with gold coins (Deeg 2005: 306–7, 536–9; Legge [1886] 1965: 55–9). While it is difficult to ascertain a specific founding date for the religious complex at Gion, most scholars agree that the Buddhist monk Ennyo 円如 (fl. ninth century) built a temple called Kankeiji 観慶寺 on the Gion site in the late ninth century. The site had originally housed a private residence of Regent Fujiwara no Mototsune (already mentioned above as a participant in the court lectures on the *Nihon shoki* held between 878 and 881), who is said to have donated it to Ennyo (McMullin 1987: 165–6). Possibly the name "Gion" was attached to the site to honor Mototsune's generosity by likening him to Sudatta, the great benefactor of Buddhist tradition.

Since its beginnings, the history of the Gion complex was intimately linked to the development of the belief in *goryō* 御霊, that is, the vengeful spirits of persons who had died a premature (often violent) death. If not placated properly, these vengeful spirits were believed to cause epidemics and other calamities. This belief seems to be very old; its origins probably predate the Nara period (710–794). However, interest in *goryō* belief, especially among the common populace, surged in the eighth century as the first major cities such as Heijōkyō 平城京 (Nara) and Heiankyō 平安京 (Kyoto) were built. This marked the first time in Japanese history that a large number of people lived together in a confined space; and due to a lack of hygiene, epidemics were a constant threat. In the Nara and early Heian periods, the city population also had to endure frequent catastrophes such as fires, floods, typhoons, and many others (cf. Nagai 2011: 131–3).

The *goryō* belief contained a political dimension as well; since reprehensible political activities were thought to produce vengeful spirits (for instance, if a political rival was murdered), catastrophes were regarded as a "barometer of political injustices" (McMullin 1988: 272). It was believed, however, that such disasters could be prevented if appropriate rituals were performed to pacify the vengeful spirits. These rituals were commonly referred to as *goryōe* 御霊会 and combined practices from various religious traditions.

The first *goryōe* mentioned in a written source was hosted in 863 by Mototsune and his kinsman Fujiwara no Tokitsura 藤原常行 (836–875) at the imperial garden Shinsen'en 神泉苑 in Heiankyō (NSJ VII [Jōgan 5/5/20]: 112–13). The alleged reason for this ritual was to stop a tuberculosis epidemic, which had claimed many victims during that year. The spread of the disease was attributed to the vengeful spirits of six aristocrats who were well known as political rivals eliminated by the northern branch of the Fujiwara family. The present head of that eminent family was none other than Mototsune. The shrewd statesman, Neil McMullin (1988: 287–9) argues, succeeded in directing popular fear of *goryō* against the spirits of his family's political enemies, thus depicting the rivals of the northern Fujiwara, whether dead or alive, as enemies of the people.

While Mototsune managed to employ this *goryōe* to his political advantage, it is apparent that the *goryō* belief also had the potential to become a threat to the ruling elite. For this reason, the Fujiwara endeavored to gain control of the *goryō* cult in the mid-ninth century (McMullin 1988: 290). This aim is reflected in a promulgation from 865, recorded in the *Nihon sandai jitsuroku* 日本三代実録

(True History of Three Reigns of Japan; 901), which prohibited the populace to assemble for *goryōe* without imperial permission (NSJ XI [Jōgan 7/6/14]: 159).

It is not entirely clear at what time the court-sponsored *goryōe* first became associated with the Gion complex. According to the shrine record *Gionsha hon'enroku* 祇園社本縁録 (Record of the Origin of Gion Shrine; date unknown), a *goryōe* was conducted in 869 under the supervision of Urabe Hiramaro 卜部日良麻呂 (?–881). In the course of this festival, 66 poles were erected and a portable shrine (of the Gion complex?) was brought to the Shinsen'en. Significantly, the text tells us that this festival was called "Gion Goryōe." Another shrine record—the *Gionsha hon'en zatsu roku* 祇園社本縁雑録 (Miscellaneous Records of the Origin of Gion Shrine; date unknown)—contains an entry for the same year, which states that pestilence deities (*ekijin* 疫神) were worshiped in the village Yasaka (Gotō 2002: 52–3). While the early dating of these events is disputed, there is strong evidence that during the next century the *goryō* rituals came to be centered at Gion (Suzuki 2019: 88–90), where the tradition has survived to the present day in the form of the famous Gion Matsuri 祇園祭. Fujiwara no Mototsune's central role in the founding of both the Kankeiji and the *goryōe* of 863 leads McMullin (1988: 291) to suspect that his sponsorship of the Kankeiji's construction was a part of his effort to gain control over the *goryō* cult. If this was really the case, Mototsune's ploy was remarkably successful: a century later, Gion was included in the list of the twenty-two major shrines in the country; from that time up to the present, *goryōe* have been held regularly at the shrine-temple complex.

Susanoo became associated with Gion at a much later date. The first textual evidence linking Susanoo to Gion is the tale of Somin Shōrai 蘇民将来 recorded in the *Shaku Nihongi*. This text played a central role in redefining Susanoo's character by linking him with the pestilence deity Mutō 武塔.

Somin Shōrai, Mutō Tenjin, and Susanoo

Urabe Kanekata 卜部兼方 (fl. thirteenth century), the *Shaku Nihongi*'s author, opens the tale of Somin Shōrai with the words "The *Bingo no kuni fudoki* 備後国風土記 says," thus creating the impression that the tale had been put to writing in the early eighth century. While it is probable that Bingo Province (present-day Hiroshima Prefecture) presented such a document to the imperial court in compliance with Empress Genmei's command of 713 (see Chapter 2), no other fragments of the work survive. There are good reasons to doubt the tale's antiquity—at least in the form that is recorded in the *Shaku Nihongi*.

Kanekata presents the story as the foundation legend of Enokuma 疫隅 Shrine in Bingo. Curiously, in the discussion that follows after the tale, Kanekata quotes his father Kanefumi 兼文 (life dates unknown) as saying, "This is the origin (*honen* 本縁) of Gion Shrine" (SNG: 172). This strange remark—why should the alleged foundation legend of Enokuma Shrine in Bingo, which does not mention Gion with one syllable, be considered the "origin" of Gion Shrine?—is one of the indicators that point to a medieval origin of the tale of Somin Shōrai as quoted in the *Shaku Nihongi*. During the medieval period, Enokuma Shrine seems to have housed a branch shrine (*bunsha* 分社) of Gion Shrine. Thus, the connection between the two shrines would only have occurred to a medieval author. The *Bingo fudoki* was probably only invoked to endow the tale with greater authority—a strategy similar to that employed in the medieval *Nihongi* (Saitō 2012: 138–40). A translation of the tale, as recorded in the *Shaku Nihongi*, follows below:

The Provincial Shrine of Enokuma

In the past, when the deity Mutō, who resided in the Northern Sea, went to wed the daughter of the deity of the Southern Sea, the sun set. There were two [brothers called] Somin Shōrai at this place. The elder brother Somin Shōrai was exceedingly poor, [whereas] the younger brother Shōrai was abundantly rich, calling a hundred buildings and granaries his own. Here the deity [Mu]tō asked shelter for the night, but, out of avarice, he [i.e., the younger brother] did not accommodate him. The elder brother Somin Shōrai [however] accommodated him. He provided him with a cushion made of millet stalks and served him cooked millet to eat.

After he had finished [his stay], some years passed and he came back, accompanied by eight divine children (*yahashira no miko* 八柱子). He spoke: "I want to reward Shōrai," and asked: "Are your descendants in your house?"

Somin Shōrai answered and spoke: "My daughter and wife are here."

Then [Mutō] spoke: "Take wreaths of cogon grass (*chi no wa* 茅輪) and make them wear these around their waists."

Following the deity's instructions, [Somin Shōrai] let them wear [the wreaths of cogon grass around their waists], and in the night [the deity] killed and devoured everyone with the exception of Somin's daughter alone. Then he spoke: "I am the god Haya-Susanoo 速須佐雄.[3] If in later times there is a plague, everybody who says that he is a descendant of Somin Shōrai and wears a wreath of cogon grass around his waist shall surely be spared." (SNG: 172)

Leaving the question of the narrative's antiquity aside for the moment, it seems obvious that it was Kanefumi who linked the tale with Gion and the deity Mutō with Susanoo. Even if we allow for a certain measure of creativity in the medieval reception of myths, Susanoo's appearance in the tale seems completely unmotivated. What was the rationale behind the association of Susanoo with the pestilence deity Mutō? Fortunately, the *Shaku Nihongi* itself provides us with some hints. In the text, the section containing the tale of Somin Shōrai and the discussion of its significance (to which I will return shortly) is placed under the heading "Susanoo no Mikoto asked the myriad deities for shelter." This is an allusion to a variant of the *Nihon shoki* that relates how Susanoo, after his banishment from the Plain of High Heaven, asked for shelter from the rain but was turned down by all the deities (NSK I [7, var. 3], vol. 1: 86/87). Thus, the motif of a wandering deity asking for shelter may have led to the identification of Susanoo and Mutō (Suzuki 2019: 122–3).

After the narrative of Somin Shōrai, the *Shaku Nihongi* records a dialogue between Kanefumi and the former chief advisor to the emperor (*kanpaku* 関白) Ichijō Sanetsune 一条実経 (1223–1284), which probably took place between 1274 and 1276 during a series of lectures on the *Nihon shoki* that Kanefumi gave for Sanetsune and his son Ichijō Ietsune 一条家経 (1248–1294), who served as regent (*sesshō*) at the time (Suzuki 2019: 88). The Urabe were religious specialists renowned for their knowledge of the *Nihon shoki* and ritual lore, who regularly held lectures at the court (Scheid 2001: 83–5). The dialogue between Kanefumi and Sanestune begins with the former's assertion that the legend of Somin Shōrai explains the origin of Gion Shrine. Sanetsune then asks what deities were enshrined at Gion. Kanefumi replies that Mutō Tenjin, whom he equates with Susanoo, was enshrined along with two female deities: Shōshōi 少将井, whom Kanefumi identifies with Kushiinada Hime, and the daughter of the god of the Southern Sea. The name Shōshōi is probably derived from a well situated at a temporary abode (*otabisho*) used to house one of Gion Shrine's portable shrines during the Gion Goryōe (Kawahara 2002: 292–3). Apparently surprised by Kanefumi's reply, Sanetsune inquires whether the Gion deity was not a god from a foreign land (*ikokujin* 異国神). Kanefumi quotes the *Nihon shoki*'s variant according to which Susanoo had come to Japan from Silla and surmises that this tale might have given rise to the theory that Susanoo is a foreign deity (SNG: 172–3).

This dialogue demonstrates both the *Nihon shoki*'s central role in medieval religious discourse and the creativity with which the ancient myths were reinterpreted and combined with new elements. As the first text that explicitly described Susanoo as an epidemic deity (with the power to both cause and prevent diseases), the tale of Somin Shōrai in the *Shaku Nihongi* set the tone for Susanoo's association with a number of such sinister deities. Possibly the most famous of these deities is Gozu Tennō, the "Bull-Headed Heavenly King."

Gozu Tennō: The Bull-Headed Heavenly King from India

Gozu Tennō is another god who is mentioned early on as a deity worshiped in Gion. The deity's name first appears in the *Honchō seiki* 本朝世紀 (Chronicle of the Reigns of Our Realm; latter half of the twelfth century). This text reports a fire that destroyed the Gion complex's treasure hall in 1070. The text specifies that the fire damaged the feet of a Gozu Tennō statue (Suzuki 2019: 94–5).

The encyclopedia *Iroha jiruishō* 伊呂波字類抄 (Characters Classified in *iroha* Order and Annotated; early Kamakura period) provides some background on this deity. The entry on "Gion" contains the following text under the heading "Gozu Tennō's provenance (*in'en* 因縁)":

> To the north of India there is a country called Nine Phases (*kusō* 九相). In this country there is a place called Auspiciousness (*kisshō* 吉祥). In this country there is a castle. The king of this castle is Gozu Tennō. He is also known as Mutō Tenjin etc., etc. His father is called King Father of the Eastern Skies and his mother is called Queen Mother of the Western Skies. The prince born to them was called Mutō Tenjin. This divine king took the Dragon King Sāgara's daughter Sakkada 薩迦陁 as wife, who bore him eight royal children (*hachiōji* 八王子). He had a retinue of eighty-four thousand six-hundred fifty-four deities. (Quoted in Nishida 1966: 261–2)

This seemingly simple text combines an astonishing number of ideas and concepts from various religious traditions. "Nine Phases" (Skt. Navasaṁjñā) refers to a form of Buddhist meditation with the goal to curb desire by meditating on the nine successive phases of a decomposing corpse (Tinsley 2017: 17–19). *Kisshō* refers to an auspicious omen (Skt. Śrīvastaya) or to Lakṣmī, the Hindu goddess of fortune (Eitel [1904] 1970: 158–9; Soothill and Hodous [1937] 1995: 204). The Queen Mother of the West is one of the most prominent goddesses of Daoism. She is "queen of the immortals and symbol of highest *yin* [and] the spouse of … the Lord King of the East, … the representative of pure *yang*" (Despeux 2000: 385–6). Interesting in our context is that she was also seen as "the goddess of epidemics who resided in the west and ruled over the demons of pestilence" (ibid.). Sāgara is the nāga king of the northern ocean, who possesses priceless pearls (Soothill and Hodous [1937] 1995: 323). According to the twelfth chapter of the Lotus Sutra, an unnamed eight-year-old daughter of Sāgara attained Buddhahood (Deeg 2007: 200–2).

The text offers an impressive example of the multitude of religious traditions that were seemingly undiscriminatingly combined in religious discourses in medieval Japan. All these foreign names and ideas (which are not explained in the text and apparently unrelated to its plot) emphasize the foreignness of Gozu Tennō and, by extension, of Mutō Tenjin, who is equated with him. The use of religious concepts, such as Nine Phases and Auspiciousness, that clearly belong to the domain of divine power (death, fortune) as names for places located beyond India, moreover, reinforces the association of foreign countries with mythical otherworlds.

As seen above, the *Shaku Nihongi* also reports that Mutō fathered eight children on his spouse. However, the term *hachiōji*, employed in the *Iroha jiruishō*, commonly refers to the children born during Susanoo and Amaterasu's *ukei* in the Plain of High Heaven. It is therefore not surprising that Gozu Tennō in a further step was equated with Susanoo as well.

In his recent monograph on Gozu Tennō in medieval religious discourse, Suzuki Kōtarō emphasizes Ichijō Kaneyoshi's 一条兼良 (1402–1481) significance as the thinker who harmonized these disparate strands of Gion belief. As a descendant of Sanetsune and the head of the Ichijō family, Kaneyoshi possessed detailed knowledge of the Urabe family's secret teachings on the *Nihon shoki*, including the *Shaku Nihongi* (Suzuki 2019: 129–30).

In 1422, Kaneyoshi wrote *Kuji kongen* 公事根源 (Roots of Court Administration and Ceremonies), a treatise on annual court rites and their origins. This work contains a section dedicated to the Gion Goryōe, in which Kaneyoshi quotes the *Shaku Nihongi*'s tale of Somin Shōrai and the *Iroha jiruishō*'s entry on Gozu Tennō with only slight alterations. For instance, he specifies that eight years passed before Mutō's return to Somin Shōrai, whose niggardly brother's name he gives as Kotan Shōrai 巨旦将来, and he claims that it was Somin himself, rather than his daughter, who was spared from the epidemic. But the most significant innovation of the work is that it associates not only Mutō Tenjin but also Gozu Tennō with Susanoo. According to Kaneyoshi, Mutō Tenjin and Gozu Tennō are different names for the same deity. However, this deity is not identical with Susanoo but rather his acolyte (*warawabe* 童部) (Suzuki 2019: 131–7).

Kaneyoshi was to revise this view in his *Nihon shoki sanso* 日本書記纂疏 (Explanations on Selected Passages of *Nihon shoki*), a commentary on the *Nihon shoki*'s divine age fascicles he completed sometime between 1455 and 1457. In this work, Kaneyoshi attempted to completely incorporate the legends of Mutō Tenjin and Gozu Tennō into the *Nihon shoki*'s myth-history. He achieves this by elaborating on an idea only hinted at by Kanekata in *Shaku Nihongi*, namely on the commonality between Susanoo and Mutō Tenjin as wandering gods seeking shelter. He uses this commonality to merge the two deities and insert the tale of Somin Shōrai into the *Nihon shoki*'s plot. In Kaneyoshi's reading, "according to one variant" of the *Nihon shoki*, Susanoo asked for shelter and was turned away by all the gods. "At that time, there were the brothers Somin Shōrai and Kotan Shōrai." After the rich Kotan had turned him away as well, Somin welcomed the god in his humble home. In the evening, Susanoo ordered Somin to have all members of his family wear wreaths of cogon grass. That night, an epidemic broke out and killed everyone except Somin's family. The god prophesized that in the case of future epidemics everyone would be spared who carried a wreath of cogon grass and a small wooden plate with the inscription "I am a descendant of Somin Shōrai" on his or her body (Suzuki 2019: 141–2).

According to the *Bingo fudoki*, Kaneyoshi continues, the above happened when the god Mutō of the northern sea was on his way to meet the daughter of the god ruling over the south sea. Mutō, he explains, is a different name for Susanoo. The Gion Shrine is a "vestige" (*keshaku* 化迹) of Susanoo. The shrine worships (1) Gozu Tennō, who is also known as Mutō Tenjin; (2) Harime 婆利女, who is also known as Shōshōi and Inada Hime and who, "according to one theory," is a daughter of Sāgara; and (3) Jadokke no Kami 蛇毒気神 (Deity of Serpent Poison Spirit), who might be a manifestation (*kegen* 化現) of the giant eight-headed serpent defeated by Susanoo. All of these deities, Kaneyoshi explains, are pestilence deities (*gyōyakujin* 行疫神), about whom the *Nihon shoki* said that they "had caused many people in the land to die" (Suzuki 2019: 142).

The last phrase is a quotation from the *Nihon shoki*'s main text describing the disastrous consequences of Susanoo's incessant weeping. Not much is known about Jadokke no Kami, but a statue of this deity is mentioned in the *Honchō seiki*'s description of the great fire that destroyed the Gion Shrine's treasure hall in 1070. Kaneyoshi's equation of Susanoo, Mutō Tenjin, and Gozu Tennō forced him to equate their respective spouses as well, thus leaving one of the Gion Shrine's worship sites vacant. Kaneyoshi filled this vacancy with Jadokke no Kami, a deity who had a documented connection to the shrine and through its name offered a further opportunity to link the Gion Shrine's tradition to the *Nihon shoki* and Susanoo (Suzuki 2019: 142–9).

With his interpretation in *Nihon shoki sanso*, Kaneyoshi succeeded in completely integrating the narratives of Mutō Tenjin and Gozu Tennō into the *Nihon shoki*'s mythical plot. However, in doing so, he not only altered the tales of those two foreign deities substantially but also transformed Susanoo into a pestilence deity. This example nicely illustrates the workings of medieval mythology. Although Kaneyoshi remains remarkably faithful to the sources and prior interpretations at his disposal, he ends up creating a completely new myth due to his unshakable conviction that the tales centering on Gion where nothing else than alternate formulations of the universal truths recorded in the *Nihon shoki*.

Myth and Ritual: Talismans and Cogon Grass Wreaths

The tale of Somin Shōrai served as foundation legend for two central rituals that are practiced up to the present day at Yasaka Shrine and many other shrines throughout Japan. The first of these is the sale or distribution of talismans carrying the inscription "I am a descendant of Somin Shōrai" or an image of Gozu Tennō. These talismans are thought to bestow the deity's protection upon the person who wears them. They come in various forms and materials and are either carried around as charms for individual protection or, more commonly, pasted to the house door to offer protection to the entire household (Nagai 2011: 208-9; Oka 2002: 102-4). The second practice has already been described by Engelbert Kaempfer (1651-1716) in his *History of Japan*:

> On the doors and houses of ordinary people (for men of quality seldom suffer to have theirs thus disfigur'd) there is commonly pasted a sorry picture of one of their *Lares*, or House-Gods, printed upon one half sheet of paper. The most common is the blackhorn'd *Giwon*, otherwise call'd *Godsu Ten Oo*, that is, according to the literal signification of the characters, this word is express'd by, *the Ox-Headed Prince of Heaven*, whom they believe to have the power of keeping the family from distempers and other unlucky accidents, particularly from the *Sekbio*, or Small-pox, which proves fatal to great numbers of their children. (Kaempfer 1727, vol. 2: 418)

Amulets bearing the inscription "I am a descendant of Somin Shōrai" seem to be even older than the ones showing a depiction of Gozu Tennō. Wooden tablets (*mokkan* 木簡) bearing Somin Shōrai's name have been unearthed from various sites on the archipelago. Judging from the number of excavated wooden tablets, the regions of modern Ōsaka and Niigata prefectures seem to have been important centers of Somin Shōrai belief. Most of these wooden tablets, thin plates with a length of about 10 centimeters and a breadth of 2 to 3 centimeters, date from the Kamakura and Muromachi periods. In many cases, they show dents on both sides in the upper part to which a cord might have been affixed in order to put the talisman around the neck or waist of little children; written documents attest this custom for the Edo period (Oka 2002: 104).

However, the oldest Somin Shōrai *mokkan* were found in Kyoto Prefecture: one wooden tablet, dating from the early Heian period, was found in the precincts of Mibudera 壬生寺 in former Heiankyō and an even older *mokkan* was unearthed in 2001 in Nagaokakyō 長岡京. The latter dates from the decade preceding the founding of Heiankyō, during which Nagaokakyō served as the capital (784–794). This wooden tablet is very small, measuring only 2.7 centimeters in length and 1.3 centimeters in breadth, and carries the inscription "I am a descendant of Somin Shōrai" on both sides. A little hole in the upper part of the tablet suggests that it was worn around the neck with a cord (Kawamura 2007: 6–8; Oka 2002: 109). Although this important discovery does not prove the authenticity of the *Shaku Nihongi*'s alleged quote from the *Bingo fudoki*, it at least demonstrates that the tale was known in some form on the archipelago as early as the eighth century.

The most visible remnants of Gion belief in present-day Japan, however, are surely the giant cogon grass wreaths that are hung up at a large number of shrines each summer. Shrine-visitors pass through these wreaths, praying for protection from illness and misfortune. This custom is derived from the Great Purification of the Last Day of the Sixth Month, mentioned in the *Engi shiki*. At the Yasaka Shrine, the wreath is hung up on the last day of July and the custom is not explicitly associated with *ōharae*, but rather referred to as Ekijinja Nagoshisai 疫神社夏越祭. Ekijinja (Epidemic God Shrine) is a subshrine dedicated to the worship of Somin Shōrai. After passing through the wreath, shrine-visitors receive a talisman with the inscription "I am a descendant of Somin Shōrai" that is believed to enable them to make it through the summer (*nagoshi*) without getting sick or meeting with other calamities (Kawara Shoten Henshūbu 2019, vol. 2: 133). At most other shrines, the wreaths are hung up at the last day of June and the accompanying ritual is called *nagoshi no harae* 夏越の祓 (purification to pass the summer).

While it is difficult to discern how far these rituals in their present form can be traced back, the merging of the Somin Shōrai legend with the *ōharae* ritual is further evidence of Susanoo's incorporation into the Gion cult and his perception as a god of the otherworld. As mentioned in Chapter 3, Susanoo was associated with the ritual of Great Purification in the early ninth-century *Kogo shūi*, which claimed that the misdeeds he committed in the Plain of High Heaven were the Heavenly Sins. The *ōharae* ritual was intended to wash these sins (along with the Earthly Sins) away to Ne no Kuni, where, according to the *Engi shiki*, the goddess Haya-Sasura Hime 速佐須良比咩 "dwells ... [and] will wander off with them and lose them" (Philippi 1990: 48; cf. EGSK VIII: 480/481). The *Nakatomi harae kunge* 中臣祓訓解 (Kamakura period)[4] goes one step further than the *Kogo shūi* and identifies Susanoo with both Haya-Sasura Hime and Enra-ō 閻羅王, the ruler of the Buddhist underworld (Teeuwen and van der Veere 1998: 44). The association of cogon grass wreaths with the *ōharae* ritual further merged Susanoo's roles as a god of the underworld and a pestilence deity.

This negative perception of Susanoo should probably not surprise us, as the Gion cult was centered in the capital and influential court aristocrats (for instance, several members of the Fujiwara and Ichijō families) played a central role in the process of its creation and shaping. As we have seen, the imperial court's antipathy toward Susanoo, the divine rival of the imperial progenitress, can be traced back to the ancient court chronicles. But how was Susanoo perceived in his homeland Izumo during the medieval period? The next section will shed light on this question.

Susanoo's Rise and Fall in Medieval Izumo

If one surveys the medieval mythology that was produced at Izumo Shrine, the first thing that springs to the eye is Susanoo's position as unquestioned paramount deity of Izumo Province. While the *Kojiki*, the *Izumo fudoki*, and (to a lesser extent) the *Nihon shoki* depict Susanoo's descendant Ōkuninushi as the region's culture hero who completed the task of "creating the land" and was rewarded with a glamorous palace for his cession of the land to Amaterasu's descendants, and while the *Izumo fudoki* ascribes the task of pulling land across the ocean to enlarge Izumo to the deity Yatsuka Mizuomitsuno 八束水臣津野 (see below), in Izumo's medieval mythology Susanoo usurps those two deities' roles and emerges as the Izumo Shrine's main deity. At the same time, the shrine's increasing institutional fusion with nearby Gakuenji, the major Tendai temple in the province, resulted in Susanoo's absorption into a fundamentally Buddhist worldview. In addition, numerous medieval myths and theories attempted to pinpoint the site of Susanoo's retreat to Ne no Kuni and thus reinforced his association with death.

Susanoo as Izumo's Paramount Deity

According to a short text written by the head priest of Izumo Shrine in 1336,

> The Great Illuminating God (*daimyōjin*) enshrined at this shrine is Susanoo, the son of Izanagi and Izanami, the younger brother of Amaterasu, and the god of All under Heaven (*tenka*). … He built a high shrine to protect the Four Seas; he also uses it to hide himself in the Floating Mountain (*furō-san*). (*Kokusō Izumo Noritoki gejō dodai utsushi* 国造出雲孝時解状土代写; quoted in Zhong 2016: 20)

Yijiang Zhong (2016: 22) emphasizes Susanoo's central role in the Izumo Shrine's medieval ritual calendar as a powerful deity who was invoked in several yearly ceremonies to secure "every step of the yearly agricultural cycle" and who was believed to command the authority to summon all gods to Izumo Shrine once a year.

The Buddhist overtones in the text quoted above are rather subdued, as is to be expected from a text composed by a shrine's head priest who wanted to defend his vested rights against the encroachment of Buddhist clergy. Only the term "Floating Mountain" (Furōsan 浮浪山) suggests that the institutional and doctrinal fusion with Gakuenji was already underway at this point in history. The significance of this term becomes clear if one takes a look at the oldest extant version of Gakuenji's founding legend, recorded in the *Gakuenji shūtora kanjin jōan* 鰐淵寺衆徒等勧進状案 (Draft for Temple Solicitation by the Priesthood of Gakuenji; 1254). According to this text, the mountain on which the temple was erected was actually a broken-off part of the famous Indian Vulture Peak Mountain (Skt. Gṛdhrakūṭa, Jap. Ryōjusen 霊鷲山), where Śākyamuni is said to have taught the *dharma* (Deeg 2005: 552). A part of this mountain, the text asserts, floated over the ocean till it reached Japan. Thus, it became called Furōsan—Floating Mountain (Yamamoto 2010: 267). To contemporaneous readers, the term Furōsan probably called this legend to mind. It is therefore significant that the Grand Shrine's head priest chose this term rather than one of the other names by which the mountain was known (or rather than not mentioning the mountain at all).

As the associations between the temple and the Grand Shrine deepened in the following centuries, their founding legends merged. This process can be traced in a number of texts from the thirteenth to the sixteenth century (cf. Izumo Yayoi no Mori Hakubutsukan 2013: 4–7). The closest ties between the two religious centers existed during the sixteenth century, when warlord Amago

Tsunehisa 尼子経久 (1458–1541) ruled over Izumo Province. In order to consolidate his own power base, Tsunehisa consistently endeavored to weaken the influence of the Grand Shrine's head priests. Not only was the head priest family descended from the former provincial rulers of Izumo, but the shrine also possessed significant land holdings and thus constituted a major political power that threatened to undermine Tsunehisa's authority in the region. To weaken the head priests' position, Tsunehisa promoted the buddhification of Izumo Grand Shrine. In the early sixteenth century, he ordered the construction of several Buddhist buildings within the shrine's precincts and sponsored Buddhist rituals to be held there by priests of Gakuenji. Moreover, he strengthened the position of the so-called *hongan* 本願, Buddhist monks who had originally been hired by the head priests to solicit donations. In this way, the head priests' authority was increasingly undermined and the institutional fusion with the Gakuenji proceeded to such an extent that Gakuenji was even referred to as Izumo Taisha's 出雲大社 "shrine temple" (*jingūji* 神宮寺) (Inoue 2013: 35; Zhong 2016: 23–5, 50).

The close ties between the two religious centers are also reflected in a founding legend of Gakuenji dating from 1570–3 (Saitō 2012: 104):

> This temple [Gakuenji] was constructed by Susanoo when he stopped a floating land that broke off from the northeast[5] corner of Gṛdhrakūṭa Hill. It is then known as Floating Mountain (*furō-san*). He built a shrine at its foot to nurture life and made it the place for all gods to descend to; he built a shrine on the top to accommodate the original essence of divinity and marked off a realm for the Buddha to manifest in all forms … As such, Kizuki and Gakuen are but one; the Way of the Buddha and the Way of the Gods never alienate from one other. (*Gakuen jisō nanigashi shojō dankan* 鰐淵寺僧某書状断簡; modified from Zhong 2016: 20)

Kizuki 杵築 is the old name of Izumo Taisha. The text thus equates Gakuenji and the Grand Shrine. The detail that the floating mountain broke off from the *northeast* corner of Vulture Peak is significant. The northeast corresponds to the Demon Gate, a direction that calls for special spiritual protection. The Tendai head temple Enryakuji, situated on Mount Hiei 比叡 to the northeast of the imperial palace, fulfilled this function for the imperial family (Faure 2016a: 43–4). The directional symbolism thus links Gakuenji and Izumo Taisha to Enryakuji and the Tendai school. Another remarkable point is that Susanoo affixes the floating mountain to the headland of Shimane, thus turning it into the western-most portion of the Shimane peninsula in a way remarkably similar to the land-pulling myth recorded in the *Izumo fudoki* (Takioto 2001: 163). According to this ancient tale, the deity Yatsuka Mizuomitsuno pulled portions of land from Silla and other regions across the ocean and affixed them to Izumo, thus creating the Shimane peninsula (IF: 134–9).

A further version of this legend from 1575 takes up another motif from the *Izumo fudoki*:

> Long ago, in the Age of the Gods, the northeastern part of Vulture Peak in India broke off and was carried by the blue waves of the boundless sea to this land of the sun in the eastern sea. At that time Susanoo no Mikoto, graciously knowing of its origin, took a pestle, affixed the mountain, and left his trace at its foot. Therefore, the mountain is called Furōsan Gakuenji and the shrine is called Kizuki Shrine. (*Hondō saikō kanjin chō* 本堂再興勧進帳; quoted in Yamamoto 2010: 268)

This version was obviously inspired by a further myth contained in the *Izumo fudoki*. In the section on the township of Kizuki it says:

> After Yatsuka Mizuomitsuno no Mikoto had performed the Land-Pulling, all of the august deities assembled and pounded the ground with a pestle (*kizuki* [*tamahiki*]) in order to build a palace for the great deity who created the earth (*ame no shita tsukurashishi ōkami* 所造天下大神). For this reason, [the place] is called Kizuki. (IF: 210/211)

In the *Izumo fudoki*, the appellation "great deity who created the earth" refers to Ōkuninushi (Aoki 1997: 18). It is therefore commonly believed that Ōkuninushi, rather than Susanoo, was worshiped at the Kizuki Shrine in ancient times.[6] But in the myths and legends of medieval Izumo, Susanoo took over the roles of the two major deities of the region: Yatsuka Mizuomitsuno and Ōkuninushi. At the same time, Susanoo's connection to the afterworld was emphasized through several tales dealing with the site of his grave.

Susanoo's Grave

The interest in Susanoo's grave, that is, the site of his entry into the afterworld in medieval Izumo is probably related to Susanoo's and Izumo's connection to Ne no Kuni and Yomotsu Kuni in both the ancient court chronicles and the *Izumo fudoki*. As mentioned in the preceding chapter, one variant of the *Nihon shoki* and the *Sendai kuji hongi* relate that Susanoo entered Ne no Kuni via the "peak of Kumanari." While a later passage in the *Nihon shoki* associates this toponym with the Korean peninsula, Inbe Masamichi 忌部正通 (life dates unknown) suggests another location in his work *Jindaikan kuketsu* 神代巻口訣 (Secret Transmissions on the Divine Age Fascicles; 1367): "The peak of Kumanari is in Izumo Province" (NSC, vol. 2: 82).

While Masamichi does not specify the mountain's exact location in Izumo, later thinkers identified the site with Furōsan, the site of Gakuenji. An alternate name for this mountain, which was first attested in 1151–3, is Wanibuchi 鰐淵 Mountain.[7] The already mentioned thirteenth-century *Gakuenji shūtora kanjin jōan* explains this name—from which the name Gakuenji is derived (*gakuen* being the Sino-Japanese reading for the same Chinese characters)—thus: when the temple's founder Chishun 智春 (trad. sixth century) accidentally dropped a bowl into a pool on said mountain, a shark (*wani*)[8] appeared and restored it to him; hence the pool came to be called "shark pool" (*wanibuchi*) (Izumo Yayoi no Mori Hakubutsukan 2013: 5). Probably in order to identify this mountain with the *Nihon shoki*'s peak of Kumanari, medieval religious thinkers started to impose the reading *waninari* on the mountain mentioned in the ancient court chronicle.[9] This conclusion is suggested by an entry on Gakuenji recorded in the *Un'yōshi* 雲陽誌 (Record of Sun and Cloud), a topography of the Izumo region compiled by Kurosawa Nagahisa 黒沢長尚 (?–1737) under the auspices of the lord of Matsue domain in 1717:

> The summit of Hirō 飛瀧 Shrine is called peak of Waninari. It is one of the eight lotus petals, also called Mount Meru (Jap. Misen彌山).[10] It is said that Susanoo no Mikoto is reverently interred here. In the sacred scripture (*shinsho* 神書) [= *Nihon shoki*] it is also recorded that he divinely passed away on the peak of Waninari. Therefore, Susanoo no Mikoto is worshiped on the peak of the mountain and venerated as Matarajin 摩多羅神. (UYS IX: 274)

As we will see below, the deity Matarajin played an important role in Tendai esotericism. His equation with Susanoo thus allows us to situate this legend in the context of the Sengoku-period amalgamation of Izumo Taisha and Gakuenji.[11]

A further shrine that played an important role in this context is the Hinomisaki 日御碕 Shrine, situated about 10 kilometers to the north of Izumo Grand Shrine. In the sixteenth century, this shrine expanded its influence with the support of Amago Tsunehisa, who used the shrine to counterbalance Izumo Grand Shrine's influence (Zhong 2016: 23). A record of this shrine, which probably dates from the early Edo period, states:

This shrine is [situated at] the north-western border of the land of Yamato. It is also [situated at the north-western border] of this province [i.e., Izumo]. This is the outermost border of *yin* and *yang*, the sacred ground from where everything originates. Susanoo no Mikoto was born in the land of *yin*. Therefore, he became a god of *yang*. The place from where he governs the world is also a site of extreme *yin*. When he had finished his meritorious work, he made this site his hidden palace {There is the mystery of the Hidden Mound}. It is also said that Ne no Kuni is the land of the first zodiac sign (*ne no kuni* 子国). This means that all things originate from there. (*Hinomisaki ryōhonsha narabi shaji enso no koto* 日御碕両本社並社司遠祖事; quoted in Saitō 2012: 115)

This text absorbs Susanoo into *yin-yang* philosophy and emphasizes the significance of Izumo's geographical position in relation to Yamato (as suggested by Saigō) from a *yin-yang* perspective. Moreover, it seems to acknowledge the location of Ne no Kuni in Izumo. The term "hidden palace" brings to mind the site of Izanaki's final retreat on the island of Awaji, quoted in the preceding chapter, as well as Ōkuninushi's government over "hidden matters" after his withdrawal from the world. Hence, it probably refers to Susanoo's grave or the site of his entry to Ne no Kuni.

The gloss "There is the mystery of the Hidden Mound" is inserted in smaller script in the text. Again, it is the *Un'yōshi* that sheds light on this comment. In the section on Hinomisaki, this work contains the following short entry: "Hiki 秘基 Shrine: Is called Hidden Mound. There is a fence but no shrine" (UYS X: 315). The same section contains an entry titled "Divine Emblem Stone" (*shinmonseki* 神紋石) partly reproduced below:

On Hinomisaki Mountain in Izumo Province there is a stone with an oak leaf emblem. Long ago, in the Age of Gods, [Susanoo], having pacified the land, ascended to the peak of Waninari. He used an oak leaf to make a divination, saying: "I want to reside at the place where this oak leaf alights." At last [the leaf] was blown away by the wind and alighted on this site. (UYS X: 314)

The *Un'yōshi*'s author equates Hinomisaki Mountain with the peak of Waninari. He also provides the following alternate names: Mount Yakumo 八雲, Mount Izumo, Mount Furō 不老, Snake Mountain, Miyama, and Uka no Yama 宇迦能山 (UYS X: 301). The last of these names is mentioned in the *Kojiki* (KJK I: 84/85) and calls to mind the following passage from the entry on the Township of Uka 宇賀, which is recorded in the *Izumo fudoki*'s section on Izumo District:

On the northern seashore there is a ridge called Ridge of Nazuki 脳礒. Its height is about ten *shaku* [*c.* 3.03 meters]. On the top, pine trees grow so profusely that [their branches] touch the ridge. It looks as though the villagers were walking to and from the cliff at dawn and dusk and the branches of the trees resemble humans clambering up the cliff. On the west side of the cliff, there is a cavern. Its height and breadth are six *shaku* [*c.* 1.8 meters]. Inside the cavern there is an opening. One cannot enter there, and no one knows how deep it is. If one approaches this cavern in a dream, one will surely die. Therefore, from ancient times to the present the local people have called it the Slope of Yomi or the Cavern of Yomi. (IF: 212/213)

Although Susanoo is not mentioned in this passage, it seems possible that this motif from the *Izumo fudoki*, like so many others, was associated with the deity in the religious discourse of medieval Izumo. While Susanoo's usurpation of Yatsuka Mizuomitsuno and Ōkuninushi's roles in medieval mythology resulted in his rise to prominence as the paramount deity of Izumo Province, the numerous tales and theories about the site of Susanoo's grave or his entry to Ne no Kuni reinforced his and Izumo's association with realms of the dead (Yamamoto 2010: 275). This second aspect accords well with Susanoo's role as epidemic deity in Gion belief discussed above. There is some evidence that this is not a coincidence. As mentioned at the outset of this chapter, the Gion complex was integrated into the Tendai network as a subtemple of Enryakuji during the tenth century. Gakuenji, on the other hand, was the first branch temple (*matsuji* 末寺) of Enryakuji. Several wooden statues of Gozu Tennō are preserved at Gakuenji, attesting to the presence of a Gozu Tennō cult at the temple, though no details are known. What is known is that Matarajin, a secret Buddha of the Tendai school, was worshiped at Gakuenji's Jōgyōdō 常行堂 (Hall of the Walking Meditation Practice) (Kim 2014: 194–6). As we have already seen in one example above, the Gakuenji's institutional ties with Enryakuji resulted in a fusion of Susanoo and Matarajin. This suggests that Susanoo's transformation into an epidemic deity associated with death took place within the framework of Tendai thought.

Susanoo's Demotion at Izumo Shrine

The Tendai network in Izumo was dealt a serious blow, however, when in the mid-seventeenth century Ōkuninushi was "reinstated" as the main deity worshiped at Izumo Shrine. The elevation of Ōkuninushi was part of shrine priests' deliberate effort to dissociate themselves from Gakuenji and to "purify" the shrine and its ritual practices from Buddhist elements. This process was set in motion with the appointment of Matsudaira Naomasa 松平直政 (1601–1666) as lord of

Matsue domain in 1638. In the same year, Naomasa issued a code requiring the Izumo Shrine to revive the practices of old Shintō and to repair and rebuild shrine buildings (Zhong 2016: 39). For centuries, the shrine's main sanctuary had existed only in the form a "provisional hall" (*karidono* 仮殿), so the priests petitioned Naomasa for funds to rebuild the main hall. Naomasa, in turn, asked the bakufu for assistance. For both Naomasa and the bakufu the sponsorship of one of the most prestigious shrines in the country provided an opportunity to legitimate and consolidate their rule. Thus, in 1661 the shrine was informed of the bakufu's sponsorship of the rebuilding project (Scheid 2003: 215; Zhong 2016: 40–1).

As Yijiang Zhong (2016: 17–18) has shown, Kurosawa Sekisai 黒沢石斎 (1612–1678), the domainal Confucianist (*hanju*) employed by Naomasa, played an important role in this process. During a visit to Izumo Shrine in 1653, Sekisai expressed his disappointment about the countless Buddhist buildings dotting the shrine's precincts. These included a Dainichi Hall, a three-story pagoda, and a temple bell. Like his teacher, the bakufu Confucianist Hayashi Razan, Sekisai was opposed to all forms of Buddhist-Shintō combinatory practices and thus strove for Izumo Shrine's purification from Buddhist elements.

The rebuilding of the main sanctuary required the performance of a complicated inauguration ceremony. Since the last such ceremony had occurred centuries earlier, many open questions had to be addressed. The most important of these was what deity was enshrined at Izumo Shrine. While medieval founding legends of Izumo Shrine and Gakuenji identified Susanoo as the shrine's main deity, the *Nihon shoki* and the *Izumo fudoki* state that the shrine was built for Ōnamuji (Ōkuninushi) (cf. Stockdale 2013: 255–6). Thus, even Razan, who strove for the revival of a pre-Buddhist Shintō, was uncertain which deity was originally enshrined at Izumo Shrine. In his *Honchō jinja kō* 本朝神社考 (A Study of Shrines in the Realm; date unknown), he suggests that Susanoo and Ōkuninushi were coenshrined at the Grand Shrine (Zhong 2016: 31–2). Bernhard Scheid (2003: 216) rightly points out that the real issue at stake was "whether the inauguration ceremonies should be conducted according to the Buddhist *engi* (which meant combinatory rituals, such as reading sutras to the kami), or according to ancient shrine manuals."

In 1661, the shrine priests announced their decision to rebuild the main sanctuary according to the slogan "Restore One-and-Only Shintō" (*yuiitsu shintō saikō* 唯一神道再興). While *yuiitsu* Shintō usually signifies a special school of Shintō founded by Yoshida Kanetomo 吉田兼倶 (1435–1511), better known as Yoshida Shintō (more on this below), in this instance it probably refers to allegedly "pure" pre-Buddhist practice (Scheid 2003: 216–17). The architectural plans for the new shrine included the removal of Buddhist elements. To achieve this goal, the head priest removed the *hongan* from their position as mediators between the shrine and sponsors and sent one member of each branch of the head priest family to Edo to directly negotiate with the bakufu. The bakufu's Temple and Shrine Magistrate (*jisha bugyō* 寺社奉行) Inoue Masatoshi 井上正利 (1606–1675) was a disciple of the neo-Confucian scholar Yamazaki Ansai 山崎闇斎 (1619–1682), who—like Razan—attempted a synthesis of neo-Confucianism and Shintō and was thus opposed to Shintō-Buddhist combinatory practices. In Ansai's synthesis, Ōkuninushi played a prominent role. When the priests assured Masatoshi that none other than Ōkuninushi was to be enshrined in the new main sanctuary, the magistrate approved the considerable funds for the rebuilding project (Zhong 2016: 41-3).

Through their negotiations with the domain and the bakufu, the shrine priests regained their autonomy from Gakuenji and support for their agenda of removing Buddhist elements from the shrine precincts and its ritual practice. In 1664 the priests began to dismantle Buddhist buildings and to transfer Buddhist treasures to nearby temples. In 1666, Gakuenji's monks were notified that they would no longer be allowed to practice Buddhist rituals at the shrine. In 1667, the "purification" of Izumo Shrine from Buddhist elements was completed with the enshrinement of Ōkuninushi in the new main sanctuary (Zhong 2016: 43-6). In this way, Susanoo was replaced by Ōkuninushi as the paramount deity of Izumo and Izumo Shrine stopped being a part of the mythicoritual Tendai network.

Susanoo's Inclusion in the Tendai Network

The development in Izumo Province was exceptional, however. In other parts of the country, the combinatory practices and doctrines of Tendai Buddhism continued to flourish throughout the early modern period. Within this mythicoritual network, Susanoo was associated with several allegedly foreign epidemic deities such as the already mentioned Matarajin, Sekizan Myōjin 赤山明神, or Shinra Myōjin 新羅明神. These associations, it will be argued in the following section, reinforced the perception of Susanoo as a foreign deity connected to disease and death.

Matarajin, Sekizan Myōjin, and Shinra Myōjin are so similar in character and so closely associated through shared narratives that it has been suggested they are in fact multiple names for a single deity (Faure 2016a: 305; Kawamura

2017: 89-90). Like Gozu Tennō, they are commonly regarded as foreign deities (*ijin*). But, in this case, a non-Japanese prototype can be identified on whom these deities seem to have been modeled. Bernard Faure (2016a: 309, 318) has shown that all three deities are avatars of the Chinese deity Taishan Fujun 泰山府君 (Jap. Taizan Fukun), a Daoist version of King Yama (Jap. Enra-ō), ruler of the underworld. This distinguishes them from Gozu Tennō, who seems to have been invented in Japan based on mythical ideas surrounding ox-head sandalwood (Skt. *gośīrṣa candana*; Jap. *gozu sendan* 牛頭栴檀), a sacred wood that was believed to grow on a mountain on the mythical continent of Uttarakuru, said to be shaped like the head of a cow. This wood was believed to be impervious to fire and to possess curative qualities (Eitel [1904] 1970: 60).[12] The three deities discussed in this section, on the other hand, were all thought to have been brought to Japan by prominent Tendai monks such as Ennin 円仁 (794–864), Enchin 円珍 (814–891), or the Tendai school's founder Saichō 最澄 (767–822) on their return trips from China.

Matarajin: God of Obstacles and Guardian of the Back Door

Matarajin, who was associated with Susanoo at Gakuenji, is surely the most complex and multifaceted member of the triad. His name is thought to derive from *mātarah*, the Sanskrit word for "mothers" and thus links him to the Indic deities of that name (Iyanaga 2002: 570–1). The Mothers are goddesses that protect the fetus inside the womb if placated properly (which means that they must be placated in order not to attack the fetus). This associates Matarajin with disease (Faure 2016a: 310; Kawamura 2017: 43–5).

Matarajin's aspect as epidemic deity comes to the fore in the Kōryūji's 広隆寺 Ox Festival, traditionally held on the twelfth day of the ninth month according to the lunar calendar (or in modern times, on October 12) in the Uzumasa 太秦 district of Kyoto. On the festival night, a priest impersonates Matarajin, wearing a white mask and white robes. The priest rides on a black ox and is flanked by four monks disguised as demons. The priest then reads a ritual prayer aimed at the elimination of diseases and other calamities and retreats to the Jōgyōdō. Both his role as epidemic deity and his association with the ox connect Matarajin with Gozu Tennō (Kim 2014: 206–8). A remarkable point about the Kōryūji's Ox Festival is its carnivalesque nature. The priest impersonating Matarajin becomes the victim of the bystanders' jokes and insults, rather than being venerated. Some depictions, moreover, show him riding the ox backward (Kawamura 2017: 23–8). This example of "symbolic inversion" links Matarajin to Susanoo, who reversely flayed a horse and principally acted contrary to expected behavior in his sister's realm (see Chapter 3). Like Susanoo, Matarajin is fundamentally "a kind of trickster figure" (Faure 2016a: 324).

It is not coincidental that after reading the ritual prayer, the priest impersonating Matarajin retreats to the Jōgyōdō, since one of the deity's primary functions in the Shingon and the Tendai schools was the protection of the *nenbutsu* 念仏 practice, which in Tendai was performed at the Jōgyōdō. Therefore, Matarajin was enshrined at the back door (*ushirodo* 後戸) of the Jōgyōdō in Tendai monasteries, that is, behind the main altar or at the northeastern corner (corresponding to the Demon Gate) of the hall. This suggests Matarajin's own demonic nature before being placated and becoming a protector against demons (Faure 2016a: 318–19).

While not mentioning Matarajin's name, the famous Noh playwright Zeami Motokiyo 世阿弥元清 (c. 1363–c. 1443) in his *Fūshi kaden* 風姿花伝 (Transmission of the Flower of Acting Style; c. 1400) associates the rituals performed at the back door with the origins of *sarugaku* 申楽,[13] which he traces back to Jetavana. When Śākyamuni wanted to teach the *dharma* there, his adversary Devadatta brought ten thousand heretics, who shouted and danced around to obstruct the dissemination of the Buddha's teachings. Some of Śākyamuni's disciples managed to lure the heretics to the monastery's back door by playing drums and flutes, thus enabling Śākyamuni to preach without any obstruction. This, according to Zeami, was the beginning of *sarugaku* (Kawamura 2017: 7–8).

This brings us to another aspect of Matarajin, namely his role as a patron of the performing arts. In pictorial representations, Matarajin is normally flanked by two young acolytes, one of whom is beating a drum, while the other is dancing wildly. Probably, it is this image that led to Matarajin's association with performing arts. In the *sarugaku* tradition, Matarajin became linked to the figure of Okina 翁 (Old Man), a symbol of longevity and wealth that was also linked to Shinra Myōjin (Faure 2016a: 303). Hata no Kawakatsu 秦川勝 (fl. seventh century), the founder of the Hata 秦 lineage, is said to have started the *sarugaku* tradition in Japan. The Hata are thought to have come to Japan from Silla, and Matarajin is connected to this lineage as well. Kōryūji, the site of Matarajin's Ox Festival, was in fact founded by none other than Kawakatsu (Kawamura 2017: 11–14). Sujung Kim (2014: 205–6) suggests that the threatening image of Silla during the Nara and early Heian periods resulted in the association of Silla deities (such as Matarajin or Shinra Myōjin) with disease.

What connects Matarajin most obviously with Shinra Myōjin and Sekizan Myōjin is the legend of his encounter with the Tendai master Ennin. According to the *Keiran shūyōshū* 渓嵐拾葉集 (Collection of Leaves Gathered in a Misty Valley; c. 1311–1347):

> When the great teacher Jikaku [Ennin] returned from China [in 847] to transmit the ritual for the extended vocalized *nenbutsu*, on his ship he heard a voice in the empty sky, which told him: "My name is Matarajin, and I am a god of obstacles (*shōgejin* 障礙神). Those who do not worship me will not be able to attain rebirth [in the Pure Land]." Consequently, Matarajin was enshrined in the Constantly Walking Samadhi Hall (Jōgyō-zanmai-dō). (Quoted in Faure 2016a: 304)

As a self-proclaimed god of obstacles, Matarajin shares the ambiguous character of epidemic deities like Gozu Tennō or Mutō Tenjin in that he can either obstruct peoples' attainment of rebirth or—once properly worshiped—can protect the *nenbutsu*, that is, the very ritual practice that enables rebirth in the Pure Land (Kawamura 2017: 191). Faure (2016a: 303) therefore fittingly describes Matarajin as a "typical liminal deity … standing on the threshold between life and death"—a characterization that again links him to Susanoo.

Other medieval texts claim that Matarajin first appeared to Saichō himself either on his return trip to Japan, on Mount Tiantong in Shandong, or on Mount Tiantai. His strong connection to China and to Tendai masters who visited China links Matarajin to two further tutelary deities in Tendai Buddhism, namely Sekizan Myōjin and Shinra Myōjin.

The Bright God from Chishan and the Bright God from Silla

According to the *Sekizan daimyōjin engi* (On the Origin of Sekizan Daimyōjin; 948), it was Sekizan Myōjin, rather than Matarajin, that appeared to Ennin on his return voyage to Japan. During a storm, the text tells us, the deity appeared in the form of an old man. With Sekizan Myōjin's protection, the Tendai master was able to return safely to Japan. Ennin's official biography does not mention the name Sekizan Myōjin. It states, however, that in 838 he prayed to a mountain god at Chishan 赤山 in Shandong Province. Since Sekizan Myōjin's name translates to "Bright God of Chishan," it seems likely that the two passages refer to the same deity. Possibly a generic term referring to a deity of Chishan was turned into the proper name Sekizan Myōjin after Ennin's death (Kawamura 2017: 111). Ennin pledged to build a temple for this deity upon his return to Japan. The fulfilment of this pledge was left to Ennin's disciples, who built Sekizan Zen'in 赤山禅院 at the western foot of Mount Hiei in 888 (Kim 2020: 38–9). The *Shintōshū* 神道集 (Collection of Shintō [Tales]; fourteenth century) identifies Sekizan Myōjin with Susanoo's alter ego Gozu Tennō (Kawamura 2017: 90). Sekizan Myōjin's demonic character is emphasized by the Sekizan Zen'in's location on the northeastern outskirts of the capital, that is, at the Demon Gate, as well as through the color red, which is usually associated with pestilence deities: Sekizan Myōjin is commonly depicted wearing a red dress and the toponym Chishan (Sekizan) in his name means "red mountain" (Faure 2016a: 312–13).

The alleged site of Sekizan Myōjin's origin, the monastery Fahua yuan 法華院 at Chishan, where Ennin had stayed for an extended period of time during his sojourn in China, was an enclave of Silla merchants and a mecca for Silla monks. The region was under the political control of the powerful merchant Chang Pogo 張保皐 (fl. ninth century), who organized trade between Chishan port in China, Chŏnghaejin 清海鎮 in Silla, and Dazaifu 太宰府 in Japan. The monastery itself was at times called "Silla monastery." Ennin had close ties with Silla merchants and monks during his stay there (Kawamura 2017: 96, 108–9; Kim 2020: 37–8).

In Japan, Sekizan Myōjin rose to prominence during the feud between the Sanmon 山門 School and the Jimon 寺門 School of Tendai Buddhism. The Jimon, based at Onjōji 園城寺 (Miidera 三井寺) in Ōmi Province, demanded its own ordination platform in order to become independent from the Sanmon with its center at Enryakuji on Mount Hiei. The Sanmon used all its influence to prevent this from happening. The dispute reached a climax in 993, when a group of Jimon monks attacked the Sekizan Zen'in, destroying various religious icons (Kim 2020: 19). In the course of this sectarian rivalry, Sekizan Myōjin came to be viewed as the tutelary deity of the Sanmon branch, whereas the Jimon monks, who saw themselves as followers of Enchin, venerated Shinra Myōjin as their paramount deity.

The legend of Shinra Myōjin's origin is almost identical to that of Sekizan Myōjin, just with different protagonists. In the *Onjōji ryūge-e engi* 園城寺龍華会縁起 (Origin of the Onjōji Assembly under the Dragon-Flower Tree; 1062) and several later sources, we are told that Shinra Myōjin appeared on Enchin's boat, when the Tendai master returned from Tang China to Japan, and promised to protect Enchin's practice of Buddhism until the arrival of the Buddha Maitreya (Kim 2020: 26–7). Shinra Myōjin means "Bright God of Silla." Considering Sekizan Myōjin's connection to Silla monks and the similarity of the two deities' origin legends, it seems likely that both names originally referred to the same deity differing only in the fact that one was associated with Ennin and the other with Enchin (Kawamura 2017: 111).

But after the schism between the Sanmon and Jimon branches, the two deities were transformed into bitter rivals symbolizing their respective factions. In popular tales disseminated by Jimon and Sanmon followers, both Shinra Myōjin and Sekizan Myōjin intervened in the dispute about an ordination platform for the Jimon branch. According to one such story, after Emperor Shirakawa 白河 (1053–1129; r. 1072–1086) had promised Onjōji an independent ordination platform, the intimidating figure of Sekizan Myōjin carrying bow and arrow appeared to him in a dream, causing him to deny the Jimon's request. According to another legend, Shinra Myōjin cursed Emperor Nijō 二条 (1143–1165; r. 1158–1165), who had taken the Sanmon's side. The deity voiced his discontent with the emperor and Nijō died shortly afterward (Kim 2020: 51–3). In this episode, Shinra Myōjin is portrayed as a typical vengeful deity (*tatarigami* 祟り神), an aspect that links him to Gozu Tennō and Matarajin.

By the thirteenth century, Shinra Myōjin was associated with Susanoo in more direct ways. The *Onjōji denki* 園城寺伝記 (Record of Onjōji; fourteenth century) explains that Shinra Myōjin manifested himself as Susanoo in Japan:

> From the Hi River in Izumo he went to Soshimori in Silla. There he supported the king and also preached to both the monks and the laity. Afterwards, in the twelfth year of the Tang Emperor Dazhong's reign (857), the deity appeared to Enchin on the boat during his return trip to Japan and became a protector deity of Miidera. (Slightly modified from Kim 2020: 96–7)

From the toponym Soshimori, we can infer that the two deities' association is based on the *Nihon shoki*'s account of Susanoo's sojourn to Silla. The *Onjōji denki* also foreshadows the imperialistic use to which Susanoo would be put five centuries later, by stating that Shinra Myōjin became a king of Silla "to display Japan's power" (quoted in Kim 2020: 94).

In his *Hyakushu kashō* 百首歌抄 (Selection of One Hundred Poems, 1468), Yoshida Kanekuni 吉田兼邦 (fl. late Muromachi period) elaborates on the *Onjōji denki*'s equation of Susanoo and Shinra Myōjin. According to this treatise, Susanoo, wearing a straw hat and a straw coat against the rain, arrived in Silla after being banished to hell (*jigoku*) by the myriad deities. Here he was accommodated by a person called Soshimori. Susanoo stayed in Silla and later appeared there to Enchin in the shape of an old man. He introduced himself as a protector of the *dharma* and accompanied Enchin to Japan, where he was enshrined at Onjōji (Yagi 2002: 104). This fascinating treatise connects the origin legend of Shinra Myōjin not only to the *Nihon shoki*'s account of Susanoo's sojourn in Silla, as the

Onjōji denki had done, but also to Susanoo's banishment from the Plain of High Heaven and his subsequent search for shelter in the rain (Yamamoto 2010: 265–6). Interestingly, Kanekuni identifies Soshimori as the name of a person rather than a place. Probably, he was influenced by the *Shaku Nihongi*'s fusion of the two wandering deities Susanoo and Mutō and used Soshimori to replace the figure of Somin Shōrai. It seems likely that, as a member of the Urabe lineage, Kanekuni had access to the *Shaku Nihongi*.[14] Significantly, Kanekuni equates Silla with hell. He reinforces Susanoo's association with death even more strongly by claiming that one of the deity's two souls ascended to heaven, turning into Taishan Fujun, while the other sank down into earth, becoming the king of the underworld Yama. The latter soul then appeared to Enchin in the form of Shinra Myōjin, thus linking Silla to the underworld (Yagi 2002: 106, 110).

Shinra Myōjin's association with Susanoo was also emphasized through ritual. During the Shinra Myōjin festival held in 1210, the narrative of Susanoo was enacted and eight youths portraying Susanoo as well as eight youths representing his wife Kushiinada Hime took part in the parade. Already at the first festival held in 1052, swords representing the weapon Susanoo had used to slay the eight-headed serpent were offered to Shinra Myōjin (Kim 2020: 69).

Through this association, both Susanoo's connection to Silla and his sinister side became emphasized. Besides the aspect of a wrathful deity, Shinra Myōjin was regarded as a pestilence deity who even ruled over his own hell (Kim 2014: 189). His equation with Susanoo thus reinforced the latter deity's connection to the realm of the dead. During an epidemic in 1084, the court decided to pray to Shinra Myōjin. After reporting the success of the prayer (the epidemic immediately stopped), the *Jimon denki horoku* 寺門伝記補録 (Complementary Record of the Jimon; 1394–1427) notes that "Shinra Myōjin is none other than Susanoo. Therefore, the talisman of 'Somin Shōrai' originated in the Shinra Myōjin shrine" (Kim 2014: 191). This passage shows the extent to which the figures of Susanoo, Shinra Myōjin, and Gozu Tennō (or, more precisely, Mutō Tenjin) had become entangled in the Jimon tradition by the early fifteenth century. It also reinforces the idea of Silla as the source of epidemics (cf. Kim 2020: 95–7).

Susanoo's Role in Yoshida Shintō

Not only did the mythicoritual network that associated Susanoo with foreign deities such as Gozu Tennō, Shinra Myōjin, or Matarajin remain influential throughout the medieval and early modern periods, it even spread beyond the Tendai school and its associated temples and shrines. One factor that contributed to this development was Yoshida Shintō's adoption of substantial parts of Tendai doctrine. Yoshida Kanetomo's thought was framed by his reinterpretation of the Buddhist *sangoku* worldview.[15] According to this worldview, Japan was the third and least important Buddhist center beside India and China since it was spatially remote from the site of Buddhism's origin and temporally late to receive its teachings. Kanetomo turned the hierarchy between the three countries on its head by proposing the primacy of Shintō over Buddhism (India) and Confucianism (China). To endow his claim with greater authority, he put the following words into the mouth of the great Japanese benefactor of Buddhism Shōtoku Taishi:

> Japan produced the seed, China produced the branches and leaves, India produced the flowers and fruit. Buddhism is the fruit, Confucianism is the leaves, and Shinto is the trunk and the roots. Buddhism and Confucianism are only secondary products of Shinto. Leaves and fruit merely indicate the presence of the trunk and roots; flowers and fruit fall and return to the roots. Buddhism came east only to reveal clearly that our nation is the trunk and roots of these three nations. (Grapard 1992b: 153)

This way of thinking also affected Yoshida Shintō's take on the *honji suijaku* paradigm. The Japanese *kami* were now perceived as primary, while the Buddhist divinities were nothing more than their traces (Scheid 2001: 244–5, 354). According to Yoshida doctrine, the *kami* had created all countries and all teachings (Hardacre 2017: 252). While this interpretation moved Japan from the margin to the center of the universe, it, in large part, took over the mythicoreligious network elaborated within medieval Japanese Buddhism. As the preceding discussion of combinatory teachings in Tendai has demonstrated, this network was much too complex to allow for easy hierarchization between the various deities it connected and could therefore be reconciled with Yoshida Shintō's Japanocentric worldview without major modifications.

In a 1481 lecture on the *Nihon shoki*, Kanetomo argued that Mutō Tenjin[16] and Gozu Tennō were just foreign names under which Susanoo was venerated at Gion Shrine. These foreign names were used, Kanetomo explains, since the capital was frequently ravaged by epidemics (NSC, vol. 3: 81). This explanation reinforces Susanoo's role as a pestilence deity and the association of epidemics with foreign countries. Since Kanetomo, like Kanefumi and Kanekata, was a member of the Urabe (Yoshida) lineage, it is not surprising that he was influenced by the interpretations they put forward in *Shaku Nihongi* (and by Ichijō Kaneyoshi's elaboration thereof) (Suzuki 2019: 154).

However, in the same lecture, Kanetomo goes much further than his predecessors in identifying Susanoo not only with Gozu Tennō and Mutō Tenjin but also with Pangu, the primordial giant of Chinese mythology, from whose corpse the universe was born. Under these three names, Kanetomo maintains, Susanoo was venerated in China, while in India he was known as Konpira[17] or Matarajin. Kanetomo also identifies the Tendai deities Sekizan Myōjin and Shinra Myōjin with Susanoo (NSC, vol. 3: 36, 86–7). In his *Nihon shoki jindai maki no shō* (Selection from the *Nihon shoki*'s Divine Age Fascicles; 1536), he adds Enra-ō (the Buddhist judge of the dead) to his list of Susanoo's alter egos (NSC, vol. 3: 201). As Saitō Hideki (2012: 168–9) remarks, Kanetomo seems intent to identify every single foreign or immigrant deity with Susanoo. The crucial difference to Tendai doctrine is Susanoo's position as the undisputed center (rather than one of many traces) of this network of foreign deities in Yoshida Shintō.

Beside his almost wholesale adoption of the Tendai mythicoritual network surrounding Susanoo, Kanetomo was influenced by another aspect of Tendai philosophy. The *Nakatomi harae kunge* had categorized Susanoo, together with the other "Violent Gods of Izumo," as a "god of no-enlightenment" and contrasted him with the "gods of original enlightenment" worshiped at Ise (Teeuwen and van der Veere 1998: 50–1). Arguably, this passage translates the adversarial relationship between Susanoo and his sister Amaterasu into Buddhist terms. However, while using the term "original enlightenment" (*hongaku* 本覚), the *Nakatomi harae kunge*'s classification actually contradicts the fundamental idea of *hongaku*, according to which ignorance is the source of both evil and enlightenment (Faure 2016a: 337–8, 348). Ichijō Sanetsune in a passage recorded in the *Shaku Nihongi* expresses a deeper understanding of the Tendai notion of original enlightenment when he remarks that although Susanoo might appear like an evil deity, in fact good and bad were not divided and wrong and right were one and the same (*zen'aku funi jashō ichinyo* 善悪不二邪正一如). Kanetomo takes a similar stance by contradicting the view that Susanoo was as evil as the sun goddess was good. Without Susanoo's apparently evil deeds, he argues, Amaterasu would not have come out of the Heavenly Rock Cave and the cycle of the four seasons would not have proceeded as it ought to (NSC, vol. 3: 81).

While the concept of original enlightenment relativized Susanoo's role as mythical villain, Yoshida Shintō's doctrinal and institutional dominance throughout the early modern period made sure that the perception of Susanoo as a foreign deity with close associations to pestilence and death became established and broadly disseminated throughout Japan. As we will see in the next chapter, it continued to influence scholars and ideologues in the modern period.

6

Korea as a Realm of Death: Susanoo and Korea in Modern Discourses

At this time, wishing to meet again with his spouse, Izanaki no Mikoto followed her to Yomotsu Kuni. When he ... peered inside, he saw squirming maggots oozing from her body. ... Hereupon, the great god Izanaki proclaimed: "How horrible it is, this foul and filthy land I have been to! I should cleanse my noble body."
—*Kojiki*, fasc. I

Nowhere else, I believe, do the living walk and work so near the dead as in this land. The hills and fields are literally strewn with graves. ... The bleached bones of a nameless ancestor are kicked about on the roadside. ... A people so closely related to death are themselves more than half-dead. ... The Korean habits of life are the habits of death. ... Death presides over the peninsula.
—Nitobe Inazō 1906

During the early modern period, the Buddhist framework of medieval mythology was increasingly criticized by neo-Confucian and, later, *kokugaku* scholars. Both these emerging schools of thought strived for the restoration of a primordial, pre-Buddhist form of Shintō. Their historicist, evidentiary approach to the study of myth paved the way for the Western-inspired positivistic studies of the modern period. The early Meiji separation of *kami* and buddhas effectively erased the combinatory discourses that had characterized medieval Japanese religiosity. However, vestiges of the *honji suijaku* paradigm, such as the perception of Susanoo as a foreign deity, remained at the shrine level and reemerged in new forms. As will be discussed below, in the course of Gion Shrine's dissociation from shrine legends related to India and Buddhism, Susanoo's connection to Korea, in fact, became emphasized. This reinterpretation of Gion Shrine's founding legends entered academic circles and deeply influenced the emerging theory of common ancestry of Japanese and Koreans. In the colonial context, Korea was equated with the mythical realms of death mentioned in the ancient court chronicles. Korea's role as a source of disease and calamity, which had in the medieval period been expressed through figures such as the pestilence deity Shinra Myōjin, was thus reemphasized and placed on a new foundation. In this way, modern interpretations of the ancient Japanese myths justified the colonial order by contrasting a corrupt, impure, and sinister Korea with the shining Japanese metropole. As will become clear in this chapter, Susanoo played a central role in this process.

Confucian Exegeses of the Ancient Myths

While the Buddhist *honji suijaku* paradigm framed discussions of deities and myths in the medieval period, the early modern period saw the emergence of new exegetical paradigms that attempted to interpret Shintō within a neo-Confucian framework.[1] Neo-Confucian exegetes tended to view the ancient myths as allegorical expressions of neo-Confucian metaphysics or as embellished accounts of historical events. They habitually turned to the Confucian-style chronicle *Nihon shoki* as the ultimate source of truth. This signified a sharp rupture from the *honji suijaku* paradigm and its reliance on secret transmissions and initiations. In the discussion of Ōkuninushi's reinstatement as the Izumo Shrine's main deity, we have already encountered an instance of this new exegetical paradigm. Hayashi Razan, whose influence on the Izumo Shrine's dissociation from Gakuenji is palpable, was vehemently opposed to Buddhist interpretations of Shintō. By claiming that the *kami*, whom he regarded as shapeless entities dwelling in the mind, were the basis of heaven and earth, Razan attempted to reconcile the ancient court myths with neo-Confucian cosmology. For him, Shintō and Confucianism were not only compatible, but essentially identical. The myths were thus turned into allegorical expressions of the workings of metaphysical forces such as *ri* 理 (Ch. *li*), the principle that permeates all things; *ki* 気 (Ch. *qi*), the substance that gives form to *ri*; and *yin* and *yang*, the male and female components of *ki*. According to this neo-Confucian reading, the sexual union of Izanaki and Izanami that gave birth to the Japanese islands was an allegorical expression of the fusion of *yin* and *yang*. Razan argued that Shintō existed before Japan had a written language. In this bygone golden age, there were only divine words (Kracht 1986: 121–35; Ooms 1985: 86–93). He envisioned the restoration of this ancient form of Shintō untainted by Buddhist influences. By reestablishing this primordial Shintō, he thought, it would become possible to realize a perfect society (Zhong 2016: 31–3).

A more historicist approach can be observed in a preface Razan's son and successor Hayashi Gahō 林鵞峰 (1618–1680) contributed to an annotated version of the Korean chronicle *Tongguk t'onggam* 東國通鑑 (Comprehensive Mirror of the Eastern Kingdom; 1484) commissioned by Tokugawa Mitsukuni 德川光圀 (1628–1701) in 1667.[2] Here, Gahō draws attention to Susanoo's sojourn in Silla as related in "our national history" (*wa ga kokushi*) and implies that Susanoo is more worthy of being called the founder of the three Han states than Pak Hyŏkkŏse, Chumong, and Onjo, who are presented in the Korean chronicle as the national founders of Silla, Koguryŏ, and Paekche, respectively. "Alas," Gahō laments, "this is not yet known in that country (*ka no kuni*)" (TT, preface: 5–6).

Gahō's privileging of Japanese sources (especially the *Nihon shoki*) over foreign chronicles shows that he shares Kanetomo's Japanocentric outlook. The possibility that a Korean chronicle might be more trustworthy with regard to Korean history than the *Nihon shoki* (here equated with "our national history") does not even seem to have occurred to him.

It is striking that in the passage quoted above Gahō treats both Susanoo and the mythical founders of the Korean states basically as historical personages. Nothing suggests their divine nature. While Gahō does not explicitly discuss the nature of the deities mentioned in the ancient myths, another prominent Confucian scholar, his younger contemporary Arai Hakuseki (1657–1725), argued that they were indeed nothing more than rulers of ancient communities. According to Hakuseki, the word *kami* used in the texts, even if written with the Chinese character for "deity" (*kami, shin* 神), referred to those who are "above" (*kami, jō* 上), that is, those in power. This euhemeristic paradigm[3] allowed Hakuseki to read the ancient myths as embellished accounts of historical events (Burns 2003: 62–6)—a strategy that was followed not only by some later Confucian and *kokugaku* scholars but also by positivistic historians in modern Japan.

Gahō was not the only Confucian scholar who linked Susanoo to the Korean peninsula. In his *Nihon shoki tsūshō* 日本書紀通證 (Compendium Treatise on the *Nihon shoki*; 1762), Tanigawa Kotosuga 谷川士清 (1709–1776) suggests that Susanoo was the founding deity of Korea. Kotosuga was a proponent of Suika Shintō, Yamazaki Ansai's synthesis of Shintō and neo-Confucian thought. Ansai shared Razan's ambition to retrieve a pre-Buddhist form of Shintō. Like Razan, he believed that both Shintō and neo-Confucianism were expressions of a universal way that consisted in the workings of abstract forces such as *ri, ki, yin* and *yang* (Burns 2003: 42–3). He based this theory on his idiosyncratic reading of the *Nihon shoki*'s myths, which is characterized by his search for a hidden meaning beneath the text through highly imaginative etymologies that allowed him to associate the Japanese myths with neo-Confucian concepts. Ansai explicitly claimed the *Nihon shoki*'s superiority over other chronicles such as *Sendai kuji hongi* or *Kojiki* (Ooms 1985: 221–32, 238–44). It is therefore not surprising that Kotosuga chose this work as his object of inquiry. However, though initiated into Suika Shintō, he went beyond Ansai's neo-Confucian interpretative framework and is commonly regarded as a forerunner of National Learning due to his interest in the ancient Japanese language that is at odds with Ansai's creative etymologies (Burns 2003: 63–6).

The *Nihon shoki* contains a passage in which a minister of the Soga lineage, after the king of Paekche had been killed by Silla troops,[4] advises his son to build a shrine to the "deity who founded the land." This deity, the minister claims, had already helped Paekche in the times of Yūryaku, when the armies of Koguryŏ had conquered the Paekche capital and threatened to destroy the kingdom. "The deity who founded the land," the Japanese minister explains, "is the god who descended from Heaven and created the state at the time when Heaven and Earth became separated and when grass and trees were able to speak" (NSK XIX [Kinmei 16/2], vol. 2: 434–9). Kotosuga argues that the "deity who founded the land" is none other than Susanoo. Quoting a passage from the *Tongguk t'onggam*, he also mentions the possibility that Tan'gun might be intended (NT XXIV: 20r [1545]). Significantly, he does not equate Susanoo and Tan'gun but just provides two possible interpretations for the *Nihon shoki*'s report. However, as we have seen in Chapter 1, Atsuta Jingū's head priest Tsunoda Tadayuki was to use exactly the same passage to equate the two deities and request Tan'gun's enshrinement at the Chōsen Shrine one and a half centuries later.[5]

Another interesting theory that links Susanoo with the Korean peninsula was proposed by Tō Teikan 藤貞幹 (1732–1797), a thinker from Kyoto with connections to both Confucians and proponents of National Learning. In his work *Shōkōhatsu* 衝口発 (A Blunt Discharge of Words; 1781), Teikan claims that Susanoo was, in fact, a ruler of Chinhan 辰韓, the region in the southeast of the Korean peninsula that was later to become the kingdom of Silla (SH: 2). He bases this claim on a passage from the "Original History of Silla" (*Silla ponsa* 新羅本史)[6] quoted in *Tongguk t'onggam*. This passage relates that among the kings of Silla "one was called *ch'ach'aung*.[7] *Ch'ach'aung* or *chach'ung* means shaman in the [Silla?] dialect, perhaps this is a title revering [the king] as a god" (TT I: 2). After quoting this passage, Teikan remarks, "I think ch'ach'aung is Susanoo. The old pronunciation [of Susanoo] corresponds [to ch'ach'aung]. In that case, it is apparent that Susanoo was a king of Silla" (SH: 2). Teikan's treatise elicited a sharp rejoinder from his contemporary Motoori Norinaga. As the text's title *Kenkyōjin* 鉗狂人 (Silencing a Madman) suggests, Norinaga was not at all amused by Teikan's provocative hypothesis, which he described as "the words of a madman" (MNZ 8: 273).[8]

The first person to mention the theory that Susanoo was identical with Tan'gun seems to have been Ban Kōkei 伴蒿蹊 (1733–1806), a man of letters, who wrote in his *Kanden kōhitsu* 閑田耕筆 (Plowing Uncultivated Fields with my Brush; 1801):

> The first king of Chosŏn is called Tan'gun; the people on Tsushima say that he is [identical with] Susanoo no Mikoto. They say that the place from where Susanoo no Mikoto deigned to cross over to Chosŏn is [located in the] north-west [-ern part] of Tsushima and is called Tobisaki. Moreover, they say that the place from where Empress Jingū set sail from Tsushima to Kyushu on her return trip from Chosŏn is also called Tobisaki and is located in the south of the province. {I think it is mentioned in one variant of the chronicle of the Age of the Gods [contained in the *Nihon shoki*] that Susanoo no Mikoto once crossed over to Silla.} (KK: 32)

Kōkei does not present Susanoo's alleged identity with Tan'gun as a scholarly theory but rather as a story he picked up during a journey to Tsushima. That he mentions both Tan'gun and Jingū in this passage, emphasizes Tsushima's strong association with the peninsula as the bakufu's gate to Chosŏn. Kōkei can hardly be called a Confucian scholar. In fact, he is often described as a proponent of National Learning since he authored two manuals on how to write in ancient Japanese under the influence of *kokugaku* pioneer Kamo no Mabuchi (Kazama 1999: 5). Moreover, *Kanden kōhitsu* is a collection of anecdotes rather than a commentary on ancient myth. Nonetheless there are some points of contact with the Confucian discourse: (1) like many Confucian exegetes, he treats Susanoo and Tan'gun (and Jingū) as historical persons rather than as divine beings or fictional characters; and (2) he turns to the *Nihon shoki* as the ultimate source of historical authority. But Kōkei's observation seems to have been taken seriously by neither Confucian nor *kokugaku* scholars, since it was rarely quoted in their works. Susanoo's connection with Tan'gun was rather discovered (or invented) independently at the Gion Shrine during the mid-nineteenth century. In the next section, we therefore return to the discourse surrounding Gion Shrine and Gozu Tennō.

Gozu Tennō, Gion Shrine, and the Separation of *Kami* and Buddhas

In contrast to Izumo Shrine, the combinatory practices and doctrines surrounding Susanoo and Gozu Tennō at Gion Shrine were upheld throughout the early modern period. But the theoretical framework underlying worship at Gion increasingly became the target of Confucian and *kokugaku* scholars' criticism. An early example is Amano Sadakage 天野信景 (1663–1733), who (like the already mentioned Tanigawa Kotosuga) belongs to a group of scholars called *kojitsuka* 故実家 (experts on the truth of ancient times) that emerged in the early eighteenth century. Through evidentiary research on ancient sources, these scholars endeavored to retrieve an ancient, unadulterated Shintō. While many of them took Suika Shintō as their point of departure, they criticized some of its tenets (Endō 2003: 146–7).

In his *Gozu tennō ben* 牛頭天王辨 (Clarification on Gozu Tennō; 1704), Sadakage criticizes both Buddhist monks' endeavors to identify *kami* as traces of the Buddha and shrine priests' attempts to turn foreign deities (*iikijin*) such as Matarajin, Konpira, Sekizan Myōjin, Shinra Myōjin, or Gozu Tennō into native deities (*wagakuni no kami*) by equating them with deities of the divine age. He denounces such teachings as "erroneous," "heterodox," and "misguided," and singles out Susanoo as a native deity and Gozu Tennō as a foreign deity who were victims of such forced analogies (SHAZ 7: 355-8). In contrast to the combinatory teachings of medieval Buddhism and Yoshida Shintō, Sadakage claims that Gozu Tennō is of pre-Buddhist Indian origin, linking him with ideas surrounding ox-head sandalwood. This wood, Sadakage argues, can heal fever and grows on a mountain shaped like a bull's head in southern India. He supports his claim by providing Gozu Tennō's Sanskrit name: Gomagriva Devaraja (which is the literal translation of the four characters making up Gozu Tennō's name: bull, head, heaven, and king) (SHAZ 7: 359–60).

In 1823, Hirata Atsutane in a similar vein denounced the theory of Susanoo and Gozu Tennō's identity as "eloquent priests' irresponsible words" that would "mislead people" (SHAZ 7: 339). According to Atsutane, this far-fetched theory could be traced to Kibi no Makibi 吉備真備 (695–775), an influential scholar and statesman of the Nara period, who spent about two decades of his life in

Tang China—more than enough time, by nativist reasoning, to become spoiled by the abhorred "Chinese Spirit" (*karagokoro*). In China, Atsutane argues, Makibi heard the Indian stories about ox-head sandalwood and learned about the bull-headed guardian deity of Jetavana. After his return to Japan, Makibi turned this deity into a calendrical deity and equated him with the native *kami* Susanoo to enhance the prestige of the calendrical and *yin-yang* teachings he had brought back from China. This combinatory deity was then worshiped at the capital's Kanjin-in. Makibi called the shrine Gion in order to emphasize its connection to the Jetavana monastery and thus reinforce Susanoo's association with Gozu Tennō (SHAZ: 342–7).

Considering Sadakage's and Atsutane's critical texts and the high level of influence *kokugaku* ideas exerted in the first years of the Meiji period, it is perhaps not surprising that Gozu Tennō was singled out as a symbol of the undesired combinatory deities of the medieval period in an edict issued by the Council of State (*dajōkan* 太政官) on March 28, 1868:

> Item: Since the Middle Ages, no small number of shrines have been using expressions like so-and-so *gongen*, Gozu Tennō, or other Buddhist terms to refer to *kami*. In all these cases, a detailed record of the history of the respective shrine has to be compiled and shortly reported. ...
>
> Item: Shrines that use a Buddhist statue as the main object of worship (*shintai* 神体) have to change this practice henceforth.
>
> Addendum: If Buddhist statues are installed in front of shrines as original sources (*honji*) [of the *kami*] or under similar claims, or if objects like temple gongs, temple bells, or other Buddhist implements are present, they have to be removed shortly. (Quoted in Kubota 1974: 7)[9]

In compliance with the edict and its implications, the Gion complex's main deity was exclusively called Susanoo from that time on. Moreover, the institution had to be renamed, since, as Atsutane had criticized, the name "Gion" carried strong Buddhist connotations. Consequently, the shrine came to be called Yasaka Shrine after a toponym mentioned in the sixteenth-century *Nijūnisha chūshiki* 二十二社註式 (Explanations on the Twenty-two Shrines) and the shrine record *Gionsha hon'en zatsu roku* mentioned in the preceding chapter (Kubota 1974: 12–14). Since religious beliefs and practices connected to Gion Shrine and Gozu Tennō had by that time spread over large parts of the archipelago, many ritual centers all over the country had to be renamed. In this context, Kawamura Minato (2007: 128–34) draws attention to a further aspect, beside the Buddhist connotations, that might have motivated the Meiji ideologues to erase the name of Gozu Tennō, namely that some shrines dedicated to this deity had been called Tennōsha. If people before the Meiji Restoration used the expression "*tennō*," Kawamura points out, it was more likely to refer to Gozu Tennō than to the emperor.[10] Of course, such a practice could not be tolerated by the architects of the Meiji Restoration, who strived to establish the emperor as the central axis of the modern Japanese state. Therefore, Gozu Tennō was written out of Japanese history.[11]

By that time, the main ritualist (*shamushiki* 社務職) of the shrine, Ki Shigetsugu 紀繁継 (life dates unknown), had already become laicized and transformed himself into a priest of the *kami*. Shigetsugu did not waste any time to demonstrate his support of the new regime: he shed his Buddhist robes as early as February 1868, one month before the Council of State ordered Buddhist priests working at shrines to become laicized on March 17 (Kubota 1974: 5–6).

Despite Shigetsugu's swift reaction to the new government's demands, the paradigm shift from combinatory practices to imperial Shintō presented a major problem for the shrine. After all, Gion Shrine was first and foremost associated with the prevention or cure of sickness. People visited the shrine to pray for their good health and buy amulets to prevent diseases. The shrine's income and prestige to a large extent rested on its reputation as an efficacious apotropaic site. But, as was apparent to anyone who read the amulets' inscription, this reputation was based on the shrine's founding legend, the tale of Somin Shōrai. The ancient court chronicles did not explicitly link Susanoo to pestilence. If the shrine wanted to keep attracting visitors to pray for their good health, it somehow had to retain the legend, which by that time had become inextricably linked with Gozu Tennō. At the same time, it was not allowed to keep worshiping the purportedly Indian pestilence deity. Shigetsugu therefore had to find a way to connect Susanoo directly with Somin Shōrai or to purify Gozu Tennō of his Buddhist aspects. In order to retain the association with healing ox-head sandalwood, it was desirable for the shrine not to purge the name Gozu Tennō completely from shrine records and ritual practice. Shigetsugu found the key to this conundrum in a treatise by his acquaintance Matsuura Michisuke 松浦道輔 (1801–1866), a disciple of Hirata Atsutane (YKS I: 11).

In his *Kanjin-in Gozu tennō kō* 感神院牛頭天王考 (Treatise on Kanjin-in's Gozu Tennō), completed in 1863, Michisuke claims that the theory of Gozu Tennō's Indian origin was fabricated in response to Buddhist pressures once Kanjin-in had become affiliated with Enryakuji. According to Michisukue, the name Gion was also attached to the shrine at that time to emphasize Gozu

Tennō's link to Buddhism. Originally, the shrine had been built in the fifth year of Tenchi's reign (666) in Yasaka Township by an envoy from Koguryŏ.[12] The deity originally enshrined at Kanjin-in was none other than Susanoo. Michisuke uses his interpretation of Susanoo's sojourn in Silla reported in the *Nihon shoki* to link Susanoo to the Korean peninsula. He claims that Soshimori was a phonetic representation of the Korean word for "ox head." Based on this linguistic link, he identifies the "place Soshimori" mentioned in the *Nihon shoki* as Ox-Head Mountain (pronounced as Udusan in modern Korean) in Lelang 楽浪 (Kor. Nangnang; in the region of present-day Pyongyang). This mountain, Michisuke argues, was the site of Susanoo's descent from the Plain of High Heaven. In a final step, he uses the motif of a deity's descent on a mountain to equate Susanoo with Tan'gun, the mythical founder of the oldest Korean state (KGT I).

Michisuke bases his theory on the *Tongguk t'onggam*'s version of the myth of Tan'gun. In the year of the earth dragon during Emperor Yao's 堯 reign (2333 BCE), we are told, when there was no one yet to rule in Korea, a divine man descended beneath a sandalwood tree. The people called him Tan'gun (Sandalwood Prince) and made him their king. His state was called Chosŏn. He founded his first capital at Pyongyang and later transferred it to Mount Paegak 白岳. In the eighth year of Shang Wu Ding's 商武丁 reign (1317 BCE), he entered Asadal 阿斯達 Mountain and became a god (TT, *oegi*: 1). Michisuke argues that this divine man was none other than Susanoo, who due to his descent beneath a sandalwood tree came to be called Tan'gun in Korea. In Japan, he was worshiped as Gozu Tennō in reference to the site of his descent (KGT I).[13]

After the promulgation of the Meiji edicts to separate *kami* and buddhas, this theory proved useful for the priests of Yasaka Shrine. It allowed them to retain the association with Somin Shōrai and ox-head sandalwood through Gozu Tennō and to justify their reading by quoting the episode of Susanoo's sojourn in Silla mentioned in the *Nihon shoki*. At the same time, Michisuke's treatise offered them a way to cut their ties with Buddhism, such as the link to Jetavana. Hence, it is not surprising that Shigetsugu endorsed Michisuke's theory in his own work *Yasakasha kyūki shūroku* 八坂社旧記集録 (Compilation of Ancient Records on Yasaka Shrine), published shortly after the Meiji Restoration in 1870 (YKS I: 10–16). The endorsement of one of Yasaka Shrine's leading priests had the air of an official recognition of Michisuke's theory.

In 1906, the theory of Susanoo and Tan'gun's identity once and for all became official shrine doctrine, when the Yasaka Shrine published a two-volume work called *Yasaka-shi* 八坂誌 (Yasaka Record) that created a seamless narrative out of the various myths surrounding Susanoo (recorded in *Kojiki*, *Nihon shoki*, and *Shaku Nihongi*), the *Tongguk t'onggam*'s Tan'gun myth, reports on Korean embassies mentioned in the *Nihon shoki*, and various other materials. The work's aim is clearly stated in the preface: to free the shrine of the "evil customs of old" and to correct "misunderstandings" and "fallacious theories" that regarded Kanjin-in as a Buddhist institution or viewed Gozu Tennō as a Buddhist or calendrical deity (YS, vol. 1, preface: 6–8). *Yasaka-shi*'s account of the shrine's origins closely follows Shigetsugu's theory[14] and provides a striking example of the invention of tradition. By skillfully selecting and splicing together portions of various sources, the editors succeeded in creating a completely new narrative that discredited the combinatory teachings and practices followed for centuries at Gion Shrine. To legitimize their reading of the ancient myths, the priests followed the historicist approach that had become established by Confucian and *kokugaku* scholars: the hybrid narrative created by the editors is followed by verbatim quotes of all the sources used for its compilation (Shigetsugu's *Yasakasha kyūki shūroku* is treated in exactly the same manner as the ancient sources). This strategy allowed the priests to "establish continuity with a suitable historic past" (Hobsbawm 1983: 1), namely a pre-Buddhist golden age as imagined by *kokugaku* thinkers. In this way, the radical reformation of shrine teachings and practices in response to the separation edicts were touted as a return to ancient tradition. Hence, Eric Hobsbawm's (1983: 2) definition of invented traditions as "responses to novel situations which take the form of reference to old situations" certainly applies to the rewriting of the Gion complex's history, even if the old situation in this case is largely fabricated through the selective use and creative interpretation of discursive antecedents.

The text starts with a combination of elements taken from *Kojiki*, *Nihon shoki*, and *Tongguk t'onggam*: After his banishment from the Plain of High Heaven, Susanoo is said to have descended *beneath a sandalwood tree* in Soshimori in Silla together with his son Itakeru. The people of this land made him their king and called him Tan'gun. Susanoo proceeded to plant tree seeds *on the Korean peninsula* with the assistance of his children, who afterward crossed over to Kii (*Nihon shoki* I [8, var. 4 and 5]). He made a boat of clay and crossed the sea (*Nihon shoki* I [8, var. 4]) in order to marry the daughter of the deity of the Southern Sea. After having obtained his bride and having rewarded Somin Shōrai (*Shaku Nihongi*), he arrived in Izumo, where he killed the eight-headed serpent, married Kushiinada Hime, and finally entered Ne no Kuni (*Nihon shoki* I [8, main text and var. 5]). The Koreans built a shrine for Susanoo on Udusan in Lelang, which is identical to Soshimori, the place where Susanoo first descended (*Yasakasha kyūki shūroku*). In the second year of Saimei's 斉明 reign (656), an embassy from Koguryŏ arrived at the Japanese court (*Nihon shoki* XXVI [Saimei 2/8/8]).¹⁵ The narrative's conclusion follows Shigetsugu's treatise: The Koguryŏ vice ambassador built a shrine for Susanoo in Yasaka Township. Since Susanoo was the great god of Udusan (Ox-Head Mountain), he was henceforth worshiped as Gozu Tennō; in the fifth year of Tenchi (666), the shrine was named Kanjin-in (YS, vol. 1: fasc. I–III).

With the publication of this text, Yasaka Shrine once and for all cut its ties with Buddhism and distanced itself from the combinatory teachings that had flourished at the Gion complex throughout the medieval and early modern periods. At the same time, the priests managed to retain the legends surrounding the pestilence deity Gozu Tennō. The bull-headed deity's connection to India was negated and replaced with a Korean origin. In this way, the priests retained Susanoo's equation with a Korean pestilence deity even while negating the validity of the *honji suijaku* paradigm. While this might not have been the shrine priests' intention, through the erasure of deities such as Matarajin or Sekizan Myōjin and Gozu Tennō's reinterpretation as a Korean deity, they arguably connected Susanoo's negative aspect as a pestilence deity even more strongly to the Korean peninsula.

Kokugaku Scholarship on Susanoo's Connection to Korea

As mentioned in Chapter 1, many proponents of National Learning (*kokugaku*) vehemently criticized early formulations of the theory of common ancestry in the late nineteenth century. Nonetheless, Matsuura Michisuke was not the only adherent of this—far from monolithic—school of thought who theorized on Susanoo's connection to the Korean peninsula. Susanoo's son Itakeru, who is only mentioned in the *Sendai kuji hongi* and the *Nihon shoki*'s variants that associate Susanoo with the Korean peninsula, plays an important role in their interpretations.

In 1888, two years before the publication of Hoshino Hisashi's fateful article on Japanese and Koreans' alleged shared ancestry, the *kokugaku* scholar Ochiai Naozumi 落合直澄 (1840–1891) wrote in his *Teikoku kinen shian* 帝国紀年私案 (Personal Opinion on the Chronology of the [Japanese] Empire):

> Itakeru, ... Susanoo no Mikoto's honorable son, also called ... the Korean Deity (Kara no Kami) Sohori or "Itate who resides in the land of Korea" (*Kara-kuni*

ni masu Itate 座韓国伊太氏), is the son who was born while the god Susanoo travelled the myriad countries after his descent from Heaven. (Ochiai 1888: 24)

The *Kojiki* mentions Kara no Kami and Sohori no Kami as Susanoo's grandsons. While there are no tales about these two deities, their names clearly suggest a connection to Korea (see Chapter 4). None of the ancient sources equates them with Itakeru. "Itate who resides in the land of Korea" is a reference to the *Engi shiki*, which mentions six shrines dedicated to this deity's worship in Izumo (EGSK X, vol.1: 668–73; cf. Takioto 1995).[16]

After thus establishing Itakeru's connection to the Korean peninsula, Ochiai proceeds to identify him with Tan'gun. He achieves this by using the Chinese characters of Tan'gun's name accompanied by an interlinear gloss instructing his readers to read the characters as an alternate form of Itate/Itakeru:

> The god Susanoo travelled the myriad countries together with his son Tan'gun/Itakeru[17] at the time of Tang Yao's Great Flood.[18] Susanoo no Kami went east and reached Silla. This is [reported in] the [following] variant of the *Nihon shoki*: "Susanoo no Mikoto, accompanied by his son Itakeru no Kami, descended to the land of Silla and lived at the place Soshimori." Tan'gun became king of Chosŏn in the twenty-fifth year of Tang Yao, the fifth year of the sexagenary cycle. … At that time, Susanoo no Kami left Tan'gun in Chosŏn and crossed the sea to his homeland. Afterwards Tan'gun crossed the sea to Japan, carrying tree seeds, which he planted on the Eight Islands. … In the end, he resided in the land of Kii. Later, the Itakiso Shrine was erected to honor this deity's spirit. … The preceding discussion shows that Itakeru no Kami and Tan'gun are one and the same deity, who is a son of Susanoo no Kami. (Ochiai 1888: 24–5)

This interpretation is reminiscent of the one provided in the *Yasaka-shi* in that it splices together bits and pieces from different sources to create an altogether new narrative.

The view that Itakeru was identical to Tan'gun was taken up by Iida Takesato 飯田武郷 (1828–1900),[19] another scholar of National Learning, in his *Nihon shoki tsūshaku* 日本書紀通釈 (Compendium Commentary on the *Nihon shoki*; 1900–9). Iida quotes from *Nihon shunjū* 日本春秋 (Japanese Spring and Autumn), a work written by the Buddhist monk Nissho Jakuken 日初寂顕 (1701–1770). In this work, Jakuken argues that Itakiso Shrine, a shrine in Wakayama dedicated to Itakeru, was "named after Tan'gun. Here [in Japan], he is called Shinra Myōjin. Another name is Kara no Kami." Iida comments that "This hypothesis is difficult to discard. Probably Tan'gun is indeed … identical with Susanoo no Mikoto's honorable son Itakeru no Kami" (Iida 1902–9, vol. 4: 2780).

The examples of Matsuura Michisuke, Ochiai Naozumi, and Iida Takesato show that not all proponents of National Learning were strictly opposed to the ideas expressed by the theorists of common ancestry. However, with the exception of Michisuke, they did not foreground early Japan's connection to the Korean peninsula and its impact on Shintō in their works. By equating Tan'gun with a marginal deity like Itakeru rather than with Susanoo, Ochiai and Iida downplayed the significance of the Japanese–Korean connection. Nonetheless, their theories might have had a direct impact on theorists of common ancestry. As can be seen in a pioneering study on Korean history by historian Hayashi Taisuke 林泰輔 (1854–1922), the identification of Tan'gun with Itakeru made it possible to equate multiple generations of Japanese and Korean deities. In his *Chōsen-shi* 朝鮮史 (History of Korea; 1892), Hayashi equates Izanaki with Tan'gun's grandfather Hwanin, Susanoo with his father Hwanung, and Itakeru with Tan'gun, thus emphasizing the shared ancestry of Koreans and Japanese (Hayashi 1892, fasc. I: 19–20).

Susanoo in Colonial-Period Scholarship

The following section analyzes Susanoo's role in colonial-period scholarship. It will become apparent that Susanoo occupied an important position in the theory of common ancestry, which enjoyed wide support among Japanese historians, linguists, and archaeologists, especially during the early years of occupation. On the other hand, ethnologists came up with new approaches that, while not untainted by an imperialist sense of superiority, opened up new avenues for postwar research.

The Theory of Common Ancestry

In 1890, Hoshino Hisashi published his groundbreaking article, commonly viewed as the beginning of the theory of common ancestry, in which he claimed that Japan and Korea had constituted one ethnical and linguistic entity in antiquity, only to become separated by the vicissitudes of history. In this article, he quotes the works of Tō Teikan, Ki Shigetsugu, and Ochiai Naozumi summarized above. While Hoshino (1890: 18–22) rejects both the equation of Susanoo with a Silla king (Teikan) or Tan'gun (Shigetsugu) and the identification of Itakeru as Tan'gun (Ochiai) as lacking evidence, he still adopts substantial parts of the three scholars' theories. For instance, he accepts Ochiai's thesis that Itakeru was identical with Itate and had crossed over to Japan from Silla. He also accepts the interpretation of Soshimori as the Korean word for "ox head," only taking issue with Shigetsugu's localization of the alleged site of Susanoo's descent on the Korean peninsula. "Lelang is the region of present Pyŏngan Province," he points out, "Inside its borders, there is no Udu Mountain. However, there is an Udu Mountain in Ch'unch'ŏn in Kangwŏn Province" (ibid.: 20).[20] This, he was convinced, had to be the site of Susanoo's descent to the Korean peninsula.

Strictly speaking, Hoshino's article did not offer many new insights but rather quoted and rearranged earlier interpretations by *kokugaku* scholars. Overall, his approach is rather similar to the historicist interpretations espoused by Confucians and proponents of National Learning. Beside his rigorous positivism, what distinguishes Hoshino's article from these earlier works is the far-reaching conclusion he draws from his observations. Contrary to earlier exegetes of the ancient myths, Hoshino was not satisfied with illuminating the meaning of individual episodes in the form of a commentary, but he drew concrete conclusions for the history of ancient Japan's relations to the Korean peninsula. As we have seen in Chapter 1, his fellow professors at the Imperial University's Department of Japanese History shared Hoshino's view that Korea and Japan did not constitute separate entities in antiquity. In a jointly published overview of Japanese history, the three professors identify the Plain of the Sea, ruled by Susanoo according to the wishes of his father Izanaki, with Korea. They further argue that Susanoo retreated to Korea after the birth of his son Ōkuninushi (Shigeno, Kume, and Hoshino 1890, fasc. I: 2).

However, in their positivistic, historicist treatment of the sacrosanct texts of Shintō, the three professors, representing the first generation of official academic historians in Meiji Japan, went too far in the eyes of their contemporaries. Hoshino's article was severely criticized by *kokugaku* scholars and Shintō activists. Kume Kunitake was even forced to resign in 1892 for publishing an article in which he called for the removal of primitive elements—such as the worship of imperial ancestors in Ise—from Shintō and identified Amaterasu as a priestess rather than a deity.[21] A year later, the Office of Historiography, where the professors had been in charge, was closed down and Shigeno was dismissed as well (Brownlee 1999: 95–101; Yoshikawa 2017: 44–5). The closure was ordered by the minister of education, Inoue Kowashi 井上毅 (1844–1895), who in a letter to Itō Hirobumi criticized that the works produced at the office "contained impossible statements, such as that the ancestors of the imperial family were

Indians *or were of the same lineage as the Koreans*. Therefore I have crushed the Office of Historiography" (quoted in Mehl 2017: 156, emphasis added).

By 1910, when Japan annexed Korea, the situation had completely changed. The theory of common ancestry had long moved into the scholarly mainstream and experienced a veritable boom in the months before and after the promulgation of Japan's annexation of Korea on August 29, 1910. Journals and newspapers were full of articles supporting the theory of common ancestry—and Susanoo was mentioned in most of these articles. In November, the history journal *Rekishi chiri* published a special issue on Korea featuring articles by Hoshino, Kume, and other famous proponents of the theory such as Kanazawa Shōzaburō or Kita Sadakichi (the journal's editor). Hoshino elaborated on his 1890 article, repeating his argument about Susanoo and Itakeru in basically unaltered form, and concluded that "in antiquity Japan and Korea constituted one realm (*dōiki*), thus it is certain that the deities travelled to and fro." The annexation of Korea, he asserts, is a restoration of this primordial unity (Hoshino 1910: 27, 40). In his overview article of the history of Japanese–Korean interactions, Shidehara Taira 幣原坦 (1870–1953), who had graduated from the Department of Japanese History at the Imperial University in Tokyo in 1893, uses the *Nihon shoki*'s account of Susanoo's sojourn to Silla as proof that interactions with the peninsula had started in the Age of Gods (Shidehara 1910: 9–10). Similarly, Kita cites Susanoo and Itakeru's arrival from Silla as the oldest recorded contact between Japan and Korea (Kita 1910: 135).

Kume (now a lecturer at Waseda University) argues that Susanoo together with his son Itakeru came to Japan from Silla, adopting Teikan's thesis that the Silla royal title *ch'ach'aung* refers to Susanoo (Kume 1910: 60). In a talk given in 1911, Kume theorized about the unity of Japan and Korea in ancient times. He argued that, like Japan, ancient Korea had been characterized by the unity of ritual and government (*saisei itchi* 祭政一致). Susanoo, he believed, had ruled in Korea as a kind of sacred king: "Susanoo no Mikoto was the ruler of Silla and became a high priest in the territory of the Han." From this assessment of Korea's past, he drew a concrete conclusion for the policies to be implemented in the colony: "I believe that Koreans should be turned into followers of Shintō" (Kume 1989: 50, 58).

This close correlation between historical analysis and suggestions for colonial policies is characteristic for proponents of the theory of common ancestry. The opening address of the 1910 special issue of *Rekishi chiri* emphasizes history's utility for the colonial enterprise by philosophically pointing out that "the past is the parent who gives birth to the present, and the future is the child that will be born from the present" ("'Chōsen gō' hakkan no ji" 1910: 3). Yoshida Tōgo 吉田東伍 (1864–1918) argues in his article, in the same issue, that through the separation from its sibling nation Japan, Korea had become a "lonely and insecure nation of stepchildren (*"mamako" kokumin*)" that could easily be assimilated to the Japanese empire (Yoshida 1910: 91), and Kita emphasizes the importance of thorough research on the history of Japanese–Korean relations in order to achieve Korea's successful assimilation (Kita 1910: 131), while Miura Hiroyuki 三浦周行 (1871–1931) cites the naturalization of Korean aristocrats in antiquity as a precedent for Japan's ability to successfully assimilate Koreans (Miura 1910: 176).

Japanese theorists of common ancestry justified their privileging of Japanese sources by pointing out that Korean chronicles such as the *Samguk sagi* or the *Samguk yusa* had been written at a much later date and were therefore not as trustworthy as the Japanese court chronicles (Kita 1910: 133). However, this line of reasoning constituted a threat to the theory of common ancestry. The expert for Korean history Imanishi Ryū 今西龍 (1875–1932), for instance, rejected the equation of Susanoo and Tan'gun, since he considered the latter a product of later times. Tan'gun, he argued, was invented in the mid-Koryŏ period (918–1392) by Buddhist monks, who reinterpreted an earlier shamanist divinity. Tan'gun was therefore neither connected to Susanoo nor to Japan. That both Susanoo (through his identification with Gozu Tennō) and Tan'gun were connected to sandalwood was a mere coincidence (Imanishi 1910: 227–9).

While most colonial-period historians agreed on the importance of Susanoo's sojourn to Silla as the earliest contact between Korea and Japan, the correct interpretation of the passage in the *Nihon shoki* was disputed. Yoshida (1893: 34–6), for instance, agreed with Hoshino's thesis that Soshimori meant "ox head" and referred to a Korean mountain, but he disagreed with Hoshino on this mountain's location, pointing out that T'aebaek 太白 Mountain in Samchŏk 三陟 at the southeastern border of Kangwŏn Province was situated closer to Izumo and thus the more likely location for Susanoo's sojourn. Similar considerations prompted the meteorologist and oceanographer Wada Yūji 和田雄治 (1859–1918) to locate Soshimori in Southern Kyŏngsang Province. Not only was Ch'unchŏn too far removed from Izumo, he stated, but it was also incompatible with the *Nihon shoki*'s narrative (NSK I [8, var. 5]), as there was no gold or silver to be found in Ch'unchŏn and the trees Susanoo is said to have planted would not have grown so far up north. For these reasons, Wada suggested that Soshimori referred to Kaya Mountain in the region of the former Kaya Federation (cf. Ch'oe 2008: 110–12; Wada 1914).

As we have seen, the theory that Soshimori was identical with the Korean word for "ox head" was not proposed by linguists but rather by historians and *kokugaku* scholars who were unfamiliar with the concept of phonetic change (cf. Kawamura 2007: 63-4)—one might add that at least the early proponents of the theory possessed at best a rudimentary knowledge of Korean, as is attested by the partly incorrect *han'gŭl* transcriptions provided by Shigetsugu and others (cf. Imanishi 1970: 114). Linguist Kanazawa, whose book *Nissen dōsoron* (1929) was already mentioned as the locus classicus of the theory of common ancestry, rejected the "ox head" theory on linguistic grounds (Kanazawa 1994: 57). Instead, he associated Soshimori with Sŏrabŏl and Sŏbŏl, toponyms mentioned in the *Samguk yusa* as old names for Silla. A gloss in the chronicle, furthermore, states that "It is the present custom to call the capital [of Silla] Sŏbŏl" (SGYS I: 36). Hence, Kanazawa argued that Soshimori referred to the capital of Silla, that is, present-day Kyŏngju in Northern Kyŏngsang Province (Kanazawa 1994: 104).[22]

It is interesting to note that Gozu Tennō, despite his prominent position among Susanoo's medieval alter egos, did not play a comparable role in colonial-period discourses. If at all, he was mentioned only as a name reinforcing Susanoo's connection to Udusan and Tan'gun, but the legends centering on this deity were all but forgotten after the separation of *kami* and buddhas. An exception to this rule can be seen in a 1928-monograph by Imamura Tomoe 今村鞆 (1870-1943), who served as police superintendent in various regions of Korea from 1908 to 1925 and conducted research on Korean customs and folklore in his spare time (Kawamura 1996: 47). In his book, Imamura reports the discovery of red paper slips of *c.* 3 by 9 centimeters (1 by 3 *sun*) bearing the inscription "*Somin changnae ji jason haeju huip*" 蘇民將來之子孫海州后入 (Jap. *Somin shōrai no shison kaishū kōnyū*), during his fieldwork in South P'yŏngan Province in northern Korea. These paper slips, he explains, were pasted to the doors of houses as talismans offering protection from diseases. Imamura points out the similarity to the Japanese Somin Shōrai cult (Imamura 1928: 182). Kawamura (2007: 59) translates the inscription as "Somin Shōrai's descendants enter as Haeju's wives" and explains that Haeju is the name of a city in South Hwanghae, a province sharing a border with South P'yŏngan. Since both provinces are now part of North Korea, it is difficult to conduct further research. It is unknown, when the custom started and whether it is still continued today (Oka 2002: 113-14).

What makes the police superintendent's alleged discovery interesting for the present study is that Imamura, born after the early Meiji separation of *kami* and buddhas, was aware of the legends surrounding Somin Shōrai and expected his readers to be familiar with them as well. This shows the success of Shigetsugu's rewriting of Yasaka Shrine's history. The episode also shows the lasting impact of the separation edicts, however, since it reminds us that the tale of Somin Shōrai, tainted through its associations with the combinatory discourses of the Middle Ages, was not analyzed in academic works on Korean–Japanese relations although it shows striking parallels to the well-known Korean tale of Princess Pari, the legendary ancestress of Korean shamans.[23] Itō Hirobumi's refusal to enshrine Gozu Tennō at Chōsen Shrine, discussed in Chapter 1, provides a further example of the low esteem in which deities not mentioned in the court chronicles were held after the enforcement of the separation policy.

Ethnological Studies

While the theory of common ancestry certainly formed a strong current in the field of Japanese mythological studies throughout the period of colonial rule in Korea, some ethnologists took other approaches to the study of myth. Two influential scholars who published extensively on the Japanese myths and their connection to the Korean peninsula before the end of the war are Oka Masao 岡正雄 (1889–1982) and Mishina Akihide 三品彰英 (also Shōei) (1902–1971). What sets Oka and Mishina apart from the proponents of the theory of common ancestry is that they did not endeavor to derive historical events from the myths they studied. Theorists of common ancestry tended to follow the euhemeristic strategies that were established by Edo-period scholars like Arai Hakuseki. Mishina (1940: 23–4), on the other hand, clarified that

> When it comes to the relation of historical facts of the past as they happened, myths and legends can of course not be regarded as authentic history. Nonetheless myths are important documents of ancient history insofar as they reflect the ideas and the social life of the people who transmit them and, moreover, in the beginning they fulfilled the social function of providing a life model for the people of the age that gave birth to the tales.

Mishina, who is regarded as the founder of Korean mythology studies in Japan today, went to Yale University as a visiting professor in 1937. Here he studied under the anthropologist Robert Lowie (1883–1957), who introduced him to Clark Wissler's (1870–1947) concept of culture areas (Hirafuji 2008: 67–8; 2013: 86). "Culture area" refers to "a relatively narrowly delimited geographical area in which a plenitude of cultural commonalities can be observed that are caused especially by (common) historical circumstances and environmental conditions" (Rössler 2007: 14). Employing this concept, Mishina

(1971: 225–516)[24] was able to demonstrate striking similarities between the myths of Susanoo and Chumong, the mythical founder of Koguryŏ.

As Hirafuji Kikuko has recently shown, Mishina was not immune to the distorted colonial perception of Korean history. Although he kept a certain distance to the theory of common ancestry, Mishina was convinced that

> For [Japanese and Koreans] who today have been able to become compatriots under the scepter of our emperor, ancient culture is truly an appropriate means. To become real compatriots, we must first return to our ethnic origins in the Age of the Gods and start from there. It would mean unprecedented pleasure to this author if his book were to succeed to at least some extent in drawing a picture, from mythical accounts, of how we compatriots were raised in the same cradle.
>
> Just as I was preparing the manuscript for the present book, it was announced that military conscription is to be implemented on the Korean peninsula. I therefore lay down my brush convinced that the day is not far ahead when these two compatriot peoples, who in antiquity grew up together, will join in leading forward the various peoples of Great East Asia under the scepter of our emperor. (Quoted in Hirafuji 2013: 89–90, brackets in original)

Like Shiratori and Imanishi, Mishina viewed the legend of Tan'gun as a later fabrication, pushing the date of its origin back to the mid-Koryŏ period. What is more, in a work on Korean history written for a general readership in 1940, he depicted Korea's alleged dependence on outside powers—he uses the terms heteronomy (*taritsusei* 他律性) and dependency (*fuzuisei* 附随性)—as one of the distinguishing features of its history. Sandwiched between the powerful nations of China and Japan, he argued, Korea was unable to develop a unique culture of its own (Mishina 1940: 26–7, 1–11). As Hirafuji (2013: 93) convincingly demonstrates, this view of Korea also characterizes Mishina's comparative studies on mythology: "in his comparison of Japanese and Korean myths, Mishina pointed out their close relatedness and mutual influences, but he also contrasted them by attributing a composite character that remained stagnant and underdeveloped to Korean myths and a distinctive, advanced mythology to Japan."

Oka Masao, one of the most influential ethnologists in wartime and postwar Japan, followed a similar approach to the study of myth. He wrote his dissertation in Vienna in the 1930s and was therefore strongly influenced by the so-called Vienna school of ethnology.[25] This school, which was centered around the Catholic priests Wilhelm Schmidt (1868-1954) and Wilhelm Koppers (1886-1961), is associated with the extreme diffusionism that represented the dominant paradigm in German-speaking ethnology from approximately 1910 to 1940. Proponents of this school emphasized the importance of migration for the formation of cultures and endeavored to reconstruct so-called culture circles (*Kulturkreise*) (Rössler 2007: 9–14). A culture circle can be defined as a "spatial-temporal construct which is believed to unveil characteristic commonalities in different cultural elements that allegedly suggest a common origin" (Braukämper 2005: 223). These cultural elements need not be material but can also refer, for instance, to religious customs or kinship systems. By adding a large number of individual cultural elements, a culture circle is constructed. This concept was combined with evolutionistic ideas in order to trace sequences of culture circles or cultural strata (*Kulturschichten*) (Rössler 2007: 11–13).

After his return from Vienna in 1940, Oka used his connections with scholars, military authorities, and government officials to establish the so-called Ethnic Research Institute (Minzoku Kenkyūjo) in 1943. Till the end of the war, Oka served as executive director of the institute, whose main objective was to study the ethnic groups of the Japanese colonies in order to facilitate the smooth operation of colonial administration (Doak 2001: 19–23; Nakao 2005: 27–9). This is in keeping with a keynote speech delivered by Oka in 1942 during the first meeting of the newly founded Ethnological Foundation. Here Oka demanded that

> Ethnology must become the cornerstone of ethnic policies by clarifying the present actual character or structure of an ethnic group that is the object of governmental rule, by investigating its ethnic consciousness, intentions and the nature of its activities and inclinations as they are structured by the group's experience and feelings. (Quoted in Hirafuji 2013: 100–1)

This marks a clear departure from the culture–historical approach of the Vienna School he had absorbed during his long stay in Austria—and to which he was to return after the end of the war. In Vienna, he was able to observe at close range the Nazis' reform of German ethnology and "was quite impressed by the way that Germanic ethnology, under Nazi influence, had drawn a tight connection between ethnic nationality and the political requirements for a new order in Europe" (Doak 2001: 19). Possibly, these observations provided the impetus for his change of heart—and methodology—during the first half of the 1940s.

Oka's main contribution to ethnology, however, was his observation that Japanese culture was fundamentally heterogeneous and his attempt to explain this heterogeneity as the result of the overlapping of various different cultures, which could still be identified as different cultural strata within Japanese culture. In his dissertation, Oka identified two matrilineal strata characterized by horticulture, which he traced to Melanesia and southern China, followed by three patrilineal strata of hunters, fishers, planters, and nomads, which brought continental culture such as clan organization, stock raising, and wet rice cultivation to Japan. It was the last of these strata, Oka argued, that marked the beginning of the Tennō dynasty and the belief in celestial deities (Oka 2012, vol 2: 1027–43).

This culture–historical approach also becomes apparent when one looks at Oka's remarks on Susanoo: the myths of Susanoo and the moon god, he argues in his dissertation, "came to Japan before the myth of the Plain of High Heaven and were probably transmitted in another tribe than the myths of Ama-terasu. Probably they belonged to the so-called Izumo culture circle." Moreover, "the myth of Susa no wo, the myths and legends that are connected to the genealogy of the Izumo [tribe], and the findings from stone-age sites prove the Izumo tribe's relations with Korea" (Oka 2012, vol. 1: 273, 96, brackets in original). Since Oka wrote his dissertation in German and the work was only published in 2012, its contents were not widely known in wartime Japan. However, his methodology opened a new way of affirming Korean–Japanese cultural parallels without claiming the original unity of the two countries as proposed by the theory of common ancestry. As we will see in the epilogue, this approach was to become influential in postwar reinterpretations of pre- and protohistorical Japanese–Korean relations. Despite the two scholars' postwar fame, during the period of Japanese colonial rule over Korea, their ethnological approaches were far less influential than the theory of common ancestry both in public and academic discourses. One of the reasons for this was surely the latter theory's greater political utility, which will be discussed in the next section.

Korea as a Realm of Death

We have already seen the important role played by the toponym Soshimori in identifying Susanoo as the mythical founder of Korea. It was another toponym, however, that was instrumental in linking Korea with the mythical realms of death mentioned in the ancient court chronicles, namely Kumanari. As discussed in Chapter 4, according to a variant of the *Nihon shoki* and the *Sendai kuji hongi*, Susanoo retreated to the "peak of Kumanari" before entering Ne no Kuni. During the medieval and early modern periods, there were different attempts to locate Kumanari on the map. Inbe Masamichi located the site in

Izumo (see Chapter 5), whereas Motoori Norinaga suggested in his *Kojikiden* that Kumanari was located in Kumano on the Kii peninsula (MNZ 9: 442–3).

Hoshino Hisashi (1890: 21–2) rejected both these theories. Based on the textual evidence contained in the *Nihon shoki* accounts of Yūryaku's and Keitai's reigns discussed in Chapter 4, he claimed instead that Kumanari represents a Korean toponym. He proposed two possible locations of Kumanari on the Korean peninsula: (1) Ungjin, which served as the capital of Paekche from 475 to 538, and (2) Ungchŏn, a port town located in the territory of the Kaya Federation in the southern part of the peninsula. While Hoshino used this hypothesis to support his idea of primordial Japanese–Korean unity, he did not draw any further conclusions from Kumanari's link to the otherworldly Ne no Kuni. Considering his positivistic approach to historical research, the ideological implications of this association might very well have eluded him. Other scholars of the colonial period were more sensitive to the ideological utility of this hypothesis, which enabled them to equate Korea with a sinister and polluting realm of the dead. In this way, colonial Korea inherited the ideological position occupied by Izumo in the ancient Japanese myths.

One scholar who equated Korea with Ne no Kuni is the marine officer and folklorist Matsuoka Shizuo 松岡静雄 (1878–1936), a younger brother of Yanagita Kunio 柳田國男 (1875–1962), one of the pioneers of Japanese folklore studies. In his *Izumo densetsu* (Transmissions of Izumo; 1931), Matsuoka provides a euhemeristic interpretation of the Izumo myths recorded in *Kojiki* and *Nihon shoki*. He even provides a date for the deeds of Susanoo, who plays a prominent role in the work's narrative, namely the sixth century BCE—a time when, as Matsuoka emphasizes, no state yet existed on the Korean peninsula. Matsuoka regards Susanoo as a Korean migrant who managed to establish himself as ruler over Izumo. From here, he tried to expand his sphere of influence by attacking the realms of Izanaki and Amaterasu but was finally defeated and forced to retreat "to his homeland Ne no Kuni, that is, Korea (*ne no kuni sunawachi kankoku*)." Although he advocates the reading of *waninari* rather than *kumanari* for the site of Susanoo's retreat, Matsuoka locates this mountain in "Chinhae District of Ungchŏn" (Matsuoka 1931: 251, 7, 45).

Korea's connection to the realm(s) of the dead and its ideological utility was not lost on theorists of common ancestry. One representative example is Abe Tatsunosuke 阿部辰之助 (life dates unknown), who in a treatise on ancient Japanese–Korean history written in 1928 located the mythical otherworlds of the ancient court chronicles on the Korean peninsula as well. The political implications of Abe's work become abundantly clear in the conclusion to this work's first fascicle with the telling headline "Why the annexation of Korea is a restoration." Here the author writes:

> As expounded above, it could be clearly demonstrated on the basis of Japanese-Korean ancient history that the ancestors of the Japanese-Korean race (*naisen minzoku* 内鮮民族) overlap (*tagai ni kōsa shitsutsu aru*). Just as in ancient times ... the people of Yamato and the people of Izumo (a people of immigrants from ... Silla) joined country with country and people with people, so in the present time through the annexation of Korea ... the country of Japan joined with the country of Korea and the people of Japan with the people of Korea. This has to be called a truly close connection. (Abe 1928, fasc. I: 52–3)

It is interesting to note that Abe views the inhabitants of Izumo as immigrants from Silla. Under Susanoo's leadership, he argues, they founded a state on the Japanese archipelago. Finally, Susanoo died and was buried on Mount Wanibuchi. The site of his grave, however, was named after Ungjin, the capital of Paekche in Susanoo's homeland (here Abe is not entirely consistent since he argued earlier that Susanoo was of Silla rather than of Paekche origin) (Abe 1928, fasc. I: 28–9, fasc. IV: 48–50).

Another point of interest in Abe's study is his explanation of the terms Yomi no Kuni and Tokoyo no Kuni, which he consistently writes using the character for "night" to express the syllable *yo*, although this spelling is only rarely used in the ancient sources. According to Abe, both terms refer to Korea. He explains that Japanese seafarers crossing the sea to the peninsula had to travel in the direction of the setting sun, that is, the direction of nightfall, for days on end. For this reason, he argues, they came to call the southern coast of Korea Yomi no Kuni, that is, "land that sees the night" (*yoru miru kuni*), or Tokoyo no Kuni, that is, "land of everlasting night" (*tsune ni yoru no kuni*). Japan, he continues, came to be called Nihon (land of sunrise) since seafarers traveling in the opposite direction faced the sunrise when crossing the ocean to Japan (Abe 1928, fasc. I: 6–7, fasc. II: 80–3).

In Abe's theory, Japan and Korea thus take over exactly the same ideological positions attributed to Ise and Izumo in Saigō Nobutsuna's reading of the ancient court chronicles introduced in Chapter 4. This allows us to modify Table 4.2 by replacing Ise and Izumo with Japan and Korea, respectively (see Table 6.1).

The ideological implications of depicting Korea as a realm of death are obvious; it allowed apologists for Japanese colonialism to paint a negative image of Korea as the polar opposite of Japan—as a "tolerated margin of mess." This

Table 6.1 Center and Periphery in Colonial Discourse

Center	Periphery
Japan	*Korea*[a]
Sunrise	Sunset
Light	Darkness
Life	Death

[a] Note that Korea inherits the position occupied by Izumo in the myths of *Kojiki* and *Nihon shoki* (cf. Table 4.1).

ideological agenda comes to the fore in an essay by Nitobe Inazō 新渡戸稲造 (1862–1933), a professor teaching colonial studies at Kyoto Imperial University, in which he describes his impressions of a trip to Korea in 1906:

> Life is Arcadian. I feel as though I were living three thousand years back, in the age of our *Kami*. ... The very physiognomy and living of this people are so bland, unsophisticated and primitive, that they belong not to the twentieth or the tenth—nor indeed to the first century. They belong to a prehistoric age.
>
> Nowhere else, I believe, do the living walk and work so near the dead as in this land. The hills and fields are literally strewn with graves. Where I am riding even now the road is lined with mounds, and with straw coffins awaiting burial. Not a few among the latter have decayed and their contents are exposed to view. ... Children play about them while the cattle they tend are grazing. The bleached bones of a nameless ancestor are kicked about on the roadside. ... A people so closely related to death are themselves more than half-dead.
>
> The Arcadian simplicity of the folk gives no promise of primitive energy; their habits do not remind us of the untamed vigor of Homeric songs, nor of Tacitus' description of early Germans, nor indeed of the fresh chronicles of the *Kojiki*.
>
> The Korean habits of life are the habits of death. They are closing the lease of their ethnic life. The national course of their existence is well-nigh run. Death presides over the peninsula. (Nitobe 1909: 214–16)

This passage offers a striking example of an imperialist thinker's perception of colonized Korea. It denies Korea a history or culture of its own, comparing contemporary Koreans with prehistoric Japanese and Europeans (thus conveniently raising Japan to the same civilizational level as the Western powers) and judging them inferior. This is achieved through the metaphor of death. Koreans' allegedly indifferent attitude toward their ancestors' remains, which implies a lack of respect for their own history, a lack of religious and moral decorum, and inadequate concern for hygiene, is linked to the death of the Korean nation. Both Japanese and European (but not Korean) myths play an important role throughout the text, implying not only that great nations revere their myths (which Koreans do not) but also pointing to the importance of the ancient myths in Japanese colonial discourses. Although neither Matsuoka nor Abe elaborated on the ideological implications of their equation of Korea with the *Kojiki*'s and the *Nihon shoki*'s mythical realms of death, it seems likely that their readers would infer as much from the colonial discourse that filled the newspapers, magazines, and bookstores of the day.

Conclusion

This study has attempted to trace the reception of Susanoo and his association to Korea from the ancient period through the era of Japanese colonial rule over Korea. The myths surrounding Susanoo, including their various reformulations and reinterpretations, present a striking example of the workings of cultural memory. Each major historical transformation affected the understanding of the ancient myths, which were at times changed beyond recognition. Nonetheless, all interpretations and reconfigurations were by necessity built on discursive antecedents. Medieval Buddhist thinkers came up with the *honji suijaku* paradigm to incorporate the *kami* into their Buddhist worldview centering on India, China, and Japan as the three centers of Buddhist civilization rather than discarding the ancient myths as lies or deceptions. Yoshida Shintō turned the hierarchy of these three countries on its head but retained the mythicoritual network linking *kami* with Buddhist (and other) divinities. In the early modern period, neo-Confucian scholars attacked these combinatory teachings but ended up creating their own syncretic teaching that replaced Buddhist notions like original enlightenment with Confucian ones like the workings of *ri* and *ki*. While criticizing neo-Confucian scholars' rationalizing interpretations of the ancient myths, proponents of National Learning took over their ambition to restore a pre-Buddhist form of Shintō. And positivistic historians of the Meiji period, while criticizing *kokugaku* scholars' irrational theses, largely followed the same historicist approach to the ancient myths. What is more, all of these thinkers tended to base their arguments on largely the same texts, namely the *Kojiki*, the *Nihon shoki*, and, up to the mid-Edo period, the *Sendai kuji hongi* as well as on commentaries of these works. This attests to the central role of the ancient court myths in Japan's cultural memory.

The case of Susanoo's association with Korea sheds light on a further aspect of cultural memory, namely its selective reception of the past. As we have seen, almost all attempts to link Susanoo with the Korean peninsula were based on two variants of the *Nihon shoki* that are rather poorly connected to the chronicle's overall mythical plot. This is not surprising since the ancient sources do not offer much more evidence that links Susanoo to Korea. Nonetheless, this dearth of evidence did not prevent exegetes from postulating such a connection. In the medieval period, the episode of Susanoo's sojourn to Silla facilitated his association with foreign pestilence deities such as Shinra Myōjin, Sekizan Myōjin, Matarajin, or Gozu Tennō. At the same time, Susanoo's connection to Ne no (Katasu) Kuni in the ancient myths led to his equation with rulers of the otherworld such as Taishan Fujun or King Yama. These associations reinforced the image of Susanoo as the polar opposite—or "evil twin"—of the sun goddess Amaterasu. Evidence that contradicted this dichotomic juxtaposition, such as Susanoo's heroic fight against the eight-headed serpent or his peaceful character in *Izumo fudoki*, were simply glossed over in silence. This reminds us that in the construction of cultural memory the act of forgetting is as important as that of remembering (Itagaki, Chŏng, and Iwasaki 2011: 21).

Chapter 3 discussed Susanoo's liminal character in the court chronicles and suggested that it was this state of inbetweenness that linked Susanoo to colonized Koreans' precarious position at the margin of the Japanese empire and thus predestined him for his central role in colonial discourse on common ancestry. A related aspect is Susanoo's association with peripheral realms such as Izumo or Ne no (Katasu) Kuni in the ancient myths. The deity's link to regions that were situated at the margin in both geographical and cosmological respect reemerged in different historical periods and contexts. In the Japanocentric worldview that contrasted Japan as a divine country with the allegedly polluted and potentially dangerous countries beyond its borders, the distinction between mythical otherworlds and foreign countries became blurred. In the medieval *sangoku* framework, Susanoo was now perceived as a foreign deity bringing pestilence from India or China—but also as possessing the power to protect people from epidemics. Through the episode of Susanoo's sojourn to Silla recorded in the *Nihon shoki*, this threatening image of Susanoo became linked to the Korean peninsula, as demonstrated in his equation with Shinra Myōjin. With the Meiji edicts demanding the separation of *kami* and buddhas, Susanoo's association with Korea was reinforced as the priests at Gion Shrine cut Gozu Tennō's ties with India and Buddhism by reinventing him as a Korean deity. Through this process, Korea's association with mythical otherworlds that had already been suggested in medieval religious discourse became emphasized. Apologists for Japanese colonialism drew on these discursive antecedents to project contemporary perceptions of colonized Korea as a backward and unhygienic country haunted by epidemics back onto the primordial time of myth, thus highlighting Japan's superiority and justifying colonial rule.

Susanoo's link to peripheral realms demonstrates the political dimension of Japanese mythology. It would be wrong to regard Susanoo's ideological utilization in colonial discourse as the politicization of originally apolitical religious texts. As we have seen, the author-compilers of the court chronicles pursued a clear political agenda, namely the justification of the emperor's rule over Japan. To this end, they contrasted the peripheral realm of Izumo with Yamato, the center of imperial authority, and Ise, the religious center dedicated to the worship of the imperial progenitress Amaterasu. In the medieval period, this pattern of contrasting the center of imperial authority with a sinister periphery was transferred to India, China, and Korea that were perceived as threatening otherworlds beyond the sea. The juxtaposition of Korea and Japan in colonial discourse built on these discursive antecedents and placed Korea in the position Izumo had occupied in the ancient court mythology.

Aleida Assmann's distinction of functional memory and storage memory as two dimensions of cultural memory in constant dynamic exchange is extremely helpful in understanding the reception of Susanoo. As we have seen, in the medieval period Susanoo emerged as the undisputed paramount deity of Izumo since his association with deities such as Matarajin or Gozu Tennō proved useful for justifying the institutional merger of Izumo Shrine with Gakuenji. Conversely, when in the early modern period shrine priests endeavored to cut their ties with Tendai Buddhism, they retrieved Ōkuninushi from storage memory to return to the allegedly primordial form of Shintō that was in turn framed by neo-Confucian notions. In this process, Matarajin, Gozu Tennō, and Susanoo's other alter egos vanished from shrine teachings and rituals. The court chronicles played an important role in this context since they connected Ōkuninushi rather than Susanoo with Izumo Shrine. Priests could thus employ *Kojiki* and *Nihon shoki* as historical precedents that helped them to win neo-Confucian scholars' support for their reform of shrine practices and teachings.

At Gion Shrine, on the other hand, Tendai influence remained strong throughout the early modern period. The priests only began dissociating themselves from their Buddhist legacy when prompted by the Meiji edicts. While the priesthood did not spare any efforts to erase any legends or names that associated the shrine with India, they retained the figure of Gozu Tennō (or at least his name) who allowed them to identify Susanoo as a deity offering protection from pestilence. They managed to retain Gozu Tennō, whose worship was explicitly prohibited by the separation edicts, by robbing this god of his identity and instead positing that "Gozu Tennō" was nothing but an alternate name for Susanoo. In this way, they were able to base Susanoo's connection to healing ox-head sandalwood on their reading of a passage of the *Nihon shoki*, which had by then become one of the sacred texts of Shintō. Their incentive for this reinterpretation was to legitimize the apotropaic rituals (most importantly the Gion Matsuri), an important source of the shrine's prestige and income. As we have seen, shrine priests' rewriting of Gion complex's history can be described as an invented tradition that aimed to justify the new religious practices and teachings introduced in response to the separation edicts by depicting them as the restoration of the shrine's original pre-Buddhist tradition. On the other hand, the Gion complex's associations with Jetavana, which formed an important strand of the sanctuary's tradition since its founding, were relegated to storage memory, from where they might be retrieved in the future if a situation arises in which it seems advantageous for the shrine to recover its Buddhist legacy.

While Gion priests' main aim in positing Gozu Tennō as an alternate name for Susanoo was to legitimize the apotropaic rituals conducted at the shrine, their reading of Soshimori as a Korean word for "ox head" came to play a central role in linking Susanoo to Korea by equating him with Tan'gun. This equation, again based on a passage of the *Nihon shoki*, found its way into academic discourse through the writings of Hoshino Hisashi, who belonged to the first generation of western-trained historians in Japan. His positivistic outlook was in many ways similar to the historicist and evidentiary approach followed by neo-Confucian and *kokugaku* exegetes, including Matsuura Michisuke, the *kokugaku* scholar who had reinterpreted Gion Shrine's founding legend. Hoshino used the hypothesis of Susanoo's Korean origins to support his argument that Japan and Korea had constituted a single politico-cultural entity in ancient times, an idea that would probably never have occurred to Michisuke or the shrine priests who utilized his theory to justify their Meiji-period reforms. Thus, the theory of common ancestry of Japanese and Koreans was born.

After Japan's annexation of Korea, this theory was broadly disseminated through academic publications, newspapers, and magazines. It served the ideological function of establishing a genealogical connection between Koreans and Japanese and, at the same time, marginalizing Korea within the Japanese empire. The ancient Japanese myths could easily be utilized as a historical precedent for the colonial situation by placing Korea in the same ideological position that Izumo occupied in the court chronicles. Thus, the colonization of Korea and the cultural assimilation of its inhabitants in the first half of the twentieth century was framed in the same way as the incorporation of Izumo into the Yamato state, twelve centuries earlier. Like ancient Izumo, colonized Korea was depicted as a peripheral site connected to dirt, darkness, disease, and death that offered a favorable contrast to the Japanese metropole. Nonetheless, Koreans' belonging to the Japanese family state was emphasized through the genealogical link between Susanoo and Amaterasu. In this way, an imperialist reading of the ancient Japanese myths justified both the colonized Koreans' inclusion and their marginalization in the Japanese empire.

Epilogue

After the War: Susanoo in Scholarship, Tourism, and Popular Culture

After Japan's surrender in 1945, all traces of Shintō vanished on the peninsula as Koreans tore down the shrines that they perceived as hated symbols of oppression.¹ Shrine officials were well aware of the hatred their draconian policies had caused. In an attempt to prevent desecration, they removed the deities from shrines and buried objects of worship or took them along as they fled the peninsula (Hardacre 2017: 434). Similarly, the theory of common ancestry vanished from public and scholarly discourses. However, many of its tenets soon resurfaced in a new theoretical framework that radically reinterpreted relations between early Japan and the Korean peninsula, the so-called horserider theory (*kiba minzoku setsu* 騎馬民族説).

The Horserider Theory

In September 1945, when the Supreme Commander of the Allied Powers closed down the Ethnic Research Institute, its former executive director Oka Masao retreated from academic life and moved to Nagano Prefecture. But in 1948 he participated in a symposium organized by his former colleagues at the institute, Yawata Ichirō 八幡一郎 (1902–1987), Egami Namio 江上波夫 (1906–2002), and Ishida Eiichirō 石田英一郎 (1903–1968). The symposium was dedicated to a discussion of "Origins of the Japanese Ethnic Culture and Formation of the Japanese State" (Oka et al. 1948). It was at this symposium that Oka for the first time introduced the theory of cultural strata in ancient Japan he had developed in his Viennese dissertation to Japanese academic circles. But Oka's theory was overshadowed by his younger colleague Egami's reflections on Japanese–Korean relations in the fourth century.

Based on archaeological artifacts excavated from tumuli of the Kofun period, Egami claimed that the fourth century marked a rupture in Japanese prehistory that was characterized by an abrupt influx of implements belonging to a horse-riding culture. His explanation for this rupture was that North Asian horse-riding people had expanded southward over the Korean peninsula and finally crossed the Korea Strait to invade the Japanese archipelago during the fourth century (Oka et al. 1948: 43–9).[2] In a later elaboration of his theory, Egami (1964: 47) admitted that his hypothesis "coincide[s] in large measure with the main outlines" of a 1921 paper by Kita Sadakichi with the telling title "Theory that the Japanese and Korean Peoples share the same origin" (Kita 1979–82). According to Egami, his horserider theory might even be viewed as "a modern edition of Dr. Kida's theory" (ibid.).

In the article in question, Kita argues that both the Japanese and Korean peoples were of mixed ancestry, the present-day Koreans being composed of a mixture of the Wa, Puyŏ, and Han Chinese peoples, whereas the Japanese were composed of the "people of heavenly ancestry" (*tenson minzoku*), *who were closely related to the Puyŏ*, as well as the Hayato 隼人, Wa, and Izumo peoples, and Chinese immigrants (Kang 1997b: 56). Kita's genealogy of the Japanese people is in large part based on the myth-histories of *Kojiki* and *Nihon shoki*, the "people of heavenly ancestry" referring to the Heavenly Grandchild Ninigi and his descendants, that is, to the imperial family. For Egami, the Puyŏ, a Tungusic people of Manchuria, were a probable candidate for the horse-riding invaders of Japan. He saw their invasion of the Japanese archipelago reflected in the myth of the Earthly Deities' ceding of the land to Amaterasu's grandson Ninigi (Egami 1964: 50, 55–7). Thus, his argument indeed shows obvious parallels to Kita's.

But there is one crucial difference between the two hypotheses. Although Kita stated that the Puyŏ were closely related to the *tenson minzoku*, that is, the people of the imperial family, he did not elaborate on this point. This is a typical pattern for proponents of the theory of common ancestry: while their studies were based on the "tacit premise" of the imperial family's Korean (or continental) origin, they accepted the "tacit taboo" against emphasizing this point (Oguma 2002: 73)—probably due to the Kume incident in 1892 mentioned above. The main innovation of Egami's horserider theory was the transgression of this taboo.

Egami's hypothesis was warmly welcomed by Western and Korean scholars. Taking Egami's theory a step further, in 1963 the North Korean historian Kim Sŏkhyŏng 金錫亨 (1915–1996) proposed the so-called "satellite state theory" (Kor. *bunguk sŏl*, Jap. *bunkoku setsu* 分国説) according to which peninsular immigrants had founded their own states in Kyushu, Izumo, and the Kinai area. Kim claimed that these immigrants remained under the control of their mother countries (Silla, Kaya, and Paekche) until the fifth century. The subjugation of the Korean kingdoms described in the *Nihon shoki*, he maintained, actually referred to these colonies on the Japanese archipelago (Farris 1998: 65–6). In the 1970s, the horserider theory (or a modified form thereof) was supported by prominent Western Koreanists such as Gari Ledyard (1975) or James Grayson (1977). More recently, the South Korean scholar Hong Wontack took up Egami's theory. In contrast to Egami, Hong insists that the invaders were not the (Tungus) Puyŏ but the (Korean) Paekche people, hence turning the hierarchical relationship of Koreans and Japanese in the ancient period, as perceived by proponents of the theory of common ancestry, completely on its head. According to Hong's theory, Susanoo was of Silla origin and ruled in Izumo during the Yayoi period, before the authority over the region was transferred to the Paekche (*sic*!) royal family (Hong 1994: 229–32).

Today Egami's theory is rejected by most archaeologists and historians;[3] nevertheless, it is widely recognized that the hypothesis had a liberating effect on the study of ancient Japanese–Korean relations since it served as a "necessary antidote to insular chauvinistic interpretations put forward in Japan" (Farris 1998: 63) at least since the colonial period. "The enduring legacy of scholars such as Egami," archaeologist Mizoguchi Kōji (2013: 17) remarks, "has been the recognition of discontinuities in the process previously recognised as continuous and evolutionary and the importance of contact with the continent in understanding Japanese history, particularly its early periods." While Oka's culture–historical approach was carried on by scholars such as Ōbayashi Taryō 大林太良 (1929–2001) and Matsumae Takeshi 松前健 (1922–2002),[4] recent Japanese scholarship tends to discuss the ancient Japanese myths within the framework of Japanese literature, thus disregarding or at least deemphasizing possible connections to the continent.[5]

Susanoo's Presence in Shimane Prefecture

The present study examines Susanoo's position within Japan's cultural memory. While professional groups such as historians play an important role in the shaping of cultural memory, as evidenced, for instance, by the wide dissemination of the theory of common ancestry during the colonial period, it would be a mistake to confine the research object to academic discourses. Cultural memory would vanish if it were not manifested in concrete sites of memory, such as memorials, museums, national holidays, or rituals.[6] As we have seen, Susanoo has always been closely connected to the Izumo region. Numerous local legends link the deity to sites in and around Izumo, as is attested, for instance, in the *Izumo fudoki* or the *Un'yōshi*. Even today, Susanoo is very much present in the towns and villages of Shimane Prefecture, as I could observe during three months of fieldwork in summer 2013. Especially, Susanoo's fight with the eight-headed serpent is firmly entrenched in Shimane's cultural memory and manifested in various contexts, forms, and media.

A major bus company based in Izumo City bears the name Susanoo Kankō (Susanoo Sightseeing) and uses a bearded deity riding on a giant serpent as its logo; Matsue's professional basketball team is known as Shimane Susanoo Magic, the team's logo is a giant serpent devouring a basketball, accompanied by a sword; the biggest highway loop in the prefecture is called Orochi Loop; manhole covers in Izumo City and Okuizumo Town depict the horned head of a giant serpent; a major street in Izumo City is called Orochi Street; large statues representing Susanoo's fight with the eight-headed serpent can be seen in Izumo, Okuizumo, Sada Town, and Unnan City. The list could be continued.

Susanoo does not only appear as a name or logo, however. There are many publicly visible explanations of his role in the mythical narrative of the ancient court chronicles and *Izumo fudoki*. A number of small bronze statues depicting mythical scenes connected to the Izumo region decorate the sidewalks of Kunibiki chūō dōri, Izumo City's central street leading to the train station. The statues are accompanied by short explanations of the scenes depicted (including Susanoo's fight with the eight-headed serpent, the land-pulling, and various episodes connected with Ōkuninushi).[7] A similar display of mythical scenes and accompanying explanations decorates the main street of Onsen resort town Tamatsukuri. Here, the deities are depicted in a cartoonish fashion with overlarge heads that make them appear like cute children. This style, which can also be observed in many tourist pamphlets and at some of the statues mentioned above, betrays a certain playfulness (though surely not disrespectfulness) in treating the venerable myths. On Japan Rail's Kisuki line, each station displays a poster designed by students of a local design school that explains a character, site, or scene from mythology connected to the site of the station in question. The rail line passes through the alleged site of Susanoo's dragon fight; thus, it is not surprising that this episode is treated extensively (almost half of the 12 posters are directly connected to this narrative).[8]

It is no coincidence that all of these displays are situated at sites frequented by many tourists. In the public consciousness in Japan (and, through the works of

Lafcadio Hearn,[9] to a lesser extent outside Japan), the Izumo region is strongly connected to mythology. Local tourist associations try to capitalize on this image by marketing the region as the "birthplace of myths and legends," the site "where mythology comes alive," or "the homeland of myths" (En-musubi Tourism Association, n.d.; Izumo Tourism Promotion Section, n.d.; Okuizumo Kankō Kyōkai, n.d.). Local tour operators organize special tours to sites associated with the ancient myths. In 2013, for instance, Yoshida Furusatomura corporation offered two bus tours connected to Susanoo: one tour was focused on sites related to Susanoo's fight with the eight-headed serpent, the other more generally on sites connected to Susanoo. Both tours mainly visited sites in Unnan City, located to the south of Izumo and Matsue. The first tour included visits to the site where Susanoo is believed to have picked up the chopsticks floating on the Hi River, the pool where the giant serpent is thought to have lived, a shrine that worships one of the giant *sake* containers Susanoo used to inebriate the serpent, the site where the god obtained Kusanagi from the serpent's tail, and the site where he buried the monster's eight heads, planting a pine tree on each head. Local guides accompanied the tourists and explained each site's significance.

Not only tour operators but also local shrines try to profit from the tourist potential of Shimane's close connection with the best-known episodes of Japanese mythology. A striking example is Yaegaki 八重垣 Shrine in Matsue. Named after the famous poem Susanoo composed after saving the daughter of Ashinazuchi and Tenazuchi from the eight-headed serpent, when he built "eightfold fences" (*yaegaki*) to shelter his bride, the shrine claims to be the site where the newly-wed deities settled down. By focusing on this romantic episode, the shrine emphasizes Susanoo's role as a deity of *enmusubi* 縁結び, that is, of fostering marital ties. Usually, Susanoo's descendant Ōkuninushi is viewed as the deity of *enmusubi*, who calls together all *kami* at Izumo Shrine each October to decide on the next year's marriages. The main attraction at Yaegaki Shrine, which draws large numbers of predominantly young female visitors to the shrine, is the Mirror Pond located inside a small grove on the shrine precincts. According to shrine tradition, Susanoo hid his bride in this grove during his fight with the eight-headed serpent. While waiting for the arrival of her husband, Inada Hime, as the goddess is called here, drank from the pond and used it as a mirror to make herself look pretty for Susanoo. Today shrine visitors can buy special paper slips and let them float to oracle how long they will have to wait to find their partner for life.

The shrine's treatment of this romantic narrative is characterized by the same playfulness as noted above. While Susanoo and Inada Hime are worshiped as deities at the shrine, the story makes them appear very human. The atmosphere on the shrine grounds, which are filled to the brim with visitors during the summer months, is one of fun and entertainment. As with many sites of memory connected to Susanoo in Shimane, the story told at Yaegaki Shrine is only loosely connected to the myths of the ancient court chronicles. In the ancient myths, Susanoo transforms his bride-to-be into a comb, which he places in his hair during his fight with the giant serpent. He only builds the "eightfold fences" to shelter his bride after he has defeated the monster. Like many of the other sites, the shrine also exudes a sense of nostalgia. In 2013, for instance, young local women wearing summer Kimonos, served as (free) guides for shrine visitors.

One final point worth noting about the public image of Susanoo in Shimane is that he is perceived in a very positive light. Susanoo is depicted as a hero, who saved a maiden from a gruesome beast and became a good husband to her. His banishment from Amaterasu's heavenly realm is mentioned only in passing, if at all. In Shimane, Susanoo is not presented as the shady little brother of the sun goddess, but as a great deity and hero in his own right. This is probably not surprising, since there are no myths or legends connecting Amaterasu to Shimane. In contrast to Susanoo and the other deities of Izumo, she is all but invisible. This phenomenon can also be observed in Iwami Kagura 石見神楽. Kagura is a theatrical dance that is usually performed by shrine maidens at Shintō shrines. However, in many parts of Japan, Kagura has developed into a sort of folk theater. In the Western part of Shimane (former Iwami Province), this tradition is still practiced by more than hundred groups that are usually unrelated to shrines and perform more often at community halls, gymnasiums, or roadside stations than at shrines. Despite this seeming secularization, the content of the dances are mostly mythical narratives. By far the most popular and most regularly performed play is Susanoo's fight against the eight-headed serpent (Iwami Kankō Shinkō Kyōgikai 2013; Ōda-shi Kankō Kyōkai 2013; Tsuwano Tourism Association, n.d.). Thus, Susanoo's role as shining hero is also emphasized through this medium.

Susanoo in Videogames

Susanoo remains visible outside Shimane Prefecture as well. He appears as a character in many works of popular culture, including Manga, Anime, and videogames. His role here is more ambivalent than in Shimane's folklore and tourism (and thus arguably more in line with the ancient court chronicles), as an analysis of the videogames *Ōkami* 大神 (Capcom, 2006) and *Shin Megami Tensei: Imagine* 新・女神転生 IMAGINE (Atlus, 2007) shows.

Ōkami is a single player game, in which the player takes the role of Amaterasu, incarnated as a white wolf (the title is a pun on the word *ōkami* that can mean both "great deity" and, written with another Chinese character, "wolf"). The game's setting is Nippon, a fictional world heavily inspired by Japanese myths and legends. The link with ancient Japan is emphasized through the artwork, which is reminiscent of traditional ink painting—an association that is reinforced through the appearance of a giant calligraphy brush during cutscenes. It is Amaterasu's task to purify the world from pollution and finally battle the fearsome Orochi, the great eight-headed serpent. In the game, players not only solve puzzles and fight demons, but also cure the emperor from sickness, feed woodland animals, and bring dead trees back to life. For such beneficial actions, Amaterasu receives "praise," resulting in level-ups. Thus, the game depicts an idealized Shintō-inspired world that teaches the veneration of nature (Anthony 2014: 38; Hutchinson 2019: 47–9).

Susanoo also has an appearance in the game. But in contrast to Amaterasu, he is not depicted as a deity but rather as a human. What is more, he is a braggart and coward who hides away in his house, afraid of the giant serpent. Amaterasu eventually lures him out (a humorous inversion of the myth about Amaterasu hiding in the Heavenly Rock Cave following Susanoo's outrages) and convinces him to help her fight Orochi. In the end, Susanoo pledges to treat Amaterasu like his sister (Hutchinson 2019: 49).[10] In this way, the game playfully alludes to the myths of *Kojiki* and *Nihon shoki* without attempting to reproduce them faithfully. It is interesting to note that Susanoo is described in a much more negative way than in the numerous contemporary depictions in Shimane. While in Shimane he is perceived as a heroic deity in his own right, in *Ōkami* Susanoo is neither a god nor a hero. It is only through Amaterasu's help that he finds his courage. Even so, his connection to the myth of the eight-headed serpent is so well known that it was apparently not an option to leave him entirely out of the storyline.

The massively multiplayer online role-playing game *Shin Megami Tensei: Imagine* provides a stark contrast to the idyllic setting of *Ōkami*. The game is set in the near future in postapocalyptic Tokyo. A war has devastated humanity and prompted the arrival of demons, who are divided into the two opposing factions of Law and Chaos. The player character is a young Demon Buster, who can turn demons into his allies and is drawn into the conflict between Law and Chaos.[11] Many characters not only from Japanese but also foreign mythologies appear in the game as demons. Amaterasu fights on the side of Law, while Susanoo is a demon of Chaos. The game thus reflects the two deities' antagonistic relationship in the ancient myths (incidentally, the giant eight-headed serpent is neutral). Amaterasu exists in both a female and a male version. This alludes to the episode in *Kojiki* and *Nihon shoki* in which Amaterasu dons armor and binds her hair in male fashion to await Susanoo's arrival at the entrance to her realm. In *Shin Megami Tensei: Imagine*, the Japanese *kami* appear side by side with "demons" deriving from other mythical traditions such as Odin (Law), Loki (Chaos), Athena (Law), Ares (Chaos), and many others.[12]

Hirafuji Kikuko (2007a: 34–41) calls this amalgamation of elements stemming from various mythical traditions in Japanese popular culture "hyper mythology" and points to videogames' significance as sources of knowledge about myth, especially for young Japanese. In a survey among students of two universities in Tokyo, conducted in 2006, Hirafuji asked about students' familiarity with videogames and with characters and names from Japanese and foreign myths. Of the respondents who had played videogames like *Megami Tensei*, about 70 percent were familiar with the name Odin, whereas less than 30 percent of students who had not experienced such a game had heard the name. With regard to the Japanese deity Amaterasu, however, no significant difference could be observed between players and nonplayers (over 90% of both groups being familiar with the name).

These findings show that young Japanese possess certain knowledge about the myths of *Kojiki* and *Nihon shoki*. Even in popular culture, the deities appearing in Japanese myths are therefore treated more faithfully than characters from foreign mythologies, which are often used as mere names without any substantial connection to the original myths (cf. Hirafuji 2007b: 170). With regard to Susanoo, the videogames treated above suggest that his adversarial relationship with his sister Amaterasu (though treated in different ways in each game) is known to the games' audiences (or at least the developers assume such a familiarity). Both the plot of *Ōkami* and the omnipresence of Susanoo's fight with the eight-headed serpent in Shimane Prefecture suggest that it is this episode more than anything else that is today associated with the name Susanoo in Japanese cultural memory. On the other hand, his nature as a foreign deity, emphasized throughout the Middle Ages and the period of Japanese colonial rule over Korea, seems to have all but vanished from public consciousness.[13] The shady little brother of the sun goddess has become thoroughly Japanese.

Notes

Introduction

1 The inadequacy of depicting Tokugawa Japan as an isolated country that eschewed foreign trade and foreign relations has long been recognized. Both the bakufu and domain lords actively conducted trade with Korea, China, Ryūkyū, and the Dutch (Toby 1977). Nonetheless, the uncontrolled influx of Western ideas and goods after the collapse of the Tokugawa bakufu constituted a dramatic rupture that posed a serious challenge to Meiji elites, who feared the disintegration of the Japanese state.
2 A similar formulation can be found in the fifteenth-century *Yuiitsu shintō myōbō yōshū* 唯一神道名法要集 (Essentials of Terminology and Doctrine of Yuiitsu Shintō), the foundational text of Yoshida Shintō, which claimed Shintō's supremacy over Buddhism and Confucianism and consequently Japan's supremacy over India and China. See Grapard (1992b: 158). The idea of the unbroken sun lineage later became one of the main tenets of modern nationalistic Shintō. On Yoshida Shintō, see Chapter 5.
3 The custom of applying two-graph posthumous names to Japanese rulers was introduced in the mid-eighth century (Lurie 2011: xx; Ooms 2009: 154). The name Jinmu is thus an anachronism that does not appear in *Kojiki* and *Nihon shoki*. For the sake of readability, I nonetheless use the two-graph names under which the early emperors (like their posteighth-century successors) are commonly known rather than the unwieldy names used in the original sources.
4 Kenneth Ruoff (2010: 3) emphasizes the ideological significance of a national origin that predates the origin of Christian civilization.
5 It goes without saying that this date is no less fictive than that of Jinmu's alleged founding of Japan (cf. Pai 2000: 92).
6 Arguably, the most prominent supporter of Tan'gun's inclusion was Ch'oe Namsŏn (1890–1957), who emphasized Tan'gun's significance for Korean national identity. See Cha and Yi (2014); Kim (2018: 56–8).
7 The term myth-history is intended to draw attention to the complex nature of the early court chronicles that seamlessly linked myths with history, thus legitimating imperial power "by linking the this-worldly order to the sacred order of the High Heavens" (Ebersole 1989: 3).
8 As the second part of the present study will show, colonial-period scholars' reading of the ancient myths was highly selective. The episodes connecting Susanoo to

Korea, for instance, appear in the *Nihon shoki* only in the form of mythical variants that are poorly connected to the overall plot and by no means constitute the core of the *Nihon shoki*'s narrative. Other ancient sources such as the *Kojiki* do not mention these episodes at all.

9 Wendy Doniger (1988: 30) draws attention to the close connection between myth and memory by pointing out, "that the tradition of a myth begins when it is heard for the *second* time—that is, when it is remembered for the first time."

10 Of special interest for the present study are not only Saitō Hideki's (2012) and Kwŏn Dongwoo's (2013) monographs on the transformations of Susanoo from the ancient through the medieval periods but also recent works on Shinra Myōjin (Kim 2020), Gozu Tennō (Kawamura 2007; Suzuki 2019), and Matarajin (Kawamura 2017)—three deities who were associated with Susanoo in the Middle Ages. Other recent monographs focus on Amaterasu's role in the ancient (Mizoguchi 2009), medieval (Satō 2000), and modern periods (Chiba 2011).

1 At the Margin of the Divine Country: Korea in Japanese Cultural Imagination

1 On the archaeology of Yayoi and Kofun Japan and its relationship to the Korean peninsula, see Barnes (2007); Farris (1998); Harunari (2004); Seyock (2004); and Shiraishi (2004).

2 The appellation Wa is found in Chinese chronicles like the *San guo zhi* 三国志 (Reports on the Three Realms), which was first drafted in the third century, and is thought to refer to the inhabitants of the Japanese islands (and possibly of the southern-most region of the Korean peninsula) (Seyock 2004: 16).

3 The last eleven chapters of the *Weizhi*, which is one of the three parts of the *San guo zhi*.

4 According to the *Samguk yusa*, Kŭmgwan Kaya was the seat of government of King Suro, the legendary first king of the Kaya Federation. The same source also states that Kŭmgwan later became Kimhae Prefecture (SGYS I, 31).

5 Lee (2015: 159–60); Mohan (2004: 106–8). On the problem of the Kwanggaet'o stele, see Mohan (2004); Pai (2000); Takeda (1989). For transcriptions of the stele's inscription, see Szczesniak (1951: 254–68); Takeda (1989: 88–9). Boleslaw Szczesniak moreover provides a translation of the stele's text into English. While it should be treated with caution, the translation gives a good impression of the difficulties involved in interpreting the fragmentary text.

6 The *Nihon shoki* presents Mimana as a Japanese colony during the period stretching from the reign of Yūryaku (trad. 457–479) to the reign of Kinmei (trad. 539–571). The *Samguk sagi* mentions Imna Karyang 任那加良 as the home country of the famous

Confucian scholar Kangsu 強首 (?–692). According to Yi Pyŏngdo, Imna Karyang is identical to Tae Kaya 大加耶, one of the Kaya states (SGSG XLVI, vol. 2: 429/438). Hong Wontack (1994: 217) argues that Mimana was probably nothing more than "a port facility (naturally with a group of Japanese residents) at the southern tip of Kaya as a direct short-cut crossing route from Japan." For a brief summary of the Mimana controversy between Korean and Japanese scholars, see Pai (2000: 431, n. 11).

7 As will be discussed below, Confucian ideas continued to exert a strong influence within the modern ideology of Japan as a family state. But although virtues such as filial piety and loyalty were extolled in official Meiji documents like the 1890 Imperial Rescript on Education, they were commonly rebranded as traditionally "Japanese" virtues and no longer explicitly associated with Confucianism.

8 For the following, see also Horstmann (1993: 394–9).

9 "Alles Denken, Urtheilen, Wahrnehmen als Vergleichen hat als Voraussetzung ein 'Gleich*setzen*,' noch früher ein 'Gleich*machen*.' Das Gleichmachen ist dasselbe, was die Einverleibung der angeeigneten Materie in die Amoebe ist" (Nietzsche 1999, vol. 2: 209).

10 "Der Trieb der Assimilation, jene organische Grundfunktion, auf der alles Wachsthum beruht, paßt sich, was es aus der Nähe sich aneignet, auch innerlich an: der Wille zur Macht fungiert in diesem Einbegreifen des Neuen unter den Formen des Alten, Schon-Erlebten" (Nietzsche 1999, vol. 11: 631).

11 Although *kokutai* literally means "national body," it is commonly translated as "national polity" or "national essence." On this central term of modern Japanese state ideology, see Antoni (2016).

12 Nietzsche himself suggested an analogy between individual cognition and processes of social integration:

> The last organisms whose development we see (peoples, states, societies), must be used to learn about the first organisms. … Commonly consciousness only appears, when the whole wants to subordinate itself to another supreme whole—first as the consciousness of this supreme whole, the non-self (*Außersich*). Consciousness develops vis-à-vis the entity whom we could serve (*dem wir Funktion sein könnten*)—it is the means to incorporate us. (Nietzsche 1999, vol. 9: 563)

An interesting figure in this context is Uehara Etsujirō 植原悦二郎 (1877–1962), who demanded that Japanese migrants to the United States should assimilate to their host country's culture. While he also advocated Koreans' assimilation into the Japanese empire, he argued that first Japan had to be democratized. In other words, Japan had to assimilate to an ideal that in his view was most thoroughly realized in the United States (Oguma 1998: 220–5). This calls to mind Meiji Japan's intermediate position in a civilizational triad between "backward" Asia and the "modern" West.

13 On Kita's views on Korea, see Kang (1997b).
14 Scholl (2018: 141–6) calls attention to the differences between the theory of common ancestry and pan-Asianism. The most important of these is that the former regards China as a negative Other, while the latter includes it into a union of Asian peoples.
15 On this interesting personage who became prime minister in 1944, see Oguma (1998: 449–57).
16 In the *Nihon shoki*, Ōkunitama no Kami 大国玉神 is given as an alternate name for Susanoo's descendant Ōkuninushi (NSK I [8, var. 6], vol. 1: 102/103). The *Kojiki* mentions a child of the deity Ōtoshi with the name Ōkunimitama no Kami 大国御魂神 (KJK I: 96/97).

2 A Foil to Set Off the Sun Goddess: Susanoo in the Ancient Sources

1 This led Alexander Slawik (1993) to identify as many as five different characters called Susanoo in the myths recorded in *Kojiki* and *Nihon shoki*.
2 In a similar vein, Mizubayashi Takeshi (1991: 501) maintains that the stories told of Susanoo in the two sources are so different that "they could even be called diametrically opposed narratives." According to Mizubayashi, the *Nihon shoki*'s Susanoo represents an "embodiment of evil," whereas the *Kojiki*'s Susanoo is an "embodiment of good."
3 David Lurie (2011: 244) casts doubt on the trustworthiness of the *Kojiki*'s preface, which, he believes, might be no more than "a retroactive justification, … a claim of official approval or sponsorship after the fact, in which the founding role played by the sovereigns Tenmu and Genmei is exaggerated in true courtier-author fashion." Nonetheless, the date of the work's completion as well as Yasumaro's authorship is generally accepted in contemporary scholarship.
4 Quiros (2017: 306). The following summary is based on the *Shinpen Nihon koten bungaku zenshū* edition (KJK). See also the English translations of the *Kojiki* by Basil Hall Chamberlain ([1882] 1982), Donald Philippi (1968), and, more recently, Gustav Heldt (2014). For a new German translation with extensive commentary, see Antoni (2012).
5 The literal meaning of the characters is "yellow spring" or "underground spring" (Antoni 2012: 521–2; Kōnoshi 1984: 57). Thus, Yomi is commonly translated as "Underworld" (Antoni 2012: 26; Heldt 2014: 14) or "Hades" (Chamberlain [1882] 1982: 38). As Kōnoshi (1984; 2008: 80–9) and others have pointed out, however, nothing in the text suggests that the Land of Yomi was conceived as a subterranean realm. The various conceptions of the afterworld presented in the old sources will be discussed in Chapter 4.

6 If not stated otherwise, translations of deities' names are taken from Heldt's (2014) translation of the *Kojiki*.
7 The meaning of Susanoo's name is disputed. According to the most common interpretations, it is either "Impetuous Male" or "Man from Susa." These interpretations will be discussed in the second half of this chapter.
8 This term is commonly translated as "Solid Land of Roots" (Antoni 2012: 33; Naumann 1996: 59) or "the land that lies beneath the hard earth's roots" (Heldt 2014: 19), but recent scholarship casts doubt on this interpretation (see Chapter 4).
9 The translation of this term is contested. Heldt (2014: 20) translates "sacred oaths," following the older translations of Philippi (1968: 75), "oaths," and Chamberlain ([1882] 1982: 53), "swear"; Antoni (2012: 34), on the other hand, translates "evocation" (*Beschwörung*). Terakawa Machio (2009: 183–9) explains the function of *ukei* in the following way: one pronounces a statement in the form of "If A, then B," then one observes if B comes true (or not) and concludes that A is true as well (or not). In the record of Suinin 垂仁, the legendary eleventh emperor of Japan, for instance, Aketatsu no Miko 曙立王 proclaims, "If the veneration of the great deity is indeed effective, may the heron living in the tree by the Sagisu Pond fall down due to my *ukei*"—and the heron falls down (KJK II [Suinin]: 206/207). As Terakawa points out, Susanoo's *ukei* differs from this procedure in two decisive ways: (1) the conditions are not clarified in advance (what outcome would prove Susanoo's innocence?), (2) Amaterasu takes part in the *ukei* although it is only meant to prove Susanoo's good intentions. Thus, Terakawa argues, Susanoo could have actually gotten the better of his sister and tricked her into an *ukei* whose outcome he then interprets himself (see below). He describes this behavior as the intrigue of a trickster (*torikkusutā-teki takurami*).
10 For stylistic reasons, the song cannot be regarded as Japan's oldest piece of poetry (Antoni 2012: 553–4).
11 Usually translated as "Flat Slope of the Underworld" (Antoni 2012: 51), "Even Pass of Hades" (Chamberlain [1882] 1982: 87–8), or "Gentle Decline passing into the land of the Underworld" (Heldt 2014: 32). The same name is given for the site where Izanaki left Yomotsu Kuni after his failed attempt to retrieve his deceased wife, leading some scholars to equate Ne no Katasukuni with Yomotsu Kuni (see Chapter 4).
12 The central figure in this process was Motoori Norinaga, whose philological reconstruction of the allegedly pure ancient Japanese language of the *Kojiki* has been exposed as an invented tradition (Antoni 2012: 275–6, 412–37). This is a typical example of what Blumenberg (2006: 329) expressed in the formula: "The reception of the sources creates the sources of reception."
13 The characters used to write deities' names differ from those of *Kojiki*.
14 For a schematic representation of the complex structure of such a myth block, see Isomae (2009: 51).

15 The *Nihon shoki* uses other characters than the *Kojiki* to write Susanoo's name. Later sources tend to use the *Nihon shoki*'s characters. The following summary is based on the *Shinpen Nihon koten bungaku zenshū* edition (NSK I, vol. 1: 24–107) as well as on the English translation by William George Aston ([1896] 1956: 10–63) and the German translation of the divine age fascicles by Karl Florenz (1901: 13–151). On the subdivisions of the *Nihon shoki*'s first two fascicles, see Metevelis (1993).

16 The Roman digit refers to the fascicle, the Arabic one to the myth block.

17 Usually translated as "Land of Roots" (Naumann 1996: 59), "Netherworld" (Aston [1896] 1956: 20), or "Underworld" (Florenz 1901: 30), this realm is often regarded as identical with the *Kojiki*'s Ne no Katasukuni.

18 Note that Amaterasu in a later episode in the *Nihon shoki* addresses almost exactly the same words to Susanoo before she retreats into the Heavenly Rock Cave (I [7, var. 1]): "I do not want to see you face to face again."

19 For a comparison and discussion of the different variants, see Isomae (2009: 42–5).

20 Only in one version (I [6, var. 2]), the sun goddess was enraged and retreated into the Heavenly Rock Cave after Susanoo had defecated under her seat in the New Palace.

21 Note that the name is written with different characters and there is a slight difference in pronunciation compared to the *Kojiki*. However, just as in the *Kojiki*, the name can be translated as Lady Wondrous Rice Paddies.

22 Variants 3, 4, and 5 explicitly associate Susanoo with the Korean peninsula and are therefore treated separately in Chapter 4.

23 This translation follows Edwina Palmer (2016: 3).

24 This summary is based on the *Shinpen Nihon koten bungaku zenshū* edition (IF) and Michiko Yamaguchi Aoki's English translation (Aoki 1997: 75–161). On the depiction of Susanoo in the *Izumo fudoki*, see also Takioto (1994: 37–50).

25 However, the *Izumo fudoki* does record an episode that is reminiscent of the *Kojiki*'s account of Susanoo's fight against the eight-headed serpent of Koshi: the entry on the Township Mori in Ou District contains the curious statement that Ōnamochi (= Ōanamuji), "the great god who has created the world," had subdued Yakuchi (Eight Mouths) of Koshi (IF: 138–40). It is unclear how these episodes are related to each other—if at all (cf. Katō 1962: 90; Miura 2003: 251).

26 This is the translation given by Aoki (1997: 110). For Susanoo's relation to metal culture, see Ōbayashi (1974: 163–95); Weiss (2014; 2018b).

27 Yamada Hisashi (2001: 37–101) provides an excellent overview of research on Susanoo.

28 On Jihen and his role in medieval religious discourse, see Grapard (1992a: 34–6).

29 In fact, the *Kojiki* states that Susanoo wanted to follow his mother to Ne no Katasukuni.

30 While Tsukuyomi's name is indeed written with those characters in the *Nihon shoki*, the *Kojiki* uses different ones. With regard to the land of Yomi, Atsutane claims that

the characters employed by him were the original ones, which were replaced by the ones used in *Kojiki* and *Nihon shoki* after the introduction of Chinese books and concepts to Japan (TM: 96–101).
31 For Tylor's relation to nature mythology, see also Wachutka (2001: 91–2). For a more general discussion of Tylor's approach to the study of myth, see Segal (2004: 14–23).
32 Aston (1905: 140–1) rejected this interpretation, pointing out that "the *susamu* etymology ... implies a noun *susa*, impetuosity, which does not exist." For this reason, he argued that Susanoo actually means nothing more than "Man from Susa." He based this interpretation on the *Izumo fudoki*'s entry on the Township Susa quoted above.
33 The following discussion is based on Hirafuji (2004: 1–24) and Satō (2004).
34 On this important intellectual of the Meiji period, see Isomae (2014).
35 Hirafuji Kikuko (2004: 76) points out that it cannot be proved whether Florenz influenced the Japanese scholars. Müller's theories, on the other hand, were well known in Japan at the time and could have directly influenced Anesaki, Takagi, and Takayama.

3 Passion for Transgression: Susanoo's Liminal Character

1 The two groups are by no means clearly demarcated in the two chronicles. Many deities cannot be unambiguously correlated with one of the groups. Susanoo presents an especially ambiguous case (see below). Since Norinaga's times, the cosmos of the old Japanese myths has been regarded as three-layered: in this conception, the Central Land of Reed Plains was believed to be located on a vertical axis between the Plain of High Heaven above and the realms of the dead below (cf. Saigō 1967: 15–34). More recent scholarship casts doubt on this view, suggesting instead a two-layered cosmos consisting of the Plain of High Heaven and the Central Land of Reed Plains with the realms of the dead being located at the latter's margin (cf. Masuda 1984: 189). According to this hypothesis, "central" has to be understood in a horizontal rather than in a vertical sense.
2 In the Hirata School of National Learning, this episode was used to support the claim that Ōkuninushi had become the ruler of the invisible realm of the dead.
3 The strategy of associating Izumo with the realms of death and contrasting it with Yamato and Ise will be discussed in detail in Chapter 4.
4 Previous studies that focus on Susanoo's role as a trickster deity include an article by Cornelius Ouwehand (1958–9), who applies Lévi-Strauss's (1955: 441) definition of the trickster as a mediator between polar opposites to Susanoo's fight with the

eight-headed serpent; various studies by Yamaguchi Masao (1977; 2003a: 292–5; 2003b), who views Susanoo as a figure linked to marginality who complements Amaterasu's role as a symbol of central power; and an article by Robert Ellwood (1997), who links Susanoo's wanderings through the various realms of the cosmos with the model of sacred kingship. See also Weiss (2014).

5 For the following, see also Yamaguchi (1977: 161–2).
6 For an extensive discussion of Lévi-Strauss's comparison, see Yoshida (1996).
7 The *Kojiki* seems to emphasize Susanoo's role as a bringer of chaos by using almost the same wording to describe the results of the destructive crying and howling that cause Susanoo's first banishment and the outrages he commits in his sister's realm (Wittkamp 2018: 345–6).
8 Witzel (2005: 10–12) reaches this conclusion after a detailed comparison of the Japanese episode to the Vedic myth of Uṣas.
9 Babcock-Abrahams borrows this expression from Aldous Huxley (1949: 13): "The good life can only be lived in a society in which tidiness is preached and practised, but not too fanatically, and where efficiency is always haloed, as it were, by a tolerated margin of mess."
10 These "Heavenly Sins" are distinguished from the so-called "Earthly Sins" (*kunitsu tsumi* 国津罪), which include different forms of sodomy as well as various sicknesses and magical practices. Róheim (1972: 371) argues "that the mischief done to his [Susanoo's] sister's ricefield is merely the 'heavenly,' i.e. symbolical equivalent of what appears in the second list as incest." It must be emphasized, however, that the list of prohibitions does not contain incest between siblings but only incest between parents and children. Mori (2002: 89) draws attention to the ambiguous attitude in ancient Japan with regard to sibling marriages, which were, after all, depicted as the mode of marriage of some of the most important deities in the myths.
11 For an English translation, see Katō and Hoshino (1926). Recent scholarship emphasizes the *Kogo shūi*'s importance in linking and harmonizing the myths of *Kojiki* and *Nihon shoki* with religious rituals. See Kwŏn (2013: 155–81).
12 On Susanoo's role as scapegoat, see also Yamaguchi (2003b).
13 See, for example, the following motifs in Aarne-Thompson's *Motif-Index of Folk-Literature* (Thompson 1955): A736.1.4.1 *Sun and moon quarrel when sun eats up all their children*, A736.1.4.1.1. *Moon kills sun's children*, A736.9. *Sun cursed by moon*, A736.11. *Contest between sun and moon*, A737.7. *Eclipses from quarrels between moon and sun*. Based on a comparison of Indian, Chinese, Japanese, and Kekchi Maya myths, Witzel (2007: 225) reconstructs a "Late Paleolithic myth of the love, meeting and parting of the Sun and the Moon." Susanoo, he concludes, is a "stand-in for the Moon" (ibid.: 241, n. 42).
14 Matsumae (1970: 122) therefore traces the myth of Tsukuyomi's killing of the food goddess to the Ise region.

15 Considering that Matsumura Takeo began researching myths in the 1920s, it seems possible that his interpretation of Susanoo as the deity of a vanquished state was in fact inspired by colonial-period works on common ancestry, whose hypotheses he then projected onto ancient Izumo.
16 Matsuda Hiroko (2019: 151), for instance, argues, "Liminality created the space for the common people of Okinawa to exercise their agency and enabled them to make their careers in the Japanese colonial empire."

4 "I Do Not Want to Stay in This Land": Susanoo's Sojourn to Korea in the Ancient Court Chronicles

1 Note that, according to one variant of the *Nihon shoki* (NSK II [9, var. 6], vol. 1: 150–3), the peak to which Ninigi, the Heavenly Grandchild, descended from the Plain of High Heaven is called Mount Sohori 添. The parallels of this myth to Korean founding myths, especially the myth of Tan'gun, have been illuminated by a number of comparative studies. See, for instance, Egami (1964); Matsumae (1983); Ōbayashi (1984b).
2 In the *Kojiki*, the name Shirahi-wake 白日別 appears as another name for Tsukushi in the episode relating the birth of the Japanese islands (KJK I: 34/35).
3 Also known as Alla 安羅. This state emerged in the center of Pyŏnhan, one of the three Han polities in the southern portion of the Korean peninsula. Archaeologists unearthed ironware in great quantity in this region, including ring-pommeled swords. Despite close ties with Paekche and the Japanese archipelago, Ara Kaya was conquered by Silla in the middle of the sixth century (Kungnip Kimhae Pangmulgwan 2008: 131). Since it is mentioned in the Kwanggaet'o stele's inscription (line 66, cf. Szczesniak 1951: 259), Bentley (2006: 179) believes "that Alla anciently was a powerful member of the Karak [i.e., Kaya] Federation."
4 The southern Chinese kingdoms of Wu and Yue 越 were famed throughout China for the supreme quality of their swords in works dating from the Later Han Period (25–220 CE) (Ōbayashi 1974: 190).
5 The Chinese characters mean "grass-mower." However, Naumann and Miller (1995: 405) postulate a link between the sword name and the Old Korean word for "serpent." They thus regard the sword as a *pars pro toto* for the serpent. Cf. Weiss (2018b: 9).
6 On this phrase of Chinese origin, see Antoni (2012: 526–7).
7 On this difficult passage and what it reveals about ancient Japanese burial customs, see Naumann (1971: 121–32).
8 *Nihongi-kō* were held six times during the early Heian period: 812–13, 843–4, 878–81, 904–6, 936–43, and 965–? (it is unknown, when the last lecture session ended) (Saitō 2006: 66–7).

9 The name is written as "Soshihoru" 蘇之保留 in the *Shaku Nihongi*. The linguist Kanazawa Shōzaburō (1994: 105), a proponent of the theory of common ancestry, argues that *shi*—like the *shi* in "Soshimori"—was nothing more than an optional possessive particle. If it is left out, one obtains the form "Sohoru," which is reasonably close to "Sohori," the name provided for the Silla capital in Japanese sources, and "Sŏbŏl," its Korean pronunciation.

10 On the *Sendai kuji hongi* and the question of its antiquity, see Bentley (2006); Robinson (1955).

11 Based on a close textual comparison, John Bentley (2006: 41), who has recently published a complete translation of *Sedai kuji hongi* into English, argues for an earlier date of the work's completion. He claims that the work quoted from proto-forms of the *Kojiki* and the *Nihon shoki* rather than from the finished works. However, the existence of such proto-forms cannot be proved (cf. Antoni 2012: 398; Teeuwen 2007: 95–6).

12 For a full English translation of the passage, see Bentley (2006: 176–81).

13 The *Nihon shoki* contains a similar passage, in which Susanoo discloses to his father that he wants to follow his mother to Ne no Kuni (NSK I [5, var. 6], vol. 1: 50/51).

14 This interpretation is probably inspired by the *Nihon shoki*'s main text, in which Izanami is indeed described as Susanoo's mother. Stockdale (2013: 250) emphasizes the strong intertextuality between the *Kojiki* and the *Nihon shoki* with regard to this passage.

15 The text continues thus: "In the time of flowers, the inhabitants worship the spirit of this Goddess by offerings of flowers. They also worship her with drums, flutes, flags, singing, and dancing."

16 In the so-called Pantheon Dispute, Senge Takatomi 千家尊福 (1845–1918), head priest of the Izumo Shrine, attempted to capitalize on Izumo's connection to the afterworld. Drawing on the theses of Hirata Atsutane and his disciples, Senge demanded that Ōkuninushi, the main deity worshiped at Izumo Shrine, be admitted into the official state pantheon and thus be put on the same level as Amaterasu. He based this demand, which from 1875 divided the Shintō priesthood into two camps, on the assertion that Ōkuninushi's role as ruler of the otherworld was no less significant than that of Amaterasu as the ruler of the present world. See Hara (1996).

17 On this point, see Kōnoshi (1984: 62–9; 2008: 84–9, 105–15); Satō (2011: 62–3, 69–70); Yamada (2001: 162–3, 172–7); Wittkamp (2018: 190–6, 201–6).

18 A similar story is also mentioned in the *Nihon shoki* (NSK I [8, var. 6], vol. 1: 102/103; cf. Antoni 1988: 154). Interestingly, in this instance, Awashima 淡嶋 is written with the same character as Awaji, the site of Izanaki's "hidden palace" mentioned above.

19 The toponym "Kumano" is attested in both Izumo and Kii. There are also scholars who locate the site of Sukunabikona's departure in Kii. See, for instance, NSK I [8, var. 6], vol. 1: 103, n. 17; Gorai (1998: 237–8).
20 The exact location of Sukunabikona's arrival varies in the different accounts: according to the *Kojiki*, he appears at "the cape of Miho 御大 in Izumo" (KJK I: 94), whereas the *Nihon shoki* gives the "little beach of Isasa 五十狭狭 in Izumo" as the site of the deity's arrival (NSK I [8, var. 6], vol. 1: 104/105).
21 Nelly Naumann (1996: 101–2) expresses a similar view: "The special otherworld which is attributed to Susa no Wo is by no means identical with *yomi no kuni*, the 'Land of Darkness' where Izanami rules. ... No one who has entered the Land of Darkness can ever leave it again; but a *ne no kuni*, a Land of Roots, promises new life."
22 This is the reading supplied in the *Shinpen Nihon koten bungaku zenshū* edition of *Nihon shoki* for the toponym that is written with the characters meaning "below the storehouse." In a headnote, the editors remark that it is probably a word in the language of Paekche (NSK XIV [Yūryaku 21/3], vol. 2: 204, n. 6). Aston ([1896] 1956, vol. 1: 367), on the other hand, gives the name in modern Korean pronunciation as "Chhang-ha [Ch'ang-ha]." It is not clear where this site is located.
23 Aston ([1896] 1956, vol. 1: 367) turns the emperor into the subject of the sentence, thus emphasizing his role even more strongly: "They with true hearts appealed to the Emperor, who restored their country."
24 Thought to be identical with the *Samguk sagi*'s King Tongsŏng (personal name Modae 牟大; trad. r. 479–501), who ascended to the throne after the short reign of Munju's successor Samgŭn (trad. r. 477–479) (NSK, vol. 2: 207, n. 16; SGSG XXVI, vol 2: 70–1, 82–3).
25 For a full translation of the Paekche Annals, see Best (2006).
26 Cf. Robbeets (2005: 652–3). Itabashi (2003: 144) notes possible cognates from Koguryŏic and Tungusic (Evenki and Lamut). This linguistic evidence supports the hypothesis of the Tungusic (Puyŏ) origin of the Paekche monarchs, which will be discussed below.
27 The capital letters indicate syllables that are written semantographically. Bentley (2000: 427) points out several possible Tungusic cognates.
28 On this mythological conception, see Matsumae (1983); Oka (1956; 2012, vol. 1: 1–38, 444, 486); Waida (1973).
29 The following discussion is mainly based on the pioneering studies of Kenneth Gardiner (1979; 1982a; 1982b; 1988) as well as on the more recent analyses of James Grayson (2001: 59–86).
30 Gardiner (1988: 157) points out that the skepticism of Kim Pusik 金富軾 (1075–1151), the Confucian author of *Samguk sagi*, becomes apparent if one compares this

episode to the *Ku-Samguksa* version. While Haemosu's descent from heaven and his divine origin are depicted as facts in the *Ku-Samguksa*, Kim Pusik's version leaves open the possibility that he was nothing more than a fraud. In the preface to his poem, Yi Kyubo criticizes Pusik for not including a fuller version of the myth in the *Samguk sagi* out of fear that it would "mislead people" (Rutt 1973: 48).

31 For full translations of the story, see Grayson (2001: 75); Shultz and Kang (2012a: 38–9).
32 On possible routes the Puyŏ might have taken to reach southern Korea, see Gardiner (1969: 573); Beckwith (2007: 2).

5 The God with a Thousand Faces: Susanoo and His Alter Egos in Medieval Mythology

1 The term "syncretism" has fallen out of favor in recent (predominantly Western) studies on Japanese religion, since in the past it has been mostly applied with negative connotations (contamination or bastardization of a once "pure" religious tradition) and since it suggests the fusion of two full-fledged religious systems—an assumption that does not further our understanding of the complex religious discourses in medieval Japan (Hardacre 2017: 143).
2 In Japanese-language studies on myth, this concept is rarely invoked. However, scholars have attempted to widen the scope of "medieval myths" and analyze ancient and modern texts through the same lens—that is with an emphasis on reception processes and the transformability of myths. Thus, the term "medieval myths" has been turned into an analytical framework similar to Aleida and Jan Assmann's concept of cultural memory. See Kwŏn (2013: 43–52); Saitō (2006: 3–8).
3 The epithet "Haya," that is, "fast" sometimes precedes Susanoo's name in the *Kojiki*.
4 The text is thought to have been written by a monk in the late twelfth or early thirteenth century and later expanded by Watarai priests (Teeuwen and van der Veere 1998: 17–18).
5 Zhong translates "southeast," but a recent edition of documents related to Gakuenji uses the character *ushitora* 艮, which refers to "northeast." See Inoue (2018: 173).
6 As mentioned in Chapter 3, according to the *Kojiki*, the Heavenly Deities built a magnificent palace for Ōkuninushi, who ceded the land to Amaterasu's grandchild Ninigi. This passage is often interpreted as the foundation myth of Izumo Taisha.
7 The name appears for the first time on a stone tube in which, according to the inscription, eight volumes of the Lotus Sutra copied by four monks in the years Ninpei 1–3 (1151–3) were enclosed (Sone 1963: 2–13, 252).
8 The present-day meaning of the word *wani* is "crocodile." It is not clear what the term meant in medieval Izumo, but likely it referred to a dangerous aquatic animal.

The *Izumo fudoki* contains the story of a young woman being devoured by a *wani* (IF: 140–3). The *Kojiki* records the story of the White Hare of Inaba about a hare who tricks the *wani* of the sea to let him cross the water on their backs so he can reach an island (KJK I: 75–9). This story appears in the cycle of myths centering on Ōkuninushi and is set in Inaba, a province in the vicinity of Izumo. On this story and the appearance of *wani* in ancient Japanese texts, see Antoni (1982), especially 37–49.

9 While it seems strange to associate an aquatic monster (*wani*) with a bear (*kuma*), the same phenomenon is attested in Chinese mythology. Wolfram Eberhard (1942: 363–4; 1968: 193–4) traces this confusion to the similarity of the Chinese characters for "bear" and "tortoise." A similar confusion can be observed in a passage of the *Nihon shoki* mentioning a *kuma wani* (NSK I [8, var. 6], vol. 1: 104/105).

10 "Misen" is the common Japanese reading for the characters denoting Mount Meru. However, the editors of *Un'yōshi* provide the reading "Miyama" (UYS X: 301).

11 The earliest textual evidence of Susanoo being equated with Gakuenji's Matarajin seems to be the first volume of *Kaikitsudan* 懐橘談 (1653), a gazetteer of Matsue domain written by Nagahisa's father Kurosawa Sekisai 黒沢石斎. See Yamamoto (2010: 258); Zhong (2016: 17).

12 For a Buddhist legend describing the wood's medicinal efficacy, see Chattopadhyaya (1970: 222–3). Medieval Japanese texts describe Gozu Tennō as the guardian deity of the monastery at Jetavana (Gotō 2002: 37). This view is probably based on Faxian's 法顯 (337–c. 422) travelogue, in which the Chinese monk explains that the figure of an ox was standing on a pillar to the right of the door to Jetavana. The same text mentions that the first image of Buddha was built from ox-head sandalwood. This image, we are told, survived a great fire at the monastery undamaged (Legge [1886] 1965: 56–7). Probably this passage gave rise both to the belief that ox-head sandalwood is impervious to fire and (in Japan) that Gozu Tennō was the guardian deity of Jetavana (cf. Higo 1938: 322–3). As will be elaborated in the next chapter, in the modern period, Gozu Tennō's connection to sandalwood was used to identify Susanoo with Tan'gun, the mythical founder of Korea, who descended from heaven beside a sandalwood tree.

13 *Sarugaku* is a form of theater that developed into Noh during the fourteenth century.

14 Little is known about Kanekuni. Some scholars identify him as a brother of Yoshida Kanetomo or regard the name as one of Kanetomo's aliases. The only thing that can be said with some certainty is that Kanekuni moved in the same circles as Kanetomo (Yagi 2002: 99–101).

15 On Yoshida Kanetomo, see Grapard (1992a); Scheid (2001).

16 More precisely, the text uses the name Mudō Tenjin 無道天神. Since the text was not written by Kanetomo himself but rather represents the notes taken by a monk

who attended his lecture (Suzuki 2019: 154), it is not entirely clear whether the use of these characters was intended by Kanetomo. Mudō is written with the characters for "no, nothing" and "way." The same characters are used in the *Nihon shoki* when Izanaki and Izanami send Susanoo, their "cruel and violent" (*azukinashi* 無道) son, off to Ne no Kuni after his uncontrolled crying had caused "the untimely death of many people in the realm" (NSK I [5 main text], vol.1: 36). As Alan Grapard (1984: 243) has pointed out, the identification of various deities in the medieval period was often based "on games of association, on puns, and on metaphors." This might be one instance of this phenomenon, linking Susanoo with Mutō Tenjin not only through the tale of Somin Shōrai but also through a linguistic similarity that moreover highlights the two deities' similar characters as cruel and violent gods who take human lives unscrupulously.

17 Konpira (Khumbīra) was a demon king associated with a mountain in northern India, who was later turned into a protector of the Buddhist *dharma* (Thal 2005: 42). On the complex history of the development of Konpira belief in Japan, see Thal (2005).

6 Korea as a Realm of Death: Susanoo and Korea in Modern Discourses

1 On Confucian Shintō, see Antoni (2016: 79–98); Endō (2003: 128–39); Kracht (1986).
2 The *Tongguk t'onggam* is a chronicle covering the history of the Korean peninsula from the founding of the first mythical state to the end of the Koryŏ period (918–1392). The chronicle was completed in 1484 and reached Japan, at the latest, in 1667, when Tokugawa Mitsukuni, the founder of the Mito School, commissioned Tsuji Ryōteki 辻了的 (life dates unknown) with the annotation of the work and had Hayashi Gahō write a preface (Nishinaka 2013: 41).
3 "Euhemerism" refers to the exegetical strategy of interpreting mythical deities as historical persons. The paradigm is named after the Greek scholar Euhemeros, who lived around the turn of the fourth to the third century BCE. In the novel *Hiera Anagraphe*, he wrote that the Olympian deities were human rulers who came to be venerated as gods (Winiarczyk 2002: 7). Chamberlain ([1882] 1982: lxx) aptly called Hakuseki the "eastern Euhemerus."
4 This refers to King Sŏng 聖 (r. 523–554), who, according to both the *Samguk sagi* and the *Nihon shoki*, died on the battlefield in a skirmish with Silla troops in 554 (Best 2006: 336, 449–51).
5 Kotosuga also quotes an interesting theory that associates the toponym Soshimori with a Korean song with the title "Soshimari" 蘇志摩利 (NT V: 17v [484]). In his

Ishō Nihonden 異称日本伝 (Commentary on Japan in Foreign Texts; 1693), the Confucian scholar Matsushita Kenrin 松下見林 (1637–1703), after quoting the tale of Susanoo's sojourn in Soshimori, remarks that "There is a Korean song called *Soshimari* {the pronunciation is close to *soshimori*}, also called *Kaiteigaku* 廻庭樂. This song describes how Susanoo no Mikoto deigned to make a straw hat (*kasa*). The notes are recorded in the *Jinchi yōroku* 仁智要録. The people of the Three Han do not know this [song]" (IN XII: 45–6). The *Jinchi yōroku* is a score of court music completed in 1177. The statement about Susanoo making a straw hat apparently refers to the episode in the *Nihon shoki* (I [7, var. 3]) that narrates how Susanoo wandered around in the rain after being expelled from the Plain of High Heaven, wearing a self-made raincoat and hat. As we have seen, the *Nihon shoki sanso* used this episode to link the *Nihon shoki*'s account of Susanoo's banishment from the Plain of High Heaven with the legend of Somin Shōrai and Susanoo's sojourn in Silla. See also Yamaguchi (2012: 127–30).

6 This probably refers to the Silla Annals (*Silla pongi* 新羅本紀) in the *Samguk sagi*, which contain all of the information mentioned in the *Tongguk t'onggam*'s quotation. SGSG I & IV, vol. 1: 21/38, 87/106.

7 This refers to Namhae 南解, the second king of Silla (trad. r. 4 CE–24 CE), who, according to the *Samguk sagi*, was the only king called by this title.

8 On Teikan and Norinaga's dispute, see also Kwŏn (2016: 233–7); Sakamoto (2008). Norinaga's rage was not only triggered by Teikan's claim that Susanoo was of Korean origin but also by numerous other statements in Teikan's work that were diametrically opposed to the views of Norinaga and his fellow proponents of National Learning. To raise only a few examples, Teikan claims that important elements of "Japanese" culture such as the emperor system, the language, and family names had been transmitted to the archipelago from the Korean peninsula and that Jinmu Tennō was in fact a Chinese prince. This Chinese prince, Teikan maintains, became the first Japanese emperor in 60 BCE, that is, six hundred years later than the date provided in the *Nihon shoki* (Sakamoto 2008: 132–7).

9 For the consequences of the separation policy for the Gion Shrine and other shrines dedicated to the worship of Gozu Tennō, see Kawamura (2007: 127–34) and Thal (2002: 392–3). The *kokugaku* scholars' influence on the policy is discussed in Inoue (2003: 163) and Kawamura (2007: 128). Other case studies of *shinbutsu bunri* in Western languages exist for Tōnomine (Grapard 1984), Ōmiwa Shrine (Antoni 1993; 1998: 180–202; Hardacre 1989: 81–3), and Itsukushima Shrine (Flache 2018).

10 The emperor was usually called *kinrisama* 禁裏様 or *dairisama* 内裏様 at the time (Kawamura 2007: 128–9).

11 Alan Grapard (1984: 245) fittingly describes the policy of *shinbutsu bunri* as a "rewriting of history."

12 The *Nihon shoki* mentions the arrival of a Koguryŏ embassy during that year (NSK XXVII [Tenchi 5], vol. 3: 268/269).
13 In fact, the *Tongguk t'onggam* does not mention that Tan'gun descended on a mountain. Michisuke attempts to gloss over this weakness in his theory by locating the site of Susanoo's descent in Lelang, in the vicinity of Tan'gun's first capital Pyongyang.
14 In contrast to Shigetsugu himself, *Yasaka-shi* does not acknowledge Michisuke as the originator of the theory. It seems likely that Michisuke circulated his treatise only in manuscript form among his friends. Tsukuba University Library possesses a manuscript of the text, which seems to be the only one in existence. The manuscript contains many scribblings and corrections, suggesting that Michisuke was not able to complete work on this text before his demise in 1866.
15 NSK, vol. 3: 206/207.
16 Apart from the shrine names mentioned in the *Engi shiki*, the god Itate (also read as Idate) only appears in the *Harima no kuni fudoki* 播磨国風土記 (*c.* 715). Here, the name of the village Idate 伊達 in Shikama 餝磨 District is explained in the following way: "[The village] is called Idate because the god Idate who guarded the advance of the ships at the time when Okinaga-tarashi Hime no Mikoto [= Empress Jingū] crossed the sea to pacify the land of Korea (*kara no kuni*) is enshrined here. For this reason, the god's name was adopted as the village name" (HF: 42/43). This deity's equation with Itakeru can be traced to Senge Toshizane 千家俊信 (1764-1831), a member of Izumo Shrine's head priest family and a disciple of Motoori Norinaga (IKS I [18–19]).
17 The interlinear gloss actually instructs the reader to read the Chinese characters for "Sandalwood Prince" as *taki*, an alternate name for Itakeru provided by the *Nihon shunjū* (see below).
18 According to Chinese myth, the waters reached up to the sky during the reign of Yao, who asked the assistance of Gun and Yu to contain the flood (Christie 1983: 91-2). The passage is apparently intended to connect Susanoo's wandering in the rain with Yao's reign, which is mentioned in the *Tongguk t'onggam* as the time of Tan'gun's founding of Chosŏn.
19 For a biography of Iida, see Wachutka (2001: 67–79).
20 As late as 1981, Shiga Gō (1897–1990) maintained that Gozu Tennō was "the deity of Soshimori (Udu Mountain) in Ch'unchŏn in Korea" (Shiga 1981: 167)—a position that found its way into Western scholarship through the uncritical quotations of this scholar by McMullin (1988: 276).
21 Scheid, forthcoming. Bernhard Scheid argues that Hoshino and Kume triggered *kokugaku* scholars' rage by subjecting *tennō* ritualism to a scientific analysis and thus encroaching on territory that had hitherto been monopolized by traditionalist scholars. Kume himself believed that his position with regard to Korea was the

true reason behind his dismissal (in his provocative article quoted above, Hoshino remarks that Kume shared his position):

We three professors, Shigeno, Hoshino, and myself, who started the Department of Japanese History were all considered bad. I was the most hateful of the three, and ... when I expressed myself too lightly in the matter of Shinto, I had to resign the prestigious position of professor at the Imperial University. Looking back, I would say that I was a victim of the merger of Japan and Korea. (Quoted in Brownlee 1999: 98)

22 Further words that Kanazawa (1994: 104) associated with Sŏrabŏl are (1) "Sohori," which appears in the Japanese court chronicles as the name of a grandchild of Susanoo and as the name of the peak onto which the Heavenly Grandchild descended, and (2) "Seoul," the name of the present capital of Korea.
23 On these parallels, see Kawamura (2007: 70-4).
24 The work was originally published in 1937.
25 On Oka's relationship to the Vienna school, see Scheid (2014), Weiss (2021).

Epilogue
After the War: Susanoo in Scholarship, Tourism, and Popular Culture

1 In the case of Chōsen Jingū, shrine priests decided to demolish the buildings themselves in order to preempt Koreans' retaliation (Henry 2014: 206). The sole remaining Shintō structure in Korea today is a Korean-style building of former Kōgen Shrine. Likely, this building was spared destruction due to its Korean architecture (Aono 1999: 147).
2 As Scheid (2014: 17) has pointed out, Egami's horserider theory can easily be aligned with the last cultural stratum of Oka's theory. Chun Kyung-soo (2016: 154) presents strong evidence that Egami even adopted the term "horserider" from Oka. Therefore, Oka's contribution to the horserider theory should not be underestimated.
3 The most common criticism leveled at the theory is that Egami himself fabricated his perceived rupture in the archaeological record by manipulating the periodization of archaeological artifacts. Studies rejecting Egami's theory include Barnes (1988: 16-24; 2007: 9); Chiga (2004); Edwards (1983); Farris (1998: 79); Mizoguchi (2013: 17-19); Shiraishi (2004: 333-6).
4 Both scholars emphasize the similarity of Japanese and Korean kingship myths. See Matsumae (1983); Ōbayashi (1974: 214-18, 235-40; 1984a: 195-400; 1986: 115-40; 1991).

5 See Weiss (2018a: 342–6).
6 On the concept of *lieu de mémoire* (site of memory) and its application to East Asia, see Itagaki, Chŏng, and Iwasaki (2011).
7 See the website of the nonprofit organization that erected the statues: http://www.izumo-imaichi.org/monument (accessed May 8, 2021).
8 For a leaflet showing the individual posters, see the following website: http://kisuki-line.jp/evo/station/ (accessed May 8, 2021).
9 Lafcadion Hearn (1850–1904), a writer of Greek–Irish descent who lived in Shimane Prefecture from 1890 to 1891 and published the bestselling book *Glimpses of Unfamiliar Japan* (1894) that introduced local legends and myths from this region to a Western audience.
10 See also the game's Japanese Wikipedia page: https://ja.wikipedia.org/wiki/大神_(ゲーム) (accessed May 8, 2021).
11 See the game's English and Japanese Wikipedia pages: https://en.wikipedia.org/wiki/Shin_Megami_Tensei:_Imagine; https://ja.wikipedia.org/wiki/新・女神転生IMAGINE (accessed May 8, 2021).
12 See the Japanese website Shin Megami Tensei: Imagine kōryaku Wiki: https://megatenonline.wiki.fc2.com/ (accessed May 8, 2021). See also Hirafuji (2014: 75).
13 Some toponyms and local shrine legends in Shimane continue to connect Susanoo to the Korean peninsula. In the coastal town of Isotake 五十猛 (written with the same characters as Susanoo's son Itakeru) in central Shimane, James Grayson (2002) has discovered a complete cycle of myths centering on Susanoo's arrival from the Korean peninsula, which is also reflected in toponyms and the names of local shrines and the deities they worship. The town is rather remote, however, and surely does not affect contemporary perceptions of Susanoo to an extent comparable to the tourist destinations mentioned above.

Bibliography

Note: Place of publication is Tokyo unless otherwise specified.

Primary Sources (keyed to abbreviations used in citations)

EGSK. *Engi shiki* 延喜式. 3 vols. Yakuchū Nihon shiryō 訳注日本史料, edited by Torao Toshiya 虎尾俊哉. Shūeisha, 2000–17.

HF. *Harima no kuni fudoki* 播磨国風土記. In *Fudoki* 風土記. Shinpen Nihon koten bungaku zenshū 新編日本古典文学全集 5, edited by Uegaki Setsuya 植垣節也, 17–127. Shōgakukan, 1997.

IF. *Izumo no kuni fudoki* 出雲国風土記. In *Fudoki* 風土記. Shinpen Nihon koten bungaku zenshū 新編日本古典文学全集 5, edited by Uegaki Setsuya 植垣節也, 129–281. Shōgakukan, 1997.

IKS. *Izumo no kuni shikisha kō* 出雲国式社考. National Archives of Japan Digital Archive. Available online: https://www.digital.archives.go.jp/das/image/F1000000000000040615 (accessed April 22, 2021).

IN. *Ishō Nihonden* 異称日本伝. 14 fascicles. Kitamidomae, Naniwa [Osaka]: Sūbunken, 1693. Waseda University Library: Kotenseki Sōgō Database. Available online: https://www.wul.waseda.ac.jp/kotenseki/html/ri05/ri05_02260/ (accessed April 22, 2021).

KGT. *Kanjin-in Gozu tennō kō* 感神院牛頭天王考. 4 fascicles. 1863. Tsukuba University Library.

KJK. *Kojiki* 古事記. Shinpen Nihon koten bungaku zenshū 新編日本古典文学全集 1, edited by Kōnoshi Takamitsu 神野志隆光 and Yamaguchi Yoshinori 山口佳紀. Shōgakukan, 1997.

KK. *Kanden kōhitsu* 閑田耕筆. In *Kanden kōhitsu, Nennen zuihitsu, Yūkyō manroku, Kagetsu sōshi* 閑田耕筆・年々隨筆・遊京漫録・華月草紙, edited by Tsukamoto Tetsuzō 塚本哲三, 1–202. Yūhōdō Shoten, 1927.

KS. *Kogo shūi* 古語拾遺. Shinsen Nihon koten bunko 新選日本古典文庫 4, edited by Yasuda Naomichi 安田尚道 and Akimoto Yoshinori 秋本吉徳. Gendai Shichōsa, 1976.

MNZ. *Motoori Norinaga zenshū* 本居宣長全集. 23 vols. Edited by Ōno Susumu 大野晋 and Ōkubo Tadashi 大久保正. Chikuma Shobō, 1968–93.

NSC. *Nihon shoki chūshaku* 日本書紀註釈. 3 vols. Shintō taikei (koten chūshaku hen) 神道大系古典註釈編 2–4, edited by Nakamura Hirotoshi 中村啓信, Makabe

Toshinobu 真壁俊信, and Akiyama Kazumi 秋山一美. Shintō Taikei Hensankai, 1985–8.
NSJ. *Nihon sandai jitsuroku* 日本三代実録. Kokushi taikei 国史大系 4, edited by Kuroita Katsumi 黒板勝美. Ōyashima Shuppan, 1944.
NSK. *Nihon shoki* 日本書紀. 3 vols. Shinpen Nihon koten bungaku zenshū 新編日本古典文学全集 2-4, edited by Kojima Noriyuki 小島憲之, Naoki Kōjirō 直木孝次郎, Nishimiya Kazutami 西宮一民, Kuranaka Susumu 蔵中進, and Mōri Masamori 毛利正守. Shōgakukan, 1994–8.
NT. *Nihon shoki tsūshō* 日本書紀通証. Ise: Tanigawa, 1762. Berlin State Library Digital Collections. Available online: http://resolver.staatsbibliothek-berlin.de/SBB0000816D00000000 (accessed April 22, 2021).
SDK. *Sandaikō* 三大考. In *Hirata Atsutane, Ban Nobutomo, Ōkuni Takamasa* 平田篤胤・伴信友・大国隆正. Nihon shisō taikei 日本思想大系 50, edited by Tahara Tsuguo 田原嗣郎, Seki Akira 関晃, Saeki Arikiyo 佐伯有清, and Haga Noboru 芳賀登, 255–70. Iwanami Shoten, 1973.
SGSG. *Samguk sagi* 三國史記. 2 vols. Segye ŭi sasang 세계의 사상 12–13, edited by Yi Pyŏngdo 李丙燾. Seoul: Ŭryu Munhwasa, 1996.
SGYS. *Samguk yusa* 三國遺事. Edited by Yi Pyŏngdo 李丙燾. Seoul: Myŏngmundang, 2000.
SH. *Shōkōhatsu* 衝口発. 1781. Waseda University Library: Kotenseki Sōgō Database. Available online: https://www.wul.waseda.ac.jp/kotenseki/html/ri05/ri05_05003/index.html (accessed April 22, 2021).
SHAZ. *Shinshū Hirata Atsutane zenshū* 新修平田篤胤全集. 22 vols. Meicho Shuppan, 1976–81.
SKH. *Sendai kuji hongi* 先代旧事本紀. Shintō taikei (koten hen) 神道大系古典編 8, edited by Kamada Jun'ichi 鎌田純一. Shintō Taikei Hensankai, 1980.
SNG. *Shaku Nihongi* 釈日本紀. Shintō taikei (koten chūshaku hen) 神道大系古典註釈編 5, edited by Onoda Mitsuo 小野田光雄. Shintō Taikei Hensankai, 1986.
TM. *Tama no mihashira* 霊の真柱. In *Hirata Atsutane, Ban Nobutomo, Ōkuni Takamasa* 平田篤胤・伴信友・大国隆正. Nihon shisō taikei 日本思想大系 50, edited by Tahara Tsuguo 田原嗣郎, Seki Akira 関晃, Saeki Arikiyo 佐伯有清, and Haga Noboru 芳賀登, 11–131. Iwanami Shoten, 1973.
TT. *Tongguk t'onggam* 東國通鑑. Kyoto: Izumoji Shūhakudō, 1887.
UYS. *Un'yōshi* 雲陽誌. Dai Nihon chishi taikei 大日本地誌大系 42, edited by Ashida Koreto 蘆田伊人. Yūzankaku, 1971.
YKS. *Yasakasha kyūki shūroku* 八坂社旧記集録. 3 fascicles. Edited by Ki Shigestugu 紀繁継. 1870. [Japanese] National Diet Library Digital Collections. Available online: http://dl.ndl.go.jp/info:ndljp/pid/816139 (accessed April 22, 2021).
YS. *Yasaka-shi* 八坂誌. 2 vols. Kyoto: Yasaka Jinja, 1906. [Japanese] National Diet Library Digital Collections. Available online: https://dl.ndl.go.jp/info:ndljp/pid/904398 (accessed April 22, 2021).

Secondary Sources

Abe Tatsunosuke 阿部辰之助. 1928. *Shinsen Nissen taiko shi* 新撰日鮮太古史. Keijō [Seoul]: Tairiku Chōsa-kai.

Akiyama Terukazu, Andō Kōsei, Matsubara Saburo, Okazaki Takashi, Sekino Takeshi, and Mary Tregear. 1968. *Neolithic Cultures to the T'ang Dynasty: Recent Discoveries.* Arts of China 1. Kōdansha.

Allen, Chizuko T. 2008. "Early Migrations, Conquests, and Common Ancestry: Theorizing Japanese Origins in Relation with Korea." *Sungkyun Journal of East Asian Studies* 8 (1): 105–30.

Anderson, Benedict. 1991. *Imagined Communities: Reflections on the Origin and Spread of Nationalism.* London: Verso.

Andreeva, Anna. 2017. *Assembling Shinto: Buddhist Approaches to Kami Worship in Medieval Japan.* Harvard East Asian Monographs 396. Cambridge, MA: Harvard University Asia Center.

Anthony, Jason. 2014. "Dreidels to *Dante's Inferno*: Toward a Typology of Religious Games." In *Playing with Religion in Digital Games*, edited by Heidi A. Campbell and Gregory P. Grieve, 25–46. Bloomington: Indiana University Press.

Antoni, Klaus. 1982. *Der weiße Hase von Inaba: Vom Mythos zum Märchen.* Münchener Ostasiatische Studien 28. Stuttgart: Franz Steiner.

Antoni, Klaus. 1988. *Miwa, der heilige Trank: Zur Geschichte und religiösen Bedeutung des alkoholischen Getränkes (Sake) in Japan.* Münchener Ostasiatische Studien 45. Stuttgart: Franz Steiner.

Antoni, Klaus. 1993. "Die 'Trennung von Göttern und Buddhas' (*shimbutsu-bunri*) am Ōmiwa-Schrein in den Jahren der Meiji-Restauration." In *Festgabe für Nelly Naumann*, edited by Klaus Antoni and Maria-Verena Blümmel, 21–52. Mitteilungen der Gesellschaft für Natur- und Völkerkunde Ostasiens e.V. Hamburg 119. Hamburg: Gesellschaft für Natur- und Völkerkunde Ostasiens.

Antoni, Klaus. 1998. *Shintō und die Konzeption des japanischen Nationalwesens (kokutai): Der religiöse Traditionalismus in Neuzeit und Moderne Japans.* Handbuch der Orientalistik V/8. Leiden: Brill.

Antoni, Klaus. 2012. *Kojiki: Aufzeichnung Alter Begebenheiten.* Berlin: Verlag der Weltreligionen.

Antoni, Klaus. 2016. *Kokutai—Political Shintō from Early-Modern to Contemporary Japan.* Tübingen: Eberhard Karls University Tübingen, Tobias-lib. Translated by Anthony De Pasquale et al. Available online: http://hdl.handle.net/10900/68861 (accessed April 22, 2021).

Aoki, Michiko Y. 1997. *Records of Wind and Earth: A Translation of Fudoki, with Introduction and Commentaries.* Ann Arbor, MI: Association for Asian Studies.

Aono Masaaki 青野正明. 1999. "Shokuminchi Chōsen de no 'Naisen ittai' to Kōgen jinja" 植民地朝鮮での「内鮮一体」と江原神社. In *Kindai Nihon no rekishiteki isō: Kokka, minzoku, bunka* 近代日本の歴史的位相：国家・民族・文化, edited by Ōhama Testuya 大濱徹也, 135–57. Tōsui Shobō.

Aono Masaaki. 2013. "Chōsen sōtokufu no jinja seisaku to 'ruiji shūkyō': Kokka shintō no ronri o chūshin ni" 朝鮮総督府の神社政策と「類似宗教」：国家神道の論理を中心に. In *Shokuminchi Chōsen to shūkyō: Teikokushi, kokka shintō, koyū shinkō* 植民地朝鮮と宗教：帝国史・国家神道・固有信仰, edited by Isomae Jun'ichi 磯前順一 and 尹海東 Yun Hae-dong, 161–95. Nichibunken sōsho 日文研叢書. Sangensha.

Aono Masaaki. 2015. *Teikoku shintō no keisei: Shokuminchi Chōsen to kokka shintō no ronri* 帝国神道の形成：植民地朝鮮と国家神道の論理. Iwanami Shoten.

Assmann, Aleida. 2010. *Erinnerungsräume: Formen und Wandlungen des kulturellen Gedächtnisses*. C.H. Beck Kulturwissenschaft. München: Beck.

Assmann, Jan. 1999. *Das kulturelle Gedächtnis: Schrift, Erinnerung und politische Identität in frühen Hochkulturen*. Beck'sche Reihe 1307. München: Beck.

Aston, W. G. 1905. *Shinto: The Way of the Gods*. London: Longmans, Green.

Aston, W. G. [1896] 1956. *Nihongi: Chronicles of Japan from the Earliest Times to A.D. 697*. London: George Allen & Unwin.

Babcock-Abrahams, Barbara. 1975. "'A Tolerated Margin of Mess': The Trickster and His Tales Reconsidered." *Journal of the Folklore Institute* 11 (2): 147–86.

Barnes, Gina L. 1988. *Protohistoric Yamato: Archaeology of the First Japanese State*. Anthropological Papers/Museum of Anthropology, University of Michigan 78. Ann Arbor, MI: published jointly by the University of Michigan, Center for Japanese Studies and the Museum of Anthropology, University of Michigan.

Barnes, Gina L. 2007. *State Formation in Japan: Emergence of a 4th-Century Ruling Elite*. Durham East Asia Series. London: Routledge.

Batten, Bruce L. 1986. "Foreign Threat and Domestic Reform: The Emergence of the Ritsuryō State." *Monumenta Nipponica* 41 (2): 199–219.

Batten, Bruce L. 2003. *To the Ends of Japan: Premodern Frontiers, Boundaries, and Interactions*. Honolulu: University of Hawai'i Press.

Batten, Bruce L. 2006. *Gateway to Japan: Hakata in War and Peace, 500–1300*. Honolulu: University of Hawai'i Press.

Beckwith, Christopher I. 2007. *Koguryo, the Language of Japan's Continental Relatives: An Introduction to the Historical-Comparative Study of the Japanese-Koguryoic Languages with a Preliminary Description of Archaic Northeastern Middle Chinese*. Brill's Japanese Studies Library 21. Leiden: Brill.

Bentley, John R. 2000. "New Look at Paekche and Korean: Data from Nihon Shoki." *Ŏhak yŏn'gu* 36 (2): 417–43.

Bentley, John R. 2006. *The Authenticity of Sendai Kuji Hongi: A New Examination of Texts, with a Translation and Commentary*. Brill's Japanese Studies Library 25. Leiden: Brill.

Best, Jonathan W. 2006. *A History of the Early Korean Kingdom of Paekche: Together with an Annotated Translation of the Paekche Annals of the Samguk Sagi.* Harvard East Asian Monographs 256. Cambridge, MA: Harvard University Asia Center.

Biontino, Juljan. 2014. "General Utsunomiya Tarō and the Suppression of the March First Movement of 1919." In *2nd Annual Korea University Korean History Graduate Student Conference*, 149–67.

Bizeul, Yves. 2005. "Politische Mythen im Zeitalter der 'Globalisierung.'" In *Nationale Mythen—kollektive Symbole: Funktionen, Konstruktionen und Medien der Erinnerung*, edited by Klaudia Knabel, Dietmar Rieger, and Stephanie Wodianka, 17–36. Formen der Erinnerung 23. Göttingen: Vandenhoeck & Ruprecht.

Blum, Mark L. 2006. "The *Sangoku-Mappō* Construct: Buddhism, Nationalism, and History in Medieval Japan." In *Discourse and Ideology in Medieval Japanese Buddhism*, edited by Richard K. Payne, 31–51. Routledge Critical Studies in Buddhism. London: Routledge.

Blumenberg, Hans. 2006. *Arbeit am Mythos*. Suhrkamp-Taschenbuch Wissenschaft 1805. Frankfurt am Main: Suhrkamp.

Boesch, Ernst E. 1996. "Das Fremde und das Eigene." In *Psychologie interkulturellen Handelns*, edited by Alexander Thomas, 87–105. Göttingen: Hogrefe.

Bottici, Chiara. 2007. *A Philosophy of Political Myth*. Cambridge: Cambridge University Press.

Braukämper, Ulrich. 2005. "Kulturkreis." In *Wörterbuch der Völkerkunde*, edited by Walter Hirschberg and Wolfgang Müller, 223–4. Berlin: Reimer.

Brownlee, John S. 1999. *Japanese Historians and the National Myths, 1600–1945: The Age of the Gods and Emperor Jinmu*. Vancouver: UBC Press.

Buckley, Edmund. 1896. "The Shinto Pantheon." *The New World: A Quarterly Review of Religion, Ethics and Theology* 5 (20): 719–44.

Burns, Susan L. 2003. *Before the Nation: Kokugaku and the Imagining of Community in Early Modern Japan*. Durham, NC: Duke University Press.

Caprio, Mark. 2009. *Japanese Assimilation Policies in Colonial Korea, 1910–1945*. Korean Studies of the Henry M. Jackson School of International Studies. Seattle: University of Washington Press.

Cha Nam Hee 차남희, and Yi Ji Eum 이지은. 2014. "Ch'oe Namsŏn ŭi 'Chosŏn minjok' kwa Tan'gun" 최남선의 '조선 민족'과 단군. *Tamnon 201* 담론 201 17(4): 5–27.

Chamberlain, Basil H. [1882] 1982. *The Kojiki: Records of Ancient Matters*. Rutland, Tokyo: Charles E. Tuttle.

Chang Sin 장신. 2009. "Ilcheha Ilsŏndongjonon ŭi taejungjŏk hwaksan kwa Susanoo no mik'oto sinhwa" 일제하 日鮮同組論의 대중적 확산과 素戔嗚尊 신화. *Yŏksa munje yŏn'gu* 역사문제연구 21: 367–94.

Chattopadhyaya, Debiprasad, ed. 1970. *Tāranātha's History of Buddhism in India: Translated from the Tibetan by Lama Chimpa and Alaka Chattopadhyaya*. Simla: Indian Institute of Advanced Study.

Chiba Kei 千葉慶. 2011. *Amaterasu to tennō: "Seiji shinboru" no kindaishi* アマテラスと天皇：〈政治シンボル〉の近代史. Rekishi bunka raiburarī 歴史文化ライブラリー 334. Yoshikawa Kōbunkan.

Chiga Hisashi. 2004. "Kamen die Reitervölker wirklich?" In *Zeit der Morgenröte: Japans Archäologie und Geschichte bis zu den ersten Kaisern*, edited by Alfried Wieczorek, Werner Steinhaus, and Sahara Makoto, 336–41. Publikationen der Reiss-Engelhorn-Museen 11. Mannheim: Reiss-Engelhorn-Museen.

Ch'oe Namsŏn 崔南善. 1927. *Fukan (Părkăn) bunkaron* 不咸文化論. Keijō [Seoul]: Chōsen Shisō Tsūshinsha.

Ch'oe Sŏk'yŏng 최석영. 2008. "Ilcheha Soshimori p'ijŏng ŭl turŏssan nonjaengsa e taehan sogo" 일제하 소시모리 (曾尸茂梨) 피정을 두러싼 논쟁사 (論爭史) 에 대한 소고. *Chungang minsokhak* 中央民俗學 13: 101–17.

"'Chōsen gō' hakkan no ji" 「朝鮮号」発刊の辞. 1910. *Rekishi chiri* 歴史地理 (Chōsen gō): 1–8.

Chou Wan-yao. 1996. "The *Kōminka* Movement in Taiwan and Korea: Comparisons and Interpretations." In *The Japanese Wartime Empire, 1931–1945*, edited by Peter Duus, Ramon H. Myers, and Mark R. Peattie, 40–68. Princeton, NJ: Princeton University Press.

Christie, Anthony. 1983. *Chinese Mythology*. Library of the World's Myths and Legends. Rushden, Northants, England: Newnes Books.

Christy, Alan S. 2012. *A Discipline on Foot: Inventing Japanese Native Ethnography, 1910–1945*. Lanham, MD: Rowman & Littlefield.

Chun Kyung-soo. 2016. "Why Did GHQ Bring Oka's Dissertation from Vienna to Tokyo?" In *Proceedings of the International Symposium on Origins of Oka Masao's Anthropological Scholarship: Meiji University, November 27, 2015*, edited by Ishikawa Hideshi, Josef Kreiner, Sasaki Ken'ichi, and Yoshimura Takehiko, 143–66. Bonn: Bier'sche Verlagsanstalt.

Como, Michael. 2010. *Weaving and Binding: Immigrant Gods and Female Immortals in Ancient Japan*. Honolulu: University of Hawai'i Press.

Creighton, Millie. 1997. "*Soto* Others and *Uchi* Others: Imagining Racial Diversity, Imagining Homogeneous Japan." In *Japan's Minorities: The Illusion of Homogeneity*, edited by Michael Weiner, 211–38. Sheffield Centre for Japanese Studies/Routledge Series 7. London: Routledge.

Csapo, Eric. 2005. *Theories of Mythology*. Malden, MA: Blackwell.

Deeg, Max. 2005. *Das Gaoseng-Faxian-Zhuan als religionsgeschichtliche Quelle: Der älteste Bericht eines chinesischen buddhistischen Pilgermönchs über seine Reise nach Indien mit Übersetzung des Textes*. Studies in Oriental Religions 52. Wiesbaden: Harrassowitz.

Deeg, Max. 2007. *Das Lotos-Sūtra*. Darmstadt: Wissenschaftliche Buchgesellschaft.

Despeux, Catherine. 2000. "Women in Daoism." In *Daoism Handbook*, edited by Livia Kohn, 384–412. Handbuch der Orientalistik IV/14. Leiden: Brill.

Dewa Hiroaki 出羽弘明. 2004. *Shiragi no kamigami to kodai Nihon: Shinra jinja no kataru sekai* 新羅の神々と古代日本：新羅神社の語る世界. Dōseisha.

Doak, Kevin M. 2001. "Building National Identity through Ethnicity: Ethnology in Wartime Japan and After." *Journal of Japanese Studies* 27 (1): 1–39.

Doniger, Wendy. 1988. *Other Peoples' Myths: The Cave of Echoes*. New York: Macmillan.

Doty, William G. 1986. *Mythography: The Study of Myths and Rituals*. Tuscaloosa: University of Alabama Press.

Douglas, Mary. [1966] 2005. *Purity and Danger: An Analysis of Concepts of Pollution and Taboo*. Routledge Classics. London: Routledge.

Duus, Peter. 1995. *The Abacus and the Sword: The Japanese Penetration of Korea, 1895–1910*. Twentieth-Century Japan 4. Berkeley: University of California Press.

Eberhard, Wolfram. 1942. *Lokalkulturen im alten China: Erster Teil: Die Lokalkulturen des Nordens und Westens*. Leiden: Brill.

Eberhard, Wolfram. 1968. *The Local Cultures of South and East China*. Leiden: Brill.

Ebersole, Gary L. 1989. *Myth, Ritual Poetry, and the Politics of Death in Early Japan*. Princeton, NJ: Princeton University Press.

Edwards, Walter. 1983. "Event and Process in the Founding of Japan: The Horserider Theory in Archeological Perspective." *Journal of Japanese Studies* 9 (2): 265–95.

Egami Namio. 1964. "The Formation of the People and the Origin of the State in Japan." *Memoirs of the Tōyō Bunko* 23: 35–70.

Eitel, Ernest J. [1904] 1970. *Handbook of Chinese Buddhism: Being a Sanskrit-Chinese Dictionary of Buddhist Terms, Words and Expressions, with Vocabularies of Buddhist Terms in Pali, Singhalese, Siamese, Burmese, Tibetan, Mongolian and Japanese*. Amsterdam: Philo Press.

Ellwood, Robert S. 1997. "A Japanese Mythic Trickster Figure: Susa-no-o." In *Mythical Trickster Figures: Contours, Contexts, and Criticisms*, edited by William J. Hynes and William G. Doty, 141–58. Tuscaloosa: University of Alabama Press.

Ellwood, Robert S. 2009. *Tales of Darkness: The Mythology of Evil*. London: Continuum.

Endō Jun. 2003. "The Early Modern Period: In Search of a Shinto Identity." In *Shinto: A Short History*, edited by Inoue Nobutaka and translated by John Breen, 108–58. London: RoutledgeCurzon.

En-musubi Tourism Association, ed. n.d. "Izumo: Where Mythology Comes Alive."

Farris, William W. 1985. *Population, Disease, and Land in Early Japan, 645–900*. Harvary-Yenching Institute Monograph Series 24. Cambridge, MA: Harvard University Press.

Farris, William W. 1998. *Sacred Texts and Buried Treasures: Issues in the Historical Archaeology of Ancient Japan*. Honolulu: University of Hawai'i Press.

Faure, Bernard. 2016a. *Protectors and Predators*. Gods of Medieval Japan 2. Honolulu: University of Hawai'i Press.

Faure, Bernard. 2016b. *The Fluid Pantheon*. Gods of Medieval Japan 1. Honolulu: University of Hawai'i Press.

Flache, Ursula. 2018. *Die Insel Miyajima und shinbutsu bunri: Eine Fallstudie mit dem Schwerpunkt der baulichen Veränderungen während der Trennung von Shintō und Buddhismus im Spiegel Meiji-zeitlicher Reiseführer.* Tübingen: Universitätsbibliothek Tübingen. Available online: http://hdl.handle.net/10900/84639 (accessed April 23, 2021).

Florenz, Karl. 1901. *Japanische Mythologie: Nihongi "Zeitalter der Götter" nebst Ergänzungen aus andern alten Quellenwerken.* Mitteilungen der Deutschen Gesellschaft für Natur- und Völkerkunde Ostasiens Supplementband 4. Hobunsha.

Fujitani, Takashi. 1996. *Splendid Monarchy: Power and Pageantry in Modern Japan.* Twentieth-Century Japan 6. Berkeley: University of California Press.

Gardiner, Kenneth H. J. 1969. "Some Problems Concerning the Founding of Paekche." *Archiv Orientální* 37: 562–88.

Gardiner, Kenneth H. J. 1979. "Beyond the Archer and His Son: Koguryŏ and Han China." *Papers on Far Eastern History* 20: 57–82.

Gardiner, Kenneth H. J. 1982a. "The Legends of Koguryŏ (I): *Samguk Sagi*: Annals of Koguryŏ." *Korea Journal* 22 (1): 60–9.

Gardiner, Kenneth H. J. 1982b. "The Legends of Koguryŏ (II): Texts Relating to the Koguryŏ Foundation Legend." *Korea Journal* 22 (2): 31–48.

Gardiner, Kenneth H. J. 1988. "Tradition Betrayed? Kim Pu-Sik and the Founding of Koguryŏ." *Papers on Far Eastern History* 37: 149–93.

Gauntlett, John O., and Robert K. Hall. 1949. *Kokutai No Hongi: Cardinal Principles of the National Entity of Japan.* Cambridge, MA: Harvard University Press.

Gellner, Ernest. 1983. *Nations and Nationalism.* New Perspectives on the Past. Ithaca, NY: Cornell University Press.

Gladigow, Burkhard. 1988–2001. "Polytheismus." In *Handbuch Religionswissenschaftlicher Grundbegriffe.* Vol. 4, edited by Hubert Cancik, Burkhard Gladigow, and Karl-Heinz Kohl, 321–30. Stuttgart: W. Kohlhammer.

Gorai Shigeru 五来重. 1998. "Kumano shinwa to Kumano shintō" 熊野神話と熊野神道. In *Kumano sanzan shinkō jiten* 熊野三山信仰事典, edited by Katō Takahisa 加藤隆久, 232–41. Shinbutsu shinkō jiten shirīzu 神仏信仰事典シリーズ 5. Ebisu Kōshō.

Gotō Kenji 五島健児. 2002. "'Gion shinkō' nanatsu no kīwādo"「祇園信仰」七つのキーワード. In *Gion shinkō jiten* 祇園信仰事典, edited by Mayumi Tsunetada 真弓常忠, 28–59. Shinbutsu shinkō jiten shirīzu 神仏信仰事典シリーズ 10. Ebisu Kōshō.

Grapard, Allan G. 1984. "Japan's Ignored Cultural Revolution: The Separation of Shinto and Buddhist Divinities in Meiji (*shimbutsu bunri*) and a Case Study: Tōnomine." *History of Religions* 23 (3): 240–65.

Grapard, Allan G. 1991. "Visions of Excess and Excesses of Vision: Women and Transgression in Japanese Myth." *Japanese Journal of Religious Studies* 18 (1): 3–22.

Grapard, Allan G. 1992a. "The Shinto of Yoshida Kanetomo." *Monumenta Nipponica* 47 (1): 27–58.

Grapard, Allan G. 1992b. "Yuiitsu Shintō Myōbō Yōshū." *Monumenta Nipponica* 47 (2): 137–61.

Grayson, James H. 1977. "Mimana, A Problem in Korean Historiography." *Korea Journal* 17 (8): 65–69.

Grayson, James H. 2001. *Myths and Legends from Korea: An Annotated Compendium of Ancient and Modern Materials*. Richmond, Surrey: Curzon Press.

Grayson, James H. 2002. "Susa-no-o: A Culture Hero from Korea." *Japan Forum* 14 (3): 465–87.

Ha Woo-Bong. 2015. "War and Cultural Exchange." In *The East Asian War, 1592–1598: International Relations, Violence and Memory*, edited by James B. Lewis, 323–39. Asian States and Empires 9. London: Routledge.

Hara Takeshi 原武史. 1996. *"Izumo" to iu shisō: Kindai Nihon no massatsu sareta kamigami* 「出雲」という思想：近代日本の抹殺された神々. Kōjinsha.

Hard, Robin. 2004. *The Routledge Handbook of Greek Mythology: Based on H.J. Rose's Handbook of Greek Mythology*. London: Routledge.

Hardacre, Helen. 1989. *Shintō and the State, 1868–1988*. Studies in Church and State. Princeton, NJ: Princeton University Press.

Hardacre, Helen. 2017. *Shinto: A History*. New York: Oxford University Press.

Harunari Hideji. 2004. "Die Yayoi-Zeit: Eine allgemeine Einführung." In *Zeit der Morgenröte: Japans Archäologie und Geschichte bis zu den ersten Kaisern*, edited by Alfried Wieczorek, Werner Steinhaus, and Sahara Makoto, 181–4. Publikationen der Reiss-Engelhorn-Museen 11. Mannheim: Reiss-Engelhorn-Museen.

Hatada Takashi 旗田巍. 1969. *Nihonjin no Chōsenkan* 日本人の朝鮮観. Keisō Shobō.

Hatada Takashi. 1974. "The Significance of Korean History." *Japan Interpreter* 9 (2): 165–76.

Hayashi Taisuke 林泰輔. 1892. *Chōsenshi* 朝鮮史. Yoshikawa Hanshichi. [Japanese] National Diet Library Digital Collections. Available online: https://dl.ndl.go.jp/info:ndljp/pid/776361 (accessed April 23, 2021).

Hearn, Lafcadion. 1894. *Glimpses of Unfamiliar Japan*. 2 vols. Boston, MA: Houghton, Mifflin.

Hein-Kircher, Heidi. 2007. "Politische Mythen." *Aus Politik und Zeitgeschichte* 11: 26–31.

Heldt, Gustav. 2014. *The Kojiki: An Account of Ancient Matters*. Translations from the Asian Classics. New York: Columbia University Press.

Henry, Todd A. 2005. "Sanitizing Empire: Japanese Articulations of Korean Otherness and the Construction of Early Colonial Seoul, 1905–1919." *Journal of Asian Studies* 64 (3): 639–75.

Henry, Todd A. 2014. *Assimilating Seoul: Japanese Rule and the Politics of Public Space in Colonial Korea, 1910–1945*. Asia Pacific Modern 12. Berkeley: University of California Press.

Higo Kazuo 肥後和男. 1938. *Kodai denshō kenkyū* 古代傳承研究. Kawade Shobō.

Hirafuji Kikuko 平藤喜久子. 2004. *Shinwagaku to Nihon no kamigami* 神話学と日本の神々. Kōbundō.

Hirafuji Kikuko. 2007a. "Gurōbaruka shakai to haipā shinwa: Konpyūtā RPG ni yoru shinwa no kaitai to saisei" グローバル化社会とハイパー神話：コンピュータRPGによる神話の解体と再生. In *Shinwa to gendai* 神話と現代, edited by Matsumura Kazuo 松村一男 and Yamanaka Hiroshi 山中弘, 31–47. Lithon.

Hirafuji Kikuko. 2007b. "Rōrupereingu gēmu no naka no shinwagaku" ロールプレイングゲームの中の神話学. In *Shūkyō to gendai ga wakaru hon* 宗教と現代がわかる本, edited by Watanabe Naoki 渡邊直樹, 168–71. Heibonsha.

Hirafuji Kikuko. 2008. "Shokuminchi Chōsen to Nihon no hikaku shinwagaku: Mishina Akihide no Chōsen kenkyū" 植民地・朝鮮と日本の比較神話学：三品彰英の朝鮮研究. *Higashi Ajia no kodai bunka* 東アジアの古代文化 135: 67–80.

Hirafuji Kikuko. 2013. "Colonial Empire and Mythology Studies: Research on Japanese Myth in the Early Shōwa Period." In *Kami Ways in Nationalist Territory: Shinto Studies in Prewar Japan and the West*, edited by Bernhard Scheid, 75–107. Beiträge zur Kultur- und Geistesgeschichte Asiens 78. Wien: Verlag der Österreichischen Akademie der Wissenschaften.

Hirafuji Kikuko. 2014. "Deities in Japanese Popular Culture." In *Sources of Mythology: Ancient and Contemporary Myths. Proceedings of the Seventh Annual International Conference on Comparative Mythology (15–17 May 2013, Tübingen)*, edited by Klaus Antoni and David Weiss, 71–80. Religionswissenschaft: Forschung und Wissenschaft 12. Zürich: Lit.

Hobsbawm, Eric. 1983. "Introduction: Inventing Traditions." In *The Invention of Tradition*, edited by Eric Hobsbawm and Terence Ranger, 1–14. Cambridge: Cambridge University Press.

Holtom, D. C. 1943. *Modern Japan and Shinto Nationalism: A Study of Present-Day Trends in Japanese Religions*. Chicago: University of Chicago Press.

Hong Wontack. 1994. *Paekche of Korea and the Origin of Yamato Japan*. Seoul: Kudara International.

Horowitz, Donald L. 1985. *Ethnic Groups in Conflict*. Berkeley: University of California Press.

Horstmann, Axel. 1993. "Das Fremde und das Eigene: 'Assimilation' als hermeneutischer Begriff." In *Kulturthema Fremdheit: Leitbegriffe und Problemfelder kulturwissenschaftlicher Fremdheitsforschung*, edited by Alois Wierlacher, 371–409. Kulturthemen 1. München: Iudicium.

Hoshino Hisashi 星野恒. 1890. "Honpō no jinshu gengo ni tsuite hikō o nobete yo no magokoro aikokusha ni tadasu" 本邦ノ人種言語ニ付鄙考ヲ述テ世ノ眞心愛國者ニ質ス. *Shigakkai zasshi* 史学会雑誌 11: 17–43.

Hoshino Hisashi. 1910. "Rekishi jō yori mitaru Nikkan dōiki no fukko to kakutei" 歴史上より觀たる日韓同域の復古と確定. *Rekishi chiri* 歴史地理 (Chōsen gō): 21–41.

Hutchinson, Rachael. 2019. *Japanese Culture through Videogames*. Routledge Contemporary Japan Series 80. London: Routledge.

Huxley, Aldous. 1949. *Prisons: With the "Carceri" Etchings by G. B. Piranesi and a Critical Study*. London: Trianon Press.

Hwang Sun'gu 황순구. 2009. *Sŏsasi Tongmyŏng wang p'yŏn* 서사시 동명왕편. Seoul: Myŏngmundang.

Hyde, Lewis. 2010. *Trickster Makes This World: Mischief, Myth, and Art*. New York: Farrar, Straus and Giroux.

Hynes, William J. 1997. "Mapping the Characteristics of Mythic Tricksters: A Heuristic Guide." In *Mythical Trickster Figures: Contours, Contexts, and Criticisms*, edited by William J. Hynes and William G. Doty, 33–45. Tuscaloosa: University of Alabama Press.

Iida Takesato 飯田武郷. 1902-9. *Nihon shoki tsūshaku* 日本書紀通釈. 6 vols. Meiji Shoin. [Japanese] National Diet Library Digital Collections. Available online: https://dl.ndl.go.jp/info:ndljp/pid/992400 (accessed April 23, 2021).

Iida Yumiko. 2002. *Rethinking Identity in Modern Japan: Nationalism as Aesthetics*. Routledge/Asian Studies Association of Australia (ASAA) East Asia Series 3. London: Routledge.

Imamura Tomoe 今村鞆. 1928. *Rekishi minzoku Chōsen mandan* 歷史民俗朝鮮漫談. Reprint 2005. Kankoku chiri fūzoku shigyōsho 韓国地理誌叢書 398. Seoul: Nanzan Ginsha.

Imanishi Ryū 今西龍. 1910. "Dankun no setsuwa ni tsuite" 檀君の説話に就て. *Rekishi chiri* 歷史地理 (Chōsen gō): 223–30.

Imanishi Ryū. 1970. *Chōsen koshi no kenkyū* 朝鮮古史の研究. Kokusho Kankōkai.

Inoue Hiroshi 井上寛司. 2013. "Izumo taisha to Gakuenji" 出雲大社と鰐淵寺. In *Mō hitotsu no Izumo shinwa: Chūsei no Gakuenji to Izumo taisha* もう一つの出雲神話：中世の鰐淵寺と出雲大社, edited by Izumo Yayoi no Mori Hakubutsukan 出雲弥生の森博物館, 34–6.

Inoue Hiroshi, ed. 2018. *Izumo Gakuenji kyūzō, kankei monjo* 出雲鰐淵寺旧蔵・関係文書. Kyoto: Hōzōkan.

Inoue Nobutaka. 2003. "The Modern Age: Shinto Confronts Modernity." In *Shinto: A Short History*, edited by Inoue Nobutaka, 159–97. London: RoutledgeCurzon.

Isomae Jun'ichi. 2009. *Japanese Mythology: Hermeneutics on Scripture*. Nichibunken Monograph Series 10. London: Equinox.

Isomae Jun'ichi. 2014. *Religious Discourse in Modern Japan: Religion, State, and Shinto*. Nichibunken Monograph Series 17. Leiden: Brill.

Itabashi Yoshizo 板橋義三. 2003. "Kōkurigo no chimei kara Kōkurigo to Chōsengo, Nihongo to no shiteki kankei o saguru" 高句麗の地名から高句麗語と朝鮮語・日本語との史的関係をさぐる. In *Nihongo keitōron no genzai: Kokusai Nihon bunka kenkyū sentā kyōdō kenkyū hōkoku* 日本語系統論の現在：国際日本文化研究センター共同研究報告, edited by Alexander Vovin, Osada Toshiki 長田俊樹, and Kerri Gifford, 131–85. Nichibunken sōsho 日文研叢書 31. Kyoto: International Research Center for Japanese Studies.

Itagaki Ryūta 板垣竜太, Chŏng Chiyŏng 鄭智泳, and Iwasaki Minoru 岩崎稔. 2011. "'Higashi Ajia no kioku no ba' o tankyū shite" 「東アジアの記憶の場」を探求

して. In *Higashi Ajia no kioku no ba* 東アジアの記憶の場, edited by Itagaki Ryūta 板垣竜太, Chŏng Chiyŏng 鄭智泳, and Iwasaki Minoru 岩崎稔, 7–35. Kawade Shobō Shinsha.

Itō Masayoshi 伊藤正義. 1972. "Chūsei Nihongi no rinkaku: Taiheiki ni okeru Urabe Kanekazu setsu o megutte" 中世日本紀の輪郭：太平記における卜部兼員説をめぐって. *Bungaku* 文学 40 (10): 28–48.

Iwami Kankō Shinkō Kyōgikai 石見観光振興協議会, ed. 2013 "Iwami kagura: Teiki kōen jōhō" 石見神楽：定期公演情報. Hamada.

Iwashita Denshirō 岩下傳四郎, ed. 1941. *Tairiku jinja taikan* 大陸神社大観. Keijō [Seoul]: Tairiku Shintō Renmei.

Iyanaga Nobumi 彌永信美. 2002. *Daikokuten hensō* 大黒天変相. Bukkyō shinwagaku 仏教神話学 1. Kyoto: Hōzōkan.

Iyanaga Nobumi. 2003. "*Honji Suijaku* and the Logic of Combinatory Deities: Two Case Studies." In *Buddhas and Kami in Japan: Honji Suijaku as a Combinatory Paradigm*, edited by Mark Teeuwen and Fabio Rambelli, 145–76. London: RoutledgeCurzon.

Izumo Tourism Promotion Section, ed. n.d. "Izumo: Birthplace of Myths and Legends."

Izumo Yayoi no Mori Hakubutsukan 出雲弥生の森博物館, ed. 2013. *Mō hitotsu no Izumo shinwa: Chūsei no Gakuenji to Izumo taisha* もう一つの出雲神話：中世の鰐淵寺と出雲大社.

Kaempfer, Engelbert. 1727. *The History of Japan*. 2 vols. London: Printed for the Translator.

Kanazawa Shōzaburō 金沢庄三郎. 1994. *Nikkan kochimei no kenkyū* 日韓古地名の研究. Sōfūkan.

Kanda Norishiro 神田典城. 1992. *Nihon shinwa ronkō: Izumo shinwa hen* 日本神話論考：出雲神話篇. Kasama Shoin.

Kang, Etsuko H. 1997a. *Diplomacy and Ideology in Japanese-Korean Relations: From the Fifteenth to the Eighteenth Century*. Houndmills: Macmillan Press.

Kang, Etsuko H. 1997b. "Kita Sadakichi (1871–1939) on Korea: A Japanese Ethno-Historian and the Annexation of Korea in 1910." *Asian Studies Review* 21 (1): 41–60.

Katō Genchi, and Hoshino Hikoshirō. 1926. *Kogoshūi. Gleanings from Ancient Stories: Translated with an Introduction and Notes*. Meiji Japan Society.

Katō Yoshinari 加藤義成. 1962. *Izumo no kuni fudoki sankyū* 出雲国風土記参究. Hara Shobō.

Kawahara Masahiko 河原正彦. 2002. "Gion goryŏe to Shōshōi shinkō: Gyōyakujin to suijin shinkō to no teishoku" 祇園御霊会と少将井信仰：行疫神と水神信仰との抵触. In *Gion shinkō jiten* 祇園信仰事典, edited by Mayumi Tsunetada 真弓常忠, 283–97. Shinbutsu shinkō jiten shirīzu 神仏信仰事典シリーズ 10. Ebisu Kōshō.

Kawai Hayao 河合隼雄. 1996. "Susanoo no tasōsei" スサノヲの多層性. In *Nihon shinwa no shisō: Susanoo ron* 日本神話の思想：スサノヲ論, edited by Kawai Hayao 河合隼雄, Yuasa Yasuo 湯浅泰雄, and Yoshida Atsuhiko 吉田敦彦, 72–92. Minerva 21-seiki raiburarī ミネルヴァ21世紀ライブラリー 29. Kyoto: Mineruva Shobō.

Kawamura Minato 川村湊. 1996. *"Dai Tōa minzokugaku" no kyojitsu* 「大東亜民俗学」の虚実. Kōdansha sensho mechie 講談社選書メチエ 80. Kōdansha.

Kawamura Minato. 2007. *Gozu tennō to Somin Shōrai densetsu: Kesareta ijintachi* 牛頭天王と蘇民将来伝説：消された異神たち. Sakuhinsha.

Kawamura Minato. 2017. *Yami no Matarajin: Hengen suru ijin no nazo o ou* 闇の摩多羅神：変幻する異神の謎を追う. Kawade Shobō Shinsha.

Kawara Shoten Henshūbu 河原書店編集部, ed. 2019. *Kyōto Gion matsuri techō* 京都祇園祭手帳. 2 vols. Kyoto: Kawara Shoten.

Kazama Seishi 風間誠史. 1999. "Hyōgen no kokugaku: Kamo Mabuchi kara Tachibana Moribe made" 表現の国学：賀茂真淵から橘守部まで. *Nihon bungaku* 日本文学 48 (2): 1–11.

Kerényi, Karl. 1956. "The Trickster in Relation to Greek Mythology." In *The Trickster: A Study in American Indian Mythology*, edited by Paul Radin, 173–91. New York: Philosophical Library.

Kim Key-Hiuk. 1980. *The Last Phase of the East Asian World Order: Korea, Japan, and the Chinese Empire, 1860–1882*. Berkeley: University of California Press.

Kim Myung Ok 김명옥. 2018. "Tan'gun sinhwa insik e taehan yŏksajŏk koch'al" 단군신화 인식에 대한 역사적 고찰. *Yŏksa wa yunghap* 역사와융합 3: 45–86.

Kim, Sujung. 2014. "Transcending Locality, Creating Identity: Shinra Myōjin, a Korean Deity in Japan." Doctoral Dissertation, Columbia University.

Kim, Sujung. 2020. *Shinra Myōjin and Buddhist Networks of the East Asian "Mediterranean."* Honolulu: University of Hawai'i Press.

Kita Sadakichi 喜田貞吉. 1910. "Kankoku heigō to kyōikuka no kakugo" 韓国併合と教育家の覚悟. *Rekishi chiri* 歴史地理 (Chōsen gō), 129–41.

Kita Sadakichi. 1979–82. "Nissen ryōminzoku dōgenron" 日鮮両民族同源論. In *Kita Sadakichi chosakushū* 喜田貞吉著作集, vol. 8, 357–419. Heibonsha.

Kohl, Karl-Heinz. 1988–2001. "Naturmythologie." In *Handbuch Religionswissenschaftlicher Grundbegriffe*, vol. 4, edited by Hubert Cancik, Burkhard Gladigow, and Karl-Heinz Kohl, 226–30. Stuttgart: W. Kohlhammer.

Köhn, Stephan, and Michael Schimmelpfennig. 2011. "China, Japan und das Andere: Einige thematische Vorüberlegungen zu diesem Band." In *China, Japan und das Andere: Ostasiatische Identitäten im Zeitalter des Transkulturellen*, edited by Stephan Köhn and Michael Schimmelpfennig, 1–30. Kulturwissenschaftliche Japanstudien 4. Wiesbaden: Harrassowitz.

Kōnoshi Takamitsu 神野志隆光. 1984. "The Land of Yomi: On the Mythical World of the Kojiki." *Japanese Journal of Religious Studies* 11 (1): 57–76.

Kōnoshi Takamitsu. 1999. *Kojiki to Nihon shoki: "Tennō shinwa" no rekishi* 古事記と日本書紀：「天皇神話」の歴史. Kōdansha gendai shinsho 講談社現代新書 1436. Kōdansha.

Kōnoshi Takamitsu. 2008. *Kojiki no sekaikan* 古事記の世界観. Rekishi bunka serekushon 歴史文化セレクション. Yoshikawa Kōbunkan.

Kracht, Klaus. 1986. *Studien zur Geschichte des Denkens im Japan des 17. bis 19. Jahrhunderts: Chu-Hsi-konfuzianische Geist-Diskurse*. Veröffentlichungen des Ostasien-Instituts der Ruhr-Universität Bochum 31. Wiesbaden: Harrassowitz.

Kubota Osamu 久保田収. 1974. *Yasaka jinja no kenkyū* 八坂神社の研究. Shintō-shi kenkyū sōsho 神道史研究叢書 8. Kyoto: Shintō-shi Gakkai.

Kume Kunitake 久米邦武. 1910. "Kankoku heigō to Ōmi ni kōgoishi no hakken" 韓国併合と近江国に神籠石の発見. *Rekishi chiri* 歴史地理 (Chōsen gō): 49–63.

Kume Kunitake. 1989. "Wa-Kan tomo ni Nihon shinkoku naru o ronzu" 倭韓共に日本神国なるを論ず. In *Kume Kunitake rekishi chosakushū* 久米邦武歴史著作集, vol. 2, 38–59. Yoshikawa Kōbunkan.

Kungnip Kimhae Pangmulgwan 국립김해박물관, ed. 2008. *Kungnip Kimhae pangmulgwan* 국립김해박물관. Kimhae: T'ongch'ŏn Munhwasa.

Kwŏn Dongwoo 權東祐. 2013. *Susanoo no henbō: Kodai kara chūsei e* スサノヲの変貌：古代から中世へ. Bukkyō Daigaku kenkyū sōsho 佛教大学研究叢書 17. Kyoto: Hōzōkan.

Kwŏn Dongwoo. 2016. "Kŭnse chunggi Ilbon chisigin ŭi samhan insik yŏn'gu: 'Sŭsanoo' haesŏk ŭl chungsim ŭro" 근세 중기 일본 지식인의 삼한(三韓)인식 연구: '스사노오' 해석을 중심으로. *Wŏnbulgyo sasang kwa chonggyo munhwa* 원불교사상과종교문화 67: 217–50.

Langewiesche, Dieter. 2013. "Grenzüberschreitung und kulturelle Norm: Europäische Erfahrungen in der Moderne." In *Grenzüberschreitungen: Der Mensch im Spannungsfeld von Biologie, Kultur und Technik*, edited by Alfred Nordheim and Klaus Antoni, 167–85. Kultur und soziale Praxis. Bielefeld: transcript.

Ledyard, Gari. 1975. "Galloping Along with the Horseriders. Looking for the Founders of Japan." *Journal of Japanese Studies* 1 (2): 217–54.

Lee Jeong-Mi. 2013. "Views of the Neighbor: Japanese and Korean Intellectuals in the Seventeenth and Eighteenth Centuries." *Sungkyun Journal of East Asian Studies* 13 (1): 29–52.

Lee Ki-baik. 1984. *A New History of Korea*. Seoul: Ilchogak.

Lee Seong-je. 2015. "The Historical Significance of the Gwanggaeto Stele." *Journal of Northeast Asian History* 12 (1): 153–61.

Legge, James. [1886] 1965. *A Record of Buddhistic Kingdoms: Being an Account by the Chinese Monk Fâ-Hien of His Travels in India and Ceylon (A.D. 399–414) in Search of the Buddhist Books of Discipline*. New York: Dover.

Lévi-Strauss, Claude. 1955. "The Structural Study of Myth." *Journal of American Folklore* 68 (270): 428–44.

Lévi-Strauss, Claude. 1964. *Le Cru et le Cuit*. Mythologiques 1. Paris: Plon.

Lévi-Strauss, Claude. 1966. *Du Miel aux Cendres*. Mythologiques 2. Paris: Plon.

Lewin, Bruno. 1976. *Der koreanische Anteil am Werden Japans*. Vorträge/Rheinisch-Westfälische Akademie der Wissenschaften. Geisteswissenschaften 215. Opladen: Westdeutscher Verlag.

Lewis, James B. 1985. "Beyond *Sakoku*: The Korean Envoy to Edo and the 1719 Diary of Shin Yu-Han." *Korea Journal* 25 (11): 22–41.

Lincoln, Bruce. 1999. *Theorizing Myth: Narrative, Ideology, and Scholarship*. Chicago: University of Chicago Press.

Lurie, David B. 2011. *Realms of Literacy: Early Japan and the History of Writing*. Harvard East Asian Monographs 335. Cambridge, MA: Harvard University Asia Center.

Makarius, Laura. 1970. "Ritual Clowns and Symbolical Behaviour." *Diogenes* 69: 44–73.

Makarius, Laura. 1973. "The Crime of Manabozo." *American Anthropologist* 75 (3): 663–75.

Makarius, Laura. 1974. "The Magic of Transgression." *Anthropos* 69: 537–52.

Malinowski, Bronislaw. 1926. *Myth in Primitive Psychology*. New York: W. W. Norton.

Maruyama Masao 丸山真男. 1961. *Nihon no shisō* 日本の思想. Iwanami Shoten.

Masuda Katsumi 益田勝実. 1984. *Kojiki* 古事記. Koten o yomu 古典を読む 10. Iwanami Shoten.

Matsuda Hiroko. 2019. *Liminality of the Japanese Empire: Border Crossings from Okinawa to Colonial Taiwan*. Perspectives on the Global Past. Honolulu: University of Hawai'i Press.

Matsumae Takeshi 松前健. 1970. *Nihon shinwa no keisei* 日本神話の形成. Hanawa Shobō.

Matsumae Takeshi. 1983. "The Myth of the Descent of the Heavenly Grandson." *Asian Folklore Studies* 42: 159–79.

Matsumae Takeshi. 1997. *Jinja to sono denshō* 神社とその伝承. Matsumae Takeshi chosakushū 松前健著作集 3. Ōfūsha.

Matsumae Takeshi. 1998. *Izumo shinwa no keisei* 出雲神話の形成. Matsumae Takeshi chosakushū 松前健著作集 8. Ōfūsha.

Matsumoto Naoki 松本直樹. 2003. *Kojiki shinwa ron* 古事記神話論. Shintensha kenkyū sōsho 新典社研究叢書 154. Shintensha.

Matsumoto Naoki. 2010. "Jindai-ki no kōzō: Shubun to issho ga tsukuru jindai" 神代紀の構造：主文と一書が作る神代. *Kokugo to kokubungaku* 国語と国文学 87 (11): 129–42.

Matsumoto Naoki. 2016. *Shinwa de yomitoku kodai Nihon: Kojiki, Nihon shoki, Fudoki* 神話で読みとく古代日本：古事記・日本書紀・風土記. Chikuma shinsho ちくま新書 1192. Chikuma Shobō.

Matsumura Kazuo. 1998. "Alone Among Women: A Comparative Mythic Analysis of the Development of Amaterasu Theology." In *Kami*, edited by Inoue Nobutaka, 42–71. Contemporary Papers on Japanese Religion 4. Institute for Japanese Culture and Classics, Kokugakuin University.

Matsumura Takeo 松村武雄. 1951. "Dōhōjin no minzoku-bunkashiteki kōsatsu" 同胞神の民族文化史的考察. *Minzokugaku kenkyū* 民族学研究 16 (2): 87–114.

Matsumura Takeo. 1954–8. *Nihon shinwa no kenkyū* 日本神話の研究. 4 vols. Baifūkan.

Matsuoka Shizuo 松岡静雄. 1931. *Izumo densetsu* 出雲伝説. Kiki ronkyū jindai hen 紀記論究神代篇 4. Dōbunkan.

McMullin, Neil. 1987. "The Enryaku-ji and the Gion Shrine-Temple Complex in the Mid-Heian Period." *Japanese Journal of Religious Studies* 14 (2–3): 161–84.

McMullin, Neil. 1988. "On Placating the Gods and Pacifying the Populace: The Case of the Gion *Goryō* Cult." *History of Religions* 27 (3): 270–93.

McNally, Mark. 2005. *Proving the Way: Conflict and Practice in the History of Japanese Nativism*. Harvard East Asian Monographs 245. Cambridge, MA: Harvard University Asia Center.

Mehl, Margaret. 2017. *History and the State in Nineteenth-Century Japan: The World, the Nation and the Search for a Modern Past*, 2nd ed. Copenhagen: Sound Book Press.

Memmi, Albert. 1965. *The Colonizer and the Colonized*. New York: Orion Press.

Metevelis, Peter. 1993. "A Reference Guide to the *Nihonshoki* Myths." *Asian Folklore Studies* 52 (2): 383–8.

Mishina Akihide 三品彰英. 1940. *Chōsenshi gaisetsu* 朝鮮史概説. Kōbundō.

Mishina Akihide. 1971. *Kenkoku shinwa no shomondai* 建国神話の諸問題. Mishina Akihide ronbunshū 三品彰英論文集 2. Heibonsha.

Mishina Akihide. 1972. *Zōho Nissen shinwa densetsu no kenkyū* 増補日鮮神話伝説の研究. Mishina Akihide ronbunshū 三品彰英論文集 4. Heibonsha.

Miura Hiroyuki 三浦周行. 1910. "Nikkan no dōka to bunka" 日韓の同化と分化. *Rekishi chiri* 歴史地理 (Chōsen gō): 163–76.

Miura Sukeyuki 三浦佑之. 2003. *Kojiki kōgi* 古事記講義. Bungei Shunjū.

Mizoguchi Kōji. 2013. *The Archaeology of Japan: From the Earliest Rice Farming Villages to the Rise of the State*. Cambridge World Archaeology. Cambridge: Cambridge University Press.

Mizoguchi Mutsuko 溝口睦子. 2009. *Amaterasu no tanjō: Kodai ōken no genryū o saguru* アマテラスの誕生：古代王権の源流を探る. Iwanami shinsho: Shin akaban 岩波新書：新赤版 1171. Iwanami Shoten.

Mizubayashi Takeshi 水林彪. 1991. *Kiki shinwa to ōken no matsuri* 記紀神話と王権の祭り. Iwanami Shoten.

Mohan, Pankaj. 2004. "Rescuing a Stone from Nationalism: A Fresh Perspective on the King Kwanggaet'o Stele of Koguryŏ." *Journal of Inner and East Asian Studies* 1: 90–115.

Mori Asao 森朝男. 2002. *Koi to kinki no kodai bungeishi: Nihon bungei ni okeru bi no kigen* 恋と禁忌の古代文芸史：日本文芸における美の起源. Kodai bungaku kenkyū sōsho 古代文学研究叢書 7. Wakakusa Shobō.

Morris-Suzuki, Tessa. 1996. "The Frontiers of Japanese Identity." In *Asian Forms of the Nation*, edited by Stein Tønnesson and Hans Antlöv, 41–66. Studies on Asian Topics 23. Richmond, Surrey: Curzon Press.

Morris-Suzuki, Tessa. 1998. "Becoming Japanese: Imperial Expansion and Identity Crises in the Early Twentieth Century." In *Japan's Competing Modernities: Issues in Culture and Democracy, 1900–1930*, edited by Sharon A. Minichiello, 157–80. Honolulu: University of Hawai'i Press.

Mun Hea Jin 문혜진. 2018. "Singminji Chosŏn ŭi Sŭsanoo pongje sinsa wa munhwajŏk honjongsŏng" 식민지 조선의 스사노오 봉제 신사와 문화적 혼종성. *Wŏnbulgyo sasang kwa chonggyo munhwa* 원불교사상과종교문화 78: 425–56.

Murai Shōsuke. 2001. "The Boundaries of Medieval Japan." *Acta Asiatica: Bulletin of the Institute of Eastern Culture* 81: 72–91.

Nagai Hiroshi 長井博. 2011. *Gozu tennō to Somin Shōrai densetsu no shinsō* 牛頭天王と蘇民将来伝説の真相. Bungeisha.

Nakao Katsumi. 2005. "The Imperial Past of Anthropology in Japan." In *A Companion to the Anthropology of Japan*, edited by Jennifer E. Robertson, 19–35. Blackwell Companions to Anthropology 5. Malden, MA: Blackwell.

Naumann, Nelly. 1971. *Das Umwandeln des Himmelspfeilers: Ein japanischer Mythos und seine kulturhistorische Einordnung*. Asian Folklore Studies Monograph 5. Society for Asian Folklore.

Naumann, Nelly. 1979. "Umgekehrt, umgekehrt …: Zu einer Zauberpraktik des japanischen Altertums." *Oriens Extremus* 26: 57–66.

Naumann, Nelly. 1982. "Sakahagi: The 'Reverse Flaying' of the Heavenly Piebald Horse." *Asian Folklore Studies* 41: 7–38.

Naumann, Nelly. 1996. *Die Mythen des alten Japan*. München: Beck.

Naumann, Nelly, and Roy A. Miller. 1995. "Old Japanese Sword Names and Stories Relating to Swords." *Zeitschrift der Deutschen Morgenländischen Gesellschaft* 145: 373–434.

Nietzsche, Friedrich. 1999. *Sämtliche Werke: Kritische Studienausgabe in 15 Bänden*. Edited by Giorgio Colli and Mazzino Montinari. 15 vols. München: Deutscher Taschenbuch Verlag; de Gruyter.

Nishida Nagao 西田長男. 1966. *Jinja no rekishiteki kenkyū* 神社の歴史的研究. Hanawa Shobō.

Nishinaka Kenji 西中研二. 2013. "Hayashi Razan to *Tōgoku tsugan* ni tsuite: Hayashi Razan no *Nenpu* ni aru *Tōgoku shiki* wa *Sankoku shiki* ka *Tōgoku tsugan* ka" 林羅山と『東国通鑑』について：林羅山の『年譜』にある『東国史記』は『三国史記』か『東国通鑑』か. *Journal of International and Advanced Japanese Studies University of Tsukuba* 5: 41–52.

Nitobe Inazō. 1909. *Thoughts and Essays*. Teibi.

No Sŏnghwan 노성환. 2011. "Han'guk ŭi Tan'gun kwa Ilbon ŭi Sŭsanoo: Ilsŏndongjoron e iyong toen Han-Il sinhwa" 한국의 단군과 일본의 스사노오 : 일선동조론에 이용된 한일신화. *Tongbuk-A munhwa yŏngu* 동북아 문화연구 26: 43–63.

Ōbayashi Taryō 大林太良. 1974. *Nihon shinwa no kigen* 日本神話の起源. Kadokawa Shoten.

Ōbayashi Taryō. 1984a. *Higashi Ajia no ōken shinwa: Nihon, Chōsen, Ryūkyū* 東アジアの王権神話：日本・朝鮮・琉球. Kōbundō.

Ōbayashi Taryō. 1984b. "Japanese Myths of Descent from Heaven and Their Korean Parallels." *Asian Folklore Studies* 43 (2): 171–84.

Ōbayashi Taryō. 1986. *Shinwa no keifu: Nihon shinwa no genryū o saguru* 神話の系譜：日本神話の源流をさぐる. Seidosha.

Ōbayashi Taryō. 1991. "The Ancient Myths of Korea and Japan." *Acta Asiatica: Bulletin of the Institute of Eastern Culture* 61: 68–82.

Ochiai Naozumi 落合直澄. 1888. *Teikoku kinen shian* 帝国紀年私案. Iijima Makoto. [Japanese] National Diet Library Digital Collections. Available online: https://dl.ndl.go.jp/info/ndljp/pid/770223 (accessed April 23, 2021).

Ōda-shi Kankō Kyōkai 大田市観光協会, ed. 2013. "Iwami kagura shūmatsu teiki kōen: Iwami ginzan" 石見神楽週末定期公演：石見銀山. Ōda.

Oguma Eiji 小熊英二. 1998. *"Nihonjin" no kyōkai: Okinawa, Ainu, Taiwan, Chōsen, shokuminchi shihai kara fukki undō made* 〈日本人〉の境界：沖縄・アイヌ・台湾・朝鮮 植民地支配から復帰運動まで. Shin'yōsha.

Oguma Eiji. 2002. *A Genealogy of "Japanese" Self-images*. Translated by David Askew. Japanese Society Series. Melbourne: Trans Pacific Press.

Oka Masao 岡正雄. 1956. "Nihon minzoku bunka no keisei" 日本民族文化の形成. In *Zusetsu Nihon bunkashi taikei 1: Jōmon, Yayoi, Kofun jidai* 図説日本文化史大系 1：縄文・弥生・古墳時代, 106–16. Shōgakukan.

Oka Masao. 2012. *Kulturschichten in Alt-Japan*. Edited by Josef Kreiner. 2 vols. JapanArchiv: Schriftenreihe der Forschungsstelle Modernes Japan 10. Bonn: Bier'sche Verlagsanstalt.

Oka Masao 岡正雄, Yawata Ichirō 八幡一郎, Egami Namio 江上波夫, and Ishida Eiichirō 石田栄一郎. 1948. "Nihon minzoku bunka no genryū to Nihon kokka no keisei: Taidan to tōron" 日本民族＝文化の源流と日本国家の形成：対談と討論. *Minzokugaku kenkyū* 民族学研究 13 (3): 11–81.

Oka Yasushi 岡康史. 2002. "Somin mamori to Somin Shōrai no shinkō" 蘇民守と蘇民将来の信仰. In *Gion shinkō jiten* 祇園信仰事典, edited by Mayumi Tsunetada 真弓常忠, 100–17. Shinbutsu shinkō jiten shirīzu 神仏信仰事典シリーズ 10. Ebisu Kōshō.

Okuizumo Kankō Kyōkai 奥出雲観光協会, ed. n.d. "Shinwa no sato: Okuizumo." 神話の里：奥出雲. Okuizumo.

Ooms, Herman. 1985. *Tokugawa Ideology: Early Constructs, 1570–1680*. Princeton, NJ: Princeton University Press.

Ooms, Herman. 2009. *Imperial Politics and Symbolics in Ancient Japan: The Tenmu Dynasty, 650–800*. Honolulu: University of Hawai'i Press.

Ōshima Masanori 大島正徳. 1918. "Yo no kokutaikan to kokka jinkakuron" 予の国体観と国家人格論. *Tōa no hikari* 東亜の光 13 (4): 8–16.

Ouwehand, Cornelius. 1958–9. "Some Notes on the God Susa-no-o." *Monumenta Nipponica* 14 (3/4): 384–407.

Pai, Hyung Il. 2000. *Constructing "Korean" Origins: A Critical Review of Archaeology, Historiography, and Racial Myth in Korean State-Formation Theories*. The Harvard-Hallym Series on Korea 187. Cambridge, MA: Harvard University Asia Center.

Pak Soon-Yong, and Hwang Keumjoong. 2011. "Assimilation and Segregation of Imperial Subjects: 'Educating' the Colonised during the 1910–1945 Japanese Colonial Rule of Korea." *Paedagogica Historica* 47 (3): 377–97.

Palmer, Edwina. 2016. *Harima Fudoki: A Record of Ancient Japan Reinterpreted, Translated, Annotated, and with Commentary*. Brill's Japanese Studies Library 51. Leiden: Brill.

Paproth, Hans-Joachim. 1976. *Bärenjagdriten und Bärenfeste bei den tungusischen Völkern*. Skrifter utgivna av Religionshistoriska Institutionen i Uppsala 15. Uppsala: Tofters Tryckeri.

Pelton, Robert D. 1997. "West African Tricksters: Web of Purpose, Dance of Delight." In *Mythical Trickster Figures: Contours, Contexts, and Criticisms*, edited by William J. Hynes and William G. Doty, 122–40. Tuscaloosa: University of Alabama Press.

Philippi, Donald L. 1968. *Kojiki*. University of Tokyo Press.

Philippi, Donald L. 1990. *Norito: A Translation of the Ancient Japanese Ritual Prayers*. Princeton, NJ: Princeton University Press.

Piggott, Joan R. 1989. "Sacral Kingship and Confederacy in Early Izumo." *Monumenta Nipponica* 44 (1): 45–74.

Pörtner, Peter. 1986. "Madness in Japanese Literature." In *Japan: Ein Lesebuch*, edited by Peter Pörtner, 222–33. Konkursbuch 16/17. Tübingen: Gehrke.

Quiros, Ignacio. 2017. "Chapter 1: Heaven and Earth First Become Active." *Kojikigaku* 3: 295–306.

Rambelli, Fabio. 1996. "Religion, Ideology of Domination, and Nationalism: Kuroda Toshio on the Discourse of *Shinkoku*." *Japanese Journal of Religious Studies* 23 (3–4): 387–426.

Robbeets, Martine I. 2005. *Is Japanese related to Korean, Tungusic, Mongolic and Turkic?* Turcologica 64. Wiesbaden: Harrassowitz.

Robinson, G. W. 1955. "The Kuji Hongi 舊事本紀: Volumes 7, 8 and 9 Considered as a Draft of the Nihon Shoki." *Memoirs of the Research Department of the Toyo Bunko* 14: 81–138.

Róheim, Géza. 1972. *Animism, Magic, and the Divine King*. New York: International Universities Press.

Rössler, Martin. 2007. *Die Deutschsprachige Ethnologie bis ca. 1960: Ein historischer Abriss*. Kölner Arbeitspapiere zur Ethnologie 1. Köln: Institut für Völkerkunde, Universität zu Köln.

Ruoff, Kenneth J. 2010. *Imperial Japan at Its Zenith: The Wartime Celebration of the Empire's 2,600th Anniversary*. Studies of the Weatherhead East Asian Institute, Columbia University. Ithaca, NY: Cornell University Press.

Rutt, Richard. 1973. "A Lay of King Tongmyŏng." *Korea Journal* 13 (7): 48–54.

Saar, Martin. 2007. *Genealogie als Kritik: Geschichte und Theorie des Subjekts nach Nietzsche und Foucault*. Theorie und Gesellschaft 59. Frankfurt am Main: Campus Verlag.

Said, Edward W. 1995. *Orientalism*. Reprinted with a new Afterword. London: Penguin.

Saigō Nobutsuna 西郷信綱. 1967. *Kojiki no sekai* 古事記の世界. Iwanami shinsho: Aoban 岩波新書：青版 654. Iwanami Shoten.

Saigō Nobutsuna. 1973. *Kojiki kenkyū* 古事記研究. Miraisha.

Saigō Nobutsuna. 2005. *Kojiki chūshaku* 古事記注釈. 8 vols. Chikuma gakugei bunko ちくま学芸文庫. Chikuma Shobō.

Saitō Hideki 斎藤英喜. 2006. *Yomikaerareta Nihon shinwa* 読み替えられた日本神話. Kōdansha gendai shinsho 講談社現代新書 1871. Kōdansha.

Saitō Hideki. 2012. *Araburu Susanoo, shichihenge: "Chūsei shinwa" no sekai* 荒ぶるスサノヲ、七変化：「中世神話」の世界. Rekishi bunka raiburarī 歴史文化ライブラリー 346. Yoshikawa Kōbunkan.

Saitō Hideki. 2013. "Kunibiki suru Susanoo: Chūsei no Izumo shinwa no sekai e" 国引きするスサノヲ：中世の出雲神話の世界へ. In *Mō hitotsu no Izumo shinwa: Chūsei no Gakuenji to Izumo taisha* もう一つの出雲神話：中世の鰐淵寺と出雲大社, edited by Izumo Yayoi no Mori Hakubutsukan 出雲弥生の森博物館, 8–9.

Sakamoto Koremaru 坂本是丸. 2008. "Kōko e no jōnetsu to itsudatsu: Norinaga o okoraseta otoko, Tō Teikan" 好古への情熱と逸脱：宣長を怒らせた男・藤貞幹. In *Kinsei no kōkokatachi: Mitsukuni, Kunpei, Teikan, Tanenobu* 近世の好古家たち：光圀・君平・貞幹・種信, edited by Kokugakuin Daigaku Nihon Bunka Kenkyūsho 國學院大學日本文化研究所, 126–67. Yūzankaku.

Sakamoto Tarō 坂本太郎, Ienaga Saburō 家永三郎, Inoue Mitsusada 井上光貞, and Ōno Susumu 大野晋, eds. 1965–7. *Nihon shoki* 日本書紀. 2 vols. Nihon koten bungaku taikei 日本古典文学大系 67–8. Iwanami Shoten.

Satō Hiroo 佐藤弘夫. 2000. *Amaterasu no henbō: Chūsei shinbutsu kōshōshi no shiza* アマテラスの変貌：神仏交渉史の視座. Kyoto: Hōzōkan.

Satō Masahide 佐藤正英. 2011. *Kojiki shinwa o yomu: "Kami no me" "kami no ko" no monogatari* 古事記神話を読む：〈神の女〉〈神の子〉の物語. Seidosha.

Satō Masako 佐藤マサ子. 1995. *Karl Florenz in Japan: Auf den Spuren einer vergessenen Quelle der modernen japanischen Geistesgeschichte und Poetik*. Mitteilungen der Gesellschaft für Natur- und Völkerkunde Ostasiens e.V. Hamburg 124. Hamburg: Gesellschaft für Natur- und Völkerkunde Ostasiens.

Satō Masako. 2004. "Suson ranjin ronsō" 素尊嵐神論争. In *Susanoo shinkō jiten* スサノオ信仰事典, edited by Ōbayashi Taryō 大林太良, 195–207. Shinbutsu shinkō jiten shirīzu 神仏信仰事典シリーズ 7. Ebisu Kōshō.

Scheid, Bernhard. 2001. *Der eine und einzige Weg der Götter: Yoshida Kanetomo und die Erfindung des Shinto*. Österreichische Akademie der Wissenschaften. Philosophisch-Historische Klasse. Sitzungsberichte 687. Wien: Verlag der Österreichischen Akademie der Wissenschaften.

Scheid, Bernhard. 2003. "'Both Parts' or 'Only One'? Challenges to the *Honji Suijaku* Paradigm in the Edo Period." In *Buddhas and Kami in Japan: Honji Suijaku as a Combinatory Paradigm*, edited by Mark Teeuwen and Fabio Rambelli, 204–21. London: RoutledgeCurzon.

Scheid, Bernhard. 2014. "Das Erbe der Wiener Kulturkreislehre: Oka Masao als Schüler Wilhelm Schmidts." *Minikomi. Informationen des akademischen Arbeitskreises Japan* 83: 5–20.

Scheid, Bernhard. 2016. "'Sie stach sich in den Schoß und verstarb': Zwei seltsame Todesfälle in den *Kiki*-Mythen." In *Werden und Vergehen: Betrachtungen zu Geburt und Tod in japanischen Religionen*, edited by Birgit Staemmler, 95–114. Bunka/Wenhua—Tübinger Ostasiatische Forschungen. Tuebingen East Asian Studies 24. Berlin: Lit.

Scheid, Bernhard. Forthcoming. "Lost in Religion: Meiji-Period Shintō as Mirrored in the Kume Incident, 1892." In *Religion and Power*, edited by Martin Lehnert and Steffen Döll. Wien: Verlag der Österreichischen Akademie der Wissenschaften.

Scholl, Tobias. 2018. *Konstruktion von Gleichheit und Differenz: Der Kolonialdiskurs einer gemeinsamen Abstammung von Japanern und Koreanern, 1910–1945*. Tübinger Reihe für Koreastudien 2. München: Iudicium.

Segal, Robert A. 2004. *Myth: A Very Short Introduction*. Very Short Introductions 111. Oxford: Oxford University Press.

Seyock, Barbara. 2004. *Auf den Spuren der Ostbarbaren: Zur Archäologie protohistorischer Kulturen in Südkorea und Westjapan*. Münster: Lit.

Shakespeare, William. [1598] 1908. *Henry IV. Part First*. Boston, MA: Ginn.

Shidehara Taira 幣原坦. 1910. "Nikkan kōtsū no gaiyō" 日韓交通の概要. *Rekishi chiri* 歴史地理 (Chōsen gō): 9–21.

Shiga Gō 志賀剛. 1981. "Nihon ni okeru ekijin shinkō no seisei: Somin Shōrai to Yasaka jinja no saijin kenkyū" 日本に於ける疫神信仰の生成：蘇民将来と八坂神社の祭神研究. *Shintō-shi kenkyū* 神道史研究 29 (3): 148–75.

Shigeno Yasutsugu 重野安繹, Kume Kunitake 久米邦武, and Hoshino Hisashi 星野恒. 1890. *Kōhon kokushigan* 稿本国史眼. Taiseikan.

Shinjō Tsunezō 新城常三. 1998. "Kodai no Kumano sankei" 古代の熊野参詣. In *Kumano sanzan shinkō jiten* 熊野三山信仰事典, edited by Katō Takahisa 加藤隆久, 383–91. Shinbutsu shinkō jiten shirīzu 神仏信仰事典シリーズ 5. Ebisu Kōshō.

Shiraishi Taichirō. 2004. "Die Kofun-Zeit: Eine allgemeine Einführung II—Der Beginn einer kulturellen Erneuerung auf der japanischen Inselwelt." In *Zeit der Morgenröte: Japans Archäologie und Geschichte bis zu den ersten Kaisern*, edited by Alfried Wieczorek, Werner Steinhaus, and Sahara Makoto, 328–36. Publikationen der Reiss-Engelhorn-Museen 11. Mannheim: Reiss-Engelhorn-Museen.

Shultz, Edward J., and Hugh H. W. Kang, eds. 2012a. *The Koguryŏ Annals of the Samguk Sagi*. Translated by Kenneth H. J. Gardiner, Daniel C. Kane, Hugh H. W. Kang, and Edward J. Shultz. Seongnam: Academy of Korean Studies Press.

Shultz, Edward J., and Hugh H. W. Kang, eds. 2012b. *The Silla Annals of the Samguk Sagi*. With the assistance of D. C. Kane. Seongnam: Academy of Korean Studies Press.

Skya, Walter A. 2002. "The Emperor, Shintō Ultranationalism and Mass Mobilization." In *Religion and National Identity in the Japanese Context*, edited by Klaus Antoni,

Kubota Hiroshi, Johann Nawrocki, and Michael Wachutka, 235–48. BUNKA 5. Münster: Lit.

Slawik, Alexander. 1993. "Die Susanowos: Vielerlei Gestalten unter einem Namen, ihre Mythen, Sagen und die ältesten chinesischen Japanberichte." In *Festgabe für Nelly Naumann*, edited by Klaus Antoni and Maria-Verena Blümmel, 341–51. Mitteilungen der Gesellschaft für Natur- und Völkerkunde Ostasiens e.V. Hamburg 119. Hamburg: Gesellschaft für Natur- und Völkerkunde Ostasiens.

Smith, Anthony D. 1991. *National Identity*. London: Penguin.

Smith, Anthony D. 2003. *Chosen Peoples*. Oxford: Oxford University Press.

Snellen, J. B. 1937. "Shoku Nihongi: Chronicles of Japan, Continued, from A. D. 697 to 791." *Transactions of the Asiatic Society of Japan*, second series, vol. 14: 209–78.

Sone Kenzō 曽根研三. 1963. *Gakuenji monjo no kenkyū* 鰐淵寺文書の研究. Gakuenji Monjo Kankōkai.

Song Sun-hee. 1974. "The Koguryo Foundation Myth: An Integrated Analysis." *Asian Folklore Studies* 33 (2): 37–92.

Soothill, William E., and Lewis Hodous. [1937] 1995. *A Dictionary of Chinese Buddhist Terms: With Sanskrit and English Equivalents and a Sanskrit-Pali Index*. Richmond, Surrey: Curzon Press.

Stockdale, Jonathan. 2013. "Origin Myths: Susano-o, Orikuchi Shinobu, and the Imagination of Exile in Early Japan." *History of Religions* 52 (3): 236–66.

Street, Brian V. 1972. "The Trickster Theme: Winnebago and Azande." In *Zande Themes: Essays Presented to Sir Edward Evans-Pritchard*, edited by André Singer and Brian V. Street, 82–104. Oxford: Blackwell.

Suga Kōji 菅浩二. 2004. *Nihon tōchika no kaigai jinja: Chōsen jingū, Taiwan jinja to saijin* 日本統治下の海外神社：朝鮮神宮・台湾神宮と祭神. Hisaizu jinja shōkyōin sōsho 久伊豆神社小教院叢書 1. Kōbundō.

Suga Kōji. 2010. "A Concept of 'Overseas Shinto Shrines': A Pantheistic Attempt by Ogasawara Shōzō and Its Limitations." *Japanese Journal of Religious Studies* 37 (1): 47–74.

Suzuki Kōtarō 鈴木耕太郎. 2019. *Gozu tennō shinkō no chūsei* 牛頭天王信仰の中世. Kyoto: Hōzōkan.

Szakolczai, Arpad. 2015. "Liminality and Experience: Structuring Transitory Situations and Transformative Events." In *Breaking Boundaries: Varieties of Liminality*, edited by Agnes Horvath, Bjørn Thomassen, and Harald Wydra, 11–38. New York: Berghahn Books.

Szczesniak, Boleslaw. 1951. "The Kōtaiō Monument." *Monumenta Nipponica* 7 (1/2): 242–68.

Takagi Toshio 高木敏雄. 1973a. "Susanoo no mikoto shinwa ni arawaretaru takamgahara yōso to Izumo yōso" 素戔嗚尊神話に現われたる高天原要素と出雲要素. In *Zōtei Nihon shinwa densetsu no kenkyū* 増訂日本神話伝説の研究 1, edited by Ōbayashi Taryō 大林太良, 208–56. Tōyō bunko 241. Heibonsha.

Takagi Toshio. 1973b. "Suson ranjin ron" 素尊嵐神論 In *Zōtei Nihon shinwa densetsu no kenkyū* 増訂日本神話伝説の研究 1, edited by Ōbayashi Taryō 大林太良, 135–60. Tōyō bunko 241. Heibonsha.

Takeda Yukio. 1989. "Studies on the King Kwanggaito Inscription and Their Basis." *Memoirs of the Research Department of the Toyo Bunko* 47: 57–89.

Takii Kazuhiro. 2014. *Itō Hirobumi: Japan's First Prime Minister and Father of the Meiji Constitution*. Nichibunken Monograph Series 16. Translated by Takechi Manabu. London: Routledge.

Takioto Yoshiyuki 瀧音能之. 1994. *Izumo no kuni fudoki to kodai Nihon: Izumo chiikishi no kenkyū* 出雲国風土記と古代日本：出雲地域史の研究. Yūzankaku Shuppan.

Takioto Yoshiyuki. 1995. "Karakuni Itate jinja no sōken to sono haikei" 韓国伊大氏神社の創建とその背景. In *Izumo sekai to kodai no San'in* 出雲世界と古代の山陰, edited by Takioto Yoshiyuki 瀧音能之, 297–322. Kodai ōken to kōryū 古代王権と交流 7. Meicho Shuppan.

Takioto Yoshiyuki. 2001. *Kodai no Izumo jiten* 古代の出雲事典. Shin Jinbutsu Ōraisha.

Tanaka, Stefan. 1993. *Japan's Orient: Rendering Pasts into History*. Berkeley: University of California Press.

Teeuwen, Mark. 2007. "*Sendai Kuji Hongi*: Authentic Myths or Forged History?" *Monumenta Nipponica* 62 (1): 87–96.

Teeuwen, Mark, and Fabio Rambelli. 2003. "Introduction: Combinatory Religion and the *Honji Suijaku* Paradigm in Pre-Modern Japan." In *Buddhas and Kami in Japan: Honji Suijaku as a Combinatory Paradigm*, edited by Mark Teeuwen and Fabio Rambelli, 1–53. London: RoutledgeCurzon.

Teeuwen, Mark, and Hendrik van der Veere. 1998. *Nakatomi Harae Kunge: Purification and Enlightenment in Late-Heian Japan*. Buddhismus-Studien 1. München: Iudicium.

Terakawa Machio 寺川眞知夫. 2009. *Kojiki shinwa no kenkyū* 古事記神話の研究. Hanawa Shobō.

Thal, Sarah. 2002. "Redefining the Gods: Politics and Survival in the Creation of Modern Kami." *Japanese Journal of Religious Studies* 29 (3–4): 379–404.

Thal, Sarah. 2005. *Rearranging the Landscape of the Gods: The Politics of a Pilgrimage Site in Japan, 1573–1912*. Studies of the Weatherhead East Asian Institute, Columbia University. Chicago: University of Chicago Press.

Thomassen, Bjørn. 2014. *Liminality and the Modern: Living through the in-Between*. Burlington: Ashgate.

Thomassen, Bjørn. 2015. "Thinking with Liminality: To the Boundaries of an Anthropological Concept." In *Breaking Boundaries: Varieties of Liminality*, edited by Agnes Horvath, Bjørn Thomassen, and Harald Wydra, 39–58. New York: Berghahn Books.

Thompson, Stith. 1955. *Motif-Index of Folk-Literature*. Copenhagen: Rosenkilde and Bagger.

Tinsley, Elizabeth. 2017. "The Composition of Decomposition: The *Kusōzu* Images of Matsui Fuyuko and Itō Seiu, and Buddhism in Erotic Grotesque Modernity." *Journal of Asian Humanities at Kyushu University* 2: 15–45.

Toby, Ronald P. 1977. "Reopening the Question of Sakoku: Diplomacy in the Legitimation of the Tokugawa Bakufu." *Journal of Japanese Studies* 3 (2): 323–63.

Toby, Ronald P. 1984. *State and Diplomacy in Early Modern Japan: Asia in the Development of the Tokugawa Bakufu*. Princeton, NJ: Princeton University Press.

Toby, Ronald P. 1986. "Carnival of the Aliens: Korean Embassies in Edo-Period Art and Popular Culture." *Monumenta Nipponica* 41 (4): 415–56.

Toby, Ronald P. 2001. "Three Realms/Myriad Countries: An 'Ethnography' of Other and the Re-Bounding of Japan, 1550–1750." In *Constructing Nationhood in Modern East Asia*, edited by Chow Kai-wing, Kevin M. Doak, and Fu Poshek, 15–45. Ann Arbor: University of Michigan Press.

Toby, Ronald P. 2008. *"Sakoku" to iu gaikō* 「鎖国」という外交. Nihon no rekishi 日本の歴史 9. Shōgakukan.

Tōgō Kazuhiko. 2011. "Japanese National Identity: Evolution and Prospects." In *East Asian National Identities: Commonalities and Differences*, edited by Gilbert Rozman, 147–68. Washington, DC: Woodrow Wilson Center Press.

Toyoshima Osamu 豊島修. 1998. "Kumano shugendō no seiritsu" 熊野修験道の成立. In *Kumano sanzan shinkō jiten* 熊野三山信仰事典, edited by Katō Takahisa 加藤隆久, 286–95. Shinbutsu shinkō jiten shirīzu 神仏信仰事典シリーズ 5. Ebisu Kōshō.

Tsuda Sōkichi 津田左右吉. 1963. *Nihon koten no kenkyū* 日本古典の研究 1. Tsuda Sōkichi zenshū 津田左右吉全集 1. Iwanami Shoten.

Tsuwano Tourism Association, ed. n.d. "Tsuwano Iwamikagura." Tsuwano.

Turner, Victor. 1967. "Betwixt and Between: The Liminal Period in *Rites de Passage*." In *The Forest of Symbols: Aspects of Ndembu Ritual*, 93–111. Ithaca, NY: Cornell University Press.

Turner, Victor. 1968. "Myth and Symbol." In *International Encyclopedia of the Social Sciences*, vol. 10, edited by David L. Sills, 576–82. New York: Macmillan.

Tylor, Edward B. 1877. "Remarks on Japanese Mythology." *Journal of the Anthropological Institute of Great Britain and Ireland* 6: 55–60.

Uchida, Jun. 2011. *Brokers of Empire: Japanese Settler Colonialism in Korea, 1876–1945*. Harvard East Asian Monographs 337. Cambridge, MA: Harvard University Asia Center.

van Baaren, Theo. 1984. "The Flexibility of Myth." In *Sacred Narrative: Readings in the Theory of Myth*, edited by Alan Dundes, 217–24. Berkeley: University of California Press.

van Gennep, Arnold. 1909. *Les Rites de Passage*. Paris: Nourry.

Verschuer, Charlotte v. 2006. *Across the Perilous Sea: Japanese Trade with China and Korea from the Seventh to the Sixteenth Centuries*. Translated by Kristen Lee Hunter. Cornell East Asia Series 133. Ithaca, NY: East Asia Program, Cornell University.

Vescey, Christopher. 1997. "The Exception Who Proves the Rules: Ananse the Akan Trickster." In *Mythical Trickster Figures: Contours, Contexts, and Criticisms*, edited by William J. Hynes and William G. Doty, 106–21. Tuscaloosa: University of Alabama Press.

Vlastos, Stephen. 1998. "Tradition: Past/Present Culture and Modern Japanese History." In *Mirror of Modernity: Invented Traditions of Modern Japan*, edited by Stephen Vlastos, 1–16. Twentieth-Century Japan 9. Berkeley: University of California Press.

Vollmer, Klaus. 1986. "Grundstrukturen japanischen Außenseitertums: Spekulationen über Susano-o-no-mikoto." In *Japan: Ein Lesebuch*, edited by Peter Pörtner, 203–21. Konkursbuch 16/17. Tübingen: Gehrke.

Vovin, Alexander. 2010. *Koreo-Japonica: A Re-evaluation of a Common Genetic Origin*. Honolulu: University of Hawai'i Press; Center for Korean Studies, University of Hawai'i.

Wachutka, Michael. 2001. *Historical Reality or Metaphoric Expression? Culturally Formed Contrasts in Karl Florenz' and Iida Takesato's Interpretations of Japanese Mythology*. BUNKA 1. Münster: Lit.

Wachutka, Michael. 2012. *Kokugaku in Meiji-Period Japan: The Modern Transformation of "National Learning" and the Formation of Scholarly Societies*. Leiden: Global Oriental.

Wada Yūji 和田雄治. 1914. "Soshimori wa Kaya-san naru no shinsetsu" 曾尸茂梨は伽倻山なるの新説. *Kōkogaku zasshi* 考古学雑誌 4 (10): 645–47.

Waida Manabu. 1973. "Symbolism of 'Descent' in Tibetan Sacred Kingship and Some East Asian Parallels." *Numen* 20 (1): 60–78.

Wakabayashi, Bob T. 1986. *Anti-Foreignism and Western Learning in Early-Modern Japan: The New Theses of 1825*. Harvard East Asian Monographs 126. Cambridge, MA: Harvard University Press.

Waldenfels, Bernhard. 2011. *Phenomenology of the Alien: Basic Concepts*. Translated by Alexander Kozin and Tanja Stähler. Northwestern University Studies in Phenomenology and Existential Philosophy. Evanston, IL: Northwestern University Press.

Weiner, Michael. 1997. "The Invention of Identity: 'Self' and 'Other' in Pre-War Japan." In *Japan's Minorities: The Illusion of Homogeneity*, edited by Michael Weiner, 1–16. Sheffield Centre for Japanese Studies/Routledge Series 7. London: Routledge.

Weiss, David. 2014. "The Japanese Trickster and His Connection to Metallurgy: The Myth of Susanoo." In *Sources of Mythology: Ancient and Contemporary Myths. Proceedings of the Seventh Annual International Conference on Comparative Mythology (15–17 May 2013, Tübingen)*, edited by Klaus Antoni and David Weiss, 337–47. Religionswissenschaft: Forschung und Wissenschaft 12. Zürich: Lit.

Weiss, David. 2018a. "Die politische Dimension der japanischen Mythologie: Forschung und Ideologie." In *Religion, Politik und Ideologie: Beiträge zu einer kritischen Kulturwissenschaft*, edited by Michael Wachutka, Monika Schrimpf, and Birgit Staemmler, 338–49. München: Iudicium.

Weiss, David. 2018b. "Slaying the Serpent: Comparative Mythological Perspectives on Susanoo's Dragon Fight." *Journal of Asian Humanities at Kyushu University* 3: 1–20.

Weiss, David. 2021. "Oka Masao in Wien: Ein japanisch-österreichisher Kulturkontakt mit Auswirkungen auf die japanische Ethnologie und die deutschsprachige Japanologie." In *Wissen über Wissenschaft: Felder—Formation—Mutation*, edited by Manshu Ide, Haruyo Yoshida, and Shizue Hayashi. Tübingen: Stauffenburg.

Winiarczyk, Marek. 2002. *Euhemeros von Messene: Leben, Werk und Nachwirkung*. Beiträge zur Altertumskunde. München: Saur.

Wittkamp, Robert F. 2014. *Altjapanische Erinnerungsdichtung: Landschaft, Schrift und kulturelles Gedächtnis im Man'yōshū (萬葉集)*. 2 vols. Beiträge zur kulturwissenschaftlichen Süd- und Ostasienforschung 5. Würzburg: Ergon.

Wittkamp, Robert F. 2018. *Arbeit am Text: Zur postmodernen Erforschung der Kojiki-Mythen*. Deutsche Ostasienstudien 34. Gossenberg: Ostasien Verlag.

Witzel, Michael. 2005. "Vala and Iwato: The Myth of the Hidden Sun in India, Japan, and Beyond." *Electronic Journal of Vedic Studies* 12 (1): 1–69.

Witzel, Michael. 2007. "Releasing the Sun at Midwinter and Slaying the Dragon at Midsummer: A Laurasian Myth Complex." *Cosmos: The Journal of the Traditional Cosmology Society* 23: 203–44.

Witzel, Michael. 2012. *The Origins of the World's Mythologies*. Oxford: Oxford University Press.

Yagi Ichio 八木意知男. 2002. "Kanekuni *Haykushu kashō* no kisoteki kenkyū: Gion shinkō-shi no hitokoma" 兼邦『百首歌抄』の基礎的研究：祇園信仰史の一齣. *Shintō-shi kenkyū* 神道史研究 50 (1): 91–124.

Yamada Hisashi 山田永. 2001. *Kojiki Susanoo no kenkyū* 古事記スサノヲの研究. Shintensha kenkyū sōsho 新典社研究叢書 137. Shintensha.

Yamaguchi Hiroshi 山口博. 2012. *Tsukurareta Susanoo shinwa* 創られたスサノオ神話. Chūkō sōsho 中公叢書. Chūōkōron Shinsha.

Yamaguchi Masao 山口昌男. 1977. "Kingship, Theatricality, and Marginal Reality in Japan." In *Text and Context: The Social Anthropology of Tradition*, edited by Ravindra K. Jain, 151–79. Philadelphia, PA: Institute for the Studies of Human Issues.

Yamaguchi Masao. 2003a. "Dōke no minzokugaku" 道化の民俗学. In *Dōke* 道化, edited by Imafuku Ryūta 今福龍太, 3–304. Yamaguchi Masao chosakushū 山口昌男著作集 3. Chikuma Shobō.

Yamaguchi Masao. 2003b. "Tennōsei no shinwa: Engekironteki kōzō" 天皇制の神話：演劇論的構造. In *Shūen* 周縁, edited by Imafuku Ryūta 今福龍太, 223–60. Yamaguchi Masao chosakushū 山口昌男著作集 5. Chikuma Shobō.

Yamamoto Hiroko 山本ひろ子. 1998a. *Chūsei shinwa* 中世神話. Iwanami shinsho: Shin akaban 岩波新書：新赤版 593. Iwanami Shoten.

Yamamoto Hiroko. 1998b. *Ijin: Chūsei Nihon no hikyōteki sekai* 異神：中世日本の秘教的世界. Heibonsha.

Yamamoto Hiroko. 2010. "Izumo no Matarajin kikō (kōhen): Kuroi Susanoo" 出雲の摩多羅神紀行（後篇）：黒いスサノオ. *Bungaku* 文学 11 (5): 256–80.

Yi Pyŏngsŏn 李炳銑. 2003. *Nihon kodai chimei no kenkyū: Nikkan kochimei no genryū to hikaku* 日本古代地名の研究：日韓古地名の源流と比較. Tōyō Shoin.

Yi Sŏngsi 李成市. 2011. "Sankan seibatsu" 三韓征伐. In *Higashi Ajia no kioku no ba* 東アジアの記憶の場, edited by Itagaki Ryūta 板垣竜太, Chŏng Chiyŏng 鄭智泳, and Iwasaki Minoru 岩崎稔, 36–65. Kawade Shobō Shinsha.

Yoshida Atsuhiko 吉田敦彦. 1996. "Susanoo no yōjisei to senshisei" スサノヲの幼児性と戦士性. In *Nihon shinwa no shisō: Susanoo ron* 日本神話の思想：スサノヲ論, edited by Kawai Hayao 河合隼雄, Yuasa Yasuo 湯浅泰雄, and Yoshida Atsuhiko 吉田敦彦, 2–47. Minerva 21-seiki raiburarī ミネルヴァ21世紀ライブラリー 29. Kyoto: Mineruva Shobō.

Yoshida Tōgo 吉田東伍. 1893. *Nikkan koshi dan* 日韓古史斷. Fuzanbō.

Yoshida Tōgo. 1910. "Kan hantō o gappei seru daikyokumen" 韓半島を併合せる大局面. *Rekishi chiri* 歴史地理 (Chōsen gō): 83–97.

Yoshikawa, Lisa. 2017. *Making History Matter: Kuroita Katsumi and the Construction of Imperial Japan*. Harvard East Asian Monographs 402. Cambridge. MA: Harvard University Asia Center.

Yoshino Yutaka 吉野裕. 1972. *Fudoki sekai to tetsuō shinwa* 風土記世界と鉄王神話. San'ichi Shobō.

Zhong, Yijiang. 2016. *The Origin of Modern Shinto in Japan: The Vanquished Gods of Izumo*. Bloomsbury Shinto Studies. London: Bloomsbury Academic.

Ziomek, Kirsten L. 2015. "The Possibility of Liminal Colonial Subjecthood: Yayutz Bleyh and the Search for Subaltern Histories in the Japanese Empire." *Critical Asian Studies* 47 (1): 123–50.

Zöllner, Reinhard. 2007. *Einführung in die Geschichte Ostasiens*. Erfurter Reihe zur Geschichte Asiens 1. München: Iudicium.

Index

Abe Tatsunosuke 阿部辰之助 166–7, 169
Age of the Gods 8, 42, 67, 111, 115, 129, 131, 149–50, 159, 163, 168
Agi (province) 56, 95
Aizawa Seishisai 会沢正志斎 25
Alalu 68
Allen, Chizuko 2
Amago Tsunehisa 尼子経久 127–8, 130
Ama no Fukine 天之葺根 92
Ama no Haha-kiri no Tsurugi 天蠅斫之剣 90–1
Amano Sadakage 天野信景 150–1
Amaterasu 天照 24, 49, 54, 158
    in colonial discourse 31, 40–6
    as imperial progenitress 3–7, 33, 40–2, 47, 64, 66–8, 72, 76, 78, 171
    See also Susanoo and Amaterasu
amatsu kami 天神. *See* Heavenly Deities
amatsu tsumi 天津罪. *See* Heavenly Sins
ame no shita 天下 54, 129
    See also tenka
Ame no Uzume 天宇受売 50
Ancient Chosŏn 6, 107, 149, 153
Anesaki Masaharu 姉崎正治 62–3
Anime 180
Aono Masaaki 青野正明 42, 44
Arai Hakuseki 新井白石 25, 147, 162
Ara Kaya 阿那加耶 91, 191 n.3
Arcadia 168
archaeology 17–18, 43, 91, 104, 157, 176–7
Ares 182
Arima 有馬 (village) 96, 99
Arinare 阿利那礼 (river) 39
Asadal 阿斯達 (mountain) 153
ashihara no nakatsu kuni 葦原中国. *See* Central Land of Reed Plains
Ashinazuchi 足名椎 50–1, 95, 179
Asia
    Japan as leader of 163
    Japan's ambiguous attitude toward 11, 27–9

    as Japan's primitive Other 27
assimilation 32, 42, 45, 80–3, 160
    See also assimilation policy; cultural assimilation
assimilation policy 1, 8, 30–3, 37–8, 44, 80–1, 83
Assmann, Aleida 10, 12, 171
Assmann, Jan 9, 17
Aston, William George 60–1, 102, 105
Athena 182
Atsuta Jingū 熱田神宮 (shrine) 41, 148
Auspiciousness 121–2
autonomy 30, 79, 83, 134
Awaji 淡路 (island) 96, 131, 192 n.18
Awashima 粟嶋 (island) 100

Babcock-Abrahams, Barbara 74
back door 135–6
backwardness
    Asia as backward 185 n.12
    colonized Koreans as backward 29–30, 64, 171
    Matarajin riding an ox backward 135 (*see also* reverse behavior; symbolic inversion)
    Susanoo's backward flaying (of a horse) 50, 56, 72–3 (*see also* reverse behavior; symbolic inversion)
bakufu 幕府. *See* Tokugawa bakufu
Ban Kōkei 伴蒿蹊 149
Batten, Bruce 17, 22
bear cult 108–9
bear/river/mountain (cluster of motifs) 106–10
Bentley, John 105, 192 n.11
Best, Jonathan 103–4
betsuin 別院. *See* subtemple
Bingo (province) 118–19
Bingo no kuni fudoki 備後国風土記 118–19, 123, 125

Blumenberg, Hans 7, 111
Bottici, Chiara 7
branch family
　Japan as 36
　Korea as 35, 38, 64
branch temple 132
Buckley, Edmund 61–3
Buddhism 113–16
　corrupting influence on Japan/
　　Shintō 8, 14, 61, 146–7, 151–4
　Gion Shrine's Buddhist
　　associations 116–7
　influence on Izumo Shrine 127–8
　as secondary to Shintō 141
　transmission to Japan from Paekche 20
　worldview. See *sangoku* worldview
　　See also Tendai Buddhism
bunguk sŏl 分國說. See satellite
　state theory
bunka seiji 文化政治 44
bunkoku setsu 分国説. See satellite
　state theory
bunmei 文明 27
　See also civilization: Western concept of

calendrical deity 151, 154
canonical texts of Japanese myth (*Kojiki*
　and *Nihon shoki* as) 7, 12
Cavern of Yomi 100, 132
center and periphery 64, 68–9, 76–80,
　98–9, 101, 111, 115, 168,
　170–1, 173
Central Land of Reed Plains 66, 77,
　97–9, 101
cession of the land 66–7, 69, 126, 176
ch'ach'aung 次々雄 (*chach'ung* 慈
　充) 148, 159
Chamberlain, Basil Hall 62, 65–6
Chang Pogo 張保皐 138
Ch'angwŏn (city) 106
chaos (Susanoo as bringer of) 65, 72, 74,
　76, 78, 181–2, 190 n.7
Chiba Kei 千葉慶 3–4
China
　civilization 17, 135, 137, 151
　　(see also *ka*)
　Korea and 35–6, 79–80, 138, 163
　and *sangoku* worldview 20, 114–15,
　　141–2, 169–71

Chinese learning (Chosŏn as
　center of) 21
Chinese Spirit 8, 151
Chinhae (district) 106, 166
Chinhan 辰韓 148
chi no wa 茅輪. See cogon grass wreaths
Chishan 赤山 (mountain) 137–8
Chishun 智春 130
Ch'oe Namsŏn 崔南善 36
Chŏnghaejin 清海鎮 138
Chōsen Grand Shrine. See Chōsen Jingū
　(shrine)
Chōsen Jingū 朝鮮神宮 (shrine) 31,
　41–2, 44–6, 148, 162, 199 n.1
Chōsen Kenkyūkai 朝鮮研究
　会 35, 41, 81
Chōsen kōron 朝鮮公論 (journal) 43
Chōsen-shi 朝鮮史 (Hayashi) 157
Chosŏn (Korea) 21, 25, 31, 149
　See also Ancient Chosŏn
Chosŏn il'il sinmun 朝鮮日日新聞
　(newspaper) 42
Christianity 28, 163
Christy, Alan 27
citizenship 81–3
civilization
　Buddhist civilization. See *sangoku*
　　worldview
　Chinese concept of. See
　　China: civilization
　civilizing mission (colonialism) 82–3
　Eastern civilization (Korea's role in the
　　development of) 36
　Korea as a land of advanced 18–21,
　　27, 30
　Western concept of 11, 27
civilizational triad (West/Japan/Asia) 27,
　168–9, 185 n. 12
Chūai 仲哀 (emperor) 19–20, 25
chūkō itchi 忠孝一致 3
Chumong 朱蒙 (king) 107, 109–10,
　147, 163
Ch'unchŏn 春川 (district) 42–4, 158, 160
chūsei shinwa 中世神話. See medieval
　mythology
cogon grass wreaths 119, 123–6
collective amnesia 81
collective identity 2, 5, 8–10, 27, 44,
　81, 87–8

collective memory 9, 17
colonizer and colonized 1, 5, 29–30, 35, 45, 64–5, 78–84, 168–73
combinatory paradigm. *See* Shintō-Buddhist combinatory practices
communicative memory 9
Confucianism
   civilization and ethics 3, 11, 27–9, 37
   China and 8, 141
   scholarship 14, 25, 93–4, 104, 133, 146–50, 154, 158, 169
   See also neo-Confucianism
Confucian Shintō 146–48 (*see also* Suika Shintō)
Council of State 151–2
court lectures on the *Nihon shoki*. *See Nihongi-kō*
court mythology
   genesis of 55, 76–8
   Izumo's relation to Yamato in 111
   in Japan's cultural memory 169–71
   Korean influences on 106
   neo-Confucian interpretations of 146
   Susanoo's role in 12, 58, 63–4, 83–4
Creighton, Millie 29
cultural assimilation 8, 11, 34–6, 173
cultural identity 1, 17, 24, 31, 80–1, 83
cultural imagination 11, 17–18, 20, 26
cultural memory
   and collective identity 81, 87–8
   concept 9–10, 17, 171
   Jingū in 26
   Kojiki and *Nihon shoki* in 78–9, 169
   Korea in 37
   reception of myths in 115
   selectivity of 170
   Susanoo in 14, 47, 78, 83, 169, 177–8, 182
Cultural Rule 44
cultural strata 164–5, 175, 199 n.2
culture area 162
culture circle 36, 164–5

dajōkan 太政官. *See* Council of State
Dazaifu 太宰府 138
Dazhong 大中 (emperor) 139
Demon Gate 128, 136, 138
Department of Japanese History (Tokyo Imperial University) 33–4, 158–9, 198 n.21

dependency (of Korea) 163
Devadatta 58, 136
Dewa Hiroaki 出羽弘明 90
dharma 127, 136, 139
diffusionism 163
dirt 29, 73–4, 173
discrimination 37, 80, 82
discursive antecedents 9–11, 13, 37, 84, 88, 154, 169, 171
disease deities. *See* pestilence deities
divine age. *See* Age of the Gods
divine age fascicles (*Nihon shoki*) 53–4, 58, 63, 123, 130, 142, 149
divine country 22–3, 115, 170
divine order 63, 73–6
Dōgen 同源 (journal) 35
dōgen dōshu 同源同種. *See* same origin, same race (of Korea and Japan)
dōiki 同域. *See* one realm (Korea and Japan as)
dōka seisaku 同化政策. *See* assimilation policy
domainal lords (*daimyō* 大名) 20, 25
Douglas, Mary 74
Dragon King. *See* Sāgara
Dutch studies 23
Duus, Peter 29, 33

E 可愛 (river) 56, 95
ear mound 25
Earthly Deities 12, 65–9, 78–9, 83, 176
edicts to separate *kami* and buddhas 8, 14, 151, 153–4, 162, 170–2
   See also separation of *kami* and buddhas
Edo period 3, 21, 59, 125, 130, 162, 169
Egami Namio 江上波夫 175–7, 199 n.2
eight divine children 119
eightfold fences 51, 179
eight-headed serpent 50, 56–7, 61, 77, 90, 95–6, 123, 140, 154, 170, 178–82
eight million deities 50, 56
eight royal children. *See hachiōji*
ekijin 疫神. *See* pestilence deities
Ekijinja 疫神社 (shrine) 125
Enchin 円珍 135, 138–40
engi 縁起 115, 133, 137–8
Engi shiki 延喜式 74, 90, 98, 125–6, 156
enmusubi 縁結び 179
Ennin 円仁 135, 137–8

Ennyo 円如 116
Enokuma 疫隅 (shrine) 119
Enra-ō 閻羅王 126, 135, 140, 142, 170
Enryakuji 延暦寺 116, 128, 132, 138, 152
epidemic deities. *See* pestilence deities
ethnic community 32, 37, 80
ethnic identity 17, 32, 80, 163–4
Ethnic Research Institute 164, 175
Ethnological Foundation 164
ethnology 157, 162–5
  colonial administration and 164
  culture–historical approach 164–5, 177
euhemerism 147, 162, 166, 196 n.3
evidentialism 145, 150, 172
evil twin (Susanoo as
  Amaterasu's) 63, 170

Fahua yuan 法華院 138
family empire 1, 37
family registration system 82
family state 1–6, 28, 32, 36–8, 87, 173
Farris, William 19
Faure Bernard 113, 135, 137
Floating Mountain 127–8
Florenz, Karl 60, 63
folklore studies 108, 161, 166, 180
food goddess 50, 55, 60, 75
foreign deities 2, 13, 110, 114, 120, 124,
  134–5, 140–3, 145, 150, 170, 182
foster children 38
Fujiwara no Mototsune 藤原基
  経 93, 116–18
Fujiwara no Tokitsura 藤原常行 117
Fukumoto Nichinan 福本日南 41
functional memory 10, 47, 171
Furō 不老 (mountain) 131
Furōsan 浮浪山. *See* Floating Mountain
Fūshi kaden 風姿花伝 136
Fu-yü 扶餘. *See* Puyŏ
fuzuisei 附随性. *See* dependency
  (of Korea)

Gakuenji 鰐淵寺 (temple) 13, 126–30,
  132–35, 146, 171
Gakuenji shūtora kanjin jōan 鰐淵寺衆徒
  等勧進状案 127, 130
Gakuen jisō nanigashi shojō dankan 鰐淵
  寺僧某書状断簡 128
Gellner, Ernest 5

gender
  in depicting colonial relationship 38
  masculinization of Meiji emperor 4
genealogical analysis 2, 9, 11, 13, 84–5, 88
Genmei 元明 (empress) 48, 118
Genshō 元正 (empress) 52
German-speaking ethnology 163–4
Gion 祇園 (shrine) 13–14, 116–26, 132,
  141, 145, 149–52, 154–5, 170–2
Gionsha hon'enroku 祇園社本縁録 118
Gionsha hon'en zatsu roku 祇園社本縁雑
  録 118, 151
Gladigow, Burkhard 68
gods of no-enlightenment 142
god of obstacles 137
gods of original enlightenment 142
golden ages 8, 146, 154
Gomagriva Devaraja 150
gongen 権現 151
goryō 御霊 117–18, 120, 122
gośīrṣa candana. *See* ox-head sandalwood
Government-General 6, 34–5, 42–5, 80
Governor-General 43–4, 81
gozu sendan 牛頭栴檀. *See* ox-head
  sandalwood
Gozu Tennō 牛頭天王 41, 121–4, 132,
  135, 137–42, 150–5, 160–2, 170–2
Gozu tennō ben 牛頭天王辨 150
Grapard, Allan 72
Grayson, James 108, 177, 200 n.13
Gṛdhrakūṭa. *See* Vulture Peak (mountain)
Great Eight Islands 49, 54, 92, 95
Great Mountain God 50, 89
Great Purification 23, 74–5, 98, 125–6
Guma 固麻 105
gyōyakujin 行役神. *See* pestilence deities

Hachiman 八幡 25
Hachiman gudōkun 八幡愚童訓 24
hachiōji 八王子 121–2
Haeju 海州 (city) 161
Haemosu 解慕漱 107–8, 193 n.30
Han 韓 19, 159
hanju 藩儒 (domainal Confucianist) 133
Hansŏng (city) 103, 109
Hard, Robin 98
Harime 婆利女 123
Hata 秦 (lineage) 136
Hatada Takashi 旗田巍 33

Hata no Kawakatsu 秦川勝 136
Hattori Nakatsune 服部中庸 59–60
Haya-Sasura Hime 速佐須良比咩 126
Hayashi Gahō 林鵞峰 147
Hayashi Razan 林羅山 25, 133–4, 146–7
Hayashi Shihei 林子平 23
Hayashi Taisuke 林泰輔 157
Hayatama 速玉 (Kumano Hayatama Taisha 熊野速玉大社) 99
Hayato 隼人 176
head family
   imperial household as (in relation to Japanese citizens) 28
   Japan as (in relation to Korea) 35, 38, 64
Hearn, Lafcadio 179, 200 n.9
Heavenly Deities 3, 12, 65–9, 101
Heavenly Rock Cave 50, 56, 61, 73, 75, 142, 181
Heavenly Rock Dwelling. *See* Heavenly Rock Cave
Heavenly Sins 74–5, 126, 190 n.10
Heiankyō 平安京 (city) 117, 125
Heian period 24, 94, 113, 117, 125, 136
Heijōkyō 平城京 (city) 117
Hein-Kircher, Heidi 26
Hesiod 98
heteronomy (of Korea) 162
Hi 簸 (river) 50–1, 56, 91, 95, 139, 179
Hiba 比婆 (mountain) 100
hidden matters 66, 131
Hiei 比叡 (mountain) 128, 138
hierarchy
   between center and periphery 99
   between three Buddhist civilizations (*sangoku*) 141, 169
   in Confucian relationships 28
   in family relations 2, 36–8
   in Japanese-Korean relations 36–8, 177
Hiki 秘基 (shrine) 131
Himuka (province) 49
Hinomisaki 日御碕 (mountain) 131
Hinomisaki (shrine) 130–31
Hinomisaki ryōhonsha narabi shaji enso no koto 日御碕両本社並社司遠祖事 131
Hirafuji Kikuko 平藤喜久子 163, 182
Hirano Kuniomi 平野国臣 26

Hirata Atsutane 平田篤胤 3, 25, 41, 60, 150–2
Hirō 飛瀧 (shrine) 130
Hiroshima (prefecture) 56, 118
Hiruko 蛭児 54–5
historical consciousness 11, 34, 83
historical continuity (construction of) 8–9, 87–8, 154
historical precedent
   ancient myths as precedent for separation of *kami* and buddhas 171
   ancient myths as precedent for colonization of Korea 25–6, 32, 34, 84, 159, 172
   naturalization of Korean aristocrats as precedent for assimilation policy 160
   order of the divine age as precedent for Yamato rule 111
historicism 145, 147, 154, 158, 169, 172
History of Japan (Kaempfer) 124
Hobsbawm, Eric 9, 154
Hōki (province) 100
Hōki no kuni fudoki 伯耆国風土記 100
Homer 98, 168
Honchō jinja kō 本朝神社考 133
Honchō seiki 本朝世紀 121, 123
Hondō saikō kanjin chō 本堂再興勧進帳 129
hongaku 本覚. *See* original enlightenment
hongan 本願 128, 134
Hongū 本宮 (Kumano Hongū Taisha 熊野本宮大社) 99
Hong Wontack 177
honji suijaku 本地垂迹 13, 113–14, 141, 145–6, 150–1, 155, 169
   See also Shintō-Buddhist combinatory practices
Honorable Country of Night 49, 55, 59–60
honseki 本籍 82
horserider theory 14, 175–7
Hoshino Hisashi 星野恒 14, 33–4, 42, 155, 157–60, 166, 172, 198 n.21
Huainanzi 淮南子 53
Huxley, Aldous 78
Hwanin 桓因 107, 157
Hwanung 桓雄 107, 157

Hyakushu kashō 百首歌抄 139
Hyde, Lewis 69, 73
hyper mythology 182

Ichijō Ietsune 一条家経 120
Ichijō Kaneyoshi 一条兼良 122–4, 142
Ichijō Sanetsune 一条実経 120, 122, 142
Iida Takesato 飯田武郷 156–7
iikijin 異域神. *See* foreign deity
ijin 異神. *See* foreign deity
Iki (province) 22
ikokujin 異国神. *See* foreign deity
imagined community 37, 78
Imamura Tomoe 今村鞆 161
Imanishi Ryū 今西龍 160, 163
imperial family
    continental origin of 158–9, 165, 176
    as head family of the family state 28
    mythical origins of 49, 65, 67, 69, 76, 101
    unbroken line 3–4, 42, 183 n.2
    See also Amaterasu: as imperial progenitress
Imperial Household Ministry 90
imperialization 82
imperial Shintō. *See* State Shintō
Inada Hime 稲田媛 56, 123, 179
Inai 稲永 34, 99
Inbe no Hironari 斎部広成 74
Inbe no Masamichi 忌部正通 130, 165
inbetweenness 12, 69–70, 79, 83, 170
incest 71–2, 190 n.10
independence
    Korean independence movement 34–6, 41 (*see also* March First Movement)
    Korean independence as an accident of history 8
    promise of Korean independence after successful modernization 30
India
    Gion Shrine's associations with 116, 121–2, 145, 150–2, 155, 170–1
    Indian ancestors of imperial family 158–9
    Indian parallels to Japanese myths 62–3, 68
    Izumo Shrine's associations with 127, 129

in *sangoku* worldview 20, 114–5, 141–2, 169–71
individual identity 27, 79
Indra 62–3
Inoue Kowashi 井上毅 158
Inoue Masatoshi 井上正利 134
Insei period 99
invented tradition
    concept 9
    and discursive antecedents 37, 84
    Gozu Tennō as 135, 170
    Susanoo's connection to Korea as 13, 110, 149
    Susanoo myth as 67, 77
    Susanoo's role in medieval mythology as 115–16
    Tan'gun myth as 160
    theory of common ancestry as 33
    Yasaka Shrine's rewriting of history as 154, 172
Iroha jiruishō 伊呂波字類抄 121–2
Ise (province) 77, 100–1, 110, 167
Ise 伊勢 (shrine) 142, 158, 171
    See also Izumo (province): Ise and
Ishida Eiichirō 石田英一郎 175
Island of Yomi 100
Isonokami Jingū 石上神宮 (shrine) 95
Itakeru 五十猛 87, 89, 91–2, 95, 99–100, 154–9
    See also Tan'gun: Itakeru and
Itakiso 伊太祁曽 (shrine) 156
Itate 伊太氏 155–6, 158, 198 n.16
Itō Hirobumi 伊藤博文 28, 30, 41, 158, 162
Itsuse 五瀬 99
Iuyazaka 伊賦夜坂 100
Iwami Kagura 石見神楽 180
Iware Biko. *See* Jinmu
Iyanaga Nobumi 彌永信美 114
Izanaki 34, 48, 53–4, 127, 146, 157–8, 166
    final retreat 96, 131
    ritual cleansing 59, 61, 96
    visit to Yomotsu Kuni 49, 100, 145
Izanami 127
    as ruler of Yomotsu Kuni 97
    birth of deities and Japanese islands 48–9, 53–5, 146
    grave 96, 99–100
Izumo 出雲 (city) 178–9

Izumo (district) 131
Izumo (mountain) 131
Izumo (province)
    connection to otherworld 95, 97, 100–2, 110–11, 129, 131–2
    Ise and 101, 110, 142, 167, 171
    Korea and 78, 139, 156, 160, 165–8, 176–7
    Susanoo in 12–13, 47–51, 56–7, 77, 91, 95, 126–34, 154
    Yamato and 6, 60, 65–9, 76–7, 110–11, 131, 170–73
Izumo (shrine) 126–30, 132–4, 146, 150, 171, 179
Izumo densetsu 出雲伝説 166
Izumo fudoki 出雲風土記 12, 57, 100–1, 126, 131–2, 178
    See also Susanoo in *Izumo fudoki*
Izumo Taisha 出雲大社. *See* Izumo (shrine)

Jaddoke no Kami 蛇毒気神 123
"Japan and Korea as one body" 31, 45, 82
Japanization 44, 82
Japanocentrism 141, 147, 170
Jetavana 116, 136, 151, 153, 172
Jian 集安 21
jigoku 地獄 (hell) 139
Jihen 慈遍 58
Jikaku 慈覚. *See* Ennin
Jilin 吉林 21
Jimon 寺門 (school of Tendai Buddhism) 138–40
Jimon denki horoku 寺門伝記補録 140
jindaikan 神代巻. *See* divine age fascicles
Jindaikan kuketsu 神代巻口訣 130
Jingū 神功 (empress) 19–20, 22–6, 34, 39, 149
jingūji 神宮寺 128
Jinjakyoku 神社局 43
Jinmu 神武 (emperor) 4, 6, 8, 33–4
jisha bugyō 寺社奉行 134
Jōgyōdō 常行堂 (Hall of the Walking Meditation Practice) 132, 135–7

ka 華 27
Kaempfer, Engelbert 124
Kaero 蓋鹵 (king) 102–3
Kagura 神楽 180

kaitaku sanshin 開拓三神 45–6
kakuretaru koto 幽事. *See* hidden matters
Kamakura period 113, 121, 125–6
Kamayama 竈山 (mountain) 99
Kamimusuhi 神産巣日 75
Kamo no Mabuchi 賀茂真淵 62, 149
Kamu-ōichi Hime 神大市比賣 89
Kanazawa Shōzaburō 金沢庄三郎 35, 159, 161
Kanda Norishiro 神田典城 101
Kanden kōhitsu 閑田耕筆 149
Kangwŏn (province) 42, 158, 160
Kanjin-in 感神院 116, 151–5
Kanjin-in Gozu tennō kō 感神院牛頭天王考 152
Kankeiji 観慶寺 116, 118
kanpaku 関白 120
karagokoro 漢意. *See* Chinese Spirit
Kara-kuni ni masu Itate 坐韓国伊太氐 155–6
    See also Itate
Kara no Kami 韓神 89–90, 155–6
karidono 仮殿 (provisional hall) 133
Katsu Yasuyoshi 勝安芳 23
Kawamura Minato 川村湊 151–2, 161
Kaya 伽倻 (federation) 19, 21–2, 24–6, 91, 104–5, 107, 160, 166, 177
    See also Ara Kaya; Kŭmgwan Kaya
Kaya (mountain) 160
Keijō 京城 (shrine) 45
Keiran shūyōshū 渓嵐拾葉集 137
Keitai 継体 (emperor) 106, 166
Kenkyōjin 鉗狂人 149
Kerényi, Karl 75
ki 気 146, 148, 169
Ki Shigetsugu 紀繁継 152–5, 157–8, 161
kiba minzoku setsu 騎馬民族説. *See* horserider theory
Kibi 吉備 95
Kibi no Makibi 吉備真備 150–1
Kido Takayoshi 木戸孝允 23, 26
Kii (province) 92, 95–7, 99–100, 154, 156, 166
Kim Sŏkhyŏng 金錫亨 176–7
Kim, Sujung 17–18, 20, 24, 136
Kim Suro 金首露 (king) 107
Kinai 畿内 (region) 177
King Father of the Eastern Skies 121
King Yama. *See* Enra-ō

Kinmei 欽明 (emperor) 41
kisshō 吉祥. *See* Auspiciousness
Kisuki 木次 (rail line) 178
Kita Sadakichi 喜田貞吉 (also Kida Teikichi) 35, 38, 159–60, 176
Kizuki 杵築 (shrine). *See* Izumo (shrine)
Kizuki (township) 129
Kofun period 19
Kōgen 江原 (shrine) 43
Kogo shūi 古語拾遺 74, 90, 93–4, 110, 126, 190 n.11
Koguryŏ 高句麗 21–2, 24, 102–3, 105, 107–9, 147–8, 153, 155, 163
Kōhon: kokushigan 稿本国史眼 34
Koiso Kuniaki 小磯國昭 1, 43–4
Kojiki 古事記 *passim*
 as canonical text 12, 87, 168–9
 comparison with *Nihon shoki* 47–8, 52–6, 94
 and National Learning 3, 52–3, 58–60, 62
 on Korea 23–4, 88–90, 156
 See also Susanoo in *Kojiki*
Kojikiden 古事記伝 58–9, 62, 166
kojitsuka 故実家 150
kokugaku 国学. *See* National Learning
kokuhei shōsha 国幣小社 43, 45
kokuminka 国民化 82
kokuseki 国籍 82
kokushika 国史科. *See* Department of Japanese History (Tokyo Imperial University)
Kokusō Izumo Noritoki gejō dodai utsushi 国造出雲孝時解状土代写 127
kokutai 国体 32
kokutai meichō 国体明徴 31
Kokutai no hongi 国体の本義 28
kōminka 皇民化 82
Kōno Bansei 河野万世 42–3
Konoe Fumimaro 近衛文麿 4
Kōnoshi Takamitsu 神野志隆光 48, 53–4
Konpira 金毘羅 142, 150, 196 n.17
Koppers, Wilhelm 163
Korea
 annexation of 1–2, 14, 29, 40–1, 43, 80
 annexation as restoration of primordial unity 8, 26, 33–5, 38–9, 159, 167, 172
 chauvinistic attitude toward 24, 157, 163, 168, 177
 colonial education in 1, 5, 30–1, 40, 44
 contradictory attitude toward 11, 17, 20, 80–2
 cultural exchange with Japan 18, 162–3, 165, 176–7
 denial of unique culture 17, 163, 168
 and Japanese identity 17, 78, 84, 167–8, 171
 invasion of (Hideyoshi) 20–1
 Japanese perceptions of 17–27, 83–4, 163
 as land of treasures and civilization 18–21, 27, 30
 as realm of death 97, 140, 146, 165–9, 173
 as source of epidemics 22, 140, 146, 155, 170–1, 173
 as threat to Japanese security 21–3
 as vassal state (of Japan) 23–6, 41
Korean embassies (to Edo) 21, 25
Korean history (colonial view of) 36, 44, 81, 157, 160, 163, 166, 168
Korea Strait 19, 22, 176
Koreyoshi no Sukune Takahisa 惟良宿祢高尚 93
Koryŏ period 160, 163
Kōryūji 広隆寺 (temple) 135–6
koseki 戸籍 (family register) 82
Koshi 高志 (region) 50, 95, 188 n.25
Kotan Shōrai 巨旦将来 122–3
Kronos 68
Kuhn, Adalbert 59
Kuji kongen 公事根源 122
Kulturkreis. *See* culture circle
Kulturschichten. *See* cultural strata
Kumanari 13, 88, 92, 95–9, 102–10, 129–30, 165–66
Kumano 熊野 (region) 96, 99–100, 102, 111, 166, 193 n. 19
Kumaso 熊襲 20
Kume Kunitake 久米邦武 34, 158–9, 176
Kŭmgwan Kaya 金官伽耶 19
kunaishō 宮内省 (Imperial Household Ministry) 90
kuni-biki 国引き. *See* land-pulling
Kunibiki chūō dōri くにびき中央通り (street) 178

Kunitama 国魂 44–5, 186 n.16
kunitsu kami 国神. *See* Earthly Deities
kuni-yuzuri 国譲り. *See* cession of the land
Kurosawa Nagahisa 黒沢長尚 130, 195 n.11
Kurosawa Sekisai 黒沢石斎 133, 195 n.11
Ku-Samguksa 舊三國史 107–9
Kusanagi 51, 92, 95, 179
Kushiinada Hime 寄稲田姫 (Kushinada Hime 櫛名田比売) 50–1, 56, 95–6, 120, 140, 154
    See also Inada Hime
Kushimura 久斯牟羅 (village) 106
kusō 九相. *See* Nine Phases
Kwanggaet'o 廣開土 21, 25, 107
Kwansei Association for Shrine Priests 40
Kwŏn Dongwoo 権東祐 48, 58
Kyoto (city) 13, 25, 116–17, 135, 148
Kyoto (prefecture) 125
Kyoto Imperial University 168
Kyushu 20, 22–3, 25, 40, 65, 149, 177
Kyūshū nippō 九州日報 41

Lakṣmī 121
land of the gods. *See* divine country
land-pulling 57, 129, 178
Langewiesche, Dieter 75
Lay of King Tongmyŏng, The 107
Ledyard, Gari 177
Leipzig (University of) 63
Lelang 樂浪 153–4, 158
Lévi-Strauss, Claude 71–2, 96
li 理. *See ri*
lieu de mémoire. *See* site of memory
liminality 13, 70, 78–84, 87, 137, 170
    See also Susanoo as liminal figure
Lincoln, Bruce 7
linguistics 17, 32–6, 43, 63, 79, 104–5, 153, 157, 161
Loki 68–9, 182
Lotus Sutra 122
Lower Takori 哆呼利 (district) 102
Lowie, Robert 162
Lunheng 論衡 107
Lurie, David 52

main family (Korea as) 36
Maitreya 138

Makarius, Laura 71, 73, 75
'*mamako*' *kokumin* 「ママコ」国民. *See* nation of stepchildren (Korea as)
Manchuria 31, 36, 107–9, 176
Manga 180
Mansen 満鮮 31
Man'yōshū 万葉集 98
March First Movement 34–5, 38, 40–1, 44
marginality
    Itakeru as marginal deity 157
    Izumo at the margin of Yamato 6, 68–9
    Japan at margin of Asian civilization 20
    Korea's marginal position in the Japanese empire 65, 79–80, 170, 172–3
    marginalization of regions associated with otherworlds 97
    Susanoo as a symbol of 2, 64, 76, 78, 170
    of variants connecting Susanoo with Korea in *Nihon shoki* 95
    zainichi Koreans' marginal position in Japan 29
Mata 末多 (king) 102–3
mātarah 135
Matarajin 摩多羅神 130, 132, 134–7, 139–40, 142, 150, 155, 170–1
Matsudaira Naomasa 松平直政 132–3
Matsue 松江 (city) 178–9
Matsue (domain) 130, 133
matsuji 末寺 132
Matsumae Takeshi 松前健 177
Matsumoto Naoki 松本直樹 11, 54, 58, 101
Matsumura Takeo 松村武雄 67–8, 77, 191 n.15
Matsuoka Shizuo 松岡静雄 166, 169
Matsuura Michisuke 松浦道輔 152–3, 155, 157, 172
McMullin, Neil 117–18
medieval mythology 13, 115–16, 124, 126, 132, 145, 194 n.2
medieval *Nihongi* 115, 119
Meiji 明治 (emperor) 1, 4, 41–2
Meiji constitution 28
Meiji government 3–4, 8, 26
Meiji period 26–7, 82, 101, 151, 169, 172
Meiji Restoration 2, 8, 11, 23, 26–7, 152–3
Memmi, Albert 45, 82

Meru (mountain) 130
metropole 34–5, 42, 45, 82–4, 146, 173
Mibudera 壬生寺 (temple) 125
Miidera 三井寺 (temple) 138–40
Mike-irino 三毛入野 99
military conscription (for Koreans) 81, 163
Mimana 任那 25–6, 34, 102, 106, 184 n.6
mimizuka 耳塚 25
Minami Jirō 南次郎 81
Ministry of Education 28, 35, 158
Minzoku Kenkyūjo 民族研究所. *See* Ethnic Research Institute
Minzoku to rekishi 民族と歴史 (journal) 35
Mirror Pond 179
Misen 彌山 (mountain) 130, 195 n.10
Mishina Akihide 三品彰英 (also Shōei) 162–3
Mito 水戸 School 3, 25
Miura Hiroyuki 三浦周行 160
Miwa 神 (village) 99
Miyama 彌山 (mountain) 131, 195 n.10
Mizoguchi Kōji 溝口孝司 177
modernization 6, 28, 30, 39, 83
mokkan 木簡. *See* wooden tablets
Mongol invasions 23–4
Mononobe 物部 (lineage) 94–5
Mori Asao 森朝男 72
Morris-Suzuki, Tessa 82
Motoori Norinaga 本居宣長 3, 58–9, 62, 149, 166
Müller, Friedrich Max 59, 63
Munju 汶洲 (king) 102–4
Muromachi period 113, 125, 139
Mutō 武塔 118–24, 137, 140–2, 195 n.16
Myth
  as collective narrative 7
  collective identity and 78, 81, 87
  of common ancestry 8, 32, 44
  comparative studies of 48, 68, 163
  genesis and reception of 7, 66, 76–8, 88, 101, 111, 115–16, 120
  history and 145, 147–9, 162, 176–7
  justification by precedent 8–9, 66, 76, 84, 87, 111, 167, 171, 173
  legitimating function of 8–11, 67, 69, 84, 87, 101
  reconfiguration and reinterpretation of 9, 79, 87–8, 115–16, 120, 124, 154, 169
  sacred authority of 8, 11, 78, 87, 119, 130, 172
  selective reception of 38, 47, 170
  social and political functions of 7–11, 162
myth-history 8, 13, 49, 58, 66, 69, 77–8, 97, 123, 176, 183 n.7
mythicoritual network 13, 113–14, 134, 140–2, 169

Nachi 那智 (Kumano Nachi Taisha 熊野那智大社) 99
Nagano (prefecture) 175
Nagaokakyō 長岡京 (city) 125
Nagato (province) 22, 25
nagoshi no harae 夏越の祓 125
Nagoya (city) 41
naichi 内地 31, 43, 79
naisen dōka 内鮮同化 42
naisen ittai 内鮮一体. *See* "Japan and Korea as one body"
naisen minzoku 内鮮民族 (Japanese-Korean race) 167
Nakatomi 中臣 74
Nakatomi harae kunge 中臣祓訓解 126, 142
Nangnang 樂浪. *See* Lelang
Nara period 117, 150
National Association for Shrine Priests 40
national identity 3–5, 27, 29, 78, 164
nationality (*kokuseki*) 82
nationalization 82
National Learning
  criticism of combinatory teachings 13–14, 145–51
  criticism of theory of common ancestry 34
  and family state ideology 3
  interpretations of myths 147, 154, 169, 172
  on Jingū 25
  political influence in early Meiji period 161
  and pre-Buddhist golden age 8, 154
  rediscovery of *Kojiki* 53
  on Susanoo 58–9, 62, 155–61

national shrine, third rank 43, 45
nation of stepchildren (Korea as) 160
native deities 150-1
nature mythology 59-63
Naumann, Nelly 72
Navasaṁjñā. *See* Nine Phases
Nazi ethnology 164
Nazuki 腦礙 (Ridge of) 131
nenbutsu 念仏 136-7
Ne no Katasukuni 根堅州国 49-51, 89, 96-100, 110, 170
Ne no Kuni 根国 54-7, 75, 89, 92, 95-102, 106, 110, 126, 129-32, 154, 165-6, 170
ne no kuni 子国 131
neo-Confucianism
    Chosŏn as center of neo-Confucian learning 21
    criticism of combinatory teachings 13, 145, 169
    interpretation of myths 146-50, 172
    privileging of *Nihon shoki* 146-50
    synthesis with Shintō 134, 169, 171
Nietzsche, Friedrich 32
Nihongi-kō 日本紀講 13, 52, 92-3, 116, 191 n.8
Nihonjinka 日本人化 44, 82
Nihon ryōiki 日本霊異記 73
Nihon sandai jitsuroku 日本三代実録 117-18
Nihon shoki 日本書紀 *passim*
    as canonical text 12-13, 52-3, 87, 92, 130, 169, 172
    comparison with *Kojiki* 48, 52-5, 94
    on Korea 19-20, 22-5, 39, 41, 88-9, 90-3, 102, 105-6, 154-5, 160, 166
    medieval interpretations of 115, 120, 122-4, 141-2
    See also neo-Confucianism: privileging of *Nihon shoki*; Susanoo in *Nihon shoki*
Nihon shoki jindai maki no shō 日本書紀神代巻抄 142
Nihon shoki sanso 日本書記纂疏 122-4
Nihon shoki tsūshaku 日本書紀通釈 156
Nihon shoki tsūshō 日本書紀通證 147
Nihon shunjū 日本春秋 156
Nijō 二条 (emperor) 139
Nijūnisha chūshiki 二十二社註式 151

Nine Phases 121-2
Ninigi 4, 65-6, 68, 176
ninku danren 忍苦鍛錬 31
Nissen dōsoron 日鮮道祖論. *See* theory of common ancestry (of Japanese and Koreans)
Nissho Jakuken 日初寂顕 156
Nitobe Inazō 新渡戸稲造 168
Nora, Pierre 24
Northern Kyŏngsang (province) 161

Ōanamuji 大穴牟遅 51-2, 99, 188 n.25
Ōbayashi Taryō 大林太良 177
object of worship (*shintai*) 151, 175
Ochiai Naozumi 落合直澄 155-8
Odin 68, 182
Office of Historiography 158-9
Ōgetsu Hime 大気都比売 50, 55
Oguma Eiji 小熊英二 37, 80
ōharae 大祓. *See* Great Purification
Ōjin 応神 (emperor) 25
Oka Masao 岡正雄 162-5, 175, 177, 199 n.2
Ōkami 大神 (videogame) 181-2
Okina 翁 136
Okinaga-tarashi Hime 気長足姫. *See* Jingū
Okuizumo 奥出雲 (town) 178
Ōkuma Shigenobu 大隈重信 39
Ōkuninushi 大国主 51-2, 56, 65-9, 77, 95-7, 100-1, 126, 129-34, 146, 158, 171, 178-9
    See also Ōanamuji
Old Chosŏn. *See* Ancient Chosŏn
Ōmi 相見 (district) 100
Ōmi (province) 138
Ōmi no Kena no Omi 近江毛野臣 106
one realm (Korea and Japan as) 159
Onjo 溫祚 (king) 109, 147
Onjōji 園城寺 (temple) 138-40
Onjōji denki 園城寺伝記 139-40
Onjōji ryūge-e engi 園城寺龍華会縁起 138
Onmyōdōdō 陰陽道. *See yin-yang*
Ō no Yasumaro 太安万侶 48
Oriental History. *See tōyōshi*
Orientalism 29
original enlightenment 58, 142, 169
Orochi Loop 178

Orochi no Ara-masa 蛇之麁正 90–1, 95
Orochi no Kara-sai no Tsurugi 蛇韓鋤之剣 90–1
Orochi Street 178
ōsei fukko 王政復古 8
Oshihomimi 忍穂耳 33
Ōshima Masanori 大島正徳 38
Ōshima Tomonojō 大島友之允 23
Osiris 68
otherworlds
    deities enter otherworld when their task is fulfilled 96–7
    foreign countries as 114, 122, 171
    Korea's association with 166, 170
    Kumano and 99–100
    otherworld conceptions in Japanese myth 97–9
    Susanoo as god of 125, 170
    Susanoo travels to 69
    See also Izumo (province): connection to otherworld; Ne no Katasu Kuni; Ne no Kuni; Tokoyo no Kuni; Yomotsu Kuni
Ōtoshi 大年 89
Ouranos 98
Ox Festival (Kōryūji) 135–6
Ox-Head Mountain. *See* Udu (mountain)
ox-head sandalwood 135, 150–3, 172, 195 n.12
Ōya Biko 大屋毘古 99–100
Ōyamatsumi 大山津見 50, 89
Ōyatsu Hime 大屋津姫 92, 99–100

Paegak 白岳 (mountain) 153
Paekche 百済 20–2, 24, 26, 41, 93, 102–6, 109–10, 147–8, 166–7, 177
Pak Hyŏkkŏse 朴赫居世 (king) 147
Palace of the Great Harvest Festival 50, 56, 72, 74
pan-Asianism 37, 39
Pangu 盤古 62, 142
periphery. *See* center and periphery
pestilence deities
    foreign deities as 114
    Gozu Tennō as 41, 123–5, 141, 152, 155, 170, 172
    Matarjin as 134–6, 170
    Mutō as 118–20, 123, 141

    Queen Mother of the Western Skies as 121
    Sekizan Myōjin as 134, 138, 170
    Shinra Myōjin as 134, 140, 146, 170
    See also Susanoo as pestilence deity
Piggott, Joan 67
Plain of High Heaven 12, 49–56, 66–74, 77, 90, 95, 98, 101, 120–2, 126
Plain of the Sea 34, 49, 55, 60, 62, 158
playful attitude toward ancient myths 178–81
Pledge of Imperial Subjects 30–1
political exclusion (of colonized Koreans) 11
political mythology 14, 26, 88, 102, 171
pollution 13, 22, 59, 89, 96, 101, 114, 166, 170, 181
Poseidon 68
pre-Buddhist Shintō 14, 133–4, 145–7, 150, 154, 169, 171–2
Princess Pari 162
positivism 145, 147, 158, 166, 169, 172
postwar period 14
protectorate (Korea as) 29, 40, 80
Provisional Government of the Republic of Korea 35–6
Pure Land 137
Pure Weaving Hall 50, 56, 71–2
Purham culture 36
purity 22, 50, 72, 74
Puyŏ 夫餘 107–9, 176–7
Pyŏngan 平安 (province) 158
Pyongyang 平壤 153
Pyŏnhan 弁韓 19, 25

Queen Mother of the Western Skies 121
qi 気. *See ki*

rangaku 蘭学. *See* Dutch studies
regent 93, 116, 120
Rekishi chiri 歴史地理 (journal) 35, 159–60
Residency-General 40
Resident-General 30, 41
"Restore One-and-Only Shintō" 133
reverse behavior 73, 135–6
    see also symbolic inversion
rewriting of history 77–8, 106, 154, 162, 172

ri 理 146, 148, 169
rites of passage 70, 79–80
ritsuryō 律令 8, 113
Róheim, Géza 72, 190 n.10
Russia 23, 79–80
Ryōjusen 霊鷲山. See Vulture Peak (mountain)

Saar, Martin 88
Sabi 泗沘 109
sacred texts (*Kojiki* and *Nihon shoki* as)
  of the Japanese nation 78
  of Shintō 8, 158, 130, 172
Sada 佐田 (town) 178
Sāgara 121–3
Saichō 最澄 135, 137
Said, Edward 29
Saigō Nobutsuna 西郷信綱 48, 100–1, 131, 167
Saimei 斉明 (empress) 154
Saimochi 鋤持 99
saisei itchi 祭政一致 159
Saitō Hideki 斎藤英喜 52, 115, 142
Saitō Makoto 斎藤実 44
Sakkada 薩迦陁 121
sakuhinron 作品論 48
Śākyamuni 20, 58, 116, 127, 136
Samchŏk 三陟 (city) 160
same origin, same race (of Korea and Japan) 83
Samguk sagi 三國史記 103–5, 108–9, 160
Samguk yusa 三國遺事 6, 105, 107–9, 160–1
Samgŭn 三斤 (king) 103
samhan 三韓. See three Han
sanbu no honsho 三部本書 93
Sandaikō 三大考 59
sandalwood 107, 135, 150–4, 160, 172, 195 n.12
sangoku 三国 worldview 20, 115, 141, 170
San guo zhi 三国志 107, 184 n.2
Sanmon 山門 (school of Tendai Buddhism) 138–9
Sanuki (province) 22
Sanwu liji 三五暦紀 53
sarugaku 申楽 136
satellite state theory 176–7
Scheid, Bernhard 66, 71–2, 76, 133
Schmidt, Wilhelm 163

Scholl, Tobias 36
Schwartz, Wilhelm 59
Second Sino-Japanese War 30, 44, 81
Seiwa 清和 (emperor) 23
Sekizan daimyōjin engi 赤山大明神縁起 137
Sekizan Myōjin 赤山明神 134, 137–9, 142, 150, 155, 170
Sekizan Zen'in 赤山禅院 137–8
Sendai kuji hongi 先代旧事本紀 13, 88–9, 93–5, 97, 100, 169
  See also Susanoo in *Sendai kuji hongi*
Sengoku period 130
Seoul 31, 35, 41, 45, 103
separation of *kami* and buddhas 145, 154, 161–2, 170, 172
  at Gion Shrine 150–5
  See also edicts to separate *kami* and buddhas
Seth 68
sesshō 摂政. See regent
settlers (in colonized Korea) 35, 42–5, 79, 81
Seyock, Barbara 19
Shaku Nihongi 釈日本紀 93, 100, 118–25, 140–2, 154
shamushiki 社務職 (main ritualist) 152
Shandong 山東 (province) 137
Shang Wu Ding 商武丁 (emperor) 153
Shidehara Taira 幣原坦 159
Shigeno Yasutsugu 重野安繹 34, 158, 198 n.21
Shimane (prefecture) 14, 47, 177–82
Shimane peninsula 128–9
Shimane Susanoo Magic (basketball team) 178
shinbutsu bunri 神仏分離. See separation of *kami* and buddhas
shinbutsu bunri no rei 神仏分離令. See edicts to separate *kami* and buddhas
shinbutsu shūgō 神仏習合. See Shintō-Buddhist combinatory practices
shinkoku 神国. See divine country
Shin Megami Tensei: Imagine 新・女神転生 IMAGINE (videogame) 181–2
shinmonseki 神紋石 131
Shinra Myōjin 新羅明神 134, 136–40, 142, 146, 150, 156, 170
Shinsen'en 神泉苑 117–18

shintai 神体. *See* object of worship
Shintō. *See* Confucian Shintō; pre-Buddhist Shintō; State Shintō; Suika Shintō; Yoshida Shintō
Shintō activists 34, 40, 43–6, 158
Shintō-Buddhist combinatory practices 8, 13–14, 114, 133–4, 145, 150–5, 162, 169
  See also honji suijaku
Shintōshū 神道集 138
Shirahi no Kami 白日神 89–90, 191 n.2
Shirakawa 白河 (emperor) 139
Shiratori Kurakichi 白鳥倉吉 6, 29, 163
shōgejin 障礙神. *See* god of obstacles
shōgun 将軍 20
Shōkōhatsu 衝口発 148, 197 n.8
Shoku Nihongi 続日本紀 57
Shōshōi 少将井 120, 123
Shōtoku Taishi 聖徳太子 93–4, 141
Shrine Bureau 43
Shunsen 春川 (shrine) 43
Shunsen fudoki 春川風土記 42
sibling nations (Japan and Korea as) 1, 5–6, 40, 84, 160
Silla 新羅 17, 20–4, 26, 33–4, 87–95, 103–6, 110, 120, 129, 136–40, 147–9, 153–61, 167, 170, 177
Silla ponsa 新羅本史 148
Sinbuk 新北 (township) 42
Singung Ponggyŏnghoe 神宮奉敬會 40
sinosphere 20
site of memory 24, 178, 180
Skya, Walter 37
Slope of Yomi 100, 132
smallpox 22, 124
Smith, Anthony 5, 8, 32
sŏbŏl 徐伐 (*sŏrabŏl* 徐羅伐) 89, 161, 192 n.9
Soga 蘇我 (lineage) 148
Sohori no Kami 曾富理神 89, 155
Somin changnae ji jason haeju huip 蘇民將來之子孫海州后入 161
Somin Shōrai 蘇民将来 118–25, 140, 152–4, 161–2
Sono Kami 園神 89
Soshimori 曾尸茂梨 1, 13, 43, 87–8, 91–5, 110, 139–40, 153–61, 165, 172, 196 n.5
South Hwanghae (province) 161
Southern Kyŏngsang (province) 106, 160

South P'yŏngan (province) 161
Śrīvastaya. *See* Auspiciousness
State Shintō 12, 40, 44–6, 152
stereotypes (about colonized Korans) 29–30, 83–4
Stockdale, Jonathan 68
storage memory 10, 12, 171–2
Street, Brian 75
subtemple 116, 132
Sudatta 116–17
Suga Kōji 菅浩二 45
Suika Shintō 垂加神道 147–8, 150
Suiko (empress) 推古 49
Sukunabikona 少彦名 96, 100
sun goddess. *See* Amaterasu
sun lineage. *See* imperial family
Supreme Commander of the Allied Powers 175
Susanoo and Amaterasu
  as antipodes 1–2, 12, 58–63, 67–9, 84, 87, 110, 142, 170, 181–2
  in colonial discourse 1, 6, 32, 38–42, 63–4, 173
  in court mythology 47–51, 54–6, 77–8, 100
  incest 71–2
  as siblings 127, 173
Susanoo and Tsukuyomi 54–5, 59–61, 77, 165
Susanoo as liminal figure 2, 12, 65, 69–70, 77, 79, 83–4, 87, 170
Susanoo as pestilence deity 110, 114, 126, 143
  association with Gozu Tennō 123–4, 152, 155, 170, 172
  association with Matarajin 132, 134, 170
  association with Mutō 119–21, 123–4
  association with Sekizan Myōjin 134, 170
  association with Shinra Myōjin 134, 170
Susanoo as storm god 59, 61–3
Susanoo as taboo breaker 65, 70–3, 87
Susanoo as tourist attraction and mascot 14, 177–80
Susanoo in colonial discourse 12–13, 18, 32, 38–47, 63–4, 83–4, 87, 146, 157–65, 170
  See also Tan'gun: Susanoo and

Susanoo in *Izumo fudoki* 12–13, 47–8, 57, 64, 110, 170, 178
　See also Izumo (province): Susanoo in
Susanoo in *Kojiki* 12–13, 39, 47–52, 59–60, 64, 88–90, 96, 110, 153–4, 156, 166
Susanoo in *Nihon shoki* 12–13, 39, 41, 47–8, 54–7, 59, 64
　connection to Korea 88–93, 95–6, 102, 110, 120, 139, 153–5, 159, 165–6
Susanoo in public consciousness 14, 178, 182
Susanoo in *Sendai kuji hongi* 13, 88–9, 93–6, 102, 110, 155, 165
Susanoo in videogames 14, 180–2
Susano Kankō スサノオ観光 (Susanoo Sightseeing) 178
Susanoo's connection to Korea
　in ancient mythology 13, 19, 87–95, 102, 110
　in medieval mythology 120, 139–40
　in early modern and modern scholarship 14, 33–4, 145, 148–9, 153–60, 163, 165–7
Susanoo's connection to realms of the dead
　in colonial discourse 14
　in court mythology 13, 89, 95–7, 106, 110
　in medieval mythology 114, 125–6, 129–32, 134, 140, 143, 170
Suseri Bime 須勢理毘売 51–2, 57
Suzuki Kōtarō 鈴木耕太郎 122
symbolic inversion 135
　See also reverse behavior

taboos 12, 62, 65, 70–3, 75, 87, 108, 176
Tachibana 橘 river 49
Tacitus 168
T'aebaek 太白 (mountain) 160
Taehan maeil sinbo 大韓毎日申報 (newspaper) 40
Taejo (king) 太祖 40
Taishan Fujun 泰山府君 135, 140, 170
Taiwan 37, 79, 82
Taizan Fukun 泰山府君. *See* Taishan Fujun
takaama no hara 高天原. *See* Plain of High Heaven

Takagi Masutarō 高木益太郎 42
Takagi Toshio 高木敏雄 60, 62–3, 67, 77
Takayama Rinjirō 高山林次郎 62–3
talismans 124–5, 140, 161
Tama no mihashira 霊能真柱 60
Tamatsukuri 玉造 (village) 178
Tanaka, Stefan 29, 31
Tang 唐 22, 33, 138–9, 151
Tan'gun 檀君 36, 107, 153
　as fabrication 6, 81, 163
　Itakeru and 156–8
　Susanoo and 6, 14, 33, 40–6, 78–9, 84, 148–9, 153–61, 172
Tanigawa Kotosuga 谷川士清 147–8, 150
taritsusei 他律性. *See* heteronomy (of Korea)
tatarigami 祟り神. *See* vengeful deity
Teikoku kinen shian 帝国紀年私案 155
Temple and Shrine Magistrate 134
Tenazuchi 手名椎 50, 95, 179
Tenchi 天智 (emperor) 153, 155
Tenchi jingi shinchin yōki 天地神祇審鎮要記 58
Tendai 天台 Buddhism 13, 58, 116, 126–32, 134–42, 171
　See also Jimon (school of Tendai Buddhism); Sanmon (school of Tendai Buddhism)
tenka 天下 127
　See also ame no shita
Tenmu 天武 (emperor) 48, 52, 76
Tennō dynasty. *See* imperial family
Tennōsha 天王社 (shrine) 152
tenson minzoku 天孫民族 (people of heavenly ancestry) 65–7, 176
theory of common ancestry (of Japanese and Koreans) 5–6, 11–14, 29, 31–47, 64, 78–80, 84, 146, 155–62, 165–6, 170–2, 175
Thomassen, Bjørn 80, 83
three gods of colonization 45–6
three Han 19
three kingdoms. *See sangoku* worldview
Three Kingdoms period 21
Tiantai 天台 (mountain) 137
Tiantong 天童 (mountain) 137
Tobisaki 飛前 149
Tokoyo no Kuni 常世郷 97, 99–100, 167

Tokugawa bakufu 徳川幕府 2, 8, 23, 25–6, 88, 133–4, 149
Tokugawa Mitsukuni 徳川光圀 147
Tokugawa period. *See* Edo period
Tokyo 181
Tokyo Imperial University 14, 33–4, 38, 62–3, 158–9
"tolerated margin of mess" 74, 78, 84, 190 n.9
Toneri 舎人 52
Tongguk t'onggam 東國通鑑 147–8, 153–4, 196 n.2
Tongmyŏng 東明. *See* Chumong
Tongmyŏng-wang p'yŏn 東明王篇 107
Tongnip sinmun (newspaper) 36
Tongsŏng 東城 (king) 103
toponyms. *See* Kumanari; Soshimori
Torikami 鳥上 50, 91
Totsuka no Tsurugi 十握剣 90, 95
Tottori (prefecture) 100
tōyōshi 東洋史 6, 29
Toyotomi Hideyoshi 豊臣秀吉 20, 25–6
tribute missions (Korean embassies as) 23–5
trickster 65, 69–76, 136
Tripitaka Koreana 20
Tsuda Sōkichi 津田左右吉 67
Tsukihoko-tooyoru Hiko 衝杵等呼而留比子 57
Tsukushi 筑紫 65–6, 77, 92
Tsukuyomi 月読 49, 55, 59–60, 77
　See also Susanoo and Tsukuyomi
Tsumatsu Hime 枛津姫 92
tsune ni yoru no kuni 常に夜の国 (land of everlasting night) 167
Tsunoda Tadayuki 角田忠行 40–1, 148
Tsurezuregusa 徒然草 58
Tsurugi Hiko 都留支日子 57
Tsushima (province) 22–3, 149
Turner, Victor 2, 65, 70, 76
2,600th anniversary (of Japan) 4–6, 31
Tylor, Edward Burnett 61–2

Uchida, Jun 81–2
Uchida Ryōhei 内田良平 39–40
Udu 牛頭 (mountain) 43, 153–5, 158, 161
Udu (village) 42

Udusan. *See* Udu (mountain)
Uka 宇賀 (township) 131
Uka no Yama 宇迦能山 (mountain) 131
ukei 49, 90, 94, 122, 187 n.9
Ukemochi 保食 55
unahara 海原. *See* Plain of the Sea
Ungchŏn 熊川 105–6, 109–10, 166
Ungjin 熊津 103–5, 109–10, 166–7
Ungsim 熊心 107–9
Ungsin 熊神 108
unity of ritual and government 159
unity of loyalty and filial piety 3, 185 n.7
Unnan 雲南 (city) 178–9
Un'yōshi 雲陽誌 130–1, 178
Urabe 卜部 (lineage) 120, 122, 140–1
Urabe Hiramaro 卜部日良麻呂 118
Urabe Kanefumi 卜部兼文 119–20, 141
Urabe Kanekata 卜部兼方 118–19, 123, 141
ushirodo 後戸. *See* back door
Utsunomiya Tarō 宇都宮太郎 38
Uttarakuru (mythical continent) 135
Uzumasa 太秦 (district) 135

van Gennep, Arnold 70, 81
vengeful deity 139–40
vengeful spirits. *See goryō*
Vienna 163–4, 175
Vienna school of ethnology 163–4, 199 n.25
Vlastos, Stephen 10
Vovin, Alexander 105
Vulture Peak (mountain) 127–9

Wa 倭 19, 21, 25–6, 176
Wada Yūji 和田雄治 160
wagakuni no kami 我国神. *See* native deities
Wakayama (city) 156
wakon yōsai 和魂洋才 28
wandering deities 65, 69, 76–7, 87, 120, 123, 140
wani 鰐 130, 194 n.8
Wanibuchi 鰐淵 (mountain) 130, 167
Waninari 熊成 130–1, 166
Waseda University 67, 159
Wei-shu 魏書 109
Weizhi Dongyi zhuan 魏志東夷伝 19
West 35

as Japan's modern Other 27
    See also civilizational triad (West/Japan/Asia)
Western colonialism. *See* Western imperialism
Western imperialism 11, 27, 36–7
westernization 27–8
Wissler, Clark 162
wooden tablets 124–5
wrathful deity. *See* vengeful deity
Wu 呉 91

Xiao Yi 蕭繹 105

yaegaki 八重垣. *See* eightfold fences
Yaegaki (shrine) 179–80
yahashira no miko 八柱子. *See* eight divine children
Yakumo 八雲 (mountain) 131
Yale University 162
Yalu (river) 108–9
Yama. *See* Enra-ō
Yamaguchi (prefecture) 40
Yamaguchi Masao 山口昌男 76
Yamamoto Hiroko 山本ひろ子 114–15
Yamanaka Tomotarō 山中友太郎 42
yamata no orochi 八俣遠呂知. *See* eight-headed serpent
Yamato 19, 21–2, 60, 101, 103–6, 110–11, 167
    See also Izumo (province): Yamato and
Yamazaki Ansai 山崎闇斎 134, 147–8
Yanagita Kunio 柳田國男 166
Yao 堯 (emperor)
Yasaka 八坂 (shrine) 116, 124–5, 151, 153, 155, 162
Yasaka (township) 118, 151, 153, 155
Yasakasha kyūki shūroku 八坂社旧記集録 153–4
Yasaka-shi 八坂誌 153–4, 156
Yatabe no Kinmochi 矢田部公望 93–4
Yatsuka Mizuomitsuno 八束水臣津野 126, 129, 132
Yawata Ichirō 八幡一郎 175
Yayoi period 18–19, 91, 177
Yi dynasty 40, 106

Yi Kyubo 李奎報 107
yin-yang 52–4, 58, 114, 116, 121, 131, 146, 148, 151
Yi Pyŏngsŏn 李炳銑 104
Yi Sŏngsi 李成市 24
Yomi no Ana 黄泉之穴. *See* Cavern of Yomi
Yomi no Kuni. *See* Yomotsu Kuni
Yomi no Saka 黄泉之坂. *See* Slope of Yomi
Yomi no Shima 夜見嶋 100
Yomotsu Hirasaka 黄泉比良坂 52, 97–8, 100
Yomotsu Kuni 黄泉国 49, 54, 59–60, 96–101, 145, 167
Yonago (city) 100
yonaoshi 世直し 3
yoru miru kuni 夜見る国 (land that sees the night) 167
yoru no osu kuni 夜之食国. *See* Honorable Country of Night
Yoshida Furusatomura 吉田ふるさと村 (tourism company) 179
Yoshida Kanekuni 吉田兼邦 139–40, 195 n.14
Yoshida Kanetomo 吉田兼倶 133, 141–2, 147
Yoshida Kenkō 吉田兼好 58
Yoshida Shintō 13, 93, 133, 140–3, 150, 169
Yoshida Tōgo 吉田東伍 160
yūgō 融合 (fusion) 42
Yuhwa 柳花 107–8
yuiitsu shintō saikō 唯一神道再興 133
Yūryaku 雄略 (emperor) 102–3, 105–6, 110, 148, 166

Zeami Motokiyo 世阿弥元清 136
zen'aku funi jashō ichinyo 善悪不二邪正一如 142
Zenkoku shinshokukai 全国神職会 40
Zeus 68
Zhi-gong tu-juan 職貢図巻 105
Zhong, Yijiang 127, 133

www.ingramcontent.com/pod-product-compliance
Lightning Source LLC
Chambersburg PA
CBHW062137300426
44115CB00012BA/1953